ZORA
ARKUS-DUNTOV

The Legend
Behind Corvette

The Authorized
Biography
by Jerry Burton

www.
BentleyPublishers
.com

ZORA
ARKUS-DUNTOV

Chapter 1: In his early teens Zora showed a clear penchant for taking risks.

Chapter 5: After leaving Europe, Zora and Elfi were caught up in the social whirl of New York.

Chapter 11: At Le Mans in 1954 Zora drove to his first—and biggest—racing win.

Chapter 15: The CERV I encompassed many of the engineering agendas Duntov held dear.

Chapter 16: Zora found that control over Corvette design was very elusive at GM.

Chapter 20: Zora tests a third-generation, L88-powered Corvette.

Chapter 24: In retirement, Zora, along with Elfi, was a fixture at many Corvette events.

Bentley Publishers, a division of Robert Bentley, Inc.
1734 Massachusetts Avenue
Cambridge, MA 02138 USA
800-423-4595 / 617-547-4170

www.
BentleyPublishers
.com

Information that makes
the difference®

Copies of this book may be purchased from selected booksellers, or directly from the publisher. The publisher encourages comments from the reader of this book. These communications have been and will be considered in the preparation of this and other books. Please write to Bentley Publishers at the address listed at the top of this page or e-mail us through our web site.

Since this page cannot legibly accommodate all the copyright notices, the Art Credits page constitutes an extension of the copyright page.

Library of Congress Cataloging-in-Publication Data

Burton, Jerry, 1950–
   Zora Arkus-Duntov : the legend behind Corvette / by Jerry Burton.
     p. cm
   Includes index.
   ISBN 0-8376-0858-9 (alk. paper)
    1. Arkus-Duntov, Zora. 2. Automobile engineers--United States--Biography. 3.
 Corvette automobile--History. I. Title.

TL140.A 75 B87 2002
629.222'092--dc21
[B]
                                                2002019532

ISBN 0-8376-0858-9

Bentley Stock No. GCZA

05 04 03 02   10 9 8 7 6 5 4 3 2

The paper used in this publication is acid free and meets the requirements of the National Standard for Information Sciences-Permanence of Paper for Printed Library Materials. ∞

Zora Arkus-Duntov: The Legend Behind Corvette, by Jerry Burton

Front Cover: Photo of Zora from Zora Arkus-Duntov Collection. Photo of Corvette by Mike Mueller.
Inside Front Flap: Photos by Mike Mueller.
Back Cover: Photos from Zora Arkus-Duntov Collection.
Inside Back Flap: Photo of the author by Jonathan A. Stein.
Endleaf: Photo © 2002 General Motors Corporation. Used with permission. GM Media Archives.

I dedicate this book to the late Dan Gale, the founding president of the National Corvette Museum. Dan was a close friend and a visionary in the Corvette community. He was a long-time member of the National Corvette Restorers Society and the man who urged me to take on this project. His encouragement and dry humor helped carry me through the difficult moments. Dan died of a stroke in October 2000. I will always cherish our friendship and that of his wife Karen.

Special Acknowledgement

Elfi Arkus-Duntov devoted hundreds of hours of her time and hospitality to make this project possible. She also provided me with complete access to all of Zora's personal papers and business materials. As we worked together, her undying love for Zora became increasingly apparent to me. Her steadfast goal was to see Zora's story published and preserved for future generations. There is no way I could have written this book without her.

Acknowledgements

I thank all of my interview subjects for their time and their insights. I also thank the following people who played a special role in bringing this book to fruition.

John Allard, who tirelessly and proactively helped me connect some vital pieces of the puzzle during the Allard era.

Janet Barnes of Bentley Publishers who came along relatively late in the project, but helped give it the final momentum it needed.

David E. Davis Jr., former editor and publisher of *Automobile* magazine and a former Chevy creative director at Campbell-Ewald advertising whose entertaining recollections added perspective, color and texture to the story.

Lawrence R. Dolph, a friend and former GM consultant, who provided unrelenting wise counsel and provided me with a number of valuable interview sources.

Herb Fishel, the head of the GM Motorsport Technology Group, for his perspectives on what Zora faced in trying to run a corporate racing program in the Fifties and Sixties.

Dave Hill, Corvette chief engineer who was able to contrast for me the differences in engineering automobiles between Zora's day and today.

Gib Hufstader, for many years Zora's right-hand man, who provided many personal insights and was extremely helpful in identifying and locating interview sources.

John Kittredge, my initial editor at Bentley Publishers, challenged me early and often while helping me shape the thematic elements of the book.

Ralph Kramer, the former director of Chevrolet Communications; **John L. Stein**, the fine editor of *Corvette Quarterly;* **Tony Hossain**, catalog writer/supervisor extraordinaire at Campbell Ewald; and **Paul Zazarine**, former editor of *Corvette Fever,* who were all kind enough to review and offer valuable input on the original manuscript.

George Damon Levy, who first introduced me to Zora, and became a trusted friend and sounding board during the times I needed counsel.

Bob Lutz, now vice chairman at General Motors, who provided valuable insight into the role of mavericks like Zora in major corporations.

Pete Lyons, an author who recorded many hours of personal conversation with Duntov while Zora was still alive and was kind enough to make them available to me.

Dr. Robert Pasick and his Ann Arbor, Michigan-based writers group consisting of **John Bacon**, **Randy Milgrom**, **Rick Ratliff**, **Dave Stringer** and **James Tobin** who afforded an honest and trusted forum for critical discussion.

Mark Patrick of the National Automobile History Collection of the Detroit Public Library for his eager cooperation in my research.

Jim Perkins, the former general manager of Chevrolet, who provided me valuable insights into Zora's never-say-die attempts to influence the C5 Corvette.

D. Randy Riggs, the former editor of *Vette* and *Sports Car International*, who graciously offered his time and resources.

Jim Schefter, the late author of *All Corvettes Are Red*, who guided, coached and encouraged me every step of the way.

Don Sherman, for providing valuable missing pieces of information as well as his late-inning assistance in reviewing the final manuscript.

Alvie Smith, the former executive in the General Motors corporate public relations department who helped me understand the GM corporate climate as it affected Zora.

Vicki Staniszewski and **Sue Stepek** of the Campbell-Ewald Advertising reference center, who also eagerly gave of their time in helping me chase down loose ends.

Jonathan A. Stein, former publishing director of *Automobile Quarterly* and currently an editor at Bentley Publishers, who served as my second editor at Bentley and became my champion.

Jay Thomsen, a close personal friend of the Duntovs, who rendered some valuable introductions and personal insights.

Bill Tower, who provided his own perspectives as a GM insider in the Sixties and whose 1956 Corvette graces the cover of this book.

Last, but certainly not least, I want to thank my wife **Nancy** and son **Michael** for their incredible love, support and understanding during the five years it took to create this book.

Prologue

N**ear** Bowling Green, Kentucky, Interstate 65 was a parking lot. It was the Friday morning of Labor Day weekend 1994, and a parade of Corvettes from all over the country had gridlocked the road in both directions. From the south, traffic was backed up for over 40 miles, past the Tennessee state line. From the north, the cars formed a solid line some 50 miles north to Mammoth Cave, Kentucky. Most of the over 5,000 two-seaters on their way to the museum had been polished and primped, looking fresh off the assembly line even though many were over 40 years old. Their V-8 engines rumbled nervously on the verge of overheating in the thick 90-degree air. Yet few drivers were upset about the traffic or the weather. They were on a mission, a pilgrimage to celebrate the official grand opening of the National Corvette Museum.

The Corvettes all filed off at Exit 28 and headed toward the museum, just off the exit ramp. The building looked like it was designed in a wind tunnel, with curves and sweeping angles resembling a fast automobile. Its silver surfaces glistened like chrome. Most noteworthy, however, was a yellow cone-shaped structure flanking the main building. It was pierced by a red spire, envisioned by its architects to become a beacon for Corvette owners around the world.

Above the traffic jam, several skydivers plummeted toward the museum grounds, smoke flares and a tethered American flag tracing their descent. Several thousand feet above the Kentucky countryside, their chutes popped and they gently glided in above a crowd of over 100,000 people.

Watching the scene from a special VIP section at the front steps of the museum was a white-haired octogenarian of Russian descent. He was Zora Arkus-Duntov, former Corvette chief engineer and the man most responsible for the automobile that was being celebrated here. Wearing a white suit, sunglasses and a baseball cap, he sat with his wife Elfi and watched the parade of Corvettes file in. When introduced to the crowd just before the official ribbon cutting, he stood up and grasped his hands together

Opposite top: Corvettes from all over North America converged on Bowling Green, Kentucky, during Labor Day weekend 1994 for the grand opening of the National Corvette Museum, where Zora Arkus-Duntov would be the guest of honor.

Opposite bottom: Inspired by the legacy Zora Arkus-Duntov helped to create, the National Corvette Museum logo would be a prominent new symbol in the Corvette community.

and raised them over his head like a heavyweight champion. Despite the presence of many other celebrities, dignitaries and executives, including the lieutenant governor of Kentucky, former Corvette chief engineer Dave McLellan and his successor, Dave Hill, the standing crowd reserved its longest and loudest applause for Zora. This was the grand opening of a brand-new museum dedicated to one car—his car.

Yet few in the crowd had any idea how many risks he had taken, how many miles he had traveled, or the odds he had overcome to be able to see this day. Duntov experienced several lifetimes in his 84 years, as he had lived through some of the most tumultuous events of the twentieth century. The offspring of Russian revolutionaries, he witnessed the Russian Revolution of 1917; was educated in one of Germany's top technical schools; joined the French Air Force; escaped from Nazi-occupied France; caught a refugee ship to Ellis Island; consulted for top United States defense companies for the war effort; started his own war munitions operation in New York; helped develop an atomic compressor; raced at Indianapolis and Le Mans; and eventually found his way to General Motors, where he drove the Corvette into sports car immortality.

But during the museum grand opening, Zora wasn't pondering the past; he was contemplating what kind of motor he should install in a recently purchased airplane in order to break a piston-powered speed record....

A Fascinating Life Journey

What took Duntov from being a refugee from communist Russia to American icon status is the subject of this book. His vagabond existence carried him through five countries and four languages. Along the way, he shattered conventions wherever he went, be it engineering doctrine, corporate politics, driving styles, dress codes or social behavior.

While Duntov is often mistaken as the man who invented the Corvette, that distinction belongs to Harley Earl, the head of GM Design Staff in the early 1950s. Duntov first saw a prototype of the two-seater sports car on an auto show turntable in New York in January 1953. Although Duntov was not employed by GM at the time, he was so taken by the two-seater that he applied for a job. After years of working for under-funded operations, he was intoxicated by the prospect of using the resources of the largest corporation on earth to execute his visions. But after accepting a job offer at GM in May 1953, he may have thought he had made a deal with the devil. GM was in the business of making money, not fine sports cars, and Zora had little inkling of the road ahead.

Duntov's managers, on the other hand, may have had similar misgivings about him. Sparks flew when Duntov's entrepreneurial, maverick style ran head on into this conservative, blue-suit bureaucracy. Yet thanks to the influence of Chevy chief engineer Ed Cole, the volatile combination brought an energy to GM that helped ignite some of its greatest sales successes in the 1960s and 1970s, a time when GM's market share exceeded 50 percent.

The Spirit of Zora

Inside the museum after the ribbon cutting, the crowd absorbed the Corvette treasures inside. There were displays from American life: an old barber shop; a recreated Mobil gas station; a Chevrolet showroom circa 1963; a sweeping motor sports display; an assembly line from the old St. Louis Corvette plant; life-size figures of Corvette notables, including Zora; and dozens upon dozens of historic Corvettes.

Everywhere one looked, there were reminders of Zora. You could see him symbolized at the front entrance in the form of the metallic Corvette SS racer gracing the glass-surrounded turntable. Built in 1957, the SS represented all of Duntov's hopes and dreams for a factory-racing program that could take on the best racing organizations around the world.

Duntov was the power under the hood of the 1957 Corvette sitting at the pumps of the Mobil gas station display. Duntov had a major influence in refining fuel injection, a universal technology today, which first debuted in the United States on the Corvette.

Duntov was the soul inside the dark blue 1963 Corvette Sting Ray split window that graced the showroom of the old Chevy dealership. Duntov hated that split window and went to war with Design Staff chief Bill Mitchell because it obscured rearward visibility. Zora lost. Still, the Sting Ray became the most renowned of all Corvettes thanks to Zora's innovative independent rear suspension and, later, disc brakes.

Duntov was the risk taker who had worked inside the Aerovette show car, parked under the skylights in the main display area. This sleek silver machine was a technical masterpiece when it was built in 1973—perhaps the most sophisticated concept car GM had ever created. It featured four-wheel drive and had a powerful V-8 engine visible under a glass rear canopy that had once housed a four-rotor Wankel engine. The car represented Zora's greatest hope to build a mid-engined Corvette. But like his other mid-engined proposals, this car never made it into production, proving to be one of his greatest disappointments.

The real, live Zora could be found amid the crowd inside the halls of this new Corvette shrine. He was the guest of honor, the celebrity extraordinaire. He spent many hours signing autographs at a long table just outside the gift shop and posing for photographs with thousands of Corvette enthusiasts. He never seemed to tire, despite the endless line of people who came to pay homage.

He and his wife Elfi wore their years proudly, with an aura of world-liness that came with their multicultural background, having lived in Berlin, Paris, London and New York. He was the ultimate personification of his car, America's own Enzo Ferrari or Ferry Porsche. Elfi was still the stunning blue-eyed blonde from Berlin, who had danced with the Folies Bergère in Paris, the Copa Cabana in Miami and Off-Broadway in New York. The two had an energy and spark that kept them together most of the time despite Zora's wanderings. Together they thrived on the limelight lavished on them by the Corvette world.

As the hours wore on into the late afternoon on the final day of the festivities, it was time for the couple to go. Museum staffers in red shirts escorted them to the front entrance, where a limousine was waiting to take them to the airport, back home to Detroit. As their car left the grounds, Zora looked out the back window and surveyed the thousands of cars, tents and people on the scene. He closed his eyes. He had come a long way all right. But in his mind, not quite far enough.

ONE

Zora plays protector to his brother Yura, seven years his junior. They were inseparable especially during their early lives, and remained loyal to each other despite a very unsettled family life.

Turbulent Times in St. Petersburg

Zora Arkus stood alone on an icy shoreline outside St. Petersburg late in the Russian winter. The surrounding birch trees were still barren and the snow had melted off the lake surface, exposing a sheet of ice underneath. Wearing a tattered long coat over his thin, 12-year-old frame, Zora faced the wind, his pale blue eyes squinting out at the glazed surface. "How thick is it?" he thought. "Will it support me if I walk out to the middle and back? And what if it won't?"

He stepped forward. The ice held firm, so he took another step, then another. He was soon several hundred yards from shore, approaching the middle of the lake. As he walked, water began to ooze between small cracks in the ice under the weight of his feet. Ignoring the warning signs, he continued, guided by his own resolve. The water began spurting higher under the pressure of his leather boots until suddenly the ice gave way and he was immersed in black water. Stunned by the cold, he felt adrenaline surge through his veins. He treaded water to keep his head above the surface. What now?

To climb back onto the ice at that point wasn't possible. The ice was too thin to hold his weight and applying pressure would cause it to break away. He was too far away from shore to stand on the bottom. He had to get closer in. So he lunged up and hammered the ice with his fists. Nothing. The ice felt like concrete. He was now beginning to lose feeling in his legs. Would he survive this? He tried again, pushing up and slamming his fists to the ice with all his might. Again nothing. His strength diminished, he tried once more. This time, water spurted up through a crack.

With new hope, he lunged again, bringing his fist down against the hard surface. Finally, he punched through. Now he could break a large piece of ice away, which would allow him to get closer to shore. But he was running out of time and his muscles were beginning to feel limp. He once again forced his way up out of the water, letting the weight of his upper torso crash down on the ice. He managed to break another piece of ice off

Opposite: Zora's homeland in St. Petersburg, Russia, was a vast matrix of canals and waterways.

the floe. Now, to his great relief, he felt bottom with his boot. He would survive. The ice was thick enough here to support his weight, so he dragged himself out of the water and onto the ice. Exhausted yet exhilarated, he crawled back to shore. He craved the warmth of his fireplace at home, miles away, yet he wore his discomfort like a badge of honor. He had mastered his destiny, at least for today.

Many years later, Zora Arkus-Duntov never directly answered the obvious question of why he would attempt such a questionable venture. His only reply was a shrug and a smile. When pressed further, he hid behind the mechanics of getting off the ice: "I was instinctively applying the lesson learned—reducing specific pressure on the ice and distributing my weight over as large an area as possible."

His response was typical Zora: he shied way from the bigger picture, preferring to describe life's events in measurable engineering terms.

What Zora really sought back then was a boundary, some means of establishing the limits of his control. But solid ground was difficult to find in pre-revolution Russia. This mammoth country, ruled for over 300 years by the Romanov czars, had run head on into the twentieth century. The serfs, who dominated the Russian landscape for hundreds of years, had only recently been given their freedom, yet many continued to live as peasants. Those who left the farms flocked into the cities but found only poverty and miserable working conditions. As a result, cities like Moscow and St. Petersburg became the epicenters of unrest and environments that were not conducive to tranquil family living. It was as if entire communities were shaken to their foundations. The rules were changing, the old codes were broken. The biggest challenge a young person could have—being caught up in this swirl of history—was finding some sort of logical order to the world.

From Brussels to St. Petersburg

Although his parents were Russian, Zora was actually born in Brussels, where his parents had met as university students. At the time, sending children to study abroad was not uncommon for the more privileged families. Zora's father and mother were students at different universities near the Belgian capital. Zora's father, Yakov Myseivich Arkus, was sent by his parents to study engineering at the University of Liège in the early 1900s. Nicknamed Jacques, he was a slight man with sensitive eyes and a well-groomed mustache. He was the second of five brothers in the Arkus family, which hailed from the Latvian city of Daugavpils, more popularly known as Dvinsk. Compared to his brothers, who were involved in activities like arms smuggling and believed in hard-core political ideologies,

Jacques was quieter and more introspective. He sided with the more conservative Kadet party during the revolution.

In contrast to Jacques, Zora's mother was a bright, outspoken and striking brunette born Rachel Kogan. In a family portrait with Jacques, her fiery eyes and intense countenance stood in stark contrast to Jacques, whom she met while studying botany at the University of Brussels. Rachel was headstrong and idealistic to the degree that she joined the Socialist Revolutionary party, the most violent of all the leftist groups, prior to the revolution. She was a firm believer in equality of the sexes and would have fit well into the women's movement in the United States during the 1960s. Hailing from an accomplished family, Rachel's brother Osaf was a minister of culture, a position that Rachel would later achieve after the Russian Revolution.

Rachel and Jacques met somewhere in Brussels in 1908, and the two began a relationship. Likely drawn to each other as fellow Russians in a foreign land, their relationship was not hampered by the fact that the University of Liège was a one-hour train ride from Brussels. Following an intense but short courtship, they married in 1909. Later that year, Rachel bore a son, Zachary Yakovlovich Arkus, on Christmas Day in the St. Giles District Hospital in Brussels.

Zora's mother Rachel (seated) was bright, outspoken and intense. A member of the Russian intelligentsia, she pushed hard for social change in Russia. Zora's father Jacques (right) was considerably more mellow. Beside them is Rachel's sister.

In those days, a common derivative of Zachary was Zoria, or the more amicable "Zorka." "Zoria" and "Zorka," however, eventually became "Zora," which was easier to pronounce. Zora's middle name, Yakovlovich, translates to "Jacob's son," a symbol of both Rachel and Jacques' Jewish bloodlines.

In Russia, young Zora had two birthdays. Until February 1918, Russia used the old-style Julian calendar, which differed by 13 days from the Georgian calendar used in the West. By the Georgian calendar, Zora's birth date was actually January 7th, which made him a year younger than his classmates. Being younger and smaller than his classmates would have implications later in terms of the need to defend himself and garner respect from his larger contemporaries.

Jacques and Rachel both graduated in 1910, when Zora was a year old, and moved back home to Russia. They settled in St. Petersburg, where they both had landed government jobs that paid well. Like many university-educated people of the time, they became part of the country's intelligentsia, a left-wing group deeply sympathetic toward massive social change. Idealistic and socially conscious, they detested the poverty and repression of the Romanov era, and supported individual well-being and education for the masses.

The unrest of the serfs and factory workers, encouraged by the rhetoric of the intelligentsia, brought the country to a gradual boil. Amid the darkening storm clouds, one of Zora's first recollections was seeing the word "War" in the headline of a newspaper. He was four.

The headline Zora read came as a result of Russia going to war in support of Serbia when Austria-Hungary declared war on that Balkan nation in August 1914. Russia allied itself with France and Britain against Germany and Austria-Hungary, a conflict that evolved into World War I. The war put even more strain on the shaky political and social fabric of Russia. Even the name St. Petersburg was changed to the more Russian-sounding Petrograd, in keeping with increasingly nationalistic feelings in the country.

The situation for Zora was exacerbated by the fact that his parents, especially his mother, spent much of their time as advocates for major social change. They were frequently absent from the home attending party meetings and demonstrations. This left scant time for nurturing their children or for the basic amenities of family life. Parenting for Zora often took place in shifts, with either Rachel or Jacques in charge, but rarely did the family do anything together. Zora grew up feeling his parents were preoccupied with their own careers or the affairs of state, not taking care of him.

Though he was born Jewish, open religious observances were not part of Zora's upbringing, thanks to the government-sanctioned anti-Semitism of Czar Alexander III. Jews were restricted in where they could live. They could not live in Moscow or St. Petersburg, and their children could only attend certain schools. So the Arkus family put their religion aside. Even if they had any fervent beliefs, given the prevailing attitudes it was better to remain silent about them. Still, tradition brought the extended family together for Passover, and some aunts and uncles occasionally spoke Yiddish during these gatherings. By and large, however, Zora's parents echoed the government rhetoric in rejecting religion as an opiate to the people.

Like many Jews, Rachel may have been driven toward her left-wing views thanks to Russian anti-Semitism. The political left offered a haven for ostracized groups like the Jews. After the revolution, Jews from all over Russia migrated back to the larger cities and took job opportunities never open to them before. Despite the many social changes, the Jews didn't necessarily begin practicing their religion again. Many like Rachel kept their religious heritage private, finding that agnostic thinking was more expedient to their long-term survival.

As a result, Zora never received any religious education from his parents. He only learned to pray from a nanny. He remembered a little prayer she taught him to say as a child: "Dear God, let that night will be good to my mother and my father. Every night." Because of the relative absence of religion in his life, Zora never thought of himself as a Jew, yet knowledge of his Jewish bloodlines may have affected his later choice of a wife and friends. Like his parents, he kept quiet about his Jewish heritage his entire life, even with some very close associates.

If organized religion wasn't a part of Zora's life, the renaissance in science and the arts was. Despite the country's instability, Russia had moved to the forefront of scholarly and scientific progress by the first decade of the twentieth century—thanks to the impetus from the intelligentsia. There was a new national pride as Russian scientists began to excel in chemistry, linguistics, history, aeronautics and rocketry. Zora was exposed to these accomplishments early on. Although he wasn't particularly interested in purely academic activities, his progressive parents would push him to achieve a higher education, which fit well with their idealistic notions of a progressive society.

The Young Risk Taker

Whether Zora's parents ever found out about the ice incident isn't known. But the circumstance gives us some insight into the early Zora. He was willing to put his own life to the test to satisfy his curiosity as well as to get some sort of grip on his existence—to establish some form of control. What's more, Zora likely felt he could send a message to his preoccupied parents by doing dangerous things that would be sure to shock them into paying more attention to him. He was the child who kept acting up just to establish the limits of behavior. Encountering little resistance, he kept upping the ante.

Zora soon became a street-wise juvenile delinquent, prone to fighting and taking risks, primarily to get attention, respect and a sense of control over the world. Early on, he acquired the Russian nickname of "Servai Glavah," meaning literally "tear-off head," or reckless. Sometimes his boastfulness forced him into risks he didn't necessarily want to take.

In elementary school, Zora bragged that he not only knew how to swim, but was good at several strokes. When his friends called his bluff, Zora's pride drove him to make good on his false claim. The reckoning took place in a channel connecting two small lakes. The 10- to 15-foot-deep channel was approximately 30 to 40 feet wide, with a wooden walkway running along both sides. Zora made it across on guts alone, although his style left something to be desired.

On another occasion, on a bet, he climbed to the very top of a birch tree, and let himself sway precariously back and forth some 70 feet off the ground so he could feel the wind and imagine himself in flight like a bird.

He achieved similar exhilaration on his bike with daredevil stunts such as riding down steep slopes. Once, while riding down a 45-degree hill, he hit the lip of a footpath by mistake and became airborne. He traveled through the air above a footbridge he had planned to coast across and crashed 100 feet from takeoff, bending his bike like a pretzel.

Zora loved the feeling of being out on the edge and loved even more the respect this type of activity garnered. It established him as a man of action. He sized up his world and realized that for him actions were more important than thoughts or feelings. He began to measure himself not by what he felt or thought, but by what he did. It allowed him to feel in control, and provided great emotional satisfaction without his having to reveal his neglected soul.

While Zora didn't necessarily desire to hurt himself, he felt an odd combination of youthful invincibility and vulnerability in taking these risks. He told others he would die young after running into a couple of gypsy fortune-tellers on the streets of Petrograd. He was only 11. The gypsies looked at his palm and started to cry, saying, "You are destined to die at a very early age." Amazingly, despite the very linear thinking patterns he later exhibited as an engineer, Zora claimed he never questioned the gypsies. He accepted the inevitability of an early death. With nothing to lose, life for him became even more of a contest. Could he beat out fate and establish who was really in control? Every new risk became a feast for his senses, an exhilarating thrill ride; he sometimes felt most alive when he was brushing close to death.

Discovering the World of Machines

Underneath Zora's bravado was a sharp, fertile mind filled with a healthy curiosity about the world. If he could understand causes, he could begin to make sense of things, to develop a higher comfort level with the ways of the world. He hated mysteries and felt some solace in knowing how things worked. He was greatly bothered if he couldn't determine the answer to a riddle or trick. In 1915, when he was five, he visited his aunt in Tambov, near Moscow, and remembered seeing a Chinese magician on a wharf along the River Zna. The magician was going through his bag of tricks—making things disappear and appear again—when he spotted young Zora in the crowd.

"Come forward, lad," the magician said with a hearty laugh. Young Zora, his dark hair parted down the middle, meekly stepped through the crowd and onto a platform with the magician. "Now take a deep breath and blow onto the teacup in my hand," the magician said. Zora did what he was told, and the teacup suddenly disappeared. The magician feigned anger at Zora for losing the cup. Zora was startled and began to cry. "Don't worry, my son," said the magician, all hale and hearty. Then he had Zora once again blow on his hand and promptly the cup reappeared. Zora was greatly relieved, and order, at least for the moment, was restored.

Zora never learned the answer to how the magician did the trick, but as he grew older, cause and effect would intrigue him. It helped him make better sense of a world where nothing seemed fastened down. He soon learned that the laws of physics were constant, even if man's laws and traditions made little sense.

As a burgeoning young scientist, Zora wanted to know what reaction accompanies a given action, even at the risk of his own hide. One of his early experiments took place at his Grandfather Arkus' dacha in Latvia, about 300 miles southwest of Petrograd, where the Arkus family spent several weeks each summer. Zora came upon his Uncle Laska sleeping on the couch in the mid-day heat. The youngster had a glass of cold water in his hand and wondered how much of it he'd have to pour down his uncle's open collar to wake him up without causing an overly violent reaction.

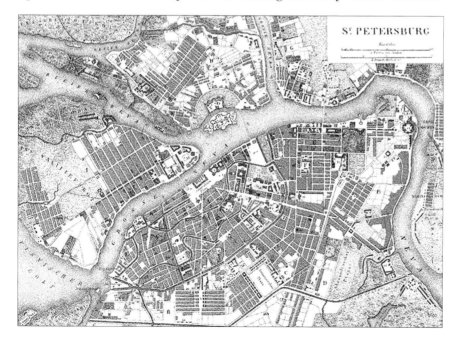

Water provided many natural boundaries in St. Petersburg. Zora's boarding school was located on the island of Elagin Ostrov on the northwest outskirts of the city.

Zora determined how much water ought to do the trick, then poured it down his uncle's collar. Laska stood up as if animated by a spring and let out a yell, then grabbed his nephew and whipped him. Later Zora said the only moral he retained was "Don't trust your eyes in assessing the level of the water in the glass."

Zora's conclusion gives insight into the mind of a future engineer. To Zora, Laska's reaction wasn't caused by the act of dumping water on him; it was the amount of water being dumped—a simple matter of trial and error. Given the same opportunity next time, Zora would understand the ramifications and use less water—not abandon the scheme.

Zora applied his flourishing curiosity to mechanical things. Ships, trains, streetcars, motorcycles and automobiles all fascinated him. These vehicles contained engaging, interworking components, but, just as important, they represented freedom and mobility. At age four, Zora drew pictures of cars on the wall of a veranda at his home. A year later, after seeing a stern-wheeler in action on the River Dvina, he deduced how steam was used in a turbine.

At age five, Zora had a chance encounter with a motorcycle as the Arkus household was preparing to view a total eclipse of the sun. Everyone in the family received a piece of glass blackened with soot through which he or she could observe the eclipse. Zora accidentally smeared the soot off his glass, and anyone he approached was indifferent to his problem, so he forgot about resooting his glass. Instead, he left the house determined to see the eclipse—with or without eye protection—from the vantage point of a nearby road. As he wandered over some sand dunes and came up to the road, a motorcycle suddenly flashed by in a blur. Startled, Zora stood mesmerized at the wonderful sight of his first motor vehicle at speed, its exhaust echoing full song into the distance. "Never saw anything move so fast," said Zora years later. "I wanted on that motorcycle."

It was a pivotal moment in Zora's life. He began to dream how he could control a powerful machine and make it do things few others had ever imagined. He never lost sight of that image. It became a powerful factor in many of the choices Zora would later make.

Still, motorcycles and cars remained relatively rare during Zora's early childhood, so whenever he saw one on the street amid the horses and buggies, it made a strong impression. He often wondered where these vehicles came from and what he might do to get closer to them.

Streetcars were much more commonplace, and Zora became an expert on them. He was well aware of the different makes, including Westinghouse and Siemens-Schuckart. He would grade each of them by speed. He liked being able to view their mechanical underpinnings as they passed by him each day on the crowded streets of Petrograd. The Westinghouse was the fastest although Zora thought it was also the ugliest.

Early on, he imagined himself one day becoming a streetcar driver. On his daily commute to school he would plant himself in a seat directly behind the conductor so that he might better learn his future craft. Once, crossing a bridge over the River Neva, the streetcar's guide structure jumped the wires. The trolley ground to a halt. The conductor climbed onto the roof to put it back in place but had forgotten to put the controls in neutral. As soon as the guide structure touched the wires, the train leapt forward, driverless, toward a dangerous sharp turn. "I realize this is the moment I get to be a tram driver," said Zora, who was not at all intimidated at the prospect of taking control of the runaway streetcar. "I jump behind the controls, forget about the man on the roof. I reduce the speed, gently apply air-brake and round the curve after the bridge and stop in the designated place." Once the conductor got off the roof, he embraced the young hero. Zora beamed with pride at the knowledge that he had become the master of this larger-than-life streetcar.

The incident made him even more interested in streetcars, as well as the switchgear that controlled their various routes in the city. He frequented the switching stations around Petrograd, where one particular old woman let him operate the switch directing each streetcar along its proper route. During the winter, he would bring salt from home to sprinkle on the rails near the switch to prevent it from freezing.

When Zora was 12, his father bought him a used bicycle, which the boy painted yellow. Zora used the bike as a device to further analyze how things worked and what he could do to make them work better. In studying how the bike functioned, Zora decided that the manufacturer was an idiot for not using a larger front sprocket to drive a smaller rear sprocket, thereby gaining ten revolutions of the rear wheel for one revolution of the front wheel. He wasn't worried about heavier pedal effort, not when it was more purposeful to engineer something without compromise. Besides, the end product would be faster, a theme Zora would often promote in his later engineering endeavors.

The streets of Zora's early youth were populated mainly by buggies and streetcars—automobiles were rare and exotic.

Facing the Gulf of Finland on the Baltic Sea, St Petersburg is surrounded by water. The area is at sea level, and tributaries of the River Neva form natural partitions of the city. Seeing a constant parade of watercraft on the river, Zora was inspired to build his own kayak. He used rectangular planks of lumber for the structure and covered it in resin-coated sackcloth. But the resin didn't cure properly, making the kayak unseaworthy, so Zora scuttled the effort. Undeterred, he recovered a sunken yacht tender from a tributary of the Neva. He reconditioned the boat, fashioned some oars and constructed a sail of burlap. He then spent many hours navigating the local waterways, enjoying the lucidity and freedom provided by the fresh air and open water.

Later, Zora talked an old man who ran a small ferryboat into letting Zora operate his craft. The ferry navigated the Bolshaya Nevka River between Elagin Ostrov and Staraya Derevnya to the north. Once again, Zora relished the feeling of control such an adventure offered him. At the helm, he cherished having the ability to set a course and potentially follow it anywhere in the world from the waterways of Petrograd. There was the added satisfaction of commanding a large, often unwieldy craft against a challenging current, a theme that characterized many of Zora's later endeavors.

Zora's first opportunity to get close to an automobile occurred after his mother was awarded a position in the government that warranted a chauffeur-driven 1909 Mercedes. Since there were only 20 or so cars in the entire city at that time, Zora could not believe his good fortune. He recalled standing outside by the car during the winter while the chauffeur, Melikov, would drink vodka in a local pub. Zora's job was to watch the car and crank the decompressor handle to start it up every ten minutes to keep the engine warm, since effective antifreeze wasn't available in Russia. It was a job Zora loved as he got behind the wheel and savored the sounds of pistons, cams and exhaust from the warmth of the cockpit. He wanted to know more about what was going on under the hood of the Mercedes. In time, he'd find out.

Zora the Protector

On February 11, 1917, a key new figure in Zora's life was born, his brother Yura. Zora was greatly excited at the prospect of having a little brother—along with the seniority being an older brother provided. He remembered traveling to the hospital with his father through the snow in a light horse-drawn carriage called a "droshka." He also recalled the first sight of his "horrible" shriveled-up newborn sibling.

Yura provided Zora with one of his first major roles in life—that of protector. He failed miserably, at least initially. When Yura reached school age, Rachel asked Zora to enroll him in the same school Zora attended. But Zora was late on the appointed day and failed to enroll Yura. Rather than take his punishment, Zora hid Yura in a cupboard inside the school. The next day, Zora knew he'd get into trouble for not having enrolled Yura the day before, so he hid Yura in the cupboard again. This continued for several weeks. Yura would come out during recess and become a hit with the girls in the class. Thinking this was school, Yura was more than content to go along, even though he'd walk home wobbly-legged after spending hours in the cupboard. Later, when Rachel went to inquire about Yura's progress, she discovered that the school had never heard of him. Zora got dressed down and Yura was transferred to another school. This was Rachel's way of punishing Zora—by removing his responsibility as a protector.

Despite his initial failure as a caretaker, Zora would develop a love for Yura that far surpassed his affection for his parents or anyone else. Later, Zora took his protector role more seriously because for much of their childhood Zora and Yura had only each other. To Zora, Yura *was* his family. Zora insisted to anyone who ever asked him that he and Yura showed more love for each other than the rest of the family ever showed for them. The two stayed together not only as best friends but also as co-conspirators. Yura was seldom very far from Zora's side. Although Yura never displayed Zora's level of bravado, the two shared many interests and would continue to support each other through many episodes of their lives.

Zora (left) and Yura get ready to go fishing. Zora looked after Yura throughout much of their youth, providing Zora with one of his first important roles in life—that of protector.

Revolution in Russia

The year Yura was born, 1917, Zora was an eyewitness to the Russian Revolution. He had felt the buildup from his early childhood. Once when playing with a friend and the friend's younger sister, Zora came across an underground printing press for *Pravda*, the communist newspaper being printed in the basement of their house. He was sworn to secrecy by his friend's parents but couldn't understand what the fuss was all about. On another occasion, this same friend invited Zora for an outing outside

Crowds and chaos in the streets were the order of the day in revolutionary Petrograd.

Petrograd to watch the friend's father practice shooting a revolver in preparation for the upcoming conflict.

The Russian Revolution occurred in two phases: a February uprising, which led to the October revolution. During the February phase, thousands of peasants and mutinous soldiers took over Znamenskii Square along the Nevsky Prospkt and raised the red flag over the Winter Palace. The mutineers stormed the security police headquarters, scattering and burning files while raiding arsenals and looting shops and private residences. Czar Nicholas II's troops were hopelessly outnumbered. That night, Zora recalled standing in a huge, cheering crowd on the streets of Petrograd watching a twin-headed wooden eagle, a symbol of the Romanov dynasty, slowly burn, melting the snow around it. Nicholas later abdicated to his brother Michael in a feeble attempt to placate the mob, but only managed to postpone the inevitable.

In October 1917, a new communist government led by Vladimir Lenin took control of Russia. The episode showed Zora first-hand that a seemingly immovable institution—the 300-year regime of the Romanov czars—could be overturned through sheer determination. The period marked perhaps the most profound economic and social change by any civilized country in history. One immediate result of the revolution was the changing of Petrograd to Leningrad in honor of the new communist leader of Russia.

The memory of the Russian Revolution would stay with Zora later as he challenged other institutions in his life. But beyond that, the immediate impact only added more hardship to an already confusing world. The revolution did little to mitigate the great instability in Russia, and the civil war that followed made obtaining basic necessities more difficult for the entire population. Zora's family was better off than most, thanks mainly to his mother's political leanings. Because she had sided with the most favored party of the Bolsheviks, the Socialist Revolutionaries, she obtained a position as director of after-school education in Leningrad. Despite her privileged position, the family was still subject to bread rationing like everyone else. Since onions were one of the few vegetables in plentiful supply, Zora and Yura subsisted on onion sandwiches for much of their youth with the result that neither could ever look at another onion again.

What food there was often had to be defended at gunpoint, which meant that guns and gunplay were prominent in Zora's youth. He used a Smith & Wesson five-shot .45 revolver for protection. He found the gun somewhere near his home in rusted-out condition and restored it to working order by soaking it in kerosene. His first test firing took place inside the family's apartment. Because he was afraid of the potential recoil, he tied the gun's handle to the back of a chair and fired the gun with a string. He carried the gun around with him along with an iron bar inside an old overcoat and used both to protect the family bread rations. For his bread pickup, he traveled along the river from Elagin Ostrov to the family's Petrograd apartment, a distance of about five miles. Many of these journeys took place during the 20-hour Russian winter nights, and he often made his way by starlight along the frozen river. Once a man approached him from the opposite direction. Zora grabbed his gun, ready to shoot because bread at that time was *life*. The man passed by, and Zora continued on his way.

David E. Davis Jr., the founding editor of *Automobile* magazine, wrote about how Zora was assigned to guard a cabbage patch at his school and was told to shoot anyone who tried to steal the school's cabbages. An old peasant woman appeared and began picking cabbages and dropping them into her satchel. Zora warned her to stop or he would shoot, but the woman ignored him and said, "No, you will not shoot. You are not stupid like adult. Adult might shoot me for some cabbages but you will not." Zora later reflected that "She was right. I see that apron full of cabbages is not worth life of old woman, so I don't shoot."

Still, Zora wasn't afraid to brandish a weapon. When a friend's mother was selling candies in a public market and a man objected to her selling at that location, Zora pulled a gun on the man. His friend's mother continued to sell.

The lack of food began to take its toll on Zora. Once, while getting off the streetcar near his apartment, Zora passed out, and an onlooker, seeing him lying near the street, brought him home. Rachel then decided to take him along on her inspection trips around the city, where he at least would be assured of receiving bread and tea.

Rachel's position benefited Zora on another level—it exposed him to the arts. The Arkus family had free access to the theaters, operas, circuses and other cultural events around Petrograd. Fostering the arts was an important propaganda advantage for the Bolsheviks in their attempt to present an idealized picture of the new regime to the outside world. It went a long way toward hiding the inadequacies of the new system. Given the city's culturally rich tradition, Zora may not have realized his good fortune. He remembered timing his arrival at an opera to watch the second act, which he knew would contain a sword fight. "After this fight is finished I depart the theater and go to another theater."

While Zora's behavior in these instances was perhaps typical of many boys his age, these episodes may have clarified in his eyes the advantages of being in control. On stage, the issues were often black and white, good versus evil, without the complications or nuances that often accompany real-world conflicts. Seeing such confrontations in sharp relief, Zora began to grasp the instant benefits of control and the gratification that came with winning.

Educating Zora

Since Rachel was without question the stronger of his two parents, Zora naturally gravitated toward her, but theirs was a complex, love-hate relationship. On the one hand, he respected her decisiveness and drive. She was strong and independent—qualities that heretofore were more acceptable in men than in women. She knew what she wanted. But her ideology caused her to hold family affairs at arm's length, and Zora and Yura often felt estranged from her.

While often neglectful of certain responsibilities as a mother, Rachel appeared to try to compensate in other areas. She was obsessed with cleanliness. She once scolded Zora for buying ice cream from a pushcart peddler. She was concerned about disease because the peddler didn't use boiling water. Zora had to turn down the peddler the next time he saw him. It was also in the interest of hygiene that led to one of the few activities the family did do together—take sauna baths. Zora remembers bursting out of a hot sauna, and then being beaten with a large tree branch to promote better blood circulation before rolling in the snow.

In spite of his feelings of neglect, Zora remained loyal to his mother and played the role of protector to her on several notable occasions. During the summer of 1920, she fell gravely ill with a kidney disorder. The family doctor lived some distance away from the central part of Petrograd where Zora and his family lived. Zora ran the distance of several miles in the early-morning twilight, panting as he snuck past the security guard at the door and up to the doctor's flat. Without opening his door, the doctor shouted, "Well, your mother will die. No use for me to come."

Zora, now exerting control as never before, drew his Smith & Wesson revolver from his belt and shot his way through the door. At gunpoint, he forced the doctor to follow him back to the family apartment, prodding him to move faster. Since the doctor had a hunched back, he was unable to move very quickly. He finally arrived back at the Arkus flat and treated Zora's mother. Rachel was saved, but the doctor died shortly thereafter. Zora felt that his pushing the doctor as hard as he did contributed to the physician's demise. Still, he showed no remorse afterwards. After all, his mother's life was at stake, and if the doctor had responded as he should have, Zora would not have had to go to such extremes.

Notwithstanding his dramatic attempt to save her life, Zora didn't agree with everything Rachel had in mind for him. In his early teens, Zora wanted to make his own decisions and displayed a stubborn determination over the issue of going away to boarding school. Rachel had already hired a Russian peasant girl to look after Yura, but Zora was too old to be supervised by the young nanny. Rachel felt that her job responsibilities were getting to be too much, so she decided to put Zora in a school on Komin Ostrov, a small island on the delta of the Neva near the center of Leningrad. But Zora objected to living away from home and arranged for a friend named Simon to secretly accompany him and his mother to the school by hiding above the rear axle of their carriage. After his mother enrolled him and left, Zora and Simon trekked back home again. Rachel was astonished to see Zora at the door, so she picked a different school, one located near the northwest outskirts of the city on a different island, Elagin Ostrov.

Zora spent several unhappy years at Elagin Ostrov. He recalled many of his classmates having shaved heads because of problems with lice in the school. There were many refugee children from the Volga area, victims of the Russian civil war. Zora felt like he had been thrown to the wolves, but he was up against the steely determination of his mother, who was the stronger player, at least at this point in his life.

Rachel's academic expectations for Zora were high despite the poor conditions. Zora was a restless student who quickly became bored with a standardized curriculum. He preferred an unstructured environment where he could pursue his own interests without restriction. Because of Rachel's high standards, she quickly became frustrated when he didn't respond to traditional educational methods. He would spend hours drawing trolleys, trains and automobiles in detail, often sketching out intricate parts. He also built devices such as a model locomotive made out of wire and a small working radio that fit inside of a matchbox. He also created a crude rheostat using a saltwater solution. Rather than recognizing Zora's genius, however, Rachel was derisive, calling him *stupitza*, a word meaning dull-witted. Because her presence loomed so large in his eyes, Zora never questioned her even later in his life, after his intelligence and abilities were well established.

While Rachel was a role model for Zora in exerting control, Jacques was not. He was a far softer personality and despite his experiments with corporal punishment when Zora was younger, his efforts failed. On one occasion, Zora refused to eat his soup and his father said, "You know what's coming." He took Zora to another room and spanked him with his suspenders. Zora cried, but when it was over, it was completely over, and Jacques acted as if nothing had happened. "And I didn't have to eat my soup," Zora shrugged. Another time, when Zora stayed out too late while fishing in a local river, his father whipped him on the back of his legs with an inch-thick rope. That turned out to be the last time Zora was ever punished physically. Years later, Zora noticed that Yura was never beaten and asked his father why. "Well, it never worked with you" was Jacques' reply.

If Jacques exerted any positive influence, it was in inspiring Zora to read. Thanks to trips to the library with his father, Zora developed an interest in Rudyard Kipling, the English author of children's popular short stories. He also liked American adventure writers Jack London and Ernest Thompson Seton, and William Shakespeare, Edgar Allen Poe, Leo Tolstoy and Nicholai Gogol, who wrote extensively about the Russian Cossacks in the classic *Taras Bulba*. These works inspired in Zora a rapacious curiosity about the world and a desire to go places outside of Russia.

Jacques' ability to influence Zora didn't go much beyond these trips to the library. His career as a mining engineer frequently took him out of town on business, which may have contributed to a pattern of poor health. He had frequent respiratory problems and would later suffer a stroke at a relatively early age.

With Rachel having her own responsibilities in her government jobs, Zora and Yura were left to fend for themselves most of the time. Zora took out his frustrations by wrestling and boxing. These sports were not only a release but another form of control. He could defend himself and garner respect, especially against physically larger classmates. Zora was a scrapper and usually emerged victorious. But the combat took its toll and Zora couldn't get out of every situation by fighting. After a year or so at Elagin Ostrov, the principal of the school told Zora either he had to leave or the principal would make life miserable for him. Zora complained to his father, but his father insisted that Zora had to solve his own problems. So without telling his parents, Zora enrolled himself in a school closer to home. "Why bother," he said. "They're working day and night."

Jacques' frequent absences helped Rachel to become increasingly restless in her relationship with him and susceptible to the lure of seeing other men. As part of her position in the government, Rachel worked with many established artists and musicians in conducting her cultural programs. She met famed artist Marc Chagall, who created a genre virtually his own with his large-scale renderings of Russian village life. Chagall was given a large studio in Vitebsk, where he taught workers to paint. During this time he met Rachel and the two began having an affair. He was quite taken by her and showered her with numerous works of art. Despite their intimacy, Rachel let the relationship progress only so far. She had no reason to change her relationship with her husband—until she met a man named Josef Duntov.

What Josef Duntov had that Marc Chagall didn't isn't known. An electrical engineer by trade, he also had a confident personality and a take-charge attitude. Perhaps Rachel was simply more comfortable with another engineer than with a famous artist like Chagall. Whatever his appeal, Rachel invited Josef to move into the household with her and Jacques and their sons.

Zora remembered that initially his father was very hurt and did not accompany the family on their annual summer vacation to the Crimea. Zora remembered crying on board the train because his father was not there. Zora also remembered his mother and future stepfather's consequent attempts to comfort him.

Josef Duntov eventually married Rachel and, despite an initial rejection, earned the respect of his stepsons; Zora and Yura would later add his surname to their own, forming "Arkus-Duntov."

Although Rachel and Jacques eventually divorced, the threesome continued to live together in a large house overlooking the ancient Peter and Paul Fortress. Despite the unusual household arrangement, Rachel never considered leaving Jacques. Even though no longer sexually attracted to her former husband, she still cared for him. Separate lodging was hard to find in Russia, and Rachel didn't want the children to be totally cut off from their natural father.

In sizing up his new stepfather, Zora deflected his hurt with practical statements. Zora decided he didn't like Josef not because of his intrusion into the family but because he didn't know much about trains. "I thought he was an ignoramus—he didn't know the difference between trams, and here he was supposed to be an electrical engineer." Likewise, Zora didn't care for his stepfather's accent, which may have been southern, possibly a Kiev accent. Rachel and Jacques had more sophisticated Leningrad (Petrograd) accents, and anyone from Kiev came across as inferior.

In the short term Josef, possessing a stronger personality than Jacques, may have provided some much-needed stability in Zora's life once the boy overcame the shock of two men sharing the affections of his mother. Josef acted more like a father was expected to behave and may have neutralized the shrillness of his mother. Still, the long-term implications of the relationship no doubt affected the type of man Zora would become. The sacred bond of the family had been broken. Never again would Zora look at relationships in quite the same way. It might also have further promoted a pattern of Zora's holding his own personal feelings at great distance.

Over time, Zora developed a healthy respect for Josef, based on his strength as a man and his accomplishments as an electrical engineer. Josef was instrumental in engineering a major hydroelectric plant, Volkovstroi, a hundred miles north of Leningrad. Zora visited the plant site twice, the first while it was under construction. He remembered the train trip north and eating hard-boiled eggs supplied by his mother. He was so tired when he arrived that he passed out along a street and took a nap under a pedestrian bridge.

Zora later took another trip to see the finished plant. He recalled a gathering in his home with his parents and their friends the night the new power plant went into operation. The lights dimmed, then went dark and suddenly came back on again, thanks to the facility. All tipped their vodka glasses to the new success. Zora got to see first hand the recognition that could come out of a major engineering success. He eventually saw Josef become the director of five different hydroelectric plants in Russia.

Out of respect, if not love, came Zora's decision many years later in New York to add his stepfather's surname to his own, creating "Arkus-Duntov." Throughout his life, Zora wore this name like a badge of honor and was quick to point out the unusual circumstances of his name to anyone willing to listen. Yet his reasons for adding Duntov to his surname appear in opposition. On the one hand, it symbolized a freewheeling life, society be damned. On the other hand, it recognized Josef's positive influence on Zora and was an attempt to formalize the connection for the entire world to see.

If Zora felt a sense of emotional loss from his real father, that feeling was exacerbated by the physical loss of other loved ones in the coming years. The raging civil war in post-revolution Russia resulted in the death of his Uncle Zelig Arkus who was hanged by the White Guards (anti-Bolsheviks) for arms smuggling in 1918. Zora also lost his Uncle Laska, who was shot during one of Stalin's purges in the 1930s, and Zora would later see another uncle, Grisha Arkus, succumb to the same purge that killed Laska.

Losing his uncles this way showed that life offered few second chances. People came and went from Zora's life and often they didn't come back. Such was the case with Zora's cousin Tamara, who was the daughter of his Uncle Zelig. Zora and Tamara met while she was visiting Leningrad from her home in Harbin, Manchuria. Both she and Zora were preadolescents at the time, and the two developed an infatuation. Romances like this were common among cousins of that era, but once Tamara returned home to Manchuria, they never saw each other again. The Tamara affair may have prompted Zora to adopt a "now or never" attitude in his later frequent attempts at sexual conquests with attractive women. In Zora's mind there may have been emotional safety in numbers.

The Young Inventor

Zora's engineering genius was not evident in his young life beyond his sketches of cars and streetcars. However, his abilities became more apparent at the high school level. While not particularly strong academically, he was most motivated when the subject matter interested him. Abstract concepts became clearer to him when applied to a real-world, hands-on activity, and he was particularly motivated when such a project had the potential to go fast.

At age 15, he conceived an idea for what could have been one of the world's earliest snowmobiles. For that he needed a couple of old airplane fuselages—one for the tail and one for the front of his sled—and a source of power. As it so happened,

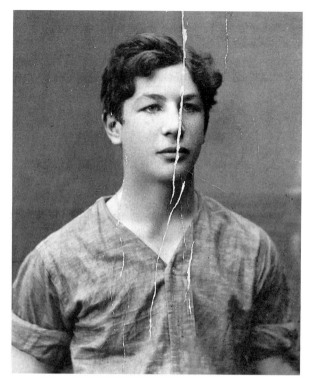

Zora in his early teens showed a clear penchant for taking risks as well as a distaste for the regimentation of the classroom.

there was a military flying school just a half mile away from his school. Zora went down to visit the commandant of the school and talked him into giving Zora the fuselages and two Hall-Scott six-cylinder aircraft engines. Zora envisioned the use of pusher-type propellers, much like those on a modern swamp craft. Some of the officers even pitched in to help. Zora took the components, put them in a building in his school and began putting the sled together. By the time the sled was finished it was summer, so Zora commenced a conversion to a waterborne craft, only to complete that in the dead of winter. The would-be snowmobile represented Zora's first attempt to build a machine largely of his own design. This provided a level of satisfaction—and control—that he had never experienced before. He vowed to do more.

TWO

Zora and Elfi went everywhere in and around Berlin in his Bugatti Type 30.

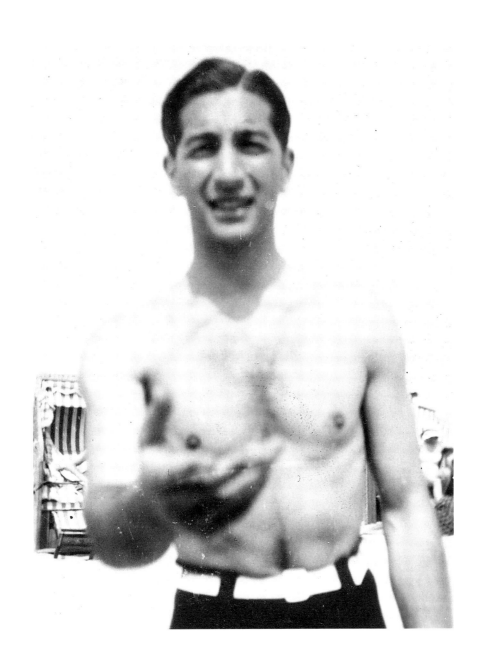

A World Beyond Russia

In 1926, when Zora was 16, his stepfather Josef was transferred to Berlin by the communist government. Josef's role in Berlin was to ensure that machinery and technical assistance going to the Soviet Union from Germany went smoothly. It would prove to be Zora's ticket to a place where he could apply his skills in one of the most technically advanced countries in the world.

Not that there weren't problems in Germany, which in the late 1920s was in many ways as unstable as the Russia that Zora had left behind. Germany was still recovering from World War I; it was paying out massive reparations and was dealing with its own communist threat. Because the country was so fractured politically, it was ripe for the nationalistic rhetoric of a demagogue like Hitler in the early 1930s. But Zora didn't know or care much about the political situation; he was more focused on what Germany might offer him. He found that the country had a tradition of engineering excellence, with many fine schools where a young man could get a solid education.

Zora didn't follow his parents to Germany right away, but instead stayed behind in Russia to finish his studies at the University of Leningrad, which would give him a better chance of getting into the German school of his choice. A year later, Rachel and Josef sent for Zora, and in 1927 he received the required state permission to go to Germany.

In the fall of 1927, Zora enrolled at the University of Darmstadt, a polytechnic engineering school located several hundred kilometers from Berlin at Hessen on the Rhine. Zora had tasted the fulfillment that came from an engineering endeavor such as building the snowmobile, and he came to see academics not as Josef and Rachel exerting control over him, but as a means of getting closer to his own natural passions.

He began a curriculum in electrical engineering, not mechanical engineering—no doubt influenced by his mother as well as by his high regard for Josef. Zora may have felt a need to please Josef, and he was certainly

Opposite: Zora in his early 20s on the beach in Germany.

impressed by his stepfather's engineering accomplishments in building the hydroelectric plants in Russia.

As a prelude to his formal classroom training, Zora spent three months in Berlin as an intern at A.E.G., a German company similar to General Electric. The Germans were big believers in mixing practical experience with academic training. It was in that factory that Zora turned what might have been an inconsequential action by anyone else into a significant personal moment. The workers had just completed a big generator and Zora was told to climb on top and stencil in the serial number. As he did so, he added a "Z" to the end of the number, and suddenly the transformer became his. This seemingly insignificant action gave Zora a sense of accomplishment he claimed he never felt again. On one level, the move was somewhat risky and therefore attractive. As an intern, he could have been dismissed for such an action. On another level, stenciling his initials provided another sense of permanence in an unstable world. Like many graffiti artists throughout history, he did it to prove he was there—and in control of a large piece of machinery. Making his mark "Z" in this way was a prelude to other indelible actions in his life, many of them involving his imprimatur "Z."

During his internship at A.E.G., Zora indulged his love of motorcycles by finding part-time employment in a Berlin motorcycle shop on the Bühringstrasse. While in the shop one day, he noticed the antics of a motorcycle daredevil outside the store. The motorcyclist was riding up and down the cobblestone street while standing on the saddle of his bike. Zora wasted no time in going outside to see this man in action. After he got off the bike, the man introduced himself to Zora. "My name is Bernd Rosemeyer," he said, extending his hand confidently. Zora shook it and was struck by the aura of this man. Zora thought he looked like a motorcycle rider ought to look: slim and muscular, with Germanic blond hair and blue eyes. They started talking about bikes and racing cars and superchargers.

The two became fast friends, and during their off hours Rosemeyer taught Duntov how to slalom his bike around the steel supports of an elevated train in Berlin. The young German was full of big dreams and vivid war stories. He fascinated Zora with tales of riding the "Wall of Death," at an annual fair in Lingen, his hometown, located near the Dutch border. The "wall" was a large cylindrical chamber where riders could cheat gravity by riding up the side of the walls at high speed.

Shortly after Zora met him, Rosemeyer's big dreams started to come true. Riding a 250-cc Zundapp, he won his first motorcycle race in 1931. He also won another 500-cc event that day and went on to win 11 grass races in 1931. Rosemeyer was distinguished company for Zora, not only for what he was then doing on bikes, but also for what he was yet to do racing grand prix cars several years later.

During their time together at the shop, Rosemeyer encouraged Zora to buy something that Zora had dreamed about since the day of the solar eclipse back in 1914: a motorcycle. For Zora the image of seeing his first motorcycle at speed that day was still as strong as ever in his mind, and the reality of owning his own machine was tantalizing. So he began to search around and through his contacts at the dealership was able to find a special 350-cc German Diamant.

Now that he had a bike, it wasn't enough for him to simply ride it on the street. He wanted to race it and feel the ultimate sense of control.

Zora loved to rip up the streets of Berlin on this Diamant, a German bike with a single cylinder 350-cc o.h.v. engine.

After seeing what Rosemeyer could do on a bike, there was no end to Zora's resolve. He had actually witnessed his first motorcycle race in Russia, on a street course close to his family's apartment. There he saw a rider lose control and crash into a lamppost, fatally crushing his skull.

The prospect that one could die racing a motorcycle didn't faze Zora. He began to enter open-class events at the Avus racetrack near Berlin. There, Zora was approached by a man named Schlesinger, who saw something he liked in the way Zora handled his bike and offered to teach him how to race. According to Zora, Schlesinger had at one time represented a German motorcycle manufacturer, Megola, which was the first and only motorcycle to use a radial engine actually located within the front wheel. The company went out of business in 1925. Whether Schlesinger in approaching Zora was hooked up with another company or whether he was acting on his own isn't documented, but Zora took Schlesinger up on his offer and began meeting him every weekend at Avus for instruction.

Zora loved the feeling of being on a bike at high speed and the ability to lean into the turns as if the bike was an extension of himself—the ultimate feeling of control. "You only need your eyes," he said years later. "It's stronger connection to my brain with motorcycle than connection with car." Racing his own motorcycle was everything he had imagined back in Russia after seeing his first motorcycle at speed.

Zora, however, neglected to tell his mother and stepfather about his racing, and when Schlesinger showed up at his home looking for Zora, his parents temporarily put a stop to his competitive career. But they couldn't suppress Zora's desire for long, and eventually he resumed his activities under their wary eyes. His mother, who now seemed to be more concerned about his safety than she had ever appeared to be in Russia, kept urging him to get into something safer. Zora persisted in his attempts to race, but Rachel refused to back off.

Eventually, Zora relented and bought a cycle-fendered "Bob" race-car, which had been built by an obscure, short-lived manufacturer of the same name. His Bob was one of only two built in 1922. It featured a three-speed transmission with a special U-joint that allowed the effective length of the drive shaft to change with the level of rear-wheel travel. It was powered by a 1500-cc. Siemens and Halske engine, which featured side valves and a three-bearing crankshaft. Zora described the sound of the engine as having boulders inside it. The Bob was set up for oval track racing. It was essentially a jalopy with no front brakes and fairly ineffective brakes at the rear. Despite its inadequacies as a practical street machine, Zora used it for everyday transportation.

Zora was a relative novice in cars and had only recently learned to drive a car because automobiles had been so rare in Russia. He learned in an Adler that belonged to a driving instructor. Zora claimed he already "knew" how to drive mentally—just like he "knew" how to swim in Russia; the Adler simply represented his first hands-on experience in a car. But this didn't stop Zora from driving his Bob as hard as he could get away with on the streets of Berlin.

Zora went everywhere in the Bob and didn't let long distances or poor weather hamper his enthusiasm for driving. When Zora began formal classes at Darmstadt in January 1928, he described driving with his stepfather Josef from Berlin to school at Darmstadt with two suitcases hung over the scuttle ahead of the cockpit like a pack mule and his tea kettle atop the Bob's pointed tail. "No Russian ever travels without a tea kettle," Zora said.

*Zora's first car was a Bob, one of only two built in 1922 by an obscure German manufacturer. It was set up for oval track racing, yet Zora used it for everyday transportation. (*Ausgang bei Gefahr: *Exit in case of Danger.)*

"On flat-land the car was all right," said Zora, "but get in the mountains and I feel screeching tires, brakes and I look over to see my stepfather's eyes rolling out."

The Bob was a disaster in the rain, with no windshield and a belly pan that held water. He eventually pulled the belly pan off the car altogether. Once in Berlin, he decided to amuse his passenger by using his feet to try to stop the car instead of the handbrake. He barely avoided ramming a bus in the process. Through it all, how-

Ausgang bei Gefahr

ever, Zora was *driving* and having the time of his life—nothing was more worthwhile than this.

The Bob also gave Zora an opportunity to demonstrate his hands-on mechanical abilities with automobiles. Although he never had any formal training as a mechanic, he had a basic knowledge of how cars worked. He also wasn't afraid to grab a set of tools and get to work to improve the power or handling of a car. He developed a reputation among his small circle of friends as a mechanic with "golden hands." Nothing pleased Zora more than diagnosing a problem, fixing it, and then driving the results of his labor. In so doing, he kept the ill-tempered Bob running, even though it required constant tinkering. In Zora's case, the result was usually a faster car, something he took great pride in. He began to think more and more about making a living around cars.

Zora the Rake

Zora was emerging as a distinguished young man with dark curly hair still parted down the middle, a thin face and a distinguished nose. He was growing ever more confident that he could take on anything. He was rail-thin and tireless. He was no longer someone's excess baggage the way he had felt growing up in Russia; he was a young adult calling his own shots now. He'd gallop up a flight of stairs two at a time as if he couldn't wait to get to the top, a habit that he continued until the very end of his life.

But things were far from perfect. His academic troubles continued after he began his formal curriculum at Darmstadt. He had received admission on a special basis because he didn't meet the school requirement for German literature. Zora flunked physics and had to take the course again, but fortunately—because of a "two strikes and you're out" policy—he passed the second time. As had been the case in Russia, it was clear that the regimentation of the classroom didn't appeal to him. He preferred hands-on projects like working on his car to abstract concepts that had at best only a theoretical connection to the real world.

Living alone in an off-campus apartment near the university at Darmstadt while his parents remained in Berlin, Zora used his newfound freedom to indulge an increasing curiosity about and attraction to the opposite sex. Although he had the brief infatuation with his cousin Tamara in his early teens, Zora was 16 when he began to notice a real change in his attitude about women. He wasn't sure where it was coming from. Duntov had vivid memories of watching several servant girls bathe nude in a special bathhouse positioned over the Dvina River when he was just four.

Despite this earthy introduction to the female anatomy, Zora put beautiful women on a pedestal at a relatively early age, thanks to idealized notions that may have come out of literature. "In my association with women, if I find physical flaw in the woman, I'm not interested. Most of my friends lost their virginity when they were 14, but it didn't bother me." His first crush was with a pretty girl named Nadia Niernberg who lived in Zora's neighborhood in Leningrad. The problem was that she didn't know who Zora was. He would often have a friend hoist him up so he could look inside the windows of her family's flat. Once he was able to view the whole family having dinner. Because she didn't respond to his gazes, he decided he had to get to her in a different way. Her brother was a middle-distance runner, so Zora decided to begin running to impress her. In the process, Zora became a competitive cross-country runner, but despite his game effort he never connected with Nadia.

While most women he encountered would agree that he was an extremely handsome man with his slender body, chiseled face and light blue eyes, Zora may have been insecure about his physical appearance. He claimed to relate to a character out of a Tolstoy novel, *Childhood, Boyhood and Youth.* "I identified with Nicolenka, the hero of *Detschva* [the title shortened and transliterated in German], so much so that when Nicolenka cried, I also cried. Nicolenka is ugly, so I conceived the idea that I too was ugly."

Zora's self-image in this regard is surprising since he spent a great part of his life acting fearless. He appeared especially fearless around the opposite sex, but this inner insecurity may explain some of his later womanizing, if indeed that behavior was based on insecurity. Still, if he had any doubts about his looks, he generally kept them to himself.

It was while he was in school at Darmstadt that Zora slept with a girl for the first time. Her name was Jenny, a 20-year-old student from the town of Wupertal in the Rhineland. "She was beautiful girl," he said. "I had to be in love to do this," although "love" in Zora's case seemed only to mean physical infatuation. Notwithstanding his verbal sentiments, Zora soon lost interest. After saying goodbye to Jenny, he took up with a girl named Dolly, but his enjoyment of women appeared to be in the chase rather than in the catch. Zora loved his freedom and at this point in his life wasn't ready for the emotional baggage of a long-term relationship.

When it came to close male friends, Zora was still a bit of a loner. University life exposed him to a host of peers, many of whom were also from abroad since German universities at that time were still open to students of means from around the world. Zora mingled with students from Iran, Latvia, Lithuania and Azerbaijan but found he had little in common with them. He befriended a student from Azerbaijan, but soon into the relationship the student felt that Zora was acting a little too superior and decided to take him down a notch. One day while the two of them were in a park on the outskirts of the city, the student suddenly pulled out a gun. The two wrestled on the ground without it going off, and when Zora finally freed himself, he stormed back to town. He remained cool, his experiences with guns in Russia no doubt having hardened him to such situations. The student followed him, still pointing the gun, but he never pulled the trigger, sensing Zora's outward lack of fear. This may have been another manifestation of Zora's belief he was going to die young.

His nothing-to-lose attitude helped Zora become an enforcer with his friends. If some outsider harassed a buddy, Zora played cop and subdued the offending party with either his fists or a can opener. While not going around looking for trouble, he didn't shy away from it either, and outsiders learned not to challenge him. Zora had learned early on that it was better to look fearless. It also made up for the fact that he was not physically large. Being cocky and self-assured was yet another means of exerting control in unpredictable situations, and most of the time it worked.

Zora first experienced flying when he took advantage of a special fare ticket offered to students at the university. He flew from Darmstadt to Berlin aboard a 12-passenger Junkers Tri-Motor and was struck by the perception of speed diminishing with altitude as well as the bright red glow of the exhaust coming out of the wing-mounted engines. He never lost his interest in aviation. In Berlin, he and some friends later fantasized about stealing an airplane and flying it west to Nova Scotia in order to break Lindbergh's trans-Atlantic speed record. After all, they mused, why should Lindbergh get all the glory?

The Mechanical Engineer

Unlike Russia, Germany was a hotbed of automotive technology and performance—thanks to companies like Daimler-Benz and Auto Union. After getting a taste of competition on his motorcycle and savoring his driving experiences in the Bob, Zora dwelled increasingly on the idea of being an auto engineer or a race driver. Engines fascinated Zora, especially the idea of how to make them more powerful. He read everything he could get his hands on regarding the subject of supercharging, which is the process of forcing more air into the engine's combustion chambers than normal atmospheric pressure can deliver, thereby creating more power.

Given this interest, he finally followed his heart and enrolled at the University of Charlottenburg in Berlin, the German equivalent of the Massachusetts Institute of Technology. In the process, he switched majors from electrical to mechanical engineering in spite of his loyalty to Josef. "I was interested in the internal combustion engine," said Zora years later. "Therefore, by hook or by crook, I learn." It was a move that would lead him to a lifelong relationship with the automobile.

As at Darmstadt, his curriculum at Charlottenburg called for long internships between courses, which included a stint in Berlin with Rinne Motoren Gesellschaft, which manufactured small three-wheeled, motorized tricycles for delivery purposes. The tricycles used a five-hp two-cycle engine. One of Zora's bosses suggested a new project for the student intern—"We have lots of moving vans drawn by horses; why not create a machine that does the same thing?" So Zora set out to create a tractor. For power, he chose a Deutz diesel engine mounted transversely and linked to the same three-speed transmission as used in the motorized tricycles. Zora designed a progressive clutch that slowly engaged to make it easy for inexperienced drivers to operate. For this purpose, Zora used a hydraulic cylinder from a door mechanism, which allowed the driver to depress the clutch, engage a gear and not worry about feathering the clutch pedal upon release. The tractor—which used a plywood body—had a five-kilometers-per-hour maximum speed and therefore could be operated on roads without a driver's license. Zora's design became known as the Primus tractor and saw limited production, an astonishing accomplishment for an intern.

Zora's views on supercharging were published in a May 1934 issue of Motor und Sport, *Germany's most prestigious automotive publication.*

But tractors weren't as exciting as race cars, and when Zora met Arnold Zoller in Berlin, the young Russian saw an opportunity to enter a much more exciting arena. Born in Switzerland, Zoller was a pioneer in supercharger engineering who became known for his work with two-stroke engines and vane-type superchargers in the 1920s and early 1930s. At the time Zora met him, Zoller was building a two-cycle, 12-cylinder, in-line racing engine that displaced 1,500-cc. Intended to compete against the likes of Mercedes-Benz, it featured a rotary compressor supercharger that Zoller himself had developed.

Apparently, Zora learned enough through Zoller and his own research to write a lengthy article on supercharging. He was just 24 when it was published in the May 1934 issue of *Motor und Sport*, now called *Auto Motor und Sport*. That Zora would approach Germany's most prestigious automotive publication for an article suggests a high level of confidence in the subject matter. Zora hoped the end result would be a high-profile piece that would get him noticed in the German auto industry. The article stated that any engine could be supercharged. "I will attempt to clarify and show that the installation of a compressor does not increase demands on engine stability, that high ignition pressures, heads flying off and other things are only the outcome of incorrect thoughts and compressors installed under incorrect conditions," wrote Zora. At the time there was concern that supercharging would cause higher temperatures, higher stress and cylinder head failures, but Zora maintained that supercharging was practical if engine temperature and pressure were regulated.

Zora produced a number of formulas and calculations in the article that demonstrated a sophisticated understanding of the subject matter. He also distinguished between supercharging, where the compressor delivers the nominal load quantity for each cylinder, and overcharging, where each cylinder is supplied not only with its piston displacement volume but also a greater mixture quantity under high pressure. Zora came out squarely in favor of supercharging as the best way to produce added performance without significant risk.

Zora's new credentials as a published expert in supercharging earned him a chance to consult with Machinen Fabrik Der Buel in Gera, Germany, on the development of several superchargers. He also designed a supercharger for a 12-cylinder, two-cycle racing engine, and it's a good bet he consulted with his new mentor, Arnold Zoller. But overall, the article did not provide the kind of long-term benefit that Zora had hoped.

Zora received his degree in mechanical engineering at Charlottenburg in June 1934. Thanks to his lengthy internships, it had taken him almost seven years from when he first enrolled at Darmstadt. Graduation provided him with additional hope that he might hook up with a major automotive concern, but no significant opportunities surfaced, and Zora bided his time in searching for his first career position. He spent most of his time in Germany in a succession of part-time jobs or consulting assignments. Although he did gain consulting roles, including the development of a V-12 Delahaye engine and six-cylinder Talbot power unit, most of his activities were anything but glamorous.

For several months, Zora worked as a testing engineer with Jlo (pronounced "Elo"), a company that manufactured two-stroke engines for chainsaws and later graduated into snowmobile engines. Zora had the unenviable task of conducting dynamometer tests in a poorly ventilated dyno room. Zora worked with a rope tied around his waist; if it went limp, a coworker would pull

Zora graduated from the University of Charlottenburg, one of Germany's top technical schools, in 1934.

him out of the room. As a result of this assignment, he walked around with constant headaches. Still, he had to make a living somehow.

But without a real career to provide a focus to his life, Zora continued to dabble in whatever was interesting or entertaining to him at the time. He loved to play poker with his friends, and it was in character for him to risk whatever assets he had. Fortunately, he didn't have much to lose.

Athletics also helped give him a sense of purpose. He continued to run in selected track events, exercised regularly and stayed in excellent physical condition despite the fact that he started smoking cigarettes. Instead of running cross-country, he developed into a sprinter. The 1936 Olympics were coming up in Berlin, and Zora claimed he was fast enough to qualify, but the Germans wouldn't accept him because he was not a natural-born German.

Besides his running, Zora also continued to use his fists and took up boxing. He fought in an amateur boxing circuit in Berlin, with a scrappy style that kept him competitive. Boxing was dangerous and he could easily have been injured, but he didn't care. During one match, he dislocated his shoulder after being slammed hard to the floor. As a friend was driving Zora home, another car hit them and Zora suffered a slight concussion and a broken arm. The incident proved to be the end of his boxing career.

Although his boxing days may have ended, Zora still took risks of a different order. In Berlin, he lived in a one-room apartment on the top floor of a three-story building. One of his favorite stunts was to climb out of his window and negotiate a six-inch-wide ledge to a hall window. One misstep would result in a three-story fall onto the street. Zora used the ledge as a faster route to a communal bathroom, but he also saw it as a kind of Russian roulette-style test. "In Russia, normally I hate to be on the high building, looking down, but I devise check on myself," he said. "If I did not manage and fall down, then it's right to die, but if I accomplish it, that's okay." Zora admitted that he often did this after having a few drinks. "If you cannot do it, what the hell, falling didn't matter anymore."

While Zora frequently performed stunts in Russia like this to attract attention from his parents and friends, this situation was a little different. Such acts could be explained by the fact that he still didn't have a career-style job or a major driving opportunity and therefore felt compelled to push the limits, just as he had on the frozen lake in Russia. Negotiating that ledge and surviving gave him a satisfaction he couldn't get anywhere else at the time. Again, it made him feel more alive than anything he could imagine as he waited for the right break to come along in his life.

High Hopes for Racing

Zora's hopes of landing a job with a major German racing concern soared after a friend from Charlottenburg named Hans Joachin Bernette introduced him to the Daimler race team at the Nürburgring, site of the German Grand Prix. At the time, Daimler-Benz had one of the most renowned racing operations in the world. Both Auto Union and Daimler-Benz were receiving massive financial support from the German government. Hitler's support allowed both Daimler-Benz and Auto Union teams to crush once-proud marques like Alfa Romeo and Bugatti yet still provide exciting racing with a German car always in the winner's circle.

Besides national pride, Hitler had a more expedient rationale behind his support of motor sports. The Versailles Treaty had prohibited the development of engines and components that could be used in bombers or fighter airplanes, but no such prohibition existed if the components were being built for a race car. According to author Peter Stevenson, "At least one competition car was powered by an engine that fit directly into a fighter aircraft."

The Daimler-Benz operation was led by Alfred Neubauer, the rotund racing czar of Daimler, long considered one of racing's most influential team managers and a pioneer in many of the disciplines of the modern-day sport such as pit boards and signal flags. Wrote Beverly Rae Kimes in her Mercedes-Benz history, *The Star and the Laurel*, "Though he was the prototype of a racing manager, there was no one else quite like him. He had a voice like a bullhorn and a vast, 280-pound physique to match. His suits hung loosely around him as if afraid to get too close; people like to say his trousers were made out of old zeppelins. He could let out torrents of invective or behave like an amiable teddy bear. Neubauer became a fixture in grand prix racing pit lanes with his trademark overcoat, fedora and a necklace of stopwatches around his neck."

Besides Neubauer, the Mercedes team had three of the world's top drivers: Rudi Caracciola, Hermann Lang and Manfred von Brauchitsch. Caracciola in particular was already a legend, having won the German Grand Prix four times prior to 1934.

Given credentials like these, Zora would have been satisfied with any toehold into the Daimler organization. Still, he made an impression on Neubauer, likely due to his published article on superchargers in *Motor und Sport* as well as his persistence and keen intellect. The bond was strong enough for the two to stay in touch, and their connection would bear fruit for Zora many years later.

Zora had similar hopes that Bernd Rosemeyer could help him get in the door at Auto Union. Rosemeyer was now using his motorcycle racing skills to come to grips with the rear-engined Auto Union grand prix cars. He got his first drive at the German Grand Prix at the Nürburgring in 1935, where he barely lost to the Mercedes of fellow German Caracciola. During the years of 1935 through 1938, Mercedes-Benz and Auto Union traded places in the winners' circles of all the major grands prix, with Caracciola and Rosemeyer usually sipping the champagne.

Rosemeyer was killed in January 1938 after setting a record speed on a German autobahn in German-sanctioned speed trials. Whether Zora expressed any personal outrage at Rosemeyer's needless death isn't known. And whether Zora would have accepted a position with either of these teams after what happened is a moot point. The fact is that Zora's background would likely have prohibited such an offer. Zora, a Russian with Jewish bloodlines, would have almost no chance—regardless of the depth of his talent. Eventually, however, the Daimler-Benz team did bring on Englishman Richard Seaman, and Auto Union recruited Italian Tazio Nuvolari in the absence of suitable German talent, but both of these men already had established reputations behind the wheel. Duntov did not and would find that Germany was not the place for him to carve out a legend in motor sports. The fact that Zora was never fully accepted in Germany—at least in this capacity—would stay with him for many years to come and would give him an added incentive later in his career when he was in a position to compete against Germany.

From Bob to Bugatti

Without a glamorous racing career to attend to, Zora channeled his energies into his own projects. If he couldn't land a position with a major racing team, at least he could upgrade his own set of wheels. He eventually replaced his Bob with a dilapidated 1922 Type 30 Bugatti he bought in Berlin from a friend named Helmut Ruihul, whose father was a banker. The Bugatti was a major step up from the Bob. It had a 2.0-liter straight eight with two side-draft carburetors and chronically leaking hydraulic front brakes. Because the car was in such poor condition, Zora was able to buy it for a low price and then quickly got it into running order. As a result he had a relatively prestigious car to drive.

Zora's style behind the wheel was hard and fast. He always pushed his cars

Zora replaced his Bob with the Type 30 Bugatti on the left, which was in poor condition at the time he bought it. Zora quickly put it into running order. It is parked next to a Type 35, the most successful road-going racecar of all time.

to the limit of their performance. The streets of Berlin after a rainstorm provided a training ground for Zora to polish his car control techniques. "Berlin after rain is like ice rink," said Zora. During one of his "training sessions," Zora managed to break the rear axle on his stepfather's Chevrolet after slamming the tail end into a curb.

Summer weekends were frequently spent on the Baltic Sea coast, and Zora grew fond of challenging other cars to impromptu races on the country roads. He claimed to be the nemesis of the Essex Terraplane, a small but powerful American car. Zora loved the feeling of taking on a competitor and finding out who had the better car or who was the better driver. Winning these road skirmishes provided enormous satisfaction for Zora—another manifestation of control—but they took their toll as well. One weekend, driving up to Herringsdorf, he lost a connecting rod in the Bugatti during a fender-to-fender duel. The car had to be transported back to Berlin on a flatbed truck, and Zora took the engine into his Berlin apartment to rebuild it.

Top: Asia Orley (left, with leather helmet) owned a stable of MGs, including a J3, Zoller-supercharged MG Q and an 1100-cc Magnette.

Bottom: Orley did most of the race driving, but Zora used the association as a means to get closer to cars and racing.

Zora and Asia

While driving around in the Bob, Zora had met another racer who would become his best friend for life. He was a Russian Jew named Asia Orley (originally Owzarow). Orley was from a successful family and worked as a banker when he wasn't racing. Despite his homely appearance, Orley attracted beautiful women. He was intelligent, witty and wealthy. Like Zora, he expressed himself through his actions and appeared not to get emotionally involved with the people in his life. That suited Zora just fine.

While Zora maintained close ties to Yura, Orley represented his closest soul mate outside the family. Yura, who was still living with Rachel and Josef in Berlin, was a regular participant in Zora and Asia's activities—often at Zora's insistence and usually to Rachel's chagrin.

Concerned about the treatment of Jews by the new Nazi government, Orley moved to Paris in 1933. Zora remained in Berlin with Yura and his parents. Once in France, Orley started racing MGs and invited Zora to join him. Zora was happy to oblige, often commuting from Berlin on race weekends.

Zora occasionally got a chance to drive himself, often in the longer races where he partnered with Orley.

Since Orley had money, he could afford to buy competitive cars, and the contemporary MGs were very competitive. Unlike the relatively affordable British sports cars of the 1950s and 1960s, the MGs of the 1930s were sophisticated and expensive race cars with graceful bodies and powerful supercharged engines. Over time, the Orley stable included an MG J3, a Zoller-supercharged MG Q and an 1,100-cc Magnette (six-cylinder). Since Orley had the most money, he did most of the driving. Zora would take over if the car was ailing or in a tight situation during a race, when more driving talent was required.

Zora was impressed and amused by Asia's imagination and ability to run a scam, which brought the two even closer together. Orley constructed elaborate ruses to keep his racing secret from his parents, including the use of assumed names. Orley's propensity to crash necessitated his keeping his parents in the dark.

Zora also loved Orley's daredevil nature, which was not unlike his own. A typical example of Orley's approach to driving was an incident during a 24-hour endurance race, the Bol d'Or at Montlhéry, the beautiful high-speed banked track outside of Paris. Orley was driving the Magnette when it caught fire. The flames chased him out of the cockpit to the tail and eventually out of the car altogether. As he abandoned the steering, he slid from the tail to the pavement at approximately 80 to 100 mph. The car continued toward the inside of the banked track and miraculously stopped without hitting anything. Orley managed to get up off the pavement and grab a fire extinguisher placed thoughtfully on the inside of the track. Then he collapsed, suffering from both fire and friction burns.

As much as he admired Orley's spirit behind the wheel, Zora loved even more the yarn Orley spun in explaining his injuries to his parents: "I fell deep asleep with a lit cigarette, the cigarette set the mattress on fire and the ensuing smoke was suffocating me. I jumped through the window, but the room was on the second floor. I hit the ledge, which inspired a rotary motion, and I landed on the ground face down."

Accidents aside, the racing continued. That same year, 1933, Zora accompanied Orley to London to investigate the purchase of another MG Magnette. This black roadster was a race car/street car hybrid. When Zora saw it, he was overjoyed with the beauty of the car. No matter how good his cars were, Asia was still Asia behind the wheel, and the results were seldom any different. But for Zora, Asia represented a way to stay close to racing—whether Zora drove or not. In the absence of any other more immediate options, Zora stayed with Asia.

The Social Side

Zora's partnership with Orley offered more than just a race car ride. Orley's banking connections had exposed Zora to an all-new social circle of influential people. By that time, Zora had matured into a handsome, self-confident young adult who was learning the finer points of how to appeal to attractive members of the opposite sex.

As a result, Zora was seeing a wide range of women. He was dating a woman named Valla Kudash, whom he had met one night while walking the ledge of his apartment building. He also had a relationship with a woman named Dolly and was seeing Rotraud Richter, an attractive German actress, but none of these women seemed to have any real impact on him.

During Whitsun holiday a few weeks after Easter, several of Zora's friends went up to Herringsdorf, a popular resort on the Baltic Sea coast. At the beach, they noticed a particularly attractive blonde, blue-eyed teenage girl practicing acrobatics and cartwheels on the warm sand. She got even more attention as she sprinted into the surf despite the fact that it was May and the water was still brisk. Their hormones racing, the boys struck up a conversation with the girl, charmed by her athletic good looks and outgoing demeanor. After chatting for a while and hoping for a reason to meet again, they finally suggested getting together later that summer.

Come August, the same group—this time with Zora in tow—spotted the girl in Berlin and remembered her instantly. She was walking near a theater on her way to a date. The young men approached her and invited her to a cafe that featured music and dancing. The girl accepted and took a chair at a table right across from Zora. He looked into her eyes and she looked into his. It was August 9, 1935.

The girl was Elfi Wolff. That night, she commented to her household nurse that she had met someone that day. "He was beautiful, with his dark hair and blue eyes," she said. "He was so confident. I think it's going to last a long time."

Elfi, short for Elfriede, was from a well-to-do Jewish family in Berlin. Her father, William Wolff, had married Clara Lapoehn in 1914 and ran one of Germany's largest greeting card companies, called Hermann Wolff. The company owned four factories in Germany, including three in Berlin and one in Dresden. Elfi was the oldest of four children. The entire Wolff family was well schooled in the arts. Grandmother Wolff was a Shakespeare fan, and William was a talented writer who composed poems and plays for Elfi to perform. He also played the mandolin and believed he would have

Young Elfi Wolff attracted the attention of Zora's friends with her fetching looks and athletic prowess.

Top: Zora and Elfi took an instant liking to each other and spent many summer days enjoying the lakes around Berlin with their friends.

Middle: Elfi and Zora share a relaxing moment in the sun. She quickly attached herself to him, and was willing to accept Zora on his terms.

Bottom: Zora's mother Rachel joins Yura, Zora and Elfi for an outing. Rachel kept close tabs on the activities of both Zora and Yura, unlike during her earlier days as a revolutionary in Russia.

been a successful actor except for his father's demand that he work in his factory. Elfi was a natural-born beauty whose first love was gymnastics. She also liked modern and primitive dance, for which she had been schooled in France.

Zora was taken by this lovely teenager and invited her to go sailing with him on Wannensee Lake, outside Berlin. She in turn was moved by this handsome, worldly Russian. Soon she was frequenting Zora's street-level one-room apartment. Zora quickly gave her a key. On one occasion, she climbed atop a freestanding wardrobe, waited for him to come home and then playfully jumped him when he came in the door.

Fortunately, Elfi's acrobatic school was close to where Zora lived so they could see each other often. Feeling much more of an attachment to this girl than one of his typical one-night stands, he decided not to rush her into bed. He waited three weeks.

But intimacy didn't necessarily equate with fidelity. This led to complications when more than one woman was sharing his bed. Zora proudly described one particular episode: "At the time, I had a delightful though somewhat under-aged girlfriend (Elfi) whom I occasionally entertained in my room. However, I also had had a torrid night with a stray girl and my tracks most definitely needed immediate covering. Since I had earlier blown the engine on my Bugatti, I kept in my room the cast-aluminum engine box containing the camshaft and its 24 actuating fingers. Out came the Bugatti casting covered with castor oil. I deposited this component on the bed and my honor, such as it was, remained unsullied."

Duntov wasn't as unsullied as he thought, however. "I knew he was cheating on me from day one," Elfi recalls. Still she found the Russian irresistible. She would spell out "Zora" in Russian with bandages on her body and then tan herself in the sun to brand herself as his girl. She had a chronically nervous stomach from always waiting for his telephone calls. She often stretched out on the carpet to get rid of the horrible pain, then seek comfort and advice from girlfriends. When one of them asked whether Zora had any money and Elfi replied "no," the friend told her confidently that he'd be back.

Early on, she likened Zora to a little devil. While visiting Austria early in the courtship, Elfi picked up a little devil on a broomstick that reminded her of Zora. She gave it to him as a good luck charm.

Her insecurity about the relationship prompted sometimes-absurd requests to Zora to demonstrate his love. She had him stand in the window of his Berlin apartment every morning between 8:00 a.m. and 8:15 a.m. to wave at a passing commuter train, just in case she was on one of those trains. Zora felt it was ridiculous to be standing in front of an open window every morning watching the blur of a train going by. When Elfi wasn't on the train, she'd have her girlfriends look for him. Zora always imagined the train's passengers thinking "Look at this idiot in the window."

Somehow, the relationship thrived against the backdrop of one of the most cosmopolitan cities in Europe. Berlin had something for everyone—the arts, theaters, and concerts. One nightclub that Zora and Elfi frequented contained a large swimming pool with artificial waves called Wellenbad. Elfi was a regular at Kadeve, a department store of the magnitude of today's Bloomingdale's in New York or Harrod's in London. She also began to work as a department store model while she attended Westend Schule, a girl's school.

The city also began to develop a seamy underside, with dozens of cabarets that featured wanton nudity and masochism. There was also plenty of sex on the streets—prostitutes walking around in shoes that tied up to the knees with color-coded strings advertising their specialty. In all, Berlin was a bizarre fantasyland about to turn into a nightmare.

By 1937–1938, Berlin was becoming increasingly inhospitable for both Zora and Elfi. Tensions steadily increased as Jews were systematically routed out of their homes, and Nazi thugs roamed the streets and the clubs. Russian-born Zora began to feel increasingly unwelcome in a racist land, but he was quite used to unrest in his life and took the attitude that this too would pass.

The signs were getting more difficult to ignore, however. One day, Zora and Elfi took his Bugatti for a Sunday afternoon drive out to a forest area outside Berlin called Grunewald and were getting passionate in the car when a Nazi Brown Shirt pulled up behind them and started harassing the young lovers. Zora responded by rushing at the Nazi with the starter crank from the Bugatti in his hand. The Nazi fled, but the experience was yet more evidence that Germany was not a place where he could stay.

Asia Orley had already reached this conclusion, having moved to Paris. And Zora—still restless to do something with his life—began to spend much more of his time in the French capital, even though Elfi remained in Berlin. The most important thing in Zora's life was not Elfi or the political situation in Germany. He wanted to make his mark in auto racing and

During her courtship with Zora, Elfi arranged for portraits made by a professional photographer. With her attractive looks, she began to pick up modeling assignments in and around Berlin.

Top: Zora and Asia Orley began to envision building their own race car, which would be known as the Arkus.

Bottom: Much of the work for the Arkus was subcontracted to various Paris garages, with the bills being paid by Asia Orley.

put his personal stamp on an automobile. Given his disappointment in not being offered a position with Mercedes or Auto Union, he felt he would have to forge his own reputation as a race car designer and driver. Asia Orley's money would give him the opportunity to do that.

In Paris, sitting in a bar on the Champs Élysées, Zora and Asia would smoke cigarettes and talk about all the possibilities in racing, sketching out their visions on the tablecloths. Looking inward, Zora knew he was a very good engineer and wanted to use his skills to build race cars. He had long discussions with Orley and others willing to listen about his compressor (supercharging) theory.

It was during these conversations that the decision to build his own car was born. It was by far the most important project Zora had yet undertaken and would have profound implications for later in his career. The car would be a racer, of course, but Zora had in mind a completely new concept—something where he could apply his knowledge about compressors. Asia and Zora started to look for a car around Paris and found an old Talbot racer, which they purchased as the basis for Zora's machine. Joining them were two other friends from Russia, Misha Gerschenovitisch and Minia Eider, who would help build the car. Then they found a basement, which became their workshop, and annexed their favorite Paris bar as their unofficial office, often bringing engine parts into the establishment, much to the consternation and amusement of the waiters and bartenders.

During April of 1935, Zora and Asia took a trip down to Monte Carlo to see the Grand Prix. Peering at the beautiful Maseratis and other grand prix cars, the two envisioned their car someday competing in the same arena. Upon returning to Paris, the team reworked the entire Talbot to their own specifications. Zora designed new connecting rods, a new crankshaft and new valves. He likened the layout of the engine to an Offenhauser Indy car motor, which necessitated disassembling the whole thing in order to change a valve. Zora also devised a second water pump to aid engine cooling.

Zora possessed a great intuition for building race cars and performed some very accurate calculations, but he and his team were battling almost impossible odds. Unlike a well-funded factory team, they had no outside help. They had to fabricate parts and they lacked the proper tools. Money was a constant obstacle and Asia's original budget was long gone, while expenses soared. The bills kept mounting and Asia began to feel the pressure.

Their goal was to get the car built and enter it in the Grand Prix de Picardie in June 1935. The team worked deep into the night, every night—by now nothing else mattered. Finally the engine was mounted into the chassis, complete with the two large compressors Zora had sourced from Germany. The car was gorgeous. Because it represented Zora's thinking, it was named "the Arkus." It even had "Arkus" embossed onto the cylinder head covers.

Zora and Orley were so enthusiastic about their modifications to the engine that they visited Talbot and told the company of their plans. The Talbot people looked on in disbelief as Zora told them he could get more than 150 horsepower out of the engine. Talbot promised him they would test the motor themselves to verify the horsepower, but the engine was never in a proper condition to test it. A litany of problems kept popping up. Chronic water leaks caused Zora to reassemble the engine several times.

Then there were other problems. Zora determined that a valve seat insert needed to be installed, so he used some liquid oxygen to cool down the block and heads to be able to install the insert. After successfully completing the job, he had some excess liquid oxygen, so the guys in the shop decided to conduct a little experiment. They set up a magneto and a little bit of gasoline as a means to ignite the liquid oxygen. But the magneto didn't ignite the mixture, so Misha got closer and tried to ignite it with a burning twig. The explosion blew out a gasoline pump, shattered all the windows of the shop and propelled shrapnel in every direction. One of the pieces embedded itself in Misha's right leg. Misha was taken to a hospital in Paris, where the doctor wanted to amputate. But Zora—showing the headstrong nature he inherited from his mother—wouldn't let him. To Zora, being an amputee was a death sentence. So the doctor took piece after piece of metal out of Misha's leg while trying to reduce the danger of blood poisoning. Misha's recovery took three weeks in the

The foundation for the Arkus was an old Talbot racer, the engine of which Zora reworked and designed new connecting rods, crankshaft, valves and a supercharger. The cam covers were clearly marked with the name "Arkus."

Zora looks over the completed Arkus, but would come to find that building a competitive race car was easier said than done.

hospital, and afterwards he had to learn how to walk again. But thanks to Zora, he still had his leg.

The team's woes were not over. Several weeks later, Asia accidentally dropped a bolt into the engine. According to Asia's diary of the episode, Zora had a look of pain on his face as he contemplated many more hours spent tearing down the engine once again. He didn't say a word; he just walked away and sat down. Fortunately, one of the mechanics was able to retrieve the bolt. Weeks later, Asia was towing Zora in the Arkus when it suddenly caught fire. The two tore off their clothes to try to smother the fire as if it were more important than family.

At Montlhéry, Zora had difficulty getting the engine started, and they spent hours pushing the car just to turn the pistons and crank. Almost miraculously the engine started, so Zora took it out on the circuit for a few laps. But the continuing problems prevented them from ever racing the car.

The Arkus was eventually sold to their mechanic, and Zora and Asia returned their attention to Asia's stable of MGs. For Zora, the Arkus was a rude lesson in trying to run his own racing operation. Clearly it made more sense to link up with an established manufacturer with greater experience and resources.

But the Arkus project wasn't a total loss. Beneath the veneer of failure was an emerging engineer learning through trial and error, taking risks and bringing his ideas to life. The lessons from the Arkus would not be forgotten. Building cars like the Arkus was exactly what Zora wanted to do with his life. It gave him the sense of control he had been seeking from the time of his youth in Russia. Now it was a matter of finding another place to do it.

THREE

The Manager and the Racer

Zora's dream of being a successful race car designer was going to take longer than planned. Europe was becoming increasingly unstable in the late 1930s and the prospect of Germany going to war against its neighbors was becoming more likely. Like it or not, Zora was about to be sucked into the vortex of a major world event and would be at the mercy of forces he couldn't control.

The signs of impending disaster were everywhere. During a road trip to Berlin in late 1938, Zora noticed dummy military equipment in the fields in an attempt to make the armed forces appear even stronger than they were. Zora and Elfi together witnessed the Nazis march on the main avenues of Berlin, goose-stepping as the crowds responded with raised hands. They stood aghast, observing this spectacle with their arms down. Zora's parents would see the inevitable in Hitler's rise to power in the 1930s. Despite not practicing any religion they were still concerned about anti-Semitism in Germany and so they immigrated to Paris.

Elfi's father also saw the writing on the wall. Despite living in one of the best neighborhoods in Berlin, he began to send his children, one by one, out of the country in 1937. Elfi was sent to Paris, Ruty to Switzerland and Warren to Scotland. William and Clara eventually also accepted the inevitable and moved to London in 1939. There, Elfi's father would reestablish his greeting card operation under a new name—Giesen-Wolff—thanks to his new English partner. The Wolffs lost almost all their possessions in the move, since sending them out of the country was extremely difficult. Elfi herself would later learn the horror of what it was like to be Jewish during this black period of history.

But Zora was reluctant to come to terms with what was happening in Europe. Perhaps he didn't want to think about the implications of Jewish ancestry in a country where Jews were being harassed and uprooted from their homes, eventually to be thrown into concentration camps. He was

Opposite: Zora enjoys the good life at a Sunday afternoon picnic, but his existence was about to be turned upside down.

more worried still about making a living. With racing jobs out of the question for the moment, Zora vowed to find employment wherever he could.

Zora had been spending a considerable amount of his time in Paris on the Arkus project, and now there were ample if not urgent reasons to leave Berlin altogether. After much foot dragging, he decided to head west to look for positions in Paris or Brussels, where he could reestablish himself in a true professional position without feeling like an unwanted foreigner.

He found a lead in Brussels through Asia Orley's father. The company was F. Société Mondiale, which manufactured machine tools as well as motorcycles. It was the motorcycles that really attracted Zora to the company. He interviewed and impressed the managers at Mondiale sufficiently to receive a job offer which he accepted. However, he never got the chance to work on motorcycles. The company had received down payments from dealers on many motorcycles but then failed to make good on delivery. Soon the company was out of the motorcycle business completely. Still, Zora tried to make the most of the job.

Zora had no previous management experience but impressed his Mondiale superiors sufficiently for them to make him a manager after several months on the job. He was assigned to supervise the machine shop, which employed about 100 people, most of whom spoke only Flemish. Zora spoke only French, Russian and German, so he had to rely on bilingual foremen to communicate his orders down through the ranks.

When Zora took over, only one person on his staff knew how to run an old, turn-of-the-century gear-cutting machine. This particular worker was unreliable and if he didn't come in on a particular day, the company was without a supply of gears, so Zora would often cut the gears himself. As a manager, he was ready and willing to jump into the fray at any time. It helped him to better understand what his subordinates were up against. In working the machine, Zora discovered that the cutter was not ground symmetrically. "When I understand that, and pay attention to which side of cutter to use, was no problem," said Zora matter of factly years later.

Over time, Zora honed his management skills and was eventually put in charge of manufacturing of hand grenades for Mondiale. This time, he had 150 people under his jurisdiction, all of whom were arriving at work pretty much when they felt like it. When one of his foremen translators didn't show up, Zora had to chase him down at a local pub. Eventually Zora imposed some discipline and standards on the group and became an effective manager, something that would serve him well in the future.

Zora was also confronted with the kind of business challenges that face many factory owners—he needed to find ways to balance quality minimums with low piece costs. In manufacturing hand grenades, Zora decided to use a cheaper stamping instead of a machined piece for the part that holds the firing pin. When he test-exploded a grenade behind a large steel plate inside the Mondiale shop, the grenade fizzled like a Roman candle. Replacing the stamping with a machined component solved the problem but also increased the unit cost.

Zora later transferred from grenades to lathes, which allowed him another opportunity to apply his engineering skills. He was assigned a project to develop an all-new lathe and called in two outside consultants to help create it. They included a University of Belgium professor named Vandepool, and one of Zora's old professors at Charlottenburg, Dr. Schlesinger. Although Zora had never created a lathe before, he sketched out his own design, which proved superior—it was the only one of the three that didn't allow any flexing, thanks to the installation of diagonal braces.

Zora likened his interest in engineering to a big detective story—one was always faced with solving some sort of a puzzle. The excitement kicks in when something turns out differently than predicted. "Then you go to work to solve the puzzle," he said. Zora went on to become the chief designer and shop superintendent of Mondiale, where he assisted with the design and manufacturing of all the company's engine lathes. He was quickly demonstrating an ability to engineer projects—from design through manufacturing.

Zora designed this lathe at his first real career job, which was at F. Société Mondiale in Brussels, a machine tool manufacturer that at one time manufactured motorcycles.

The Continued Draw of Racing

While Zora continued his work at Mondiale, racing was never far from his mind. He wrote another technical paper, this one titled "Analysis of Four-Wheel Drive for Racing Cars" for a German society of engineers. Until then, Zora had been primarily interested in engines, but here he showed considerable vision in an area where he had previously had no obvious training. By getting his article published, Zora may have wished to send a message to Mercedes and Auto Union that they had made a mistake by not hiring him.

Four-wheel drive was a radical new concept at the time, since most race cars up until then had been built for straight-line speed. Power and aerodynamics were just coming into the equation in the mid 1930s, thanks to the designs of Mercedes and Auto Union, which had won the vast majority of the grand prix races since 1934.

Zora felt he had the answer for the poor-handling, rear-engined Auto Unions—four-wheel drive.

The two German rivals, Mercedes and Auto Union, employed radically different approaches to their race cars. The Mercedes cars were more traditional, with front-mounted engines and a succession of power plants ranging from straight 8s to V-12s. The Auto Union designers, on the other hand, positioned their engines behind the driver, just ahead of the rear axle, and used V-16 and V-12 power plants.

While the Auto Unions were unbeatable on wide, fast circuits, it was a different story on the tight tracks. Their drivers had difficulty detecting impending slides from their forward position in the cockpit. Zora, who would become a strong advocate of mid-engined cars, felt that four-wheel drive might be the answer, a point he asserted in his paper. He was intrigued by the concept of extra grip coming from four tires instead of two biting into the pavement. Zora ignored the challenge of fitting such a unit within the strict 750 kg weight limit then in effect. But if this challenge could be overcome, four-wheel drive would make the Auto Union unbeatable on any track, and might have major applications for nonracing vehicles as well. Zora would champion this technology throughout his life.

In the 1937 Automobile Salon in Paris, Zora had the opportunity to meet the designer of the Mercedes-Benz' SS and SSK racers as well as the grand prix Auto Unions, Dr. Ferdinand Porsche. Whether they discussed four-wheel-drive applications on the Auto Union is unknown, but they did talk about supercharging. Even in the face of Porsche's reputation, Zora couldn't help himself. He took issue with Dr. Porsche on some technical aspects of his compressor motor. Porsche was not known for taking criticism well, and Zora felt the discussion might have soured Porsche against him. Ultimately, Zora felt that he had destroyed whatever slim chance he had of working for the Auto Union race team. It may not have made much difference, for Porsche had largely moved on to design and build Hitler's affordable "people's car," which became known as the Volkswagen Beetle.

The meeting with Dr. Porsche wouldn't be Zora's last connection with the Porsche family. Later, after World War II, Porsche created his own storied sports car marque, which would provide Zora with another opportunity to reestablish a connection.

At the same 1937 Paris show, Zora also met Ettore Bugatti, the renowned constructor of racing cars. As the owner of a Bugatti, Zora had more than a passing interest in getting to know this man. He was struck by Bugatti's dandified appearance, complete with derby hat, gray tie with diamond clip, and white gloves. Zora was particularly intrigued by Bugatti's shoes, which separated the big toe from the rest of his foot. It set Bugatti apart as a maverick, which Zora could fully appreciate, although the subject of shoes was beyond his immediate interest.

While Bugatti presented a memorable appearance, he applied a different aesthetic sense to his racing machines, which were elegantly simple and fast. Zora was even more impressed by the fact that Bugatti's cars were successful in the hands of privateers. For example, René Dreyfus and his older brother Maurice were able to buy a Bugatti and transport it from their home in nearby Nice to the 1930 Monaco Grand Prix and win the race, beating legends such as Tazio Nuvolari and Louis Chiron. The car, of course, was considered the most successful road-going race car of all time—the Bugatti Type 35. René Dreyfus went on to become the most famous Bugatti driver, and was a man Zora would get to know better several decades later.

At the time, Bugatti's star was fading in grand prix circles, thanks to the overwhelming dominance of the government-supported German teams. But his place in racing history was secure, having completely dominated the sport in the late 1920s. Even though the Germans dominated the scene in the late 1930s, the lessons of Bugatti would stick with Zora. "His cars looked right, handled right and won races not by sheer power, but by superior handling."

Elfi's Career

During Zora's tenure at Mondiale, Elfi was becoming a bigger part of his life, despite his efforts to be independent. He lived in a one-room apartment in Brussels which contained a bed and a partition for a toilet and bidet. Elfi spent much of her time with him in these cozy quarters. Since the room had no kitchen, she cooked inventive meals for him using an alcohol-fueled cooker.

But Elfi was about to get a big career break. Since he had moved to Paris in 1932, Asia Orley had gotten to know a number of dancers from the world-famous Folies Bergère. A dancer named Erna Otto introduced Elfi to Herr Funke, who ran the Spark Ballet, one of the many acts within this Paris-based dance troupe. Funke quickly recognized Elfi's talent and beauty and, despite her limited ballet experience (she had performed for a short time for a ballet troupe in Berlin), Funke offered her a chance to join the group in 1937. Elfi gladly accepted and traveled with the group for a year as they performed throughout France and Belgium.

The following year, Elfi saw more opportunity come her way. In late 1938, she joined another dance troupe under the Folies Bergère, known as the Bluebell Girls, who were named after the troupe's leader, an English dancer known as Bluebell. The troupe had 24 dancers split evenly between blondes and redheads. They performed cabaret-style reviews all over France, although they were based in Paris. They did not dance topless like some of the other acts in the Folies, but instead wore an array of very stylish yet sexy evening gowns. Elfi was the slimmest of all the dancers and was usually the one to be lifted high in the air at the climax of a number. The pace was often grueling. On weekends the dancers worked two shows, and often did not get to bed until after 3 a.m.

Zora was not apparently threatened by Elfi's new celebrity status. If anything, it opened up new opportunities for him and his friends to meet and entertain the Folies girls, frequently engaging them in all-night parties—with or without Elfi. Even Yura—who had moved to Paris with his parents—got into the act, having a fling with one of Asia's girlfriends from the Folies.

Top: Elfi got a big dancing break with the Bluebell Girls, a dancing troupe under the world famous Folies Bergère. Elfi is standing fourth from the left.

Bottom: The Bluebell Girls performed in many stylish outfits, dancing heavily choreographed routines. Elfi is third from the left.

While Zora was enjoying himself, Elfi increasingly talked of settling down together, an idea that terrified Zora. A commitment of this nature may have been one of the few risks Zora didn't want to take. He had worked hard to establish a sense of control in his life and didn't wish to lose his freedom to make decisions for himself. Furthermore, he didn't put much stock in the institution of marriage after seeing his father tossed aside by his headstrong mother. In Zora's mind, it was better to keep his options open and never give himself totally to another person.

So Zora tried to put marriage off. Ironically, it was his mother, Rachel—despite her own sordid history—who prodded Zora into making a long-term commitment to Elfi. Rachel suggested to Zora that he couldn't expect this nice young girl to keep waiting indefinitely. Still vulnerable to her suggestions, he popped the question to Elfi one day at the Berlin Zoo while they were watching some monkeys fornicate. Elfi didn't take long to ponder her response. Since the couple didn't have any money, her father paid for the rings.

Zora and Yura had their own little bachelor party in Brussels before joining Elfi at her parents' home in Berlin. Perhaps it was more of a toast to Zora's dwindling status as a totally free man. The two got drunk at the train station and Yura vomited all over Zora's blue suit. When the two arrived in Berlin, Zora's suit was still wet, and Elfi's mother Clara took the suit to the cleaners. But Elfi and Zora's engagement party went on despite Zora's wariness of what he was about to get into, and the young couple was showered with gifts.

Zora got a reprieve from marriage, however, after he suffered a severe attack of sciatica brought on by performing a Pasch dance, a sexual strut involving extreme movements of the torso and hips. The occasion was a birthday party for his friend Misha. The attack was so bad that his father picked him up and brought him back to Paris, where he was bedridden for weeks, resulting in the wedding being postponed. He was treated with Chinese needles and a vegetable diet. When these remedies proved ineffective, Rachel took him to Dax, a resort in the Pyrenees that specialized in mud baths. Elfi went there to visit and stayed after Rachel returned home. Elfi convinced Zora's mother that she needed to sleep in the same room so that she could look after her fiancé.

Designing Diesels

After Zora recovered, he still dragged his feet about getting to the altar. His excuse was that he needed to earn more money first, so he took a job in Paris at Société des Locomotives Diesel, also known as Marchak. At Marchak he designed mining locomotives, yet another example of his taking on a new endeavor with no previous experience and showing another dimension to his extraordinary design skills. Zora had sketched and built a model locomotive as a youth in Russia, but this was his first hands-on design exercise. He sketched two different narrow-gauge mining locomotives, the designs of which were successful enough to merit production in both France and the United States.

He also designed a locomotive transmission as well as several diesel engines for truck and tractor applications. Marchak had been using German-made Deutz diesels, but with the possibility of another war against Germany, the company was eager to establish its own source. Zora's design borrowed heavily from the Deutz unit, although it differed mainly in its cone-shaped combustion chamber. His engine was used in Etablissements Willeme and Sotradies, French truck and tractor manufacturers. Zora's effort proved superior to those of several other counterparts at the company and he was soon put in charge of all Marchak's in-line diesel engines, a position similar to his role at Mondiale with the engine lathes. Surely these accomplishments say something extraordinary about Zora, not only as an engineer and visionary but also as an effective manager. It was becoming increasingly clear that he would have a successful future no matter where he went. The question came down to what Zora really wanted to do and how high he wanted to go.

The Lure of Gold

While gainfully employed at Marchak, Zora was becoming restless because he was detached from any hands-on opportunities to work with race cars. He was ready for a new challenge that would allow him to feel totally in charge of his life. It didn't take long to come up with a scheme that involved danger, intrigue and a fast car. In 1936, Léon Blum, socialist minister of France, issued a decree freezing all gold transactions in and out of France. French capitalists, big and small, turned to Belgium, where the trade of gold was free and unencumbered by the government, and the price was higher. Anyone who could conceive of ways to safely transport gold from France to Belgium could benefit from the higher exchange rate across the border.

The challenge was how to smuggle gold without getting caught. Zora decided it would be best to drive the gold to Belgium and opted to use Asia Orley's Flathead Ford V-8 for that purpose. Zora devised a special tube that looked like a cross member, which ran across the chassis frame above the rear axle. With the false cross member installed, Zora made his border runs during the middle of the night. He was staying with his parents at the time and, unsure of their attitude about his clandestine activities, he decided to keep them in the dark. Zora would pretend to go to bed, then sneak out and coast the Ford down a hill before starting it, just to make sure he was out of earshot. Once on the highway, the run would take about two hours, including a document check at the border. On his high-speed runs through the darkness of the French countryside, Zora was impressed with the 5,000-rpm revving capability of his Ford Flathead V-8 and began to imagine the engine's potential if it could only breathe a little more freely.

Once he would arrive in Brussels, the Ford would be put up on a hoist, where Zora's contacts would remove the tube, count the gold and pay him. The people in Brussels nicknamed him Edison for his ingenuity in designing the tube. The return home took about the same amount of time, and Zora would slip in just before dawn. His parents eventually found out and put an immediate stop to his export business. Zora's adult status did not exempt him from the rules of his parents' house.

Before his gold smuggling was discontinued, Zora made about one run a week over the course of a year, as did his friends Orley and

Gerschenovitisch. Zora made enough money to buy a large Renault sedan, a Nerva Sport. But instead of keeping it himself, he gave it to his mother and stepfather, perhaps as a peace token, or perhaps as a symbol that despite all they had been through, he still cared for them.

Zora's smuggling episode would have a bigger payoff for him a decade later, when he could put his experience with the Ford Flathead V-8 to better—and more legal—use.

Elfi made extra money in a different way. She bought a lottery ticket in the Loterie National and won. Like the lotteries of today, this was a multimillion-franc payoff, and her share of a 50,000-franc pot was enough, along with a contribution from her father, to buy a beautiful black MG J2 Midget with a red leather interior and supercharged engine. She loved sports cars and had previously owned a couple of former race cars—a Mathis roadster as well as a Chenard—that had been converted for street use. She was well schooled by Zora in driving and learned to drive aggressively on the country roads outside of Paris.

Wedding Bells

By early 1939, Zora's back was much better, and he had more money in his pockets. He had also run out of excuses not to get married, so he finally set a date with Elfi for a wedding. The civil ceremony took place on February 11, 1939, in Billancourt, just outside of Paris. Asia—not Yura—was Zora's best man, a choice to which he attached no particular significance.

Being a nervous groom, Zora hesitated when the celebrant asked if he'd take Elfi to be his lawful wedded wife. "Yes, he will," blurted Elfi for him, and the ceremony proceeded. The newlyweds rented the Astor Bar off the Champs Élysées for the reception, and Zora invited all his racing friends, while Elfi invited her friends from the Folies Bergère. The exhausted couple stayed in their own apartment on their wedding night. They never did honeymoon because Zora had just started his job with Marchak. Elfi had a week of vacation coming, so she celebrated by going skiing at a French resort with a girlfriend.

Elfi practices dancing movements at a ski resort on her "honeymoon," which she took with a girlfriend because Zora could not get off work.

FOUR

ignature du titulaire - Handteekening des houde

Zora's World at War

When World War II finally broke out in September 1939, Zora didn't harbor any passionate feelings toward either side. His native Russia was allied with Germany at the beginning of the war. Furthermore, he had lived in Germany and had many friends there. He held a deep respect for the engineering capabilities of German companies such as Daimler-Benz and Auto Union. While he harbored a strong personal distaste for the Nazis, he—like many Europeans of the time—had little idea what a madman Hitler was. Zora was more concerned about having to uproot himself again and perhaps be forced out of Europe altogether.

Upon mobilization, Zora first considered trying to stay neutral by sticking it out at Marchak, feeling that this was just another war. "You know, fight with Germany and maybe year or two years or five years, all forgotten, and we embrace Germany," said Zora. But Yura had already joined the Armée de l'Air, the French Air Force. Zora's mother, horrified by fascism yet mellowed from her leftist thinking by her years in the West, urged Zora to follow in his brother's footsteps. "It's duty," she said. "You fight—democracy." It was a far cry from her days as a high-ranking communist official in the Soviet Union.

But also weighing on his mind was his own ego; he could once again take up his childhood role as protector of Yura and the sense of satisfaction that would provide. He ignored the fact that his brother was a young adult who had preceded Zora into the service and was perfectly capable of taking care of himself.

Elfi would have preferred he not enter the service, since it would mean not only separation from her husband but that she'd be left behind in Paris and be vulnerable to a German invasion. All things considered, it was a gamble Zora was willing to take, although he hedged his bets by urging her to move to safer territory in England, where she could live with her parents in London until the end of the war. Many of her fellow Bluebell

Opposite: Zora assumes a more serious visage in his French passport photo. He would find that proper paperwork during wartime was a particularly vexing issue.

Girls were English, and she could easily accompany them back home. But Elfi, fearful of losing all of her possessions, including items her parents left behind for her, stubbornly insisted on remaining in Paris. Zora's parents were still there, she reasoned, and could help out if anything went wrong.

Besides Elfi's safety, Zora's other consideration could have been his own survival. If he sensed any fear of getting hurt or killed in the war, however, he didn't let on. Like many young men of the era, Zora felt a certain youthful immortality, having already outlived the gypsies' prediction in Leningrad that he would die young. If anything, the chance to be around high-performance airplanes in potentially dangerous situations had a certain appeal.

The matter now settled, Zora quit his job with Marchak and enlisted in the military. French policy, however, didn't guarantee which branch of the service an enlistee would be assigned. Zora was originally assigned to an infantry group in Montpellier, away from Yura, who was training to be an air force candidate officer at Mérignac, just west of Bordeaux. Clearly, Zora was not cut out to be an infantryman. He complained about eating mess-hall-quality food, getting up at 5:30 a.m. and having to shower with cold water.

In attempting to transfer to Yura's regiment in the air force, he discovered another snag. It had been French policy since Napoleon that brothers could not serve in the same unit. When the brothers Duntov were discovered together, Private Second Class Zora Arkus was reassigned. But several weeks later, he again turned up in Yura's unit. "String pulling" was Zora's explanation, although he never indicated which strings got pulled or how he was able to maneuver around French policy. But thanks to Zora, the brothers were stationed together at the base at Mérignac. Their unit was an attachment of Potez bombers, light twin-engine airplanes with four crewmen.

Leaving Paris

Back in Paris, Elfi was alone and in limbo. At the outbreak of the war, the French government immediately issued vintage gas masks left over from World War I, which was not a reassuring gesture to Elfi or other residents. With the buildup in tension came an eerie quiet throughout the country, a period referred to as "the phony war." Little was happening militarily, and many of the armed forces grew restless waiting for the Germans to invade. This spawned a popular song in France called "We're Hanging Our Laundry on the Siegfried Line." Elfi spent the time setting up housekeeping in their West Side Paris apartment overlooking the Seine. She had just received their furniture—part of a dowry package from her parents, the day before the war broke out—as well as the rest of her parents' personal belongings that weren't confiscated by the Nazis back in Berlin.

Although Zora didn't care for writing letters, he wrote several to Elfi addressed to their apartment, located at 3 rue Général Grosetti. Sensitive about the possibility of the letters falling into the wrong hands—those of either the Germans or French collaborators—he used an assumed name, Abranovitch, and referred to himself in the third person. He also used a false return address.

In one letter drafted while he was still in Montpellier, he wrote: "My dear, I saw Zora and he's very well and nicely tanned. It's too bad I cannot telephone him because of the enemies (Germans)." He then described in the third person his own attempt to get into the same regiment as Yura.

Another letter was addressed to Elfi in Marseilles, where she was performing with the Folies. Even though the Folies had closed down in Paris on the day of general mobilization, Bluebell had arranged for an engagement in this coastal city near the Riviera, which was relatively peaceful at the time. As such, it seemed to Zora like a good place for a weekend rendezvous with Elfi, so he wrote her another letter using the same false address in Montpellier. He then told his company doctor that he needed to go to Marseilles to see a dentist. The doctor agreed but then sent him to another city. Zora missed his last chance to see Elfi before the German invasion.

While Elfi's parents were safely in London, Zora's parents were still in Paris and were in much the same predicament as Elfi—except they had emergency exit visas from the United States, the result of Rachel's work for a Jewish relief organization. As the Germans advanced westward toward Paris, Rachel and Josef knew they had to get out and encouraged Elfi to do the same, inviting her to come with them. Their plan was to head south toward Bordeaux to get close to where Zora was stationed. From there they hoped to get to Marseilles and catch a boat out or head west by land to Spain.

Rachel and Josef's pleadings finally galvanized Elfi into action, but unlike them, she had no papers. She knew the Germans were coming and she had to leave Paris immediately. She hurried to the gendarmerie to try to obtain travel papers but found the office abandoned. She tried several other government offices to no avail. Securing proper documentation would be

In this letter, Zora drew a little sketch to help explain to Elfi how to fix a mechanical problem with her MG.

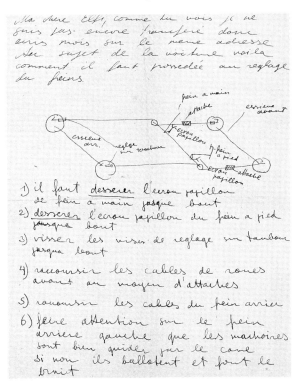

impossible. She'd have to make do with a stateless passport issued after her marriage, since she had given up her German citizenship when she married Zora. With Zora hundreds of miles away at Mérignac, he was helpless to do anything about Elfi's situation or that of his parents. Suddenly his decision to join the French Air Force didn't seem like such a good idea.

Then time ran out for Elfi. On June 13, 1940, the day before German tanks rumbled through the streets of Paris, she made the decision to go. Not wanting to leave her MG behind, she stubbornly refused Rachel and Josef's offer to ride with them. She then threw everything she could into the two-seater, including Zora's technical books and a few of her clothes. She said a tearful good-bye to Zora's father, Jacques, who planned to remain in their apartment and take his chances. She also said goodbye to everything else she owned, including a Chagall painting of a figure that was half woman and half cow, which Rachel had given to her. Her plan was to eventually link up with Rachel and Josef. But since the roads leading out of Paris were choked with refugee traffic and staying together would be next to impossible, they made arrangements to meet in Fontainebleau, a small town about 30 kilometers south of Paris.

Elfi faced just one unsettling problem. She had little gas in her MG and supplies had dried up because of military and refugee demand. Asia Orley, however, told her that she might be able to obtain fuel from an old girlfriend of Zora's named Dolly, from the Berlin days. Since then, Dolly had moved just outside Paris. Orley gave Elfi directions to Dolly's place, which was far enough away from the city to enable her to maintain a supply of gasoline in a large tank on her property. But when Elfi arrived, Dolly felt no compassion for the wife of her ex-boyfriend and refused to give her

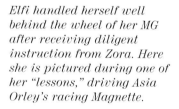

Elfi handled herself well behind the wheel of her MG after receiving diligent instruction from Zora. Here she is pictured during one of her "lessons," driving Asia Orley's racing Magnette.

any gas. After three hours of pleading, Elfi gave up and hit the road, her MG now running on fumes. Desperation set in.

Elfi remained strong. When she finally reached Fontainebleau, she searched the town futilely for Josef and Rachel. Noticing her distress, a gendarme asked her what she was doing and where she was planning to sleep that night. He made it clear she wouldn't be allowed to sleep in her car. Then he ordered her to follow him up to his personal quarters above the police station to spend the night with him. She wondered what Zora would think of the episode, but with a strong survival instinct setting in, she did as the gendarme suggested, relieved he didn't force himself on her. When he woke up early the next morning to go back on duty, she quickly snuck out and found her car. She would now have to find her way to Bordeaux on her own.

Zora Joins the Air War—Almost

Zora had to wonder what he had gotten into after he was reunited with Yura in the Armée de l'Air. He had hoped to become a pilot, so he could exercise the same control he'd had in racing motorcycles and driving cars. Because he was in a bomber unit, however, he wouldn't get the same raw thrill he would flying a fighter plane. But Zora didn't get a chance to fly at all. Instead he was assigned as a tail gunner, where he would be a sitting duck in any air-to-air engagement with the enemy.

Making matters worse, there were few airplanes for training purposes. When the war started, the French had only several hundred single-seat fighters—138 Morane 406s, 94 Curtiss Hawks and only 8 modern bombers. Five of those were twin-engine LeO 45s and three were Potez 633s. These few bombers were no match for Germany's best. Zora's airplane, the Potez 633, was at least 100 mph slower than its German counterpart, the Messerschmitt BF110. To add to the insult, the Germans had a 20-to-1 advantage in aircraft numbers alone.

Even after the French began to crank out new airplanes, the French Air Force was so disorganized that it was unable to make effective use of them. In his limited training as a tail gunner, Zora discovered that many of the available airplanes lacked guns or radios. The planes had been shipped that way from the factories. In those instances where a Potez plane did have guns, the controls tended to freeze at the high altitudes for which the aircraft was designed.

While Zora expected to be mobilized closer to the German border once the war broke out, he remained at Mérignac because his unit was under the control of the local land army, which decided to keep its planes at home. For Zora and Yura, it was probably a good thing that their unit remained in southwest France, hundreds of miles from the German front.

Nonetheless, the war came to them. Mérignac was the bombing target of a squadron of Italian warplanes that swept over the region. Zora and Yura felt the earth tremble as an unexploded bomb just missed their barracks. "It was one of the most picturesque engagements of the war," said Yura in an interview years later in *Sports Illustrated*. "We had only one squadron to send up against them—a Belgian squadron equipped with Italian fighters. When the Italian bombers encountered the Italian fighters, the confusion in the sky was total."

Overall, the French Air Force was so ineffective early in the war, before the Allied effort ramped up, that French antiaircraft batteries fired on any airplane in the sky, assuming it was German. Even though many individuals of the French Air Force would fight bravely against the Germans, the combination of inferior aircraft, inadequate training and lack of organization would prove to be their undoing.

Later, the French would get help from the United States in the form of the twin-fuselage Lockheed P38 Lightning, which was among the fastest airplanes in existence by 1943. The P38 was so fast that one American officer quipped at the time that it made the Potez look like Wilbur Wright's plane.

Word of Invasion

When Zora heard from the French authorities the news about the German invasion of Paris, he was helpless to do anything about it. He could have been arrested if he tried to leave his encampment, and he didn't trust some of the French authorities who had already adopted an occupation mentality, as evidenced by his need to disguise his letters. The French military was in disarray and it was only a matter of time before the Germans overran them. Zora and Yura seriously considered commandeering a Potez bomber and flying it to safety in England, but that would not have solved the problem of how to get Elfi and their parents out of France. Worse yet, with the Germans advancing westward, Zora's family appeared to be in immediate danger. He wondered if it might be possible to find them amid the chaos. He decided it was best to stay put and let them find him—if they were still alive.

Zora also worried about the whereabouts of his father, Jacques, who had told him earlier that if the Germans invaded Paris, he would not flee the city. Zora wondered whether Jacques honored that pledge or whether Rachel and Josef would be successful in persuading him to accompany them. If Jacques stayed in Paris, sooner or later he'd fall into the hands of the

Nazis. His Russian heritage wouldn't provide much protection as long as he had a Jewish surname. Zora didn't want to contemplate Jacques' fate.

Elfi on the Run

Elfi found her way out of Fontainebleau and arrived at a refugee station, which provided her with a bite to eat and a few liters of gas. Feeling renewed, she resumed her drive, but instead of contending with the traffic on the main roads, she chose the back ones, where she could make better time. By then she had abandoned all hope of finding Zora's parents. She just wanted to survive—one day at a time—and hope she could find her husband in Bordeaux. Out on the open road, the MG's motor humming, she could almost forget there was a war going on. But then she saw a plane go down in the distance, and the sickening sight of black smoke and flames. She didn't know whether it was German or French.

Later that day, Elfi managed to get more gas at another refugee station. Toward evening, she began to search for a place to spend the night and saw some French soldiers in a village street. She asked one of them where she could find a room. Like the gendarme the night before, the soldier too was attracted to Elfi, so they talked awhile. He finally asked her for a lift into the next village. When they arrived, he invited her to spend the night in an old peasant's house, which had a fireplace. She no longer cared what his intentions were. During wartime, one had to put one's trust in total strangers. The soldier offered her shelter and safety and she gladly accepted. There were children in the house sleeping all over the place, but Elfi and the soldier slept together that night in a giant bed. The soldier fed her strawberries the next morning and gallantly sent her on her way. Yes, she thought, there were still some good people left in the world.

The next morning, she continued along the French country roads toward Bordeaux, but trouble was still on the horizon. Later that morning, the MG sputtered and died for no apparent reason. She still had gas left in the tank, and couldn't figure out why the car wouldn't start. Desperation again set in. She didn't want to abandon the car—it held too many of her belongings. Lacking any other alternatives, she got out and started pushing. Nearing the point of exhaustion, after what seemed like hours she heard the voices of angels—English voices—and realized she was near a Scottish army camp.

Seeing a beautiful young woman in their midst, the soldiers must have thought their prayers had been answered. They eagerly took her back to their quarters, put her up in a peasant house and fed her a warm breakfast the next morning. They even got the MG running again and filled up the tank. They issued one caveat: Don't stop the engine because it might be hard to start again.

Underway again, she came to a crossroads and was stopped by another gendarme, who insisted on examining her papers. Since she didn't have any, she was forced to follow him to the police station, where he asked her about the whereabouts of her husband. They told her she'd be taken into their custody overnight. Meanwhile, several other gendarmes went out and inspected what she was carrying with her in the MG. Her heart raced at the thought they might think she was a spy. She had Zora's technical books written in German. Surely she was done for. But suddenly they announced she was free to go. Puzzled by that decision for years, she later concluded, "maybe because I had no gold, jewelry or money worth confiscating."

On the fourth day of her journey, after the French authorities had helped her get the MG started again, Elfi arrived amid the scenic Bordeaux vineyards where Zora was stationed. She was parked outside the gate of the French airfield when Zora noticed her car as he was riding by in a military truck. The sight of Elfi never looked so good. He jumped out and sprinted over to her and picked her up and smothered her with kisses. He couldn't help but marvel at how she had stayed ahead of the Germans and French authorities without money or papers. Looking at her disheveled appearance—complete with a fever blister—after five days on the open road, he saw a bit of himself in her—the risk taker who took on the odds and prevailed. Her fortitude inspired in him a whole new respect for his young wife.

In Quest of Exit Papers

Several days later, Josef and Rachel showed up at Mérignac. Elfi had beaten them by taking the less-traveled back roads. Since Zora was in the process of demobilizing when Elfi arrived, they were now free to pursue an escape route. Zora was coolheaded about the situation. If he felt any inward fear, he didn't show it.

His first move was to drive with Yura to nearby Bayonne, on the Spanish border. They stayed there several days and ran into Asia Orley, who was in a similar predicament and looking for passage to a safer place. By now, the rumor mill was rampant with speculation about what the Germans would do next. Zora and Asia decided to have a little fun and started a cruel rumor that the Germans would spare one Frenchman for every two conscientious objectors turned over to them. Bayonne at the time was a haven for conscientious objectors, and it wasn't long before the rumor came back to them.

While in Bayonne, Zora and Yura noticed French airplanes on the backs of trucks being transported toward Zora's old base at Mérignac, so they turned around and headed back toward the base, thinking the French might be mobilizing again. But a few days later, Marshall Pétain, the French military commander, declared an armistice. General Charles de Gaulle, now in London, issued a speech encouraging all Frenchmen to escape and redeploy in England. Zora and Yura considered seeking passage for everyone in their family on a Polish ship bound for England, but feared doing so because of their Russian ancestry. Stalin at the time was still allied with Hitler.

So Zora and Yura once again pursued an escape plan. Since they needed a place to stay, they rented a room on the second floor of a house in Toulouse. Located southeast of Bordeaux, Toulouse was the closest large city to the Pyrenees mountains, which represented the most logical way to escape into Spain.

While inwardly terrified, the refugees made every effort to maintain a normal existence in the house. Elfi recalled the fantastic smell of the coffee Josef would make each morning. Elfi often did the cooking, and one day Josef went to the fish market and brought home whatever was available that day, including live green eels. The house provided little more than shelter and was overrun with fleas. By necessity, Zora became an expert flea catcher. He'd catch them with his fingers and flush them down the drain.

The question for Zora became how to get everyone out of France without exit visas. He was now playing for much higher stakes than protecting just himself. A bad decision could cost him his whole family. Yet he maintained his cool persona and employed a businesslike approach to finding a way out. He and Yura spent many a day driving Elfi's MG up into the Pyrenees, to check out the border towns and look for a possible escape route. Zora approached a border agent at le Perthus, an eastern French border town, and told him about the situation. The agent said there was no way he would allow Zora to cross the border by car without papers and didn't recommend going by foot through the mountains. Zora might have tried it nonetheless, if not for concern about his mother being able to make it. Several days later, the whole group went exploring for a route to freedom, spending several days in the mountains without food while sleeping in the car.

Zora knew his window of opportunity was slipping. He wasn't having any luck obtaining exit visas in Toulouse, so he decided to try his luck in Marseilles. He took Yura and Elfi with him and instructed Rachel and Josef to remain in Toulouse until they heard from him.

In Marseilles the threesome kept a low profile, being careful not to trust anyone, since what was left of free France was slowly disappearing, and many of the French authorities had already accepted the inevitability of German conquest. The gendarmes were looking out for their own survival. Furthermore, Zora and Yura being Russians who spoke German and French, the French didn't know whether to regard them as threats. The brothers didn't want to call too much attention to their activities.

Zora evaluated the best place to lie low for a week or two. A church? A monastery? No, in Zora's mind there was only one safe place: a brothel. His logic was simple. Brothels were safer because the owners had to pay off the gendarmes in order to operate. Since Zora was low on money, he got the proprietor to believe he had an expensive fur in Paris and once he retrieved it, he'd pay. He and the proprietor sealed the deal with a glass of cognac.

Since the threesome had no rationing cards, they survived by eating pigeons. Purchased from local markets, where pigeon meat was one of the few food items not subject to rationing, they ate several a day. Open ditches provided their water supply, which they filtered and purified themselves. Elfi went out and bought fabric and spent her time making dresses during the day, while Zora and Yura went about their business of finding a way out of the country.

A week or two became several months as Zora and Yura tried in vain to seek passage out of France. The situation appeared increasingly hopeless. They had no leverage against the intransigent French authorities. Zora and Yura made daily visits to the cafes of Marseilles, where they observed the gendarmes arresting people without proper documentation. When the police got close enough, Zora and Yura would move down the street to another cafe. They tried their luck at a succession of consulate offices, but nothing seemed to work. Zora even purchased Chinese citizenship in hopes it could result in a visa.

When nothing else worked, what finally saved the day was Zora's magnetic charm with women. It started with Zora visiting the Spanish consulate in Marseilles. There the beautiful, raven-haired sister of the Spanish head consul was working behind the counter and saw Zora walk in wearing his blue French Air Force uniform, which had been stripped of all its insignias. Zora reminded her of her late husband, a Spanish officer. Zora told the consul his story—that he was a Russian who was stateless, but he had an American visa and needed help to get to America. But the consul was under pressure from French authorities to keep ex-military people in the country, despite de Gaulle's order for military personnel to escape and redeploy in England. Therefore, no exit visas would be forthcoming.

Nonetheless, Zora made the Spanish consulate a daily stop, where he engaged the consul's sister in conversation while each day wearing the same dark blue uniform. Vulnerable to his advances, she agreed to have dinner one evening with him and Yura. The threesome had a good time drinking and lost track of the hour as late night became early morning. Because her residence was a convent where the main door was locked after a certain hour, Zora and Yura had to push her up and over the wall of the convent in the early morning twilight.

Zora and Elfi seek fresh air on the deck of the refugee ship Nyassa, *which provided safe if uncomfortable passage from Lisbon to New York.*

The consul soon learned that these Russian rakes had been wining and dining his sister, so when Zora arranged a meeting with him regarding exit visas, the consul was very cool. However, to get the pair out of the picture, he provided the necessary visas immediately. To show his appreciation, Zora went out and bought the most expensive bottle of cognac he could find—Napoleon Brandy—to present to the consul. Not wanting to give these scoundrels the satisfaction, the consul wouldn't accept it.

Now armed with the right papers, Zora sold the MG to a Frenchman who wanted it for his soldier son. The money from the MG financed a train trip out of Marseilles to Lisbon by way of Madrid and then passage on a ship to America.

Zora, Elfi and Yura spent a couple of days in Lisbon staying at a fine hotel in Estoril outside the city. There they met Asia's parents and other refugees they knew. But the quality of their accommodations was about to diminish. Their ship, a Portuguese freighter named the *Nyassa,* had been converted to a passenger ship for refugees.

Before the *Nyassa* left the dock, there was a major celebration, with lots of champagne and port wine. The group, now including Rachel and Josef, was so ecstatic to be getting out of Europe safely, they weren't particularly worried about submarine attacks. Their joy was short-lived.

The boat had two classes of passengers, based on the price of the tickets. Men and women were segregated in the cabins. Zora and Elfi both

ended up in incredibly cramped cabins shared by at least eight other people. Zora speculated that the vessel might have been used previously as a slave ship.

Once the ship embarked, seasickness set in. Other passengers offered Elfi Dramamine, but it only made her sicker. Zora fared somewhat better, but his effort to help two seasick children almost ended in three drownings. He had volunteered to help the children by taking them out for some fresh air on the lower deck. As he walked them toward the bow, a huge wave washed over the ship. Zora and the children found themselves lifted from the deck by a mountain of frigid seawater, to the horror of the children's parents, who were watching from an upper deck. Fortunately, the ship's railing prevented the trio from being washed overboard.

After nine or ten days at sea, the *Nyassa* landed in Hoboken, New Jersey, during the early morning hours of December 4, 1940. All the passengers aboard the ship were processed through Ellis Island. Zora didn't harbor any particularly fond memories about the experience, or even of being in America for that matter. He and the other refugees missed Europe.

That first night in America, Zora took the family out to see this grand place called New York, ducking into a restaurant on Broadway. Having accomplished his mission of protecting his family from the Germans, he drank to his victory.

FIVE

With his silver hair and striking features, Zora in the early 1940s looked like a Hollywood leading man.

America and Ardun

America was yet another new challenge for Zora—his third different homeland since his youth in Russia. Its flagship city, New York, with its towering buildings and bustling avenues, must have seemed light years away from his early childhood in Russia. Still, he had been largely indifferent about this so-called "land of opportunity." Whether he would have eventually sought passage to America if the Nazis hadn't forced him to flee Europe is debatable. He expressed no particular desire to move to the United States prior to the war, although he had fond memories of the country from a 1922 relief effort that brought food, shoes and other supplies to Soviet children.

There was little else to attract him to the United States, largely because American car companies lagged behind Europe in the development of sophisticated racing machinery. The only thing that remotely interested Zora was the fledgling hot-rod movement centered on the West Coast. Besides, life had been good to him in Paris and Berlin and, given a choice, he would have been happy to stick it out on the Continent working gainfully on a major racing program. In reality, he didn't have a choice, and now he was an ocean away from many friends and professional contacts and even from his father, who at the time was in a Nazi concentration camp.

Like any foreign country, America posed challenges for immigrants— a new language to learn, cultural mores to understand and, in 1940, the potential for feeling like an unwanted foreigner in a country about to be swallowed up by World War II. There were no guarantees he would be able to work, given the lingering aftereffects of the Depression. Furthermore, Zora and his family had very little money in their pockets—only the remainder of their proceeds from the sale of Elfi's MG. Still, there was enough left to secure quarters in a rooming house on the West Side of Manhattan—on Riverside Drive—facing the Hudson River. The monthly rent was $7.

After a few days of walking the streets and sizing up the place, Zora concluded that America wasn't such a foreign country after all. The more

Opposite: Zora and Elfi enjoy the amenities of American life together in New York.

he looked around, the more he realized that *everyone* was a foreigner in New York, or so it seemed. Because of a steady stream of immigrants flowing through Ellis Island, New York had large neighborhoods of ethnic populations that provided support systems for newcomers.

Zora was excited to discover that New York had a significant Russian community, which contained some blood relatives. His uncle, David Arkus, Jacques' older brother, had immigrated to America and ran a pharmacy in Manhattan. David couldn't help Zora, however, because he had lost everything in the stock market crash of 1929. He never recovered and died less than a year after Zora landed in New York. Zora also had a distant cousin from Lithuania, Ossia "Josef" Arkus, who had also lived in Berlin and Paris and had arrived in New York a year earlier than Zora. Upon his arrival, Ossia had called every Arkus in the New York phone book in search of some way to make a living. He eventually found work in the fur business.

Zora saw that he could make his own breaks, just as Ossia had. There was little to hold him back here except his own imagination. This was a place, it appeared, where people with ambition and drive could succeed no matter where they came from. Life had been difficult here, to be sure, thanks to the Depression. But Zora sensed that America, through its technology and resources, was on the verge of an explosion. "Such a country!" he marveled. Walking along the streets of New York, he could feel its energy, and he wasted no time finding a way to fit in.

It was a Berlin acquaintance who gave Zora his first big break in America. A few days after his arrival, Zora bumped into Julian Hoffman, whom he had known from his days of racing motorcycles at Avus and other tracks in the Berlin area. Knowing Zora's engineering background, Hoffman suggested Zora contact a Russian patent attorney named George Rubissow, who might be able to help him find a job.

Like Zora and Hoffman, Rubissow had also lived in Berlin, which provided Zora with something in common with which to gain an audience. Zora immediately went to see Rubissow, who also lived on Riverside Drive not far from where Zora was staying with his family. A balding man with a round face, Rubissow was in the process of negotiating with aircraft engine manufacturers Pratt & Whitney and Curtiss Wright for the rights to use an improved polyharmonic damper for torsional vibration. Polyharmonic dampers serve to tune out engine vibrations on multiple orders or frequencies. This damper patent had been issued to a Frenchman, Monsieur Solomon. With all communication to France cut off because of the war, no one could contact Solomon to better understand the mechanics of the damper. Rubissow needed to find an engineer who could decipher the designer's intent.

For Zora, it was a perfect opportunity. He was able to study the drawings and understand enough of the design to produce some calculations and another rough drawing of the damper. Buoyed by Zora's success, Rubissow commissioned him to design an all-new damper for another client, General Machinery Corporation, in Hamilton, Ohio. The company produced a two-cycle, two-stroke diesel engine for minesweepers. The affected engine had a fourth-order vibration that would increase as engine speed increased. Zora borrowed a crankshaft from the engine and went to work. His design solved both the original fourth-order vibration as well as an eighth-order vibration and went into full production for use on minesweepers.

General Machinery was so impressed with Zora's work that their chief engineer, Birger Olson, wrote a letter to Rubissow dated February 12, 1941, suggesting that Zora come to their Hamilton, Ohio, plant to adjust the first engine equipped with these dampers. "In view of the fact that Mr. Archus [sic] is not a citizen," wrote Olson, "it would be desirable to apply for a permit for him to enter the plant doing confidential government work."

Zora obtained the security clearances recommended in the letter. His efforts for General Machinery attracted the attention of the United States Navy and resulted in an invitation to visit the submarine operations at the Brooklyn Navy Yard. There he solved another torsional vibration problem on a submarine engine. Soon the prestigious Massachusetts Institute of Technology came calling. They invited him to Boston to explain how polyharmonic dampers work. In only a matter of weeks, Zora had established himself in the upper echelon of a field about which he had previously known nothing.

Zora contended that most of the damper designs of that time were not truly polyharmonic because they might work at only one or two orders of vibration, so he set about designing a true polyharmonic design that involved four weights running in radial slots held in by springs. As rpm increased, they would fly outward, thus changing the effective mass of the damper assembly. Zora would receive his first patent for this design in 1947.

The Consulting Life

Zora's reputation as an engineer was growing fast, and calls for his expertise were constant. Because most diesels came from Germany, there was a high demand for diesel know-how in the United States. In addition to General Machinery, he also began consulting for Fairbanks Morse, American Locomotive and Worthington Pump & Machinery in Buffalo. He made $100 a day as a consultant and $2,000 per calculation. "In the 1940s, that was good money," said Zora. After three weeks in the United States,

Yura, Elfi and Zora smile at their good fortune in the United States, after being in the country for only a short time.

Zora was able to buy his wife a fur coat. America wasn't such a bad place after all. "I live like life of Riley," Zora said.

Zora's earnings enabled a move into a two-room apartment situated on the Columbia University campus just two blocks from Broadway. The apartment at 425 Riverside had a large bedroom and living room and rented for $80 a month. Now in more comfortable quarters, Zora continued consulting for nearly a year, as Rubissow negotiated the rights to the dampers to interested parties in France, Belgium and Luxembourg. Zora, however, asked Rubissow to cease these negotiations pending approval of the United States government to file his patent in France. The approval never came because one month later, on December 7, 1941, the Japanese bombed Pearl Harbor.

Zora smelled a major opportunity now that America was officially at war. Certainly there would be a need for machine tool shops capable of building war munitions and specialty parts, but Zora had little money to invest and couldn't afford expensive machine tools. He knew his cousin, Ossia Arkus, was earning good money from his job in the fur business and approached him about a partnership. Ossia agreed to put up about $15,000 to start the business. In addition, Zora received funding from his stepfather, Josef Duntov. Fifty percent of the company went to Ossia Arkus, 30 percent to Zora, 10 percent to Yura and 10 percent to Josef Duntov. The money was enough to buy five basic machine tools, including a drill press, a lathe and a grinder. Zora figured that hired help would run him between 50 and 75 cents an hour, based on prevailing wages in 1941.

Zora found a suitable facility at 351 West 52nd Street and purchased the necessary specialty tools. The Ardun Mechanical Corporation was born. Ardun was a derivative of "Arkus" and "Duntov." At the same time, Zora and Yura officially added Duntov to their surname, creating Arkus-Duntov. This was to demonstrate their profound esteem for Josef, who had become a fully accepted member of the family. In Zora's eyes, Josef had come a long way from the stranger with the funny accent in Leningrad who had invaded their household. Further motivating Zora and Yura was the fact that Josef had provided some of the cash to start their business.

An added incentive for Zora in creating Ardun was to provide employment for Yura. Despite earning an engineering degree from the

Institute Aéronautique at the Sorbonne during his years in Paris, Yura failed to attract any job offers in the engineering field and ended up taking a job with a furrier, thanks to a connection through Ossia Arkus. Zora still sought ways to help his brother, since Yura was the blood relative for whom Zora cared the most. Ardun would be an ideal environment to continue Zora's role as protector for Yura, while maintaining some daily connection with his family.

Ardun Mechanical soon became a runaway success. Government contracts helped pay for additional tooling, some of which was provided directly by the government. Thanks to the high quality of its machining and manufacturing, the new company quickly received a classification "A" for the Army Air Forces Quality Control. This was touted in a magazine spread advertisement for Ardun. The ad cited Ardun's entire inventory of machine tools, grinders and lathes and listed the firm's numerous customers, including Remington Rand, Wright Aeronautical Corporation, Republic Aviation and U.S. Rubber. Also listed were General Motors Corporation and Chevrolet Motor & Axle Division, which could have been Duntov's first contact with the company that he would so fundamentally influence.

The ad also featured several endorsement letters including one from the Propeller Division of Remington Rand. The letter stated: "We are manufacturers of the Hamilton Standard Hydromatic Propeller which requires the employment of a number of shops outside of our own three plants. Our parts are of the highest precision requirements comparable to those used in aircraft engines and other work of [a] most exacting nature. Among those outside shops we have employed the Ardun Mechanical Corporation of 351 West 52nd Street, New York City, on two parts requiring turning, heat-treatment, and grinding to tolerances running within three- to five-thousands."

As the war effort heated up, Ardun expanded its output, producing a number of specialty parts, including ship propeller shafts and bomb cones. A staple item was a distributor valve or breather nut, which controlled the pitch of an aircraft propeller. At the time, each piece brought in $10 from the government, which had two other sources besides Ardun for this part. Yura devised a way to use a Cincinnati centerless grinder to manufacture the valves, which substantially reduced manufacturing costs—so much so, that Zora approached Eaton, one of the other companies producing the part, and offered to sell identical valves to them with their packing for $5. The offer was too good for Eaton to refuse, and Ardun made major profits based on the sheer volume despite the lower profit margin.

Times were good—so good that Zora, now in his early 30s, was making a salary of $40,000 per year, a staggering sum at the time, and was soon able to buy out his cousin as well as his stepfather. Now, Zora and Yura each owned 50 percent of the company. The company grew and at the height of the war, Ardun Mechanical employed 100 people and required a larger facility. The company was moved to a loft space on 56th Street between 10th and 11th Avenues in Manhattan. Zora also created a second company called Hudson Mechanical for tax purposes, but it was essentially the same operation as Ardun.

Success inevitably brought a swagger to Zora's demeanor, and he began to believe he could take on anything. His storybook success was almost too good to be true. But a jet helicopter project that Yura brought in may have brought Zora back down to earth. The helicopter had been designed by a Polish engineer who contracted Ardun to build a prototype. Helicopters, of course, were relatively new in the mid-1940s and jet helicopters were strictly at an experimental stage. Zora developed a unique combustion igniter system for the jet engine that provided continuous ignition by means of a magneto.

While the project was fascinating from a technical viewpoint, it proved to be a comic disaster. The welding process caused several abrupt explosions in the shop, one of which badly singed Yura's hair. Incomplete combustion also caused one wall of the shop to be caked with unburned jet fuel. The shop was located next to a recording studio, and when Zora or Yura fired up the engine, the shrieking jet noise drowned out all other activity for blocks around. Yura made an arrangement with the recording studio to give them some advance notice before doing any testing. Eventually, after Ardun had lost over $30,000 on the deal, the jet helicopter project was scrapped. The episode suggested that in the military hardware business, it was just as easy to lose money as it was to make it.

Moving to the Penthouse

At the height of the war, Zora and Elfi moved again, to a penthouse on the 17th floor of 33 Riverside Drive. The luxurious West Side apartment rented for $150 a month and had been formerly occupied by Ira Gershwin and later by Guy Lombardo. While the unit wasn't particularly big, consisting of a single bedroom, dining room, living room and kitchen, its biggest asset was its terrace, which looked out over the Hudson. The penthouse roof was the ideal place to entertain guests on sultry evenings, and many a night Zora and Elfi would lie back on chaise lounges, toast each other with martinis and celebrate their good fortune while watching the sun set over the Hudson.

Zora was in his prime. He had movie star looks thanks to his chiseled face, light blue eyes and prematurely silver hair. Elfi was still a blue-eyed bombshell, and their magnetism attracted many guests from the racing and entertainment worlds to their frequent parties. Their social set included jazz singers, dancers, artists and actresses. Fueled by gin, cigarettes and the jazzy notes of Artie Shaw and Duke Ellington, the parties lasted into the early morning hours. The apartment had a giant mirror on one wall and after a party, Elfi would dance by herself in front of the mirror, reliving the electricity of the evening. Afterwards, she and Zora sometimes slept under the stars on the terrace, the lights of Manhattan aglow around them as they dreamed even bigger dreams.

Zora and Elfi loved their penthouse terrace as a place to soak in the sun or entertain guests.

After feeling like a vagabond much of his life, Zora finally felt accepted in America. He was making money, but more important, he felt he was in control and choosing his own course. Anything was possible in America if one was smart and persistent enough. It didn't seem to matter that much whether you were Jewish, Russian or Irish; if you didn't make it here, there was no one to blame but yourself. Success also meant fame, and a chance to make an even bigger mark on the world.

To prove it, Zora needed to look no further than the successes of his close friends. Asia Orley had immigrated to New York via Spain and worked at a high level for U.S. Army Intelligence during the war. Julian Hoffman, Zora's friend from Berlin who had made the important connection with George Rubissow, was getting rich through his numerous contacts in the business and entertainment world. And Vadim Gonsoff, a new friend of Zora's, was a suave actor working for the Soviet section of the Voice of America, which provided radio broadcasts in Russian to the Soviet Union via strategically located transmitters. Gonsoff's extensive connections in the entertainment community helped Elfi resume her dancing career in New York. These success stories were a far cry from the calamities that befell Zora's friends and loved ones under Stalin's purges and Hitler's concentration camps.

This realization caused Zora to begin to think about becoming an American citizen. Previously, citizenship wasn't a big issue for Zora, since he was able to get the security clearances he needed to conduct his business at Ardun. But at the height of the war effort, Ardun was operating

After immigrating to the United States, Asia Orley obtained a high-level position with U.S. Army Intelligence during the war. He is pictured here with Elfi and some unidentified friends.

three shifts and Duntov was living and sleeping out of his office. One night, after nodding off in his office, he went down to 40th Street to take in a movie. The movie brought back memories of Russia in 1922 and the United States relief effort at the time. America had been good to Duntov, a place where he could realize his dreams and exert control without feeling like an unwanted outsider. The following morning, Duntov called his attorney to begin the process of becoming an American citizen. But the process would take longer than he expected and wasn't completed until 1949, long after the war had ended.

The Problems of Success

Success created problems for Zora and Elfi's relationship. Despite their long journey together, Zora still carried with him an inability to totally commit himself to another person. In his eyes, it indicated a loss of control. He demonstrated this in his reluctance to get married—despite Elfi's beauty and her devotion to him—and his frequent wanderings up until the time of his wedding.

Now that he was a successful businessman in America, Zora began to equate prosperity with power. And for Zora the trappings of power meant spotting a beautiful woman and taking her on his arm. Consequently, as Ardun became more successful, Zora became increasingly bold and began to seek out women for potential affairs. Adding fuel to the fire was his cousin Ossia's urging that he was too much of a man to confine himself to one woman.

Elfi, meanwhile, was heading emotionally in the other direction. She had serious longings to raise a family, something Zora wanted no part of. He had a difficult enough time making a commitment to her and the loss of control that entailed. "Zora loved children—he just didn't want to have any of his own," lamented Elfi. Perhaps he remembered all too vividly the pain his mother's affairs had caused him. He didn't want to do the same to his own children, to have to look them in the eye and try to hide the truth about his own philandering nature. More fundamentally, Zora didn't want to have children because he somehow feared losing them, just as he had lost many other loved ones as a youth.

When Elfi became pregnant, she unilaterally decided to carry the baby instead of getting an abortion, and Zora bided his time in response. She would pay the price, sooner or later. It turned out to be sooner. She miscarried at seven months after visiting her doctor, a friend of hers who lived on Long Island. A German named Dr. Milbauer, he was married to Asia Orley's cousin Sheila. While visiting, Elfi was bending over a crib to pick up the doctor's baby when she felt a searing pain in her abdomen. After the miscarriage, Elfi was hospitalized with a blood clot in her leg.

"For Elfi, was major tragedy," shrugged Zora, "but for me, not. I did not see myself as a father of a family, enjoying the conjugal life."

After Elfi was released from the hospital, she was depressed about losing the baby. The last thing she could imagine was Zora starting an affair. Yet one afternoon she walked into a small French bistro on 52nd Street that Zora frequented and found him sitting in a cozy corner table with his arm around a blonde Russian ballerina, Luba, who lived in France. Zora slouched down in his chair after seeing Elfi storm in, trying in vain to look innocent. Seeing the two, her face beet-red, Elfi blurted in French: "That is exactly what I imagined." Zora tried to pass Luba off as Yura's girlfriend, but Elfi wasn't convinced.

The incident motivated Zora to pursue a complete separation from Elfi, at least for a while, because he was growing tired of trying to hide his affairs. He had never been totally faithful to Elfi since he had met her. If she had a problem with it, it was her problem. So he suggested that Elfi take a little vacation by herself and sent her to a dude ranch on the Hudson for a few weeks to do some horseback-riding. While she was away, he moved out. When she returned a few days later, she discovered Zora was gone. There was no note and no explanation. Zora figured that Elfi knew what was going on.

Zora had moved into an apartment with Luba on 56th Street. He would now indulge himself without limits. Luba would be his ticket to a number of other beautiful Russian ballerinas including her close friend, Genia Delarova, a well-known dancer who competed for Zora's affections and once answered the door for him wearing only an apron. Zora took care of both women and allowed all the dancers in the troupe to charge their lunches and drinks on his tab at the same French bistro where he was first discovered by Elfi.

The Russian ballerinas later opened a flower shop in New York to which Zora contributed time and capital. Once Zora stood in when they needed an extra deliveryman but put a quick stop to that when someone recognized him.

As a peace offering during their separation, Elfi bought Zora this cockapoo named Porti, but she ended up keeping the dog herself.

Now on her own, Elfi consoled herself by working and sought some out-of-town dancing engagements to try to free herself of the memory of Zora. The first out-of-town engagement was in Detroit, at the Latin Quarter. She stayed in the Motor City for three months at the Hotel Detroiter on Woodward Avenue, but she hated both Detroit as well as her separation from her husband, whom she still loved very much. She was careful not to let him know her feelings.

Elfi's new independence had a surprising effect on Zora. For the first time since he had met her, he no longer possessed her. From his vantage point, she didn't appear to be pining his absence. She received many date requests and, although she refused most of them, she commenced a brief relationship with a United States Army general who frequented the Latin Quarter when he was in town. For companionship, she kept a cockapoo named Porti, which she had originally bought for Zora. To further emphasize her independence, she took flying lessons.

Sensing he was losing her, Zora began calling Elfi every day in Detroit and even flew out for a visit. But Elfi had learned a thing or two over the years and played to his jealousy by keeping him at arm's length, despite the love she felt for him.

Besides Detroit, her dancing career also took her to Chicago's Shubert Theater where, in the fall of 1946 she performed with Richard Tauber in a production called *Yours Is My Heart*. She used the stage name Elfi Dukar to establish her own identity. Upon returning to New York she continued taking dancing lessons and picked up several dancing roles in Off-Broadway theaters. She also occupied herself by making gloves for the Air Force when she wasn't dancing. When plugged into a power source, the gloves were heated by wires woven into the linings.

Her career successes provided her with a much-needed diversion from Zora and also helped introduce her into an inner social circle of New York society, which helped her self-esteem. She became friendly with singer Pearl Bailey; Maurice Rentner, a well-known dress designer; actresses Joan Blondel and Bea Lilley; bandleader Xavier Cugat; Ben Kahn, a famous furrier in New York for whom she modeled; and Charles Addams, the brilliant cartoonist for *The New Yorker* who inspired the *Addams Family* television show in the 1960s and several feature films in the 1990s. She also frequented a society called *Escolier*, where beautiful women like her were invited to exclusive functions where artists, show business personalities and wealthy businessmen from around the world intermingled.

Zora kept a watchful eye on Elfi's activities and was intrigued by her new life without him. But he was still not ready to relinquish his ballerinas or move back together. He would frequently take Elfi to dinner, but then rubbed her face in the reality of his new situation by going back home to Luba. Elfi would return to her apartment alone. Occasionally, things got ugly. On New Year's Eve 1944, Zora visited Elfi during the early evening but planned to go out and celebrate later with Luba. In a moment of weakness, Elfi started to make a scene. So Zora, in an ultimate effort to control her, called a doctor friend of his who drugged her with a hypodermic needle. Then Zora went out and celebrated the New Year with Luba. Promptly at midnight, without a shred of remorse, he called to wish Elfi a Happy New Year. Elfi had plenty of grounds to press charges but didn't. She loved Zora too much to ever risk a permanent break.

Zora's inability to make a commitment eventually eroded his relationship with Luba as well. When the war ended in 1945, he and Luba split up and she subsequently married a French count.

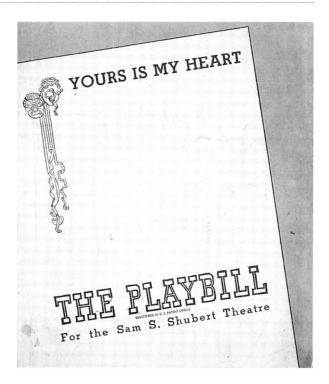

Elfi starred in the Chicago production of Yours Is My Heart *at the Shubert Theater. She used the stage name Elfi Dukar to foster a stronger sense of independence from Zora.*

SIX

Zora behind the wheel of his Indy Talbot in 1946. He saw racing as the ultimate pursuit, the embodiment of his need for control.

Shifting into High Performance

As World War II wound down in 1945, Zora knew he would have to adapt Ardun to a peacetime economy. His workforce dwindled slowly from around 300 to 25 people as his defense contracts expired. He suspended his existing union contract and reorganized under a new one. No longer needing a large manufacturing operation, Zora moved Ardun to a smaller shop located at 503 West 56th Street in New York City.

Zora's heady days as a war munitions contractor were over. It had been a great run and he had profited handsomely. Yet the end of World War II offered something more intriguing—a chance to form his own performance and racing business. Given his incredible success with Ardun, peacetime represented his biggest opportunity yet to achieve the kind of career he couldn't muster back in Germany or France. Zora could get back on track in his life, literally and figuratively. He could achieve a sense of connection to the world that had eluded him ever since his boyhood in Russia.

There were even bigger stakes. Given the absence of major players in performance and racing in America, Zora saw that he could be a founding father of the American high-performance industry. He could become as famous as Bugatti or Porsche by establishing his own marque here in America. He could beat the Europeans at their own game on the racetracks of the world.

But he had to start somewhere. Zora had been a keen observer of the American high-performance scene when he lived in Europe. He knew that on the boulevards and dry lakes of southern California, hot-rodders had squeezed 100-mph speeds from four-cylinder Model As, Model Ts, Dodges, Buicks, Essexes and Chevrolets. Naturally, the hot-rod community had high hopes for the Flathead Ford V-8 when it debuted in 1932. It was a real breakthrough—the world's first low-priced V-8, bringing power to the common man. But it was also crude and noisy. While its performance drew raves from the likes of bank robber Clyde Barrow—of Bonnie and Clyde

Opposite: Zora begins to put his ideas on paper for how to make the Ford Flathead V-8 into a powerhouse for hot-rodders.

fame—who wrote a letter to Henry Ford praising the engine, serious hot-rodders wanted something better. The engine awaited the birth of an aftermarket industry to make it go faster.

Zora reasoned that he could be an integral part of that soon-to-emerge industry. While the world of performance had taken a long moratorium during the war years, Zora saw increased postwar demand for hot cars and hot parts. He imagined a powerful yet dependable engine that was also affordable and easy to maintain. Knowing the tremendous development costs of creating his own power plant, Zora felt it was wisest to start with an established production block and make it go faster. He knew just the one.

The Flathead Ford V-8 had made an impression on him in the 1930s during those midnight runs smuggling gold out of France. He liked the revving capability of the Ford as it effortlessly turned over at 5,000 rpm, and there were already millions of them on the road. He also knew he could make it more powerful by pumping more air in and out of its combustion chambers. The way to do that, in Zora's opinion, was to convert the inverted-L side valves of the Flathead engine to an overhead valve configuration, which would provide a higher compression ratio and higher volumetric efficiency.

In 1945, Zora approached the Ford Motor Company about an overhead valve conversion project. He had no connections at Ford, however, and was probably seen as just another Joe off the street, without credibility in the vast world of automotive manufacturing. Besides, Ford was preoccupied with satisfying the tremendous demand for basic transportation in a peacetime economy, not helping aftermarket entrepreneurs offering high-performance add-ons for hot-rodders.

So Zora struck out on his own. He bought a couple of Flathead Ford V-8s and other necessary components and broke them down to study how he could create an overhead valve conversion package that didn't call for modifications to the basic engine block. He wanted a unit that customers could either install themselves or have the work done by a competent mechanic. Zora envisioned selling these conversion kits directly to consumers through speed shops and auto dealers.

Zora began mapping out his ideas on paper. All his life, he sketched ideas on notepads, napkins or scraps of paper, and if he felt the idea was worth pursuing he would then hand his rough drawing over to a professional illustrator or draftsman. Sometimes he did his own drafting at his glassed-in office at Ardun, but in most cases he used a professional draftsman.

Zora's cylinder head design incorporated hemispherical combustion chambers—just like those used on the German Auto Unions in 1938 and 1939—with radically inclined overhead valves actuated by pushrods and rocker arms. In Zora's mind, the demands put on the intake and exhaust

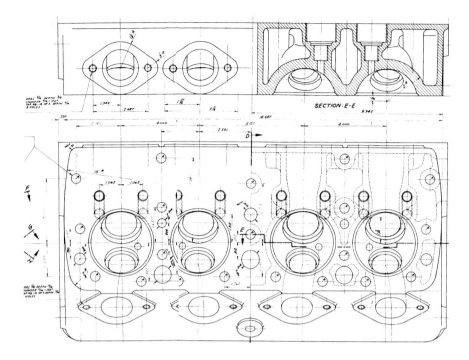

This original blueprint for the Ardun overhead valve conversion called for hemispherical combustion chambers, an idea Zora borrowed from Auto Union and Talbot.

valves were diametrically opposed, therefore there was no reason to put the valves at an equal angle, as in traditional engines. This allowed use of a larger exhaust valve and was one of the first applications of a nonsymmetrical valve arrangement, which later became common in the industry. Besides saving space, the nonsymmetrical pattern allowed the head of the exhaust valve to be exposed to the onrushing stream of cool charge, which reduced the temperature and stresses in the valve.

The Ardun cylinder head was cast from a high-tensile, heat-treated Alcoa aluminum alloy. In an industry dominated by cast-iron parts, lightweight aluminum was a very exotic engine material at the time. Besides the weight savings of the head, the hemispherical combustion configuration was designed to reduce heat buildup, allowing for a higher compression ratio. It was also designed to be more knock-resistant, given the wide variations in gasoline octane levels of the time.

The beauty of the Ardun conversion, at least on paper, was its relative simplicity. The block underneath remained unmodified from the Ford factory. This permitted replacement of pistons, rings, connecting rods, main bearings, camshaft and even the cylinder block itself. Those parts were available at any Ford dealer. Ardun tooled and manufactured most of the top end of the motor, making its own cam followers (tappets) and pushrods.

In February 1946, Zora began test runs to measure horsepower and torque on his own General Electric dynamometer. He accumulated over 1,000 hours of testing. The tests showed the engine was putting out a measured 160 horsepower versus 100 horsepower for the stock Ford Flathead, a 62 percent increase. The Ardun engine could also rev higher. During testing, he discovered that the engine could even sustain speeds of 6,000 rpm versus 5,000 rpm for the stock engine if the oil pressure was increased from 60 to 80 pounds per square inch.

Once the numbers were all in, Zora was ecstatic. His engine had the potential to grace the engine bay of every hot rod from New York to California!

Power for the Masses

After almost two years of development, temporary production tooling was completed, and in 1947 the engine was ready for the marketplace. A venture of this nature would be different from the munitions business. As opposed to having the U.S. government as his principal customer in the midst of a world war, Zora's new scheme relied on a savvy blend of engineering, manufacturing, marketing, sales and good overall business sense. Making it all come together would be a major challenge, and engineering prowess alone wouldn't ensure success.

Further complicating matters was the fact that Yura decided to go his own way after the war. Still intrigued by his unsuccessful experience with the Ardun jet helicopter project and desirous of a position where he could strike out on his own, Yura took a position as the manager of Automotive and Aircraft Hydraulics, Inc. The company was concerned with the design, manufacturing and development of jet helicopters and high-speed internal combustion engines. Yura had handled much of sales and marketing for Ardun and would be missed. Likewise, Joe Arkus, who handled many of the business affairs of the company, also left Ardun to go into the restaurant business.

Despite losing two key members of his team, Zora was still confident of success. He was convinced that if his product was good enough, the world would beat a path to his door.

The Ardun V-8 was offered either as a complete engine or as a conversion kit. To promote the engine, Duntov created a four-page brochure, which provided full specifications, a performance curve chart and line drawings. The insert stressed the performance potential of the conversion, emphasizing high horsepower, high torque and wide continuous operating range, all with low fuel consumption, low initial cost and low maintenance costs. According to the brochure, the engine was tuned to operate on 67 octane. A second purebred racing version delivered in excess of 200 hp at 5,500 rpm.

A second launch ad boasted the claim: "Speed as never before…at an unbelievably low price," and featured a tabletop photo of the Ardun heads in all their glory.

Zora also went to work on the public relations front, generating an article in *Popular Mechanics* that resulted in 2,000 inquiries about the engine. A common theme in the media stories was the novelty of hemispherical or dome-shaped heads, which allowed more charge into the combustion chambers. This was pretty exotic stuff at the time, having previously been the province of aircraft engines or grand prix racers.

But publicity and inquiries did not add up to sales. One of the obstacles in the marketplace was the price of the conversions. At $500 each, they were expensive, and that figure didn't include installation costs. Furthermore, the installation process itself was a challenge. The conversion required six hours' work by a competent mechanic and might have taken an amateur considerably longer.

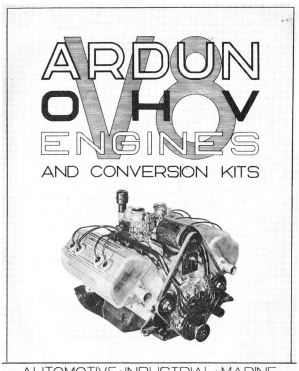

The Ardun conversion seemed too good to be true based on this four-page Ardun advertising insert. The insert touted the conversion's high horsepower, high torque and wide continuous operating range, all while claiming low fuel consumption, low initial cost and low maintenance costs.

The physical size of the heads presented another problem. They were too wide to fit into the engine compartments of many passenger cars. That limited Duntov's market to hot rods with open cowls, where the bulbous cylinder heads could be fully exposed in the engine bay, or in trucks, where there was more room under the hood.

For a time, it appeared that the truck market might be the key to commercial success for the Ardun conversion. Trucks also represented a potentially larger market than hot-rodders did, given the number of trucks on the road, many of which were underpowered for the loads they had to carry.

So Zora quickly produced a special magazine ad touting the engine's greater power and efficiency for truck fleet operators and industrial power users. The headline read: "Now More Power for Ford V-8s…160 horsepower and over…from 100 horsepower Ford V-8 engines with the new Ardun conversion kit." Featured in the ad was a Ford pickup, while at the bottom of the ad was a box soliciting potential distributors.

Potential truck applications attracted the attention of the *New York Times*, which ran a piece on the Ardun conversions on August 18, 1947.

"A major new manufacturing industry for New York City is seen as a result of development of a motor truck engine, now perfected after two years of intensive engineering and tests," wrote the *Times*. "The new engine is a result of five experimental engines built during research activities, and the present model, now under consideration for production expansion plans, assures low operating costs and higher power output at the lowest price per horsepower of any engine on the market, Mr. Arkus-Duntov disclosed." Further publicity for the conversion was generated when Zora was pictured with one of his engines in the September 4, 1947, issue of the trade magazine *Iron Age*.

Zora's press clippings finally attracted the attention of the Ford Motor Company, which showed some interest in the truck applications. But initial tests conducted by Ford demonstrated poor reliability and the auto giant didn't pursue the matter further.

Indeed, Zora's Ardun conversion delivered neither the performance nor the reliability claimed in his advertising. In fact, the engine suffered from a litany of problems. D. Randy Riggs, in an *Automobile Quarterly* article on Ardun, wrote: "Its cast-steel pushrods weighed the same as a connecting rod, and valve seats came loose from expansion differences of the aluminum and bronze materials. The stock Ardun valves were too heavy. Exhaust manifolds were constricted and head gaskets were a common failure.

"The Coke-bottle shaped lifters were originally made from Buick components and had a tendency to gall. Valve springs were inadequate. The entire valve train was heavy and unreliable, and defied high rpms. The two intake manifolds had no balance tube between them and were poorly designed. The spark plug tubes were a menace and the stock Ford ignition was not up for the task."

"The Ardun was a great hot water heater," said Ray Brock, former technical editor and publisher of *Hot Rod* magazine. "By going with the overhead valves and pushrods, the exhaust ports were too close to the water jackets and everything got too hot. The engines were famous for blowing head gaskets."

"You had to be a pretty good engineer to get them to work," said Brock. "The blocks required a lot of work as well, and many of the people who bought the kits put them on the shelf and left them there."

The two years Duntov spent bringing the conversion to market may not have been enough. Not when he had to overcome the problems associated with raising an engine's horsepower by 62 percent. His engineering strengths were stronger at the concept phase, where his originality and free-form thinking could run wild. He wasn't a development engineer adept at perfecting a technology. It appears he didn't have the patience or inclination to work through the hundreds of details associated with a project of this magnitude, despite his livelihood depending on it. While his basic concept may have been sound, the engine may have required someone with a patient, methodical approach to shore up the engine's weak spots and ensure that all of its components could handle the extra horsepower and revving capability of the Ford Flathead.

Racing for Ardun

After seeing his original hopes for street applications dashed, Zora turned to racing as a way to save his program. If he could develop a racing version of the Ardun head and show how well it could run against established power plants, it might be a much-needed source of credibility. The engine he had in mind for conversion purposes was another Ford Flathead, the V-8-60, which at the time was considered to be a cheaper alternative to the expensive Offenhauser power plant in midget racers. This was a considerably smaller market than the one Zora originally envisioned, but he saw it as a chance to generate some additional publicity in the performance community and perhaps jump-start some renewed interest in his street conversion packages.

Zora needed development money to make this happen, so he approached Alexis Thompson and Erwin Goldschmidt, owners of the New York Polo Grounds midget track. Goldschmidt was a prominent name in racing circles in the 1940s, and Thompson was the owner of the Philadelphia Eagles football team. The two made a deal with Zora. He would design the engine and if it showed potential, they would produce the money to manufacture it. The proving ground would be the Yellowjacket Speedway in Philadelphia, where Zora's "Little Ardun" had to beat the existing track record.

With Thompson and Goldschmidt's development money in hand, Zora went to work. What he did specifically to correct the deficiencies of the original Ardun conversion is not clear, but it is likely he focused his effort on the valvetrain with an eye toward increasing its revving capability. He also modified the cylinder bore using sleeves to produce the same displacement as an Offenhauser. The finished engine looked significantly different and more compact than the standard Ardun with its double-hump rocker covers.

To try to break the track record, Duntov hired experienced midget driver Johnny Renninger. Zora appropriately nicknamed him "Johnny Ringer." Renninger was no small guy—he weighed over 200 pounds, which was going to test the engine's power even more. Zora then installed the prototype Little Ardun in Renninger's #58 racer owned by Bob Volsted.

The "Little Ardun" in the engine bay of Johnny Renninger's #58 midget racer. Built on the Ford Flathead V8-60, it was designed to be a cheaper alternative to the Offenhauser power plant in midget racers.

The engine, however, was up to the task. Zora himself broke the track record at Yellowjacket before Renninger had a chance to get into the car. Zora did so on a bitterly cold winter day with a clean track, sans the rubber deposits that usually build up on the surface during racing season.

Renninger and Duntov continued working together to further develop the engine when tragedy intervened during a test session at Kingsbridge Armory, an indoor track. Zora didn't like how the throttle was working; however, Renninger insisted on getting into the car and taking it out for a few laps. While he was out lapping, the throttle stuck, Renninger lost control and the car ran through a barrier, hitting a wall. Renninger suffered two broken legs, one with multiple fractures. Because Renninger was so heavy, safety crews had a difficult time extracting him from the car. Finally they pulled him onto a stretcher and took him to a hospital, where he sat for several hours without receiving any medical attention before being transferred to another hospital. Renninger had also suffered a ruptured artery, and doctors considered amputating his leg. On hearing the news of the crash, Thompson and Goldschmidt threatened legal action against Ardun, suggesting that Zora's company was somehow negligent. The parties eventually settled, but considerable damage was done to Zora's hopes of making his engine a fixture in midget racing circles.

Still, a sliver of hope for the program remained after a German company showed an interest in the Little Ardun. "Veritas," a new name in the world of racing, was founded in 1948 by a group of ex-BMW employees. Their intention was to build sports cars based on the prewar BMW 328, but the company also developed an open-wheel racer and was seeking an alternative to the pushrod-actuated hemispherical combustion chamber six-cylinder BMW engine for this purpose. Zora—through his friend Asia Orley—licensed Veritas to build the engine in Germany. Back in New York, the company produced 20 V-8-60 Ardun heads, which are extremely rare today, being perhaps the most collectible of Ardun components. But these low volumes weren't enough to keep his fragile business afloat, and Zora's hopes for the Ardun to be a force in midget racing were dead.

Zora was finding out the hard way that being a "founding father" of a high-performance industry would be much more difficult than he realized. His Ardun engine program had been a failure and Zora didn't have any other backup projects up his sleeve. So when a Russian friend named Sacha Berger asked Zora to guarantee a loan, he consented and used Ardun for collateral. When Berger defaulted on the loan, Zora lost the company. Ardun, in Zora's eyes, was already lost. Yura and Joe Arkus, who had made the original company a business success, were long gone. Weary of the high costs and development time to create a high-performance engine that could compete with the larger auto manufacturers, Zora had already decided it was time to go work for somebody else. He had in mind a place where he could concentrate on engineering or driving, thus avoiding the headaches of running his own operation.

Ardun had been a painful lesson. On paper, it looked like a hands-down winner, but in reality, the Ardun engine had a narrow window of practicality. It arrived on the market several years too late and then quickly succumbed to a competitive market that offered more power and reliability at less cost in the guise of overhead valve engines from Cadillac in 1949 and Chrysler in 1951. Had it been more completely developed, however, it might have had a much bigger impact in the hot-rod community, if not in the larger automotive market.

While Zora was officially no longer a part of Ardun, he and Yura still held legal title to the Ardun name and negotiated the rights to use it with several parties. One of those was Franklin Motor, the now defunct aircraft engine manufacturer, which at the time was also manufacturing the engines for the Tucker automobile. The Waco Meteor acrobatic biplane used the Franklin engine as well, and the exporter for the Waco was the same man who defaulted on the loan—Sacha Berger. Talks were held about continuing to produce the Ardun conversion kits at the Franklin plant in upstate New York, but negotiations fell through. Eventually, the Duntovs sold the rights to Rudy Sternberg, whom they had met through Julian Hoffman. Sternberg continued to market the Ardun name through Ardun Power Products Corporation, located in Richmond Hill, New York. Their contract gave Zora and Yura the right to inspect and approve the quality of parts and components being manufactured by the firm.

The Ardun Legacy

Long after Ardun was sold off, the name would go on to become legendary in the hot-rod world, thanks to the efforts of a couple of enterprising southern California hot-rodders, Don Clark and Clem Tebow of C&T Automotive in Sherman Oaks, California. They followed up on Zora's vision, making the Ardun into exactly the kind of power plant that Zora conceived but could not build.

Wrote D. Randy Riggs in *Automobile Quarterly*: "This hot rod duo was famous for trying new ideas and in their experimentation, switched to Chrysler valves, changed valve spring pressures, used aftermarket cams (some with roller lifters), built equal-length headers, installed tubular pushrods and replaced the fiber camshaft gear with one made from aluminum."

Clark and Tebow found that the heads would breathe more easily if they weren't restricted by the carburetor intake equipment then being used. So they designed their own manifold injection system. They also devised a roller tappet camshaft, which made a higher peaking speed possible. Previous dynamometer tests with the engine were limited by a valve float condition common to power plants equipped with rocker arm-actuated valves.

Given Clark and Tebow's careful modifications, the engine began to make some noise out on the high-speed salt flats of Utah. As reported by Jerry Chesebrough in *Hop-Up*, the engine was installed in a George Hill/Bill Davis streamliner named "The City of Burbank." The car set a flying mile speed record of 229.774 mph at Bonneville in September 1952. This shattered a record that had been held, ironically, by Auto Union. It also set a flying kilometer record of 226.9 mph (converted) and a standing-start mile—104.01 mph—and standing-start kilometer—85.485 mph (converted).

Ardun-powered race cars were racing and winning at other venues as well in the early 1950s, as noted by Riggs. Bob Estes, a southern California Mercury dealer, entered an Ardun-Mercury-powered Kurtis Kraft at the Indy 500 for Joe James. He managed to average 124 mph around the speedway but got bumped during qualifying. Still, the engine garnered considerable attention given its "stock-block" origins. The Ardun even made some noise on an international level. At Montlhéry in France, Marcel Balsa drove his Ardun-powered car to victory. And on the southern California drag-racing circuits, Scotty's Muffler Service class B lakester (a rear-engined belly-tank record car) set record runs in excess of 185 mph driven by C. W. Scott. In addition, Don Yates drove a wedge-nosed dragster to class wins in Los Angeles, getting over 400 horsepower out of his Ardun-Mercury V-8.

Zora took tremendous pride in these accomplishments, despite the fact that outsiders had made the engine viable. Seeing his ideas achieve mass production was an elusive dream for the white-haired Russian, the result of an inability at times to see through the practical side of things. These blind spots would be the source of considerable frustration in the years ahead.

Driving Ambitions

Zora had another agenda in those postwar years—that of establishing a reputation as a driver. Driving was his ultimate means of measuring himself and would rule the other major decisions he would make in his life. It was more important than engineering; in Zora's mind engineering was simply a means to drive. Combining the two brought Zora the ultimate in satisfaction. Nothing he could imagine would give him more fulfillment than driving his own machinery to a speed record or racing championship.

Zora's main stumbling block was that he had never really made a name for himself as a driver. His experience had been primarily with Asia Orley and his MGs back in the 1930s, and Zora was largely a backup to Orley. The Arkus project never got off the ground and didn't allow any opportunity for Zora to further hone his driving skills. In 1946 Duntov was 35, an age considered by many at the time to be over the hill. Despite his lack of driving experience, Zora was confident he could learn quickly.

With his rationale established, Zora decided to go for broke. Never willing to start at the bottom, he elected to apply his accumulated knowledge toward the most famous race in the world—the Indianapolis 500. And one of his employees at Ardun, Luigi Chinetti, could help him get there.

Chinetti was the Italian-American who later became synonymous with Ferrari. He was a multiple Le Mans winner (Alfa Romeo and Ferrari) and later imported Ferraris to the United States and headed up Ferrari's North American racing efforts. Zora met Chinetti for the first time in Paris in the 1930s when Zora was attempting to race the Arkus. Chinetti was active on the local racing circuits in France, and at the time had planned to open up an exotic car repair shop. According to Stan Grayson, writing in *Automobile Quarterly*, he had come to America ostensibly to go to the Indianapolis 500 as chief mechanic with American Harry Schell in 1940 and was still in the States when America entered the war. Stranded in the United States, he remained in New York for the duration, then elected to stay in the States permanently

Like Chinetti, Zora was obsessed with the Indianapolis 500, the only race in America that garnered any real attention outside the country. Both were affected by the whole Indy mystique, from "Back Home in Indiana" to the bottle of milk served to the winner of the race.

With a goal of entering the 1946 Indianapolis 500, Zora bought a prewar

Zora partnered with Luigi Chinetti (center) on his Indianapolis 500 effort. The three-time Le Mans winner had worked at Ardun in New York and went on to become the North American importer of Ferrari automobiles. Famed driver Achille Varzi is on the left.

six-cylinder Talbot racer. As a grand prix car, the Talbot was never competitive. It ran against Mercedes and Auto Union but was hopelessly outclassed. Zora hoped that the Talbot might have better luck on American soil. The car became Chinetti's project while he was at Ardun and, like the old Arkus, also a Talbot, it was a project.

The 1946 500 was the first year the race was run following World War II. Zora felt that this could be an advantage in the fact that he wouldn't be competing against any established factory operations. The field would be dominated by prewar machinery. According to historian Donald Davidson of the Indianapolis Motor Speedway, Zora's Indy Talbot may have been the last race car at Indy to sport actual swinging doors, and it was one of 15 European cars entered that year.

The Talbot had a six-cylinder, three-carburetor naturally aspirated engine. Zora elected to race with the original engine because his own Ardun power plant was still under development.

Once committed to go to Indy, Zora contacted Speedway president Wilbur Shaw and asked for suggestions on a driving coach. Shaw suggested Cliff Bergere, an Indy veteran who finished third in the 1939 race. Since Chinetti was still preparing Zora's Talbot back in New York, Zora received permission from the Speedway to practice in one of Bergere's cars. But according to an April 29, 1946, letter from George Rodway on behalf of Wilbur Shaw, Zora was told, "You must pass the driver's test in the car in which you will qualify and start in the race." Bergere showed him all the basics, how to drive the fastest line around the track and how to handle traffic and pit stops.

Zora's Indy Talbot bore a resemblance to his old Arkus racer from the 1930s, also a Talbot.

Besides orientation at the Speedway, Zora had to prepare his Talbot for qualifying. Although he and Chinetti had rented a place in Indianapolis for the month of May, they didn't show up with the car at the Speedway until May 28, two days before the race. The Talbot had required more work than they bargained for.

Zora had to take a five-stage rookie test before he would be permitted an official qualifying attempt. The test called for doing ten laps of the two-and-a-half-mile Speedway within a prescribed minimum speed. The first phase called for maintaining 85 mph. The latter phases called for increasing speed in ten-miles-per-hour increments up to a maximum of 115 mph. Duntov passed the first phase, but on the second stage he spun out of control on the northeast turn and skidded onto the apron. Speedway officials were alarmed enough that he was not permitted a second qualifying attempt, and his hopes for running in the 1946 Indy 500 were over.

That same year, Zora ran the Talbot in AAA-sanctioned events on dirt tracks at Langhorne, Pennsylvania, and Goshen, New York. During practice in Goshen, Zora got into a dice with legendary dirt driver Rex Mays, with the two continuously switching places around the mile oval. Zora over-cooked it on the straights and paid dearly

While Zora didn't make the field at Indy, it didn't discourage him from entering the car in other AAA-sanctioned events on dirt tracks.

in the corners, where Mays would eat him for lunch. "Rex was high, wide and handsome in corner," said Zora, "while I jerky—accelerating and braking." Finally, the AAA officials called them both in and said if they used the same techniques in the race, mayhem would result.

So far, Zora had done nothing to distinguish himself as a driver. He was not smooth and consistent, but rather overaggressive and jerky, a sign of his inexperience. He had discovered the great difficulty in trying to be a great engineer as well as a great driver. Often the two didn't mix because excellence at either endeavor demanded a total commitment, something Zora wasn't prepared to give. He may not have had the temperament to be a great driver, but whatever limitations he possessed, he never stopped trying.

At Langhorne, Duntov arrived for the first time during practice and had to wait to cross over to the inside of the track. Watching the careening machines kicking up rooster tails of dirt as they lapped, he thought, "I must be crazy to enter this race." Once on the track, however, the impression of speed went away, and he immediately liked the fact that the response of the car was much slower and steering with the throttle provided a feeling of complete control. Zora liked the dirt best when he was the only one on the track and didn't have to eat the mud flying off the tires of the other cars. He also raced an Ardun-powered sprint car at Union, New Jersey. Once again, he achieved nothing remarkable at any of these venues.

He liked the dirt enough, however, to enter Pikes Peak, the most famous hill climb in North America. Duntov submitted an entry form dated July 31, 1946, listing himself as the driver and Luigi Chinetti as his mechanic. But Zora would only go if the Pikes Peak Hill Climb Association organizers were willing to offer appearance and transportation money. They weren't, and informed him so in a Western Union telegram dated August 21, 1946. A Duntov rendezvous with Pikes Peak would have to wait a few more years.

In 1947, Zora and Chinetti went their separate ways, with Chinetti pursuing an effort to drive an Alfa Romeo. Zora returned to Indy with the Talbot and a new chief mechanic whose last name was Ladd. They submitted their entry as "The Martin Special." The car was actually sponsored by the Cornelius Printing Company of Indianapolis at the request of Speedway president Wilbur Shaw. Exactly how the sponsorship came about isn't known, but it's likely, says IMS historian Davidson, that Shaw went to his friend Pem Cornelius and asked him to help Zora as a means of assuring the car got to the track. The sponsorship probably amounted to less than $250.

This time, Duntov appeared at the Speedway four days before the race to resume the rookie test at the 95-mph phase. He passed that and was running 103 mph on the third phase when the car quit. Once again, his hopes to compete in the Indy 500 were dashed.

After the 1947 race, Shaw wrote a letter to Zora in which the subject of Zora's Talbot came up. "I do not know what to recommend about the Talbot; she is a little bit short of steam to make any money out here. I think it would be advisable if you can get anything out of it to let her go."

In November of that year Duntov followed Shaw's advice and sold the Talbot to Harry Schell, a blue-blooded American born in Paris of well-to-do expatriate parents. He would later become the only American in grand prix racing, driving for a succession of different teams, including Cooper, Gordini and Ferrari, but he never won a grand prix in his 14-year career.

Schell got to know Duntov in New York and the two became close friends. Schell offered to buy the Talbot for $5,000. Zora accepted, which put an end to his days as a race car owner. He and Schell would cross paths again soon, however.

Zora never let go of his dream to compete at Indy. For the rest of his life he was an annual visitor to the track and maintained close friendships with Wilbur Shaw and later the Hulman family. But his heart ached at the fact that he was never a part of "the greatest spectacle in racing." He would have to make his mark in the world in a different way.

Driving in Europe

In 1947, Zora got a chance to drive again with his old racing partner, Asia Orley. While visiting Paris, Zora received a call from Asia, who was planning to run a Veritas—most likely powered by a little Ardun engine—in the ten-hour race at Montlhéry and asked if Zora wanted to co-drive. Asia picked Zora up shortly after his arrival and brought him to a small hotel.

"Tomorrow is training," said Asia. "Stay here and get some sleep." After Asia left, Zora planned to go out anyway because he hadn't been to Paris since before the war. However, he couldn't find his shoes. It didn't take him long to figure out who had taken them. Asia's strategy worked. Without shoes, Zora had to stay in the room and get a good night's sleep.

The next morning, Zora awoke with the sun beaming into his eyes. The room had a standing wardrobe behind which he could hear a woman singing while taking a bath. Unable to resist the sight of a woman, Zora decided to take a peek by standing on a chair, but the chair tipped backward and hit him hard on the ribcage, cracking a rib. Zora yelled out, startling the woman in the bath. He later had to have his ribs taped. Zora later admitted that the incident was "one of the many dangers of motor racing."

The Veritas was a beautiful silver machine powered by a 2.0-liter engine and rolling on modern-looking ventilated discs. Unfortunately, Orley and Duntov were up against a much tougher level of competition, competing against Ferraris, Connaughts, Gordinis and Maseratis driven by the likes of Stirling Moss, Peter Collins, Jean Behra and John Cooper. They finished well down in the field.

Zora was on and off with Elfi during the late 1940s, separated by her work engagements in Miami and Chicago and his racing endeavors at Indy

Zora and Asia Orley drove their Veritas in a handful of European races in the late 1940s, but were not a serious factor in any of the races.

and in Europe. While friendly to each other, Elfi was still well aware of Zora's proclivities and didn't want to appear too eager in following him around. So she pursued her dancing career and spent time in England with her parents.

Still, they kept in touch and got together whenever possible. When they were together in New York, they found time to entertain in the penthouse on Riverside Drive. They hosted Zora's growing list of racing celebrity friends, including Alfred Neubauer, imported car impresario Max Hoffman and German race drivers Wolfgang Seidel and Wolfgang von Trips.

To avoid the appearance of waiting around for Zora in New York, Elfi extended her dancing career after receiving an offer to work in Miami at the Copa Cabana. She drove to Miami with a girlfriend in her new Packard convertible. She was one of only four dancers from New York and was picked because she had the best legs. In Miami she joined a troupe of showgirls who intermingled with Miami's glitterati of celebrities and mobsters. One of the latter, a man from Illinois, was visiting Elfi when Zora happened to call from New York. The mobster got on the line and offered Zora a Bentley for Elfi—as if Zora owned her.

In many ways, Zora did possess Elfi. She could have stayed on in Miami after Jackie Gleason called and offered her an audition with the June Taylor Dancers. She also had offers to dance in Las Vegas or tour South America with the Katrine Dunham ballet. But she could not stay completely away from her silver-haired husband. For Zora's part, Elfi still did more for the man than any other woman could. Upon seeing her radiant and bronzed dancer's figure, he wondered why he had ever left her.

Zora Pulls a Not-So-Fast One

In 1948, after finishing the 10 heures de Paris race in a Veritas, Zora was staying at the Hotel California in Paris with Elfi when the telephone rang. It was Harry Schell. Schell wanted to know whether Duntov would be able to drive his open-wheel D046 Cisitalia at the Shelsley Walsh hill climb in England that weekend. Schell had a conflict and was looking for someone to replace him. The offer represented a departure for Schell because in the past he had used Zora as a phantom driver.

In an event at Mont Ventoux, Schell had one car but wanted the organizers to think he had two because they had paid the entrance money. So he kept his car in a nearby barn and changed the numbers on the side of the car, entering the "second" car in Zora's name. Schell then changed helmets and accents to become "Zora."

Zora decided to accept the drive. The next morning at the unholy hour of 5 a.m. a van containing the race car and driven by Schell's mechanic pulled up at the hotel. Before they departed, Zora inquired about travel money to take the ferry to England, but the mechanic told him he had none.

Schell had departed for an unknown destination the evening before, so Zora and the mechanic discussed whether to make the journey. Finally they decided to go ahead. They reasoned that Schell had somehow arranged with the British Royal Automobile Club (R.A.C.) to take care of any expenses once they arrived in England. So Zora, Elfi and the mechanic drove to Dieppe on the French coast to catch the ferry. Upon their arrival, they haggled with the captain of the ferry to let them cross without paying. Duntov promised that representatives from the R.A.C. would meet them and pay the fare. "If they don't, you can arrest us," he said. Zora's sincerity persuaded the captain and he cordially invited them aboard.

En route, Elfi started thinking about the prospects of being thrown in the slammer should the R.A.C. not be waiting on the other side. Ever the adventurer, Zora responded: "The die is cast—enjoy the sea voyage."

Upon their arrival in England, everything proceeded smoothly. As Zora had predicted, an R.A.C. representative was on hand to take care of their passage. But they weren't off the hook yet. Prior to the departure, Zora had bought a case of red wine and had stowed it in the back of the race car. The customs officer pulled back the tarp covering the race car, which exposed the wine. The customs officer exhaled and looked at Zora. "It is contraband; it has to be confiscated," he said. "And you [speaking to Zora] will be subject to heavy fines as a common criminal."

Opposite, top and middle: Zora and Elfi socialized with the crème of racing society, including Mercedes racing czar Alfred Neubauer (top photo, center) and race drivers Wolfgang Seidel (middle photo, middle) and Wolfgang von Trips (middle photo, right).

Opposite, bottom: During their separation, Elfi moved to Miami and danced at the Copa Cabana. She was also offered an audition by Jackie Gleason with his June Taylor Dancers.

His mind racing to get out of this predicament, Zora started talking. "If I intended to smuggle the wine, I would attempt to conceal it, no? The wine I bought is for self-consumption only. My French mechanic consumes two bottles a day, one for lunch and the other with dinner, and to keep him happy, I have a little extra. If you have a cat, you see to it that the cat has milk; the mechanic needs wine just as a cat needs milk—look at his nose." Fortunately, the nose of the mechanic had turned purple from the English cold. The customs official looked at his nose and let them go.

But their adventure still wasn't over. The R.A.C. representative explained the route to the Midlands and provided a certificate of insurance. But the mechanic sternly objected to driving on the left side of the road, and after the R.A.C. person explained that it's the law, the mechanic refused to drive the lorry altogether. Zora, unwilling to give up a potential race car ride, had the insurance put in his name. He then got behind the wheel of the lorry and drove the rest of the way. At about the dinner hour, the trio arrived at their destination in the Midlands.

Practice began the following morning. The course consisted of a straight climb, a left turn followed by a right turn then another straight—a total distance of less than a mile.

Zora had several years of experience running hill climbs in France at Chateau Tierry in the 1930s during his partnership with Asia Orley. This was less demanding, being straight and under a mile in length. Zora was present for the last hill climb at that location. The event was discontinued in 1937 after a driver named Catano lost control in his Bugatti and killed 25 people, mostly children. Duntov was driving an MG Q Midget in that event and was supposed to make his run right after Catano, but the starter held him at the line. "I hate to think if he had released me," Zora said later. "More people might have been killed and I possible among them."

Back at Shelsley Walsh, Duntov accomplished his practice run and found that the gearing was wrong. He changed gears on the Cisitalia and presented himself again at the starting line for a second practice run. But the officials told him that only one practice run was allowed—no exceptions. Resigned to his fate, Zora felt cheated and did not show well in the hill climb itself, registering times of 47.92 and 47.51 seconds, compared to the class winning time of 38.30 seconds. "My chance to show the capability of the Cisitalia was not to be," said Zora.

The event could have been yet another exercise in futility for Zora's driving career had it not been for the presence of Sydney Allard in the paddock. The British sports car manufacturer was at Shelsley Walsh running his own car, a single-seater powered by a rare German Steyr air-cooled

V-8. Whether Zora actually talked to Allard at the event isn't documented, but there were only 50 competitors in the event and Allard's machine, with its unusual engine and a new de Dion rear suspension, was the talk of the hill-climbing community. Certainly Zora, knowing Allard's history with Ford power plants, would have been anxious to talk to Allard and check out this particular machine. While he was at it, Zora would have been most eager to reference his own Ardun overhead valve conversion.

Zora did not distinguish himself in driving Harry Schell's Cisitalia D046 up the hill at Shelsley Walsh in 1948. But the exercise may have led to a meeting with Sydney Allard and with it a new career opportunity.

SEVEN

A natty Zora poses with the Mercedes W165 after a Nürburgring test drive in 1951. The experience had been a dream come true, even though his chances of landing a driving position for the vaunted German race team were virtually nil.

Sojourn in England

Coming off the disappointing Ardun engine endeavor and his largely ineffective outings as a racing driver, Zora contemplated his next move. He was 38 in 1948, and in a weaker moment, he might have questioned whether he had the right stuff to run his own organization, or whether he would ever be able to fulfill the dreams of becoming another Bugatti or Porsche. He realized he might be better off in an outfit where he could be the engineering virtuoso instead of the conductor, even if it meant sacrificing some of his individualism—and authority.

The failure of Ardun meant that Zora no longer had a support staff that he could use for another business venture. Yura was still on his own, having left Automotive and Aircraft Hydraulics for Curtiss Wright, and Zora's close friend Luigi Chinetti was setting himself up as the North American importer of Ferrari automobiles.

Unlike Yura and Chinetti, Zora had no firm offers. He was a vagabond once again, separated from his wife and now without a job and perhaps without a future. He needed a refuge where he could go to figure out what to do with the rest of his life. In Zora's mind, his meeting with Sydney Allard at Shelsley Walsh in 1948 represented an opportunity to find just such a shelter.

Working with Allard

Sydney Allard was building a considerable reputation manufacturing hand-built British sports cars after the war. He was a "sporting gentleman" in the finest sense of the term. Tall in stature, with a high hairline and round spectacles, Allard was known affectionately as "The Guv'nor."

Like Zora with his Arkus racer, Allard started with home-built specials when he was 23. It was a natural outgrowth of his day job managing an automotive service operation, Adlards Motors Ltd. According to Allard historian and former employee Tom Lush, Allard had named his business after a roofing company that his father had purchased. Struck by how close this

Opposite: Zora Arkus-Duntov found that several years at Allard proved to be the perfect respite between running his own business at Ardun and moving on to a major corporation at General Motors.

name was to his own, Allard apparently decided to have a little fun with that similarity, "even though he would have no idea how much confusion this was to cause in later years," Lush wrote in *Allard, the Inside Story*.

Adlards Motors Ltd. eventually became a Ford dealership, which Allard used to keep money coming in while he began to experiment with different suspension and powertrain combinations—primarily Ford—for his home-built specials.

Allard built his specials primarily for reliability trials, a hybrid between road racing and off-road racing. The courses were a diabolical combination of level sections, hills and steep descents, designed to strand competitors in mud or a ditch. The winner would be the car that completed the most stages with the fewest penalties. Before Allard showed up, honors usually went to Singers, MG Magnettes and Midgets, Austins and V-8-powered Fords.

Allard himself had been competing with a modified Ford, but it couldn't keep up with the lighter, more nimble British sports cars. So he took a V-8-powered Ford Model 48 and completely reworked the chassis and suspension and added a body from a Bugatti racer. The car became known for its British registration number, CLK 5. Its weight distribution and torque were perfect for the trials, and soon other competitors inquired about what Allard could do for them. Suddenly he was in the race car business. He thought he could make a go of it if he could keep costs low and parts interchangeable. He built a dozen "Allard Specials" by 1939, and had plans to enter the sports car and racing business full-time. But then, according to Allard historian John Allard (no relation), World War II put a stop to his racing efforts, and he shifted his attention into rebuilding Ford army trucks.

When the war ended in 1945, the pent-up demand for sports and passenger cars encouraged Allard to move forward with his plans. He formed the Allard Motor Company in early 1946 and set up a production facility in Park Hill near Clapham Common, while the showrooms and offices were situated on Clapham High Street. The small works closely resembled a blacksmith shop. There, according to *The Motor*, amid the aroma of metal, leather and castor oil, Allard's craftsmen toiled long hours in dingy quarters creating the hand-built sportsters.

A range of Ford V-8-powered Allards in two-seater, tourer, saloon and drophead forms was soon in production. This amounted to only a handful of cars per week, but the numbers steadily grew, as the world became more interested in sports cars. In 1947, the J1, a car designed strictly for trials, was introduced. The J2 debuted in 1949. It was a visual delight, with its low-slung body featuring cycle fenders, a long cowl with portholes on the cowl to aid in engine cooling, and leather hood straps.

Ardun and Allard

Zora knew that, like himself, Allard was a hot-rodder at heart. He loved big, hairy cars, especially with powerful engines installed in lightweight chassis. But Allard had a problem in the late 1940s: He couldn't obtain the kind of American V-8s he needed to make his machines fast. "It must be remembered that Allard was in a bind, performance-wise with the Ford Flathead V-8," notes John Allard. "It was inefficient, producing low horse-power for its size. But Sydney didn't have a lot of alternatives available. Most engines being manufactured in England were also of prewar design; the only modern engine on the horizon was a dual overhead cam in-line six for the new Jaguars."

Yet there was hope: Cadillac had a new overhead valve V-8 scheduled to debut in 1949. But offering the Cadillac engine—or any American V-8—was impossible because of import restrictions that were put in place by the British government. Duntov, of course, had an answer for Sydney Allard—the Ardun engine. Zora thought that if he could sell Allard on the merits of using the Ardun V-8, they could figure out a way to get around the import restrictions later.

The best way to sell the merits of the Ardun, thought Zora, was to race an Allard equipped with an Ardun engine. Zora still earned royalties on Ardun engines, so he would have more than pride at stake in seeing the Ardun succeed. Second, he could also satisfy his urge to race—still the primary motivation for many of his life's decisions. So he made Allard an offer: Zora would trade a complete Ardun engine in exchange for an Allard J2 to be consigned to him to race in the states. Allard agreed and made arrangements to give Zora a J2 that had previously run at Silverstone.

The first event Zora had in mind was sponsored by the newly formed Sports Car Club of America at Watkins Glen, New York, on September 17, 1949. Interestingly, an Ardun insert also appeared in the Watkins Glen program for that race, evidence that Duntov was still pushing Ardun components.

Racing in America

Although sports car racing was in its relative infancy in the United States, Watkins Glen was the hotbed of the fledgling sport. As the only major road-racing venue in the United States, the race captured considerable attention around the world. Broadcast to Europe through the Voice of America as well as aired locally, the race attracted crowds of over 100,000.

At the time, the course was a just a network of streets and country roads, unlike today's modern closed circuit. Racing on public roads came to an abrupt end in 1952, when the Cadillac-Allard of SCCA president Fred

Wacker was forced off course. A seven-year-old boy was killed and 14 others were injured.

The J2 arrived in Watkins Glen minus an engine, with an unpainted aluminum finish and red leather interior. Zora dropped an Ardun V-8 into the car and fitted three dual carburetors set up to run on methanol (in 1949, selection of fuel was free).

The silver car weighed only 2,500 pounds and used a de Dion rear suspension. The J2 also had Allard's trademark front suspension—a swing axle arrangement formed by cutting a straight axle in half. According to John Allard, the unit allowed the front wheels to move up and down independently of each other, but also allowed them to move in other directions as well. "This combination of swing axle front suspension, de Dion rear and well over 50 percent of the unsprung weight being in the rear, resulted in a car that understeered under acceleration and oversteered under braking," wrote Allard. Zora would later help mitigate the problem.

Trouble developed during the first practice session at Watkins Glen when Zora was not allowed out on the track. Despite the fact that Zora had never won a race, officials deemed him a professional, and this early Sports Car Club of America race was for amateurs only. This situation still wasn't resolved on race morning, with one faction on the steward committee insisting Duntov was a pro who could not race against the amateurs. The other faction maintained he was an SCCA member in good standing and therefore had a right to race. Finally, a compromise was reached and Zora was allowed to start from the back of the grid.

After the green flag dropped, Duntov quickly surged to the front of the field—thanks to the power of his Ardun engine. He marveled at the exhilaration of leading his first race while setting a blistering pace. His joy, however, was fleeting. After a lap or two, he was black-flagged and waved into the pits, after race officials determined that he was locking an inside wheel on tight turns while trail braking. The race stewards claimed that the function of the car was compromised, although to Zora it was a natural consequence of his driving style.

Briggs Cunningham took over the lead in his Ferrari 166SC, the very first Ferrari to come to America. He led until the last lap and seemingly had the race in the bag only to give way

Zora and his Ardun-powered Allard J2 on the grid at Watkins Glen, New York, in September 1949. Although he started from the back of the field, he quickly assumed the lead, only to be black-flagged by race officials who were concerned about an inside wheel that was locking under braking.

to hard-charging Miles Collier driving a Riley powered by a Ford Flathead V-8. According to *Speed Age* it had been "A most thrilling ending to a most thrilling meet, and a race that, in all probability, will be named as the turning point in American sports car racing history."

Working at Allard

Duntov's spirited showing at Watkins Glen had the desired effect. He had convinced Sydney Allard of the merits of using his Ardun engine in Allard production cars if a way could be found around the import restrictions. Even better, Zora also convinced Allard to offer him a position as a technical advisor.

Zora knew that Allard's company was a place where he could watch another maestro at work, use his engineering skills, and perhaps get a chance to race. Most importantly, he wouldn't have to worry about running a company. He eagerly accepted Allard's offer, but rather than pulling up stakes in New York, he chose to sublet his New York apartment instead of moving permanently to London.

Duntov first journeyed to England in the fall of 1949, where the weather was already turning cold. Upon his arrival in London, Zora stayed in a boarding house that had been arranged by Allard. Zora was surprised to discover the lack of certain amenities in the postwar period—like heat. The only way to get any heat was to put coins into the room's heater. Duntov told Allard that if he didn't get better accommodations, he'd go back to America. Allard eventually put Zora up at the more comfortable Mount Royal Hotel at Marble Arch. The Allard shops were cold and clammy as well. Taking a page from Elfi, who used to feed the employees in the Ardun shop back in New York, Zora brought chocolates to help fatten up his emaciated English shopmates.

Ironically, Zora's move to London would actually provide a chance to see more of Elfi, who was on an extended visit with her parents. But this proved to be more a coincidence than an orchestrated plan.

Zora still had his eye on other conquests. On one of his trips across the Atlantic, he had met 26-year-old actress Yvonne de Carlo aboard the *Mauritania*. Her most famous role was yet to come, that of Moses' wife opposite Charlton Heston in *The Ten Commandments*. In 1950 she was just coming into her own as an actress, having starred in the film *Criss Cross*, where she played the ex-wife of a hoodlum. In Zora's eyes, she was a major prize.

He engaged her in conversation and managed to intrigue her into a date that evening on the ship. Zora liked challenges, and this beautiful movie star was positively intoxicating.

At the time, Duntov was sharing a first-class cabin with his friend and associate, Julian Hoffman. Yvonne de Carlo was also in first class, and Zora arranged with the steward for Hoffman to sleep elsewhere on the ship. Very late that night Zora and Yvonne, arm in arm, scampered down to Zora's cabin. With great anticipation, he unlocked the door only to see Hoffman still sitting on a cot in the room. That broke the spell, and Zora and Yvonne went their separate ways that night.

Later Zora met Yvonne de Carlo again in London and invited her to a Christmas party being held at Allard. She made the perfect party accessory. While the boys at Allard were initially impressed to see a beautiful actress on Zora's arm, they were clearly more interested in talking about automobiles and didn't pay much attention to Miss de Carlo. She was more than a little annoyed by it all, and any hopes he had of a sexual conquest were dashed.

While she represented a tangible prize, Zora wasn't really looking to get involved with the actress. He didn't have the slightest interest in committing to someone who would have him catering to her whims, rather than her catering to him. It was just not in his constitution to let any woman run his life, so he let her go.

Elfi, it turned out, was still in the picture. It had been six years since Zora's separation from her. While they remained cordial and saw each other whenever convenient, they did not share a residence until 1951, when Zora obtained a flat in Chelsea near the Allard works. Their moving in together, however, did not represent any major change in Zora's attitude. He was willing to have her back as long as it could be on *his* terms. He had missed her during their separation, and she was still a companion he was comfortable with. Elfi had accepted the only terms by which Zora would agree to live with any woman—the freedom to do as he pleased. She was loyal to him no matter what he did.

Ardun—Made in England

When it came time to find a way around the import restrictions on engines, Zora called in Rudy Sternberg, who set up a plan to assemble the engines in England. Sternberg, who had been knighted for his efforts in promoting exports, lived near Buckingham Palace in a large home with servants. Duntov had met him originally through Julian Hoffman, who had worked for Duntov during the later days at Ardun.

Evidence suggests that Sternberg set up an arrangement to get around British import restrictions by having broken-down engine components that had been manufactured and shipped from New York assembled at one or two locations in the United Kingdom. One of these assembly points was A.E.C. in Southhall, a manufacturer of double-decker buses, while the other was Monaco Engineering in Herts. The actual exportation was handled by Dominions Export Company Ltd. Julian Hoffman traveled to England to help set up the deal, which provided a flow of engines directly to the Allard works. Allard would be the sole customer of Ardun "Made in England" power plants. He eventually took over all manufacturing and distribution rights. An Allard catalog from 1952 even referred to the Ardun engine as an "Allard" engine.

Allard also gave his non-British customers the option of ordering a car without an engine. By specifying that the engine be installed at an Allard dealer or other shop, the car would be built with the appropriate engine mounts, bellhousing adapters, fuel line routing and exhaust positioning. Various hood configurations were also available to match a given engine choice.

Allards equipped with Ardun engines, however, still suffered from many of the same valvetrain problems that had haunted Zora. As Tom Lush wrote in *Allard, The Inside Story*, "A great number of minor troubles had occurred, and the power output was well below claimed figures." Author David Kinsella echoed Lush in his assessment: "Owners who had previously driven a modified, side-valve engine found the Ardun something of a disappointment as a performance V-8 in the medium speed range."

Because of the limitations of the Ardun engine, American customers increasingly opted for alternative power plants like the Cadillac and Chrysler V-8s as these became available. Zora himself must have faced the inevitable after his own track and dynamometer tests made it clear that both the Chrysler and Cadillac overhead-valve V-8s were more reliable and more powerful than the Ardun. Willing to accept this reality, Zora concentrated on the interchangeability of Chrysler and Cadillac V-8 parts for both racing and customer cars. He also established relationships with Robert Bosch in Germany and Weber Carburetors in Bologna, Italy, to supply parts for Allard cars.

Zora also spent time working on suspensions, including Sydney Allard's controversial swing axle. He sorted out transmissions, working with a four-speed and a three-speed nonsynchronized gearbox. In addition, working with Allard, Duntov managed to squeeze a fourth gear into a Ford three-speed truck transmission, although the result wasn't necessarily successful. Zora may have had something to do with an Allard quick-change rear end, modeled after a Halibrand unit, as well. Duntov also spent much of his track testing time at MIRA, a high-speed facility near Lindley, England.

Allards became formidable sports cars during this period. Known for their stout V-8 power plants and quirky handling, they became a thorn in the side of more established racing operations like Jaguar, Mercedes and Ferrari. In this sense, the Allards provided a notable parallel to the Cunningham racers—also powered by American V-8s—and later the Ford Cobras and Chevrolet Corvettes. The Corvette comparison becomes more noteworthy when it is considered that Sydney Allard also experimented with fiberglass bodies in 1952 and early 1953. According to historian John Allard, the company constructed at least four fiberglass-bodied Palm Beaches, at least one of which survives today.

Enjoying Allard

Zora's tenure at Allard was also good therapy for a weary businessman. He was clearly having fun, no longer having to worry about running a company. Instead of agonizing about contracts, unions and payrolls, Zora could simply work from day to day without the necessity of planning ahead. It was hands-on work where he could instantly see the results of his efforts. Zora didn't have an office; he spent most of his time out on the shop floor.

After spending days and weeks in the dyno area located behind a partition, Zora hatched a practical joke on the rest of the assemblers and craftsmen in the shop. He faked the sound of an engine exploding on the dyno and simultaneously hurled pistons and connecting rods over the partition onto the shop floor. Thinking there had been a terrible accident, the entire staff came running in reaction to the "explosion." They found Zora behind the partition, laughing uncontrollably at the victims of his joke.

While Zora was staying with Rudy Sternberg before getting the Chelsea flat with Elfi, he hatched another practical joke. Julian Hoffman was also staying at the house, and Zora decided to have some fun at Hoffman's expense. Hoffman had a phobia about exposure to dirt or germs and would often wipe doorknobs and other household objects before touching them. Once when Hoffman was drawing a bath, Zora darted in just before Julian could get into the tub and jumped into the bathwater. Hoffman was aghast and chased a naked Zora into the empty parlor next door.

After hours, Zora would spend time with Sydney Allard or his managing partner, Reg Canham, hoisting pints of ale at the local pub. It was all very relaxed and friendly. Before meeting Allard, Duntov had a

Zora inside the Allard race shop in London. His years there allowed him to obtain hands-on experience without the burdens of running his own business.

stereotype of British people as all stiff upper lip. That changed quickly, and he became quite at home in yet another adopted country.

Zora and Neubauer

Being back in Europe put Duntov in a better position to maintain his friendship with Mercedes-Benz racing czar Alfred Neubauer, with whom Zora had stayed in contact since his student years in Berlin. The relationship bore fruit in 1951 when Zora had a chance to test-drive a Mercedes race car at the grueling Nürburgring.

Why Neubauer gave Zora this opportunity is subject to question, since Zora had still not done anything to distinguish himself behind the wheel of a race car. Either Neubauer felt compelled to give his old acquaintance a break, or Zora projected such utter self-confidence and persistence that he may have convinced Neubauer to at least give him a chance. Neubauer probably felt he wasn't risking a whole lot. Like the rest of Germany's industrial giants, Daimler-Benz was still rebuilding. Zora's "test" was behind the wheel of a prewar 1.5-liter Mercedes. Being 12 years old in 1951, the car was outdated. If anything, these older cars would serve a role in getting the Mercedes juggernaut up and running again.

The competitiveness of the cars probably didn't matter to Zora. He was just happy to live the moment for which he had longed all his life—to climb into the cockpit of one of the silver grand prix machines. Making it even better was having prewar legends like Caracciola, Lang and Kling in attendance, all under the watchful eye of the great Alfred Neubauer. It was Zora's own version of a modern-day fantasy camp.

Out on the course, the W25's 1.5-liter engine at a full cry, Zora set out to conquer the Nürburgring's 14 miles of diabolical twists and turns. He was protected from the unforgiving trees only by the hedges as he flew around the famous banked *Karussell*, up to *Hohe Act* and into *Wipperman*, *Eschbach*, *Brunchen* and *Pflanzgarten*. For Zora, this was his moment to follow in the footsteps of the prewar giants like Caracciola, Rosemeyer and Nuvolari.

But it wasn't reality, according to Zora's account, especially after an exhaust pipe loosened up and starting rubbing against a rear tire, forcing a spin. Zora brought the car safely under control, but his ride was over. Despite the incident not being his fault, he was quite aware that his chances of being offered a

Zora experiences the Mercedes-Benz W25 at the Nürburgring in 1951, all under the watchful eye of Mercedes racing czar Alfred Neubauer.

position as a Mercedes team driver ranged between slim and none. Strangely, Duntov wasn't discouraged by the incident, and corresponded regularly with Neubauer regarding his interest in joining the team. Neubauer, for his part, appeared to humor Zora.

Even if an offer had been tendered, Zora was less enthusiastic about returning to Germany. This was the first of several visits he would make to Germany during his tenure at Allard, and parts of the journey were not pleasant. Driving in an open-topped Allard, Zora and Elfi were sneered at by many Germans. Much of the city had not yet been rebuilt in the early 1950s, and the populace still harbored considerable bitterness toward foreigners, especially ones driving British cars. For the first time Zora felt like a total alien in his former homeland, a feeling that may have affected his willingness to pursue more aggressively a position with Mercedes or to return to Germany years later when several other legitimate job opportunities came his way.

Still, Daimler-Benz and its impressive facilities presented a powerful lure, especially compared to the crude Allard works. Many of the research and development labs that had been destroyed during the war had been rebuilt. These new facilities suggested to Zora what he could achieve with real resources behind him.

While Zora was visiting the Daimler facilities in Stuttgart, he was offered the opportunity to test his Allard on the rolling chassis dynamometer. The Allard was a prototype that incorporated the chassis and suspension from a J2X—Allard's latest assault weapon for Le Mans—and powered by a Cadillac V-8 engine.

While the Allard was being tested on the dyno, Duntov observed the "standing wave" for the first time. This was a phenomenon that occurred on the tires of old race cars at speed before the advent of radials. It manifested itself in a series of wrinkles in the tire sidewall, which would bulge and retract as the tire contact patch lost contact with the road. Once the wave built up to a certain point, the tire could explode. It was a primary factor limiting the top speeds of race cars during the period.

While the Allard was on the dyno, the engine blew up, so Mercedes engineer Rudi Uhlenhaut rounded up a Mercedes engine and installed it in the Allard. Uhlenhaut was a young whiz kid who not only knew how to engineer, but—unlike Zora—he could also drive the doors off many of the big-name factory drivers, according to Beverly Rae Kimes in *The Star and the Laurel*. Given their engineering talents, Uhlenhaut and Zora had much in common. Had Duntov secured a position on the Mercedes team, he might have functioned much like Uhlenhaut. And if it weren't for the presence of

Uhlenhaut, Zora conjectured that Neubauer might have approached him about a similar position.

After Uhlenhaut installed the Mercedes engine in the Allard, Zora and Elfi drove it back to England. Afterwards, Zora wrote Uhlenhaut a short note: "I take this occasion to thank you for the sporting attitude and kindness you have shown me during my visit." The two remained friends and stayed in touch for many years. Uhlenhaut would go on to become the chief of passenger car development at Daimler-Benz, a career path that suggested to Zora what could have been had he been German instead of Russian.

Zora and Elfi drove this Cadillac-powered Allard to Germany in 1951, their first return to their former home-land after World War II.

As for a driving position with the Mercedes team, Neubauer thanked Zora for his interest in a letter he wrote on October 16, 1952. "If we can't take you as a driver, it's because we've already got our team in place. We've also got 30 or 40 offers from drivers that include Taruffi, Farina, Chiron, etc., and I'm having to reject them all. Sorry we can't give you better news. Please be aware of our situation. Greetings—Neubauer."

In his letter, Neubauer showed great kindness to a man who had yet to prove himself behind the wheel. It is a remarkable testimony to the high overall regard Neubauer had for Duntov.

Zora was often fond of embellishing his impact on certain events. Because he had Neubauer's ear at the time, he took credit for planting the seed that led to the great Stirling Moss becoming a Mercedes team driver. According to Zora, Neubauer confided in him that he was worried that his team drivers—Caracciola, Lang and Kling—no longer had the stuff to keep up with the newest racing sensation, Juan Manuel Fangio. The Argentinean was driving for Alfa Romeo at the time. Neubauer asked Zora if he knew anyone he could recommend. According to Zora, Neubauer knew only German and was totally ignorant of what was going on in the English racing world. Zora volunteered the name Stirling Moss. "I explain to him what Stirling did and it's all business," said Duntov. "And I feel that I was instrumental that Neubauer selected Moss."

Moss, however, disputes Zora's account. "I'm slightly doubtful," he said. "My father and Ken Gregory [Moss' business manager] had already established a connection." Also, as it turned out, Fangio himself joined Mercedes in 1954, providing Neubauer with the best of both worlds.

Duntov also took some credit for encouraging Neubauer to stay with the use of fuel injection in the Mercedes Formula One car when the marque made its return to F1 at Reims in 1954. Zora stayed in close communication with Neubauer and Uhlenhaut for many years.

Zora's relationship with Neubauer and Uhlenhaut demonstrated to Zora the amazing things that could be accomplished within a larger company that was fully committed to high engineering ideals. Zora saw what these men did for their marque. He knew he could have a similar impact—perhaps not at Daimler-Benz, but with another company. The demand for automobiles in postwar America meant that the larger American companies like Ford and General Motors had even more resources at their disposal than Daimler-Benz. But they needed ideas, imagination and vision. They needed a man like him. Zora vowed to begin a systematic search for a position within a larger company, a place where he could become another Neubauer or Uhlenhaut.

Driving for Allard

No matter how unsuccessful Duntov's Mercedes test at the Nürburgring may have been, it may have helped him get behind the wheel of a racing Allard. During the first couple of years at Allard, Duntov wasn't asked to go to the races with Sydney Allard and the rest of the Allard team. Allard considered himself to be the team's main driver, and he had won the 1952 Monte Carlo Rally in 1952 driving a big 4.4-liter P1 saloon. While Allard was aware of Zora's interest in driving, he had written him off as a serious candidate for the endurance races such as Le Mans because he thought Zora didn't like to drive in the rain. At that time, talents such as Tom Cole, Peter Reece and Alfred Hitchings were also driving for Allard, and Sydney felt he already had enough depth on the team without Zora, who had done little behind the wheel to impress him.

Duntov, however, wanted to drive—it was his primary reason for being there—and the Mercedes episode was just one leg of his circuitous route to get a seat. Through journalist and race car owner Rob Walker, he also caught wind of a chance to drive a C-Type Jaguar at Goodwood in 1951. Zora scored an offer, but the Jaguar factory later objected because Duntov was an employee of Allard.

The episode caught Sydney's attention, who then offered to put Zora behind the wheel of the new J2X Le Mans at the 1952 Le Mans 24-hour. The new car was a modified J2 with a fully enclosed body, the result of a new FIA rule prohibiting mud flaps and wings. Powered by a Chrysler V-8 and with a top speed of more than 150 mph, the J2X was some 30 mph faster than the old J2 on the Mulsanne straight.

Sydney Allard and Jack Fairman shared the number one team car, while Zora was paired with Frank Curtis in a second car. Duntov and Fairman started the race. Both got off cleanly during the traditional "Le Mans-style" start, where the drivers sprinted across the track toward their waiting machines.

Both cars were running fine when, just short of the three-hour mark, Duntov lost his brakes on the Mulsanne straight at 140 mph. He went off the end of the four-mile straight-away and into the hay bales, eventually sailing down an escape road toward Tours.

Zora behind the wheel of the Allard J2X Le Mans at the 1952 Le Mans 24-hour. The car suffered from a succession of mechanical woes and was finally retired with a broken axle shaft at the 14-hour mark.

He was able to get turned around and made it back to the Allard pits, where it was discovered that a shock absorber had broken loose and pinched a brake line.

After 56 minutes in the pits, the car went back out, this time in the hands of Frank Curtis. Duntov and Curtis drove several shifts each through the misty French night before the car stopped out on the circuit with a broken axle shaft at the 14-hour mark. The lead car of Allard and Fairman had succumbed to engine problems after 13 hours.

The silver Mercedes 300SL of Hermann Lang and Karl Riess went on to win overall, the effort once again led by Zora's old friend Alfred Neubauer. Had Duntov made a better showing during his earlier Nürburgring test in the prewar grand prix car, he might have had a shot at participating in a winning effort for the German racing team.

The Le Mans Experience

Win or lose, gentleman Sydney Allard always made Le Mans a special experience for his team. He usually scouted out available hotels around Le Mans several months in advance. He selected a hotel based not only on accommodations but on a good restaurant and pub. One of his favorites was 30 kilometers from the track, to which Zora objected because the race car was also used for transportation back to the hotel.

The owner of the hotel knew that Duntov liked ecrivisses, a type of shrimp that looks like a miniature lobster. After Zora returned from a long day testing at the track, the innkeeper would have a big platter of them waiting in the refrigerator. Zora would sit at a table at 1 a.m. with a bottle of red wine, some French bread and his ecrivisses, eating to his heart's content. Sydney also had a restaurant cater elaborate spreads at the track, which were served on red and white checkered tablecloths.

But niceties didn't win races. In the future, Allard knew that he would have to come up with a more competitive car to run with the big Mercedes, Ferraris, Cunninghams and the C-Type Jaguar. Zora helped develop such a car and laid out the groundwork for his efforts in a lengthy article in the December 1952 issue of *The Automobile Engineer* titled "Vehicle Performance—A Method of Determining Drag, Engine Power Output, and Transmission Behavior Under Operating Conditions." The article described testing the J2 and J2X at MIRA. The paper attempted to reconcile the differences between controlled laboratory testing of an automobile versus real test-track situations and made extensive use of mathematical formulas. Topics included low, medium and high-speed coasting runs—used to calculate drag and rolling resistance—and full-throttle power runs. This paper provided the impetus for the development of the JR in 1953, which was another fully enveloped body developed by Dudley Hulme. It produced even less aerodynamic drag than the J2X Le Mans.

The Spanish Diversion

At the 1952 Le Mans race, representatives of Pegaso approached Duntov about a consulting project to evaluate their new sports car. The Spanish truck manufacturer had entered three cars for the 1952 event, but none of them were ready in time. Zora was mildly interested, feeling it might make a pleasant diversion. But Pegaso didn't seem like a very likely place to make sports car history. Even so, they had hired former Alfa Romeo engineer Wilfredo Ricart. Ricart designed the first Pegaso, a front-engined sports car vaguely resembling a Ferrari. The Spanish government subsidized the entire project. The Pegaso was a very competent sports car, but only 125 were built, and it never became a major player on the market. At the time, Ricart wanted Duntov to audit the entire program and write an analysis of what he felt. Zora decided to accept the offer, despite the fact that it was Ricart's car and there would be little that he could accomplish in terms of actual engineering.

The prospect of spending some time in Spain after months in cold, clammy England no doubt helped Zora to decide. As part of his deal, Duntov was given the opportunity to drive a black Pegaso from Le Mans to Barcelona, where he stayed for six weeks on a leave of absence from Allard. Zora, who was with Elfi at the time, recalled the drive in the cramped cockpit, which lacked ventilation. The problem was exacerbated by Spain's hot dry climate.

Crossing the border into Spain brought back memories for Zora and Elfi as they crossed at the same town, le Perthus, as they had when they were fleeing France in 1940. This time the experience was more a vacation than a run for their lives.

In summarizing his trip a year later, Duntov saw certain similarities between Pegaso and Ettore Bugatti's operation but indicated that the company philosophy emphasized form rather than function. "They initiate the form without understanding the spirit," wrote Zora. "The general impression is that in the pursuit of form and things external, the organization has forgotten the main purpose for which automobiles are built. The people seem to know everything about an automobile, but one is entitled to doubt if they understand what they know."

Duntov noted that while Pegaso had a qualified design staff, they sadly lacked development engineers. "Design wise," he wrote, "the engines give the expected output and there is nothing visibly wrong with elements of the chassis. However, they only look good in showrooms. On the track they don't run and don't handle."

Zora suggested that inexperienced test drivers gave enthusiastic reports to the design staff in order to please. Management in turn complimented each other in fits of self-adoration. "The management believed that the drawbacks they suffered were incidental and not inherent to the structure of their organization and that the end of troubles will come tomorrow."

Duntov noted that his frank analysis of the situation decreased his popularity considerably within the Spanish company, and he returned to Allard after the completion of his Pegaso assignment.

But his heart was no longer with the English manufacturer. He was now more determined than ever to apply his talents on a larger playing field. The Allard company was at a crossroads. After the war, there was a tremendous demand for transportation in England, and the British government had placed high tariffs on imports. Those policies were being relaxed in the early 1950s and small operations like Allard could not compete in the mass market with the larger manufacturers.

Duntov also had the feeling that Sydney Allard regarded his company as more of a hobby than as a growing business. Yet Allard had no wish to sell the company either, as evidenced by the fact that Reg Canham discovered a wire from a group in Switzerland that wanted to buy it—but the offer was two years old by the time he heard about it.

The experience at Allard had been a nice sabbatical, but Duntov longed to see what he could do with big budgets, with the kind of money big American companies like Ford and General Motors had to throw around.

Zora's introduction to GM resulted from the fact that the commander of the Eighth U.S. Air Force in England, General Francis Griswold, was an

Allard fan and actually sold an Allard K2 to General Curtis E. LeMay, the commander of the Strategic Air Command. This led to LeMay meeting Duntov during a visit to the Allard shops in summer 1952.

LeMay talked to Duntov of his high-level connections at GM, among them Chevrolet Chief Engineer Ed Cole. Knowing Duntov's interest in hooking up with an American auto company, LeMay encouraged him to write to Cole. Duntov took LeMay up on his suggestion and waited patiently for a reply that never came.

Duntov concluded that if he were going to get a job with one of the Big Three in America, he was going to have to do it from within the United States. In fall 1952, he moved back to New York.

EIGHT

Seeing the Corvette on the turntable at the GM Motorama in New York in 1953 was a major turning point in Duntov's life, and caused him to direct his job-seeking efforts toward General Motors where he might have a chance to influence this car.

GM ENGINEERING STAFF
GENERAL MOTORS CORPORATION
GENERAL MOTORS TECHNICAL CENTER
DETROIT 2, MICHIGAN

December 19, 1952

LINCOLN-MERCURY
DIVISION OF FORD MOTOR COMPANY
6200 W. WARREN AVENUE · DETROIT 32, MICHIGAN

November 26, 1952

CHRYSLER CORPORATION

Detroit 31, Michigan

December 9, 1952

ENGINEERING DIVISION
P. O. BOX 1118

Mr. Z. Arkus-Duntov
20 East 83rd Street
New York, New York

Dear Mr. Arkus-Duntov:

Your letter of November 20 has been turned over to me.

We find your letter very interesting and the description
of your many engineering connections must have given
you a lot of experience.

I really believe that a man of your varied experience would
do better to make contact with a smaller firm; one
having a variety of engineering problems which must be
solved by one individual, rather than a large corporation
are many specialists--each one having a
development of a finished

Courting the Automakers

After returning to New York in the fall of 1952, Duntov took up residence at the penthouse at 33 Riverside Drive, which he and Elfi had sublet for $150 a month while they were in England. He began to send out job application letters by the dozens, trying for a position with a large automotive company. After years of trying to secure projects with limited resources, the prospect of having millions of dollars available to execute his ideas was alluring. Zora was so motivated that he was willing to forgo a career with a smaller sports car/racing concern where his perspectives would be better understood and appreciated. In short, he was making the gamble of his life—risking a potential loss of control—in joining a large American automotive manufacturer.

There were other risks as well. Employment with a large car company would more than likely mean moving to the Midwest and having to learn yet another culture quite foreign to the social customs of New York or Europe. Elfi in turn would be separated from her contacts in the entertainment world. But Zora was no longer a young man at age 41, and the clock was ticking. In his view, the American auto industry still represented the best place to make a name for himself as an engineer and as a driver.

Zora's initial job targets were Studebaker, Ford, Lincoln-Mercury, Chrysler and General Motors. He tried his luck at Studebaker Corporation via an acquaintance named John Cuccio, at Raymond Loewy Associates, which was the automaker's design house. In an October 1952 letter, Zora wrote, "After almost two years with Allard, I am back again in old New York. I am in the process of investigating my possibilities of developing dream engines and chassis for American automobile industries. All joking aside, I am really wondering if the specialized knowledge which I have might be of interest to one of the major manufacturers here. I do sincerely feel that I can make creative contributions in the engine and chassis field." Cuccio issued a courteous, if innocuous, reply in a letter to Zora dated November 2, 1952. No interview ever took place.

Opposite: Convinced that joining a large automotive concern was the best way for Zora to achieve his dreams, he began a furious campaign to obtain a position with a major American manufacturer in the fall of 1952.

Switching to Chrysler, Zora essentially recited his entire resume in a lengthy November 1952 letter to James C. Zader. He played up his connection to the Ardun OHV V-8 project as well as his involvement with Allard, including the fact that Allards ran with Chrysler Firepower V-8s, in addition to Cadillac and Ardun power plants. "I am at your disposal for any additional information or a personal interview, if you so desire," concluded Duntov. In a postscript, Zora wrote, "For obvious reasons your Firepower was chosen for Allard factory racing cars. I carried out some development work on your engine, and subsequently drove one of the cars at Le Mans, and it was not the engine which prevented the cars from winning the race."

Despite Zora's impressive credentials, in a December 1952 letter, A. G. Herreshoff of the Chrysler personnel department suggested that Duntov put his efforts toward a position "in a smaller firm, one having a variety of engineering problems which must be solved by one individual, rather than a large corporation in which there are many specialists—each one having a small part in the design and development of a finished product."

Not willing to let the matter lie, Duntov replied to Herreshoff: "The decision on my part to seek an association with a large company is fully a conscious one. Looking upon being an engineer as a calling more than a profession, I am subordinating the financial prospect to the possibility of more efficient use of whatever abilities I have. The fact that the Ardun and Firepower are embodying the same design features (hemispherical heads) and are trying to achieve the same technical aims was the basis of the belief that I will fit well in the Chrysler team and will enjoy a hearty welcome."

Automotive authorities over the years have noted the similarity between the Ardun cylinder head and the first-generation Chrysler hemi, introduced in 1951. Duntov, however, never made any assertions in this regard, despite the fact that the Chrysler built a performance legacy on the hemi engine. Zora himself had borrowed the hemispherical concept from Auto Union and Talbot. Furthermore, he had no patents on the technology and, if anything, wanted to leverage any similarities into a possible job at Chrysler. But his strategy did not lead to an employment opportunity.

Duntov next turned his sights on the Ford Motor Company, firing off an inquiry to Benson Ford of the Lincoln-Mercury Division in late November 1952. Again, Duntov made much of the Ardun connection with Ford and Mercury. His inquiry was referred to the Ford Division. In a quick reply back to Duntov, Ford's J.J. Tigue wrote: "A review of your background indicates that your experience and talents are obviously in the developmental engineering field. Position openings of this type are a rarity within the Lincoln-Mercury Division. All developmental work and research is conducted by the Ford Motor Company's engineering staff." There is no record of Ford showing any further interest.

Zora's initial experience with GM wasn't much better. He had already written to Ed Cole in 1952 at LeMay's suggestion and had continued to knock on the door that fall. Finally, a letter he wrote to Cole later that year—in October—bore fruit. The letter offered information and technical assistance on a K3 Allard that GM had purchased for evaluation purposes. Wrote Zora: "The K3 Allard which you ordered [for GM] is one of the models for which development I am partly responsible and I would like to inform you that I am at your disposal for any information and assistance you may desire in conjunction with this car. Should the production model duplicate the characteristics of the test car, the roadworthiness and stability should be exceptionally good. For my own reasons, I would very much like the opportunity of meeting with you personally in order to determine the possibility of me associating myself with your company."

This time, Duntov received an acknowledgment directly from Cole, dated November 4, 1952. But it wasn't exactly a warm invitation, suggesting a get-together the next time Duntov was in the Detroit area. There was no offer to fly him to Detroit for a job interview. Stung by Cole's lukewarm reaction, Duntov's initial sentiment was "to hell with him."

But the door at GM was still open. A letter written by H. Kjolhede of the GM personnel department stated that Duntov might be better suited to GM's overseas operations and that GM would refer his qualifications to A. A. Maynard, chief engineer of that division.

Encouraged by this glimmer of interest, Duntov fired back an acknowledgment letter to Kjolhede as well as a separate letter to Cole that laid out the reasons Zora was attracted to GM. The Cole letter contained a copy of his article on vehicle performance for *The Automobile Engineer*. In describing the paper, Zora acknowledged the lack of resources at a company like Allard, where he had done his research. "If you will read the paper, the method described will probably make you smile," Zora wrote, "but working in the frame of a small company, one has to substitute imagination for instrumentation and go to great length to obtain precise information."

Duntov's original letter to Cole was passed on to one of Cole's key lieutenants, Maurice Olley of the research and development section. Finally Duntov was getting somewhere. Olley wrote a letter to Duntov dated January 5, 1953, stating: "If you are still available, and would consider employment with Chevrolet Engineering, we will arrange an interview." Duntov quickly responded: "I am still available and interested in employment with Chevrolet engineering."

Several weeks later Olley followed with another letter stating: "Thank you for your letter of January 9, which has been receiving attention. We are also interested in reading your article which was published in the December issue of *The Automobile Engineer*." But there was no specific mention of an interview.

In the meantime, Duntov received a letter dated January 26, 1953, from A. A. Maynard. It stated: "We are now considering whether our organization has a present requirement for a man of your training and experience. We hope within the next ten days to two weeks to be able to advise you of our decision." Zora didn't hear anything for almost three months.

The Search Continues

Discouraged but not defeated, Zora expanded his search beyond Detroit and even considered going back to England. In a late 1952 letter to L. (Lofty) England at Jaguar, Zora used an item in *Autocar* about the appointment of a new racing manager as the springboard of an inquiry with company founder William Lyons. Jaguar would have been a very attractive proposition for Duntov, given its emergence in international endurance racing with its C-Type and D-Type cars. "I propose to join your company as development engineer believing that I can efficiently contribute to the achievement of the company's aims in this field," Duntov wrote. He received a standardized reply from England that indicated there were no positions open that he could fill.

Duntov also expanded his targets beyond the automotive sector, primarily because he needed the money. When he came across an ad seeking engineers for Fairchild Aviation on Long Island, he applied for a position. Duntov had interviewed with Fairchild once before going to Allard in England, so he decided to try his luck again in a letter to C. M. Wieden, chief design engineer, dated January 7, 1953.

Wrote Duntov: "The bulk of my experience is in the automotive field. However, automobiles are built in Detroit and I would like to stay in the New York area. In the latter years I came to think of myself as being a development engineer and hope that under proper guidance, I can contribute efficiently in a field which is not exactly my own."

It is not known exactly what aspect of Zora's background appealed to the decision-makers at Fairchild, but it is clear they saw something they liked. They offered Zora a position as a development engineer. He started work in February 1953, and adopted the lifestyle of an American commuter as he took the train each day from his residence in Manhattan out to Farmingdale on Long Island. Later he started driving his own Mercury to work.

Zora's assignment was to design a turbine blade for a heavy water atomic compressor destined for a nuclear reactor. Duntov worked closely with an analytical engineer in honing the shape as well as experimenting with various metals and conducting critical speed calculations for the blade. Duntov claimed to have very little knowledge of what this compressor was being used for or whether it had any applications for nuclear weapons. It is known, however, that Fairchild had been one of several companies awarded a project by the Air Force's Aircraft Nuclear Propulsion (ANP) program to develop a nuclear-powered airplane. After being awarded the program in 1946, the company began a series of experiments.

Whether Zora actually worked on a compressor for aircraft use is not documented. According to a Fairchild corporate history, the company's involvement with the Air Force's Nuclear Energy for the Propulsion of Aircraft (NEPA) program was liquidated in 1951, and the entire ANP program was suspended in March 1953. It was resurrected again in April 1954 but eventually was scrapped in light of other options such as long-range missiles and cheaper conventional bombers like the B52 and B70. If Zora did work on an aircraft application, he did not relay this fact to anyone, either at the time or later.

Zora was up front, however, regarding his frustration at knowing such a small piece of the big picture. "They told me only what I needed to know, not any more." Clearly, such a company did not fit with Zora's swashbuckling personality, characterized by a need to control situations while achieving notoriety.

Regardless, Zora established his credentials very quickly at Fairchild. He claimed there was a grass-roots movement afoot to make him chief engineer, which was an amazing accomplishment considering his short tenure there. But while the organization seemed to embrace Duntov, he was less enthusiastic about the prospects of long-term happiness in a closed, secure environment. Furthermore, corporate policy prohibited him from traveling abroad because of the high-security nature of the job. Zora hadn't given up on his racing career and was already entertaining the idea of going back to Le Mans for Allard. Another reason for craving international mobility was that Zora's father had survived his stay in a Nazi concentration camp and had returned to Paris. Zora wanted the freedom to visit him in Europe, but couldn't do so as long as he was employed at Fairchild.

Love at First Sight

There was another factor weighing on Zora's job satisfaction at Fairchild. About a month before he started at the Long Island firm, he fell in love. It happened in the plush velvet ballroom of the Waldorf Astoria in

Manhattan at the GM Motorama. A precursor to the modern auto show, Motorama was a daring collection of concept and production cars that showcased the talents of Harley Earl and his band of bright young designers in GM's Styling department. GM was on an aggressive campaign to set new standards of design for the industry as well as fuel the continued postwar public interest in more expressive, fun vehicles. Earl himself pioneered the use of cars with concealed running boards, tail fins, curved front and rear glass and "hardtop" body styles.

Motorama was a logical place to display these daring new shapes. More than that, it was an *event*. With its lavish displays, orchestras and stage choreography, Motorama summarized much of the postwar excitement that surrounded the automobile in America.

Zora came in through the turnstiles of the Waldorf just like thousands of other patrons that January week. Wandering through a maze of people and show cars such as the limousine-like Pontiac Parisienne or the two-seat Buick Wildcat, he came across a little low-slung sports car from Chevrolet called EX-122. It stopped him in his tracks.

The car was the most gorgeous automobile Duntov had ever seen. Unlike the other chrome-laden dreamboats on the floor, this low-slung two-seater was elegant and understated. It sported a windswept plastic body and a lipstick-red interior. Scripted in chrome on her nose was the word "Corvette," a name originally used for a class of small, fast and very maneuverable lightly armed warships.

Checking out the technical specifications of the car, Zora quickly realized he was looking at more eye candy than substance. "Mechanically, it stunk," he said, "with its six-cylinder engine and two-speed automatic transmission. But visually, it was superb."

Of all the cars at Motorama, Duntov sensed that the Corvette was the jewel, the one that was most viable for eventual production. Likewise, the feeling at GM was that if the public liked the car and the name, it could have a future as America's answer to the MG TC and TD or the Jaguar XK120. These cars had whetted an American appetite for sports cars among World War II veterans who had been exposed to them in England during the war years. In the early 1950s, sports car buyers had few places to go for an American sports car. Choices included the expensive ($10,000) limited production Cunningham C-3, the Nash-Healey and the Kaiser Darrin.

While sports cars were rare in the United States, fiberglass sports cars such as the proposed Corvette and the Kaiser Darrin were virtually unheard of. There was growing interest in this new material after the war. It had been originally used for military application, but in 1946 Kaiser Darrin engineer Bill Stout had collaborated with Owens Corning on a new fiberglass body for his Stout Scarab. In 1950, a California boatbuilder named Bill Tritt founded Glasspar, a fiberglass components manufacturer, to fabricate boat hulls. But even fiberglass boat hulls didn't catch on until the early 1960s.

Glasspar's fiberglass Jeep prototype was shown at the Los Angeles Motorama. It caused a sensation, prompting *Life* magazine to publish a feature on fiberglass cars in February 1952. Later that year, a Willys dealer in Downey, California, named B. Robert Woodill commissioned Glasspar to develop a fiberglass automobile body for limited production. The result was the Wildfire, a two-seat roadster powered by a Willys F-head, six-cylinder engine. Though it was not a particularly successful effort, historian Karl Ludvigsen credits the Wildfire with setting the stage for a production fiberglass sports car.

Always looking to push new technology, Cole shared Earl's enthusiasm for this new body material called fiberglass. In fact, he hired Maurice Olley to set up a research and development department project to pursue this idea. Upon coming to Detroit, Olley immediately began experimenting with fiberglass and actually used it in building a full-sized Chevrolet convertible, which accidentally rolled over three times yet survived remarkably intact, as described by Ludvigsen in *Corvette, America's Star-Spangled Sports Car*.

The sight of the Corvette in the Waldorf Astoria ballroom stopped Zora in his tracks. While he loved the design, he knew it needed an engineering makeover in order to create a real sports car out of it—a task he would relish.

Given these factors, Earl proceeded in 1951 with his idea for a GM sports car coded Project Opel. He started working with a small group of stylists led by Henry Lauve, a Paris-educated designer who graduated from the Sorbonne. The group was housed in a small studio in an anonymous-looking brick building on Milwaukee Avenue opposite the main GM building in Detroit. Earl wanted to pursue the initial development of the car in relative secrecy.

At the time, Earl wasn't sure which division would get the Corvette. But Earl felt close to Chevy's Ed Cole, so he invited Cole and Thomas Keating, then Chevy general manager, to a meeting. Also present was GM president Harlow Curtice. The meeting took place on June 2, 1952, in an auditorium in the old GM building. When Cole saw the car, he knew it was just the thing he needed to help jump-start the stodgy Chevrolet Division.

Earl hoped to price the car at about $2,000, a sum within the reach of college-age buyers, a major market for the vehicle. This fit well into Chevrolet's marketing plans, and the support at Chevy for Earl's proposal was unanimous. The sports car would debut at the 1953 Motorama, scheduled to open at the Waldorf Astoria.

Prior to the June meeting, Earl hired Robert McLean, a Cal Tech graduate with both engineering and design credentials, to draw a layout of the car. McLean's approach to this was unconventional, both in his techniques and in the vehicle configuration, as Karl Ludvigsen recounted. McLean's design located the seats just in front of the rear axle and the engine close to the firewall, as in traditional sports car designs but quite different from contemporary passenger cars.

Still Courting GM

Zora fired off this letter to Maurice Olley at GM after witnessing the Corvette for the first time. Suddenly he knew that GM had a design on its hands that would match up with anything in the world.

While Zora had contacted GM as part of his job search effort, until now GM represented just another large corporation with a lot of resources. There was no other emotional hook. Even Ford and Chrysler had interested Zora more, thanks to tie-ins with the Ardun and its Ford engine block and Ardun's hemispherical combustion chambers, which were later adapted by Chrysler. But Zora's visit to Motorama—where he had his first glimpse of the Corvette—changed his attitude about GM. The corporation advanced to the top of his list of potential employers.

Even though he was negotiating with Fairchild Aviation at the time, he couldn't get the Corvette out of his mind, so he fired off a letter to Maurice Olley, commenting on his reaction to the car. He wrote, "Thank you for your letter of January 22. I went to Motorama and found the Chevrolet sports car breathtacking [sic]. I think this is the turning point from which european [sic] body designer can look for inspiration to Detroit."

GM had still not tendered an interview offer six weeks later, and Zora in the meantime had gone to work for Fairchild. In a letter to Olley on March 17, Duntov—now actively trying to get out of Fairchild after only six weeks on the job—tried to jump-start the process with this offer: "Should the red tape of an interview arrangement be the reason and your basic intention not changed, I would gladly make a

```
                        33, RIVERSIDE DRIVE,
                        NEW YORK 23,N.Y.
                        TELEPHONE  ENDICOTT 2-5373.
                                          Jan.28th,'53.


Mr.M.Olly,Director
Research and Development Section
Chevrolet-Central Office
Division of General Motors Corp.
Detroit,2, Mich.



Dear Mr.Olly:
Thank you for your letter of January 22.

I went to Motorama and found the Chevrolet sports car
breathtacking.
I think this is the turning point from which european
body designer can look for inspiration to Detroit.
I do think that your letter was very kind,

                              Yours sincerely,
```

trip to Detroit under my own steam." On March 24 Olley responded, inviting Duntov to Detroit two days later at GM's expense. Duntov then flew to Detroit for an interview with Cole and Olley. Duntov engaged the two men in a deep philosophical exchange about high-performance automobiles and Olley made a number of points to Duntov regarding vehicle stability. Olley even lent Zora several papers he had written on the subject. The session went well enough that on March 30, Olley's secretary, Norma Puzycki, sent Duntov an official employment application.

In early April 1953, Duntov received a telegram from Olley that said, "Please wire the following information: Are you a U.S. Citizen? Have you sent me your employment application? If not, please do so immediately. I am holding up your expense report. Please include costs of wires sent me, meals from the time of NY departure to arrival at home, hotel rooms, tips, etc. Please send receipts."

Several weeks later, Duntov received a letter from GM Overseas Operations dated March 31. The letter closed the door on any possibilities abroad in a letter from Chief Engineer Maynard: "We regret that after a careful check we find that we have no opening in our organization for a person of your qualifications, as our staff is complete in this respect at the present time."

But this hardly mattered now. It looked like something might really happen in Detroit for Duntov, as indicated in an April 8, 1953, letter from Olley: "We should have something definite to report within about a week. If this application goes through favorably, I should be wanting to know when it would be convenient for you to start working at Chevrolet. Will you drop me a line and let me know [if] either mid April or May 1st would be convenient for you?"

Duntov immediately wired back to Olley referring to the earlier discussion about vehicle stability that he had with Cole and Olley. "Since our meeting, I am thinking stability most of the time and your papers which I am holding on to are my valuable partners in the process."

Zora concluded: "Since we are practically in mid-April, now, in case of a favorable decision, I can start May 1st. Hope to see you soon." In his haste, he misspelled Olley's name in the letter, spelling it "Olly."

That same day, Duntov referenced his progress in a letter to General Curtis LeMay in which he informed LeMay that he had used him as a reference with GM. Not shy with the General, Zora also took the opportunity to inquire about the possibility of hitching a ride on a U.S. Air Force plane to Le Mans that June.

Duntov received another letter from Olley April 24 detailing living arrangements that had been made for Duntov in Detroit. "We have made a reservation for you at the Abington Hotel located at 700 Seward. We reserved a two-room apartment, which consists of a living room with Murphy bed, and a kitchen dinette. The daily charge is $6.00 for single occupancy, $8.00 for double occupancy. The monthly rate (3 months minimum) is between $160-$170 per month, single or double occupancy."

The letter went on to explain that GM does not pay moving expenses to new employees. "They only pay such expenses when a GM man is being transferred from an out-of-town Division," wrote Olley. "Looking forward to seeing you on Friday, May 1st."

Zora would be an assistant staff engineer, reporting directly to Olley. His starting salary was $14,000 a year, with the potential to double that through a bonus system.

NINE

Although Zora looks the part of a seasoned GM executive in this official corporate portrait, the real Zora would make life uncomfortable for his superiors.

Zora and the General

On May 1, 1953, Duntov walked through the doors of the General Motors Building, his shoes clicking confidently across the marble floors. He was a proud new employee of the largest corporation on the planet. In stark contrast to Sydney Allard's blacksmith shop, his new work address at 3044 West Grand Boulevard in Detroit was the industrial equivalent of the Taj Mahal. Consuming an entire city block, the 15-story limestone building was a monument to power and optimism, combining neoclassical Greek-style columns, Roman arches and rectangular windows. Designed by Detroit architect Albert Kahn in 1920, it cost the huge sum of $20 million. The building was its own insulated world, containing 1,800 offices, an auditorium, exposition hall, auto display rooms, shops, a gymnasium, a cafeteria and lounges. Atop the roofline, giant red neon letters spelled out "General Motors," inspiring the title years later for John DeLorean's book, *On a Clear Day, You Can See General Motors.*

GM was a totally different world from anything Duntov had ever experienced. It was the super company within postwar superpower America. It was in 1952, a year before Zora joined the company, that former GM president Charles Wilson uttered his famous words during a confirmation hearing to become secretary of defense under President Eisenhower: "What was good for the country was good for General Motors and vice versa." Who could argue? Zora's new employer generated revenues that rivaled many nations' gross national product. Its share of the American market was over 50 percent.

GM was a proud organization still benefiting from the brilliance of three maestros—Billy Durant, Alfred Sloan and Charles Kettering—men who combined creativity and achievement with the ability to inspire and lead. Thanks to these men, GM also developed the industry's best independent front suspensions and transmissions and emerged in the 1920s and 1930s with very clear advantages in its products versus those of competitors. This helped drive GM sales dominance in virtually every automotive segment.

Opposite: The GM headquarters building on Grand Boulevard in Detroit was a dramatic symbol of GM's status as the largest corporation in the world.

According to GM consultants Lawrence R. Dolph and Dr. Ron Westrum, Sloan and Kettering called it "keeping the customer dissatisfied" by making new models not only more stylish but also offering better performance. They were also more reliable as well as safer and more comfortable.

It was an outrageously successful formula. The legacy of these men carried GM past its competitors into its preeminent position in the industry. For several generations of Americans, GM's products really were the best in the world.

Being the best also meant being the richest. GM was teeming with resources that far exceeded anything that Duntov could ever imagine in Germany or in Russia. The corporation was mammoth, with hundreds of engineers, draftsmen, designers and development people, plus numerous testing and development facilities. The corporation was in the process of constructing a giant new technical center in suburban Warren, and it had a vast proving ground in nearby Milford. The capability to do great things was astounding.

But success also had a price. Year after year of success at GM institutionalized policy and procedure. High profitability bred arrogance and myopia. Increasingly, the corporation relied on annual styling changes to motivate buyers instead of Kettering-style engineering improvements. And to anyone who questioned the system, the retort often was: How dare any outsider dispute the greatest example of capitalism in existence, God's own General Motors?

"The essential goodness of the company was never questioned," wrote David Halberstam in *The Fifties*. "It was regarded as, of all the many places to work, the best, because it was the biggest, the most respected, made the most money, and very quietly, through bonuses and stock, rewarded its top people the most handsomely."

Because the financial stakes were high, the value system and the accompanying lifestyle were very difficult to leave behind. Wrote Maryann Keller in her book, *Rude Awakening: The Rise, Fall and Struggle for Recovery of General Motors*, "Once an executive reaches a level of prestige at General Motors, he hangs on for dear life. A visible change is seen in his demeanor. Gradually, he stops seeing the company's flaws and begins to develop a defensive posture towards critics and skeptics."

Being insular, GM was also regimented. Upon moving to Detroit, Zora's first impression of GM was that all the higher-ups wore navy blue suits and yellow wing tips (really brown). Zora was also struck by the hierarchical nature of the company where everyone knew his place and access to higher-ups was strictly controlled. Zora also noticed that all aspects of behavior were codified—at least for his superiors—from where to live, what to wear, what church to attend or where to dine or play golf.

In a hierarchy dominated by conservative white Anglo-Saxon Protestants, Duntov, a passionate Russian of Jewish ancestry, clearly stood out. As opposed to wearing dark blue suits and wing tips, Zora wore tweed sports coats and button-down shirts, sometimes with an ascot. Instead of joining a country club and playing golf, Zora went to races on the weekends or played on his boat. As for Elfi, she declined to attend stuffy bridge parties and society lunches, opting instead to socialize with her friends and various entertainment contacts from New York and Miami. When she did attend GM functions, she often showed off her dancer's body with simple yet elegant form-fitting outfits, frequently with short skirts. In short, Zora and his wife didn't fit in a corporate world that prized conservative conformity.

As Halberstam wrote in *The Fifties,* "General Motors was Republican, not Eastern sophisticated Republican, but heartland conservative Republican—insular, suspicious of anything different." Halberstam went on to quote Duntov himself to make his point: "Zora Arkus-Duntov, a top GM designer and an émigré, once complained to a friend of the insularity of the culture and noted that the problem in the company was that it was run in every department by men "who believe that the world is bordered on the East by Lake Huron and on the West by Lake Michigan."

"It's like entering the priesthood," wrote Brock Yates, describing life within GM. Yates quoted a local observer in his 1983 book, *The Decline and Fall of the American Auto Industry*: " 'They get out of college and go into the system at the zone level. From then on, the Corporation takes care of everything; it sells their houses when they move, invests their incomes, provides them with cars every few thousand miles, gets them memberships in the right clubs, and so on. They even retire together in GM colonies in the South and Southwest. You talk about a cradle-to-grave welfare state. The further they advance, the more monastic they become. They simply have no concept of the real world.' "

The GM system rewarded anonymity as much as individual brilliance. "It was the duty of the rare exceptional GM employee to accept the limits on his individual fame," wrote Halberstam. "He would be known within the company and perhaps the larger automotive industry as a man of talent, but the rest of the country would not know his name; the corporation came first and the corporation bestowed wealth but anonymity on its most valued employees. The individual was always subordinated to the greater good of the company."

Clearly Zora, a swashbuckling individualist seeking to put his personal stamp on the automobile, thought he was in the wrong place. His motivations were obviously different from those of most of his peers. He never sought titles nor wealth as ends in themselves; he wanted the sense of control in working on his own visions and the visibility and respect he hoped would accompany great accomplishment. Putting Duntov's high-performance agendas and maverick personality in the midst of this bureaucratic culture meant that the sparks would fly. And they often did.

Fortunately, Duntov was ultimately reporting to Ed Cole, a man who was a maverick himself. Cole had brought Duntov into GM—along with people like Indy 500-winning driver Mauri Rose, Maurice Olley and Frank Winchell—for the express purpose of shaking things up. Cole wanted to reestablish engineering as a primary catalyst for success.

"After World War II, Cole was the great hope of the corporation, someone who could follow in the tradition of Kettering," said former GM consultant Lawrence Dolph. "Cole had a wealth of great ideas and great vision. Unlike many typical corporate executives today, Cole was a hands-on manager who found solutions to momentous challenges by getting personally involved."

Ed Cole created the climate at GM that allowed for talented, provocative engineers like Duntov to join the company and participate in an engineering renaissance at the corporation.

Cole caught the attention of the Cadillac Division while still a student at the General Motors Institute, now named the Kettering Institute. As Karl Ludvigsen wrote in *Automobile Quarterly*, Cole became an engineering assistant at Cadillac and never finished at GMI, such was the demand for his talent. He became a full-time Cadillac engineer in 1933, working primarily on engines. During World War II, he specialized in tank design. After the war, he helped John F. Gordon develop the high-compression, overhead-valve Cadillac V-8 that ushered in a whole new era in engine design.

Cole's quickly growing reputation as a doer brought him to Chevrolet as chief engineer in 1952. Cole's presence brought about a night-and-day change at GM's largest division. "Ed Cole had *carte blanche* at Chevy to get the place moving," said Alex Mair, who held a succession of GM management jobs including general manager of Pontiac and GMC and eventually group vice president of technical operations at GM. "All of a sudden, this whole place was on fire. His job was to create a new Chevrolet and he canceled all the programs that were underway. Cole said he would arrange a transfer to another division for anyone who didn't like what was going on."

Under Cole's guidance, Chevrolet was about to reestablish itself as the "engine" of GM, the high-volume division that defined high-quality, affordable transportation in America. As such, its emerging advertising themes such as "See the USA in Your Chevrolet" resonated with millions of Americans.

Cole's motto was "kick the hell out of the status quo," an attitude that didn't ingratiate him to many of his more conservative peers. Cole took a risk in bringing in a guy like Duntov. Zora was from *Russia,* of all places, of communist parents at a time when Senator Joseph McCarthy of Wisconsin had just finished a major communist witch-hunt in Washington. GM downplayed the Russian connection. David Halberstam wrote that at the height of the anti-communism sentiment in the United States, Duntov was described in GM promotional material as being of Belgian extraction rather than Russian.

Hiring Duntov was risky for reasons other than his nationality. His career experience with Ardun and later Allard on one level had little relevance in a large corporation whose bread and butter was high-volume passenger cars and trucks. The Corvette, of course, was the one area where Duntov's experience was relevant, and Cole's decision to hire him underlined that the Russian engineer, in Cole's view, was just what Chevrolet needed to make the Corvette into a real sports car. Duntov's background with both supercharging in the 1930s and with the Ford Flathead conversion program in the 1940s put him into an excellent position to influence the final design of a new V-8 engine that was in the pipeline. Cole in fact was already eyeing the Corvette as a potential application for this new V-8 and was counting on Duntov to figure out ways to squeeze even more power out of it.

The need for this engine at Chevrolet was obvious. While Ed Cole and Harry Barr had done a commendable job of making the 1953 Corvette's Blue Flame Six into a semi-respectable power plant, the fact remained that the Corvette's performance was nothing exceptional. It would go from 0 to 60 in about 11 seconds, which put the Corvette driver in danger of being blown off by many larger passenger cars like the Oldsmobile Rocket 88. When Duntov came on the scene, Ludvigsen wrote in *Corvette, America's Star-Spangled Sports Car*, Cole's new engine—an all-new lightweight overhead valve V-8—was set to make its debut in the 1955 Chevrolets, including the Corvette.

The engine would be Cole's greatest legacy. Its light reciprocating mass made for high revving capability. Its stud-mounted rocker arms and hollow push rods made it lighter. And a sand-casting process allowed for better

Ed Cole was counting on Zora to find ways to squeeze more horsepower out of the Chevy small-block V-8 in order to satisfy the high-performance market.

control of wall thickness. Incredibly, the development process took only 28 months, yet the resulting engine was phenomenal. Hot-rod maven Vic Edelbrock Jr. called it "God's gift from heaven." All told, more than 65 million small-block V-8s had been produced by the 40th anniversary in 1995, and today a variation of this engine still powers the Corvette as well as many other GM vehicles.

The engine wasn't originally called the "small-block"; it acquired that nickname over the years thanks to its compact exterior dimensions and the fact that later in the 1950s Chevrolet developed a 348-cubic-inch truck engine that would evolve into the Chevy "big-block."

While the small-block would become a major turning point for the corporation, the future of this engine was uncertain back in the early 1950s. The engine was still controversial within conservative GM. Duntov once remarked bitterly that 90 percent of the people within the Chevrolet Division opposed this engine. Many felt Chevy had the best six in the business and questioned why they should worry about a V-8. Zora sensed that Cole was still regarded by many as a young upstart, and when the engine started eating bearings during early testing, smug comments multiplied among the naysayers. But the engine quickly proved itself and may have done more to set the table for Chevrolet's successes in the next 20 years than any other single technology.

Getting Down to Work

Duntov's first assignment was at Chevrolet R&D on the main floor of the GM Building in a converted auditorium. The working area was a matrix of partitions and desks cordoned off with drapes. There, Duntov would be linked with Cole's new team in an effort to jump-start the Chevrolet Division. Duntov would be tested early, becoming involved in a wide succession of projects during his first six weeks on the job.

On his team was Mauri Rose, and Zora was thrilled to get a chance to work with the Indy 500 winner. The two spent many hours discussing racing and engineering philosophy. "He was good engineer," said Zora, "very good." Duntov often accompanied Rose for lunch at a Danish restaurant near the GM Building, where they talked performance and racing, often feeling like redheaded stepchildren in an environment that was largely indifferent to anything that smacked of low volume.

Rose could be very abrasive and blunt and wasn't shy about telling Duntov that he was a better engineer than a race driver. "Zora couldn't drive a nail," Rose was said to remark after witnessing him during a test session at a racetrack. Still, Zora maintained a lot of respect and compassion for Rose, especially after his wife left him and he was forced to care for his two children, both of whom had polio. Many years later, in 1967, Zora claimed to go to bat for Rose in helping him be selected to drive the Indy 500 Camaro pace car.

Zora also liked a peer named Ben Griffith. Griffith adored fast driving and didn't mind riding shotgun with Zora in his assigned car, a 1953 Chevy Bel Air with a Corvette Blue Flame engine and Powerglide automatic transmission. Griffith enjoyed a good cocktail after work, which made him an instant hit with Zora. Griffith later went on to Ford Motor Company where he designed a hypoid gear that offset the center of the axle and the pinion. Zora described him as "a genius."

Zora reported to the man who interviewed him, Maurice Olley. As recounted by Maurice D. Hendry in *Cadillac: Standard of the World*, Olley was a brilliant example of the caliber of people Cole sought for his team. Born in England, he had spent the early years of his career as personal designer for Sir Henry Royce, and later became chief engineer for Rolls-Royce in America. From 1930 to 1937, he was successively special projects engineer for Cadillac and General Motors. During the war years, he served as engineering representative for Rolls-Royce Limited U.S.A. (aircraft engines) and was later appointed to the British Ministry of Supply (tanks). Beginning in 1945, he was a technical consultant to GM-owned Vauxhall Motors in England, from which Cole recruited him in 1952.

While a genius in his own right, Olley was a quiet, introspective old Englishman who disliked spontaneous displays such as whistling at work. Freewheeling Duntov provided a stark contrast to Olley, and according to Elfi Duntov, the two clashed instantly.

One of Duntov's first assignments was to analyze suspension options for a tail-heavy car. GM was looking into the possibility of rear-engined vehicles as early as the late 1940s and wanted to know how to set up a suspension for a vehicle with a 40/60 weight distribution. A special vehicle was built with a 115-inch wheelbase. It was front-engined and had rear-wheel drive, but also contained ballast to shift the bulk of the weight rearward. After working with this vehicle, Duntov didn't touch the suspension; he instead recommended the most direct, obvious solution he could think of: Increase the rear tire inflation. "When you inflate the tire proportional to the load they carry, you are in the ballpark," Duntov said. Zora claimed that his solution came from what he observed during the 1930s with the Mercedes and Auto Union grand prix teams, both of which used larger tires on the rear as well as an increase in rear tire pressure.

British-born Maurice Olley proved to be a difficult boss for Duntov, especially during Zora's early weeks on the job.

But to Olley, Duntov's "solution" was not a true engineering fix—it was borderline insubordination. A man of little patience, Olley immediately recommended that Duntov quit the company. Shocked at Olley's confrontational attitude, Zora considered taking Olley up on his offer. But after considering the matter, Zora realized he had worked too hard to get to GM and wasn't going to throw his career away based on this small incident.

Olley later realized his mistake, according to Duntov, after driving the vehicle with Zora's recommended tire pressures. Olley's attitude changed somewhat, and Zora felt redeemed by being called out to the Proving Ground to test drive variations of the tail-heavy car. Duntov in fact claimed credit for the later recommendation of a higher rear tire inflation (22 pounds front and 26 pounds rear) for the rear-engined Corvair, which debuted during the 1960 model year. Zora later factored in the advantages of varying tire pressure in designing CERV I, a mid-engined experimental vehicle in 1959.

While Zora maintained a certain suspicion about Olley, things settled down between them, and Duntov's next assignment was to address a schizophrenic handling problem on the original Corvette. The original chassis tended to oversteer in the front and understeer in the rear, with the result being oversteer at the limit and severe axle tramp around corners. The basic problem was that the two ends of the car were fighting each other.

The fact that the car was designed that way and approved by Olley was initially the source of some wonderment by Duntov. But Zora was magnanimous many years later in understanding that decisions of this nature could easily result from a large bureaucracy such as GM. "Consciously, he would not build that car," said Zora in a 1989 interview. "He knows what produces oversteer and understeer in the palm of his hand. But I'm supposing that development engineer said, 'I did that and car did this' and provided that information to Olley. Olley, in turn, said to do it this way. It was the result of not him being able to ascertain situation directly."

Zora predicted that the car's schizophrenic handling could quickly get a Corvette driver in trouble once the car turned into a tight corner and the steering got sharper by itself. If lateral acceleration forces were high enough, severe oversteer would prevail and the car would spin. He set out to neutralize these characteristics, deciding ultimately to make the leaf springs flatter in the rear, modify a ball joint in the front and increase the size of the front stabilizer bar. "Before long, I produced a car which I could put into a drift and have it respond as the car should."

Duntov also added a degree of positive caster to create a better on-center steering feel, thereby reducing wind wander. Prior to the availability of power steering, most American cars had zero caster in an effort to reduce steering effort. Duntov's changes didn't see production until the 1956 Corvette, which represented the first major overhaul of the 1953 original. "We wound up with a car that does not outdrive you," said Duntov.

Olley also asked Duntov to analyze why the exhaust system stained the back of the body and sometimes contaminated the interior. The contamination was worse when the heater was functioning. Duntov discovered that when the front vent panel or Ventiplane was opened, it would reverse the airflow from the rear to the front, so Duntov attached strands of yarn to the car and recorded what happened on film from a following car, a novel approach at the time. As he later told historians Pete Lyons and Karl Ludvigsen, Duntov determined that relocating the exhaust outlets to the tips of the rear fenders cured both this and the staining problem.

Despite these modest successes, there was still little trust between Duntov and Olley. Duntov sometimes felt that Olley was withholding information from him. Olley, for his part, may have been testing Duntov's problem-solving capability and attention to detail.

Regardless, Duntov was assigned to a project developing a two-cycle engine for GM. At the time, Chevrolet R&D was experimenting with two-cycle engines, both in normally aspirated and supercharged form. Duntov spent a considerable amount of time trying to solve problems with idle quality and a limited torque band, but finally wrote what he called a "brutal" report. Zora suggested that, given the alternatives, two-cycle engines were not yet viable for the automobiles of the day. He may have given up too early or maybe just saw the light. Regardless of the circumstances, Olley took Duntov off the project and instead gave it to another associate, Bob Schilling. Although Schilling secretly agreed with Duntov's opinion, he played the political game far better and avoided confrontations with Maurice Olley. In bowing to Olley, according to Zora, Schilling was later awarded with Olley's job, a carrot that had been held out to Duntov. Indeed, this was how the system worked at GM and at many other large corporations in America.

Rocking the Corporate Boat

Duntov clashed again with Olley when Zora "announced" that he was going to race for Allard at Le Mans. Duntov insisted this was a previous commitment, yet it was only a month and a half after he started at GM. Olley flatly refused, so Zora said he would have a word with Mr. Cole because he was going. Cole gave Zora the courtesy of a hearing, but the Chevrolet chief engineer didn't embrace the idea either, and tried to paint a picture for Zora of how important it was not to rock the corporate boat. He intimated that Olley would be retiring in the near future and that Zora was a leading candidate to succeed him as head of R&D (before Schilling was offered the position). Cole's opposition was surprising since the Allard team that year was running with Cadillac engines and several Cadillac engineers had journeyed to France to provide technical assistance. When Zora reminded him of this, Cole grudgingly acquiesced, feeling that maybe Duntov might learn something from the experience that he could bring back to Chevrolet. Still, Duntov would pay a political price for this action.

Duntov had to take a leave of absence without pay to make the trip to France. After realizing what a stir his Le Mans request had caused at GM as well as the number of run-ins he was having with Olley after only six weeks on the job, Duntov purchased a one-way ticket to France. He detested the loss of control he was already feeling and had no intention of returning to GM. He decided he would stick around in Europe and hoped to catch on somewhere else. He even flirted with the idea of joining Briggs Cunningham's operation, although he disagreed with Cunningham's choice of strong, heavy race cars. Duntov also still had an emotional link to Allard, although he saw no real future there.

Duntov's plan was to drive the race and try to forget about GM. He was anxious to get behind the wheel of the new Allard JR. The paper he had gotten published in *The Automobile Engineer* had laid some of the groundwork for the car. The Cadillac overhead valve V-8 engine underneath its bonnet replaced the Chrysler V-8 of the previous year. The Cadillac was some 100 pounds lighter than the Chrysler and was also smaller in dimension, a considerable advantage inside the narrow Allard engine bay. The Cadillac put out almost 280 horsepower—more than the C-Type Jaguar, which won Le Mans that year.

When Zora got to France, however, he discovered that he would be driving for a new set of car owners, who happened to be the very top brass of the United States Air Force. They were led by General Curtis E. LeMay, commander of the Strategic Air Command (SAC). Le May practically personified the newly formed Air Force. He had led the B-17 bombing raids over Germany and later planned and commanded the devastating B-29 firebombing of Japan.

The SAC maintained a large fleet of long-range nuclear-armed bombers from bases around the world as well as strategic missiles to protect the United States against the Soviet Union. Despite increased defense spending in this new nuclear age, most defense expenditures went for hardware, not for people programs, and it was tough to maintain the ranks of enlisted personnel. LeMay thought one way to do so was to appeal to a growing interest in automobiles among his servicemen.

For starters, LeMay set up a special garage facility in an old stable at Offutt Field, the Omaha headquarters base. It was called the Hobby Shop. He hired a couple of mechanics to help the servicemen work on their cars. LeMay started things off by picking up an old car and bringing it into the Hobby Shop for restoration work.

But LeMay didn't stop there. He and his top officers had a strong interest in racing and wanted to create a SAC racing team as a means to promote a plan to use Air Force bases as venues for sports car racing. LeMay's timing was perfect in light of the public outcry against sports car racing on closed public roads after the Watkins Glen tragedy in 1952. At the time, Thompson, Connecticut, had about the only dedicated road circuit in the United States.

Reade Tilley, who had served as LeMay's PR officer during the Berlin airlift, was already a sports car racer and got LeMay's plan rolling by running a silver Jaguar XK120 on the original public road circuit at Elkhart Lake, Wisconsin, in September 1952. Tilley was competing against an impressive grid of purpose-built racing cars—Cunninghams, Ferraris, Allards, Jaguars and Porsches—driven by accomplished racers such as Phil Hill, Jim Kimberly, Fred Wacker and Briggs Cunningham. Accompanying Tilley was LeMay himself. According to a 1992 article by Steven J. Thompson in *Car and Driver*, LeMay walked through the paddock wearing a Hawaiian shirt and khaki slacks and holding an unlit cigar. It was LeMay's baptism into road racing and he liked what he saw, even if the organization of the event didn't quite live up to military standards.

The next step in LeMay's plan was to hold a trial race on October 26, 1952, at Turner Air Force Base in Albany, Georgia. The event brought in a whopping $47,763, a considerable profit in early 1950s' dollars, according to Thompson. Encouraged by this success, LeMay scheduled seven additional races in 1953. Of the 14 SCCA national events in 1953, fully half were held on SAC bases and one on a non-SAC Air Force base. Events were held in Florida, Texas, Illinois, Ohio, Nebraska, Nevada, Georgia and California. During 1953 alone, the base races brought in over a quarter of a million dollars. According to Tilley, the money bought needed items to improve the quality of life at the bases—televisions, pool tables, mattresses, radios, washers, sofas, hobby shop equipment and more.

Now in a new role, LeMay was at Le Mans, leading a group of his fellow officers as race car owners. Without their capital, Allard would have stayed at home for lack of funds. Besides the JR owned by LeMay, the

General Curtis LeMay personified the newly formed Unites States Air Force. But sports car racing also interested him, especially the notion of using air bases as racetracks.

other two cars were purchased by David Schilling, who was a top fighter ace during World War II, and Tilley, who was a special assistant to Le May.

Fast Friends

Duntov and LeMay, who had met in London at the Allard shops back in 1952, immediately hit it off upon their reunion at Le Mans. LeMay was also an engineer by education and they talked the same language. LeMay thought Duntov was a superb driver and appreciated Duntov's advice as a consultant and test driver. According to author John Allard, LeMay even raced in several events, until Congress passed a law that forbade the commander of SAC from participating in "dangerous activities." The law specifically mentioned "sports car racing."

Zora may have been largely responsible for LeMay's enthusiasm. "We thought he was a hell of a guy, a real gentleman racer," said Tilley of Zora. "He was a little different from the racers we encountered over here. He wanted his car to be just so. Our mechanics were aircraft mechanics and volunteers who had worked on engines that only revved up to 2,800 rpm. Zora guided our guys on how to work on race engines. He was very competent, very interested and very helpful. We became very good friends."

The new JR had been put through the paces at a number of test sessions, including some high-speed runs at American Air Force bases at Heyford and Fairford in England. Cadillac engineers were present at some of these tests.

Pairing up with high-level American military officers provided some unanticipated benefits for the Allard team. Suddenly, Air Force transport planes were available to fly engine parts over from the States to England. When one of the engines developed compression trouble during practice for a major race, the Air Force was quick to assist. "Within two hours of the stoppage, the Americans had the engine out, lifted by pulley blocks slung from a tree branch and lowered on to the flat bonnet of a Jeep," wrote Tom Lush. "With one man seated beside it to keep it in place, the Jeep motored off slowly to the nearby American air base. Purely by chance (!) a four-engined transport plane was just leaving for the United States and was bound for an aerodrome quite near the specialist department that had prepared the engines. By a strange coincidence, another plane was leaving the next day for the Le Mans base, so was able to bring back a replacement engine. The new unit was installed and running by Thursday evening…."

The team had planned to take three cars to Le Mans, although the third car was not finished in time and instead was taken along as a parts source. In addition to Cadillac V-8 engines, both cars used Cadillac three-speed manual transmissions.

After experimenting with color-coded cockpit signal lights the year before as a means of communication with a driver, Sydney Allard added two-way radios for both team cars to enable drivers to communicate directly with the crew from out on the circuit. This was done at the behest of General LeMay on the basis of his aircraft experience. In the pits, the radio was hooked up to several speakers so everyone could hear what the driver needed in advance.

For the 1953 race, Duntov and Sydney Allard were slated to drive the number 4 and number 5 cars respectively. Whether Allard had dictated any type of team strategy is unknown, but just before the start, according to Duntov, one of the Allard mechanics intentionally left Duntov's car in third (high) gear instead of first, to make sure Allard got out in front. The tactic worked, as Duntov lost precious seconds fishing for the right gear to get going. "Since one cannot distinguish the noise of his own engine from others, the realization took some time—enough for a great number of cars passed me like I was a sitting duck," said Zora. As the cars came around the eight-mile circuit after the first lap, it was Allard in the lead in the number 4 Allard at a record pace, ahead of a Ferrari and Stirling Moss' Jaguar.

At Le Mans, there is always a certain distinction in leading the first lap of the race, much like the first turn at Indy. The crowd chanted "Allard, Allard," but the elation was short-lived, as Allard's car dropped out with a broken differential-mounting bracket, which severed a brake line.

Zora later attributed the problem to the insufficient bracing of the rear end housing against the prop shaft, which resulted in the housing being ripped out of the frame, severing the brake lines in the process. As Duntov noted in a 1953 memo to Olley, he also felt Allard's car may have been experiencing power hop coming out of the bends, an indication of the tremendous torque being produced by the Cadillac engines.

Allard's exit left the Allard co-driven by Zora and Ray Merrick as the sole Allard torchbearer. "I was passing everything in sight on the Mulsanne straight," said Duntov. "However, I was forced to give way on the rest of the circuit. Due to my poor handling, after passing a car, its driver's waving fist would appear in my mirror." Signals from the Allard pits indicated that Zora was running near record speed, a fact that didn't wash with Zora because other cars were regularly passing him on the curved sections. Later, Zora claimed the stopwatches were some 20 seconds slow.

An hour and a half into the race, Duntov's Cadillac V-8 began overheating. Wrote former Allard employee Tom Lush: "Duntov was lapping steadily around 4 minutes, 40 seconds [about 108 mph] until 5:20 p.m., when he came through on the RT [radio transmitter] to say that the engine was beginning to overheat. He came into the pits with a cloud of steam beneath the car on lap 17, and as no water could be added until after the 28th lap [due to race rules], he could only wait until the engine had cooled slightly. He then cruised around, with several more stops, until he had completed the 29th lap at 7:00 p.m. The car was refueled and replenished with water warmed on the tea-making stove, and Ray Merrick took over, the car now being an hour behind our planned running time."

"He continued lapping steadily at about 96 mph," continued Lush, "keeping a close watch on the temperature gauge, and maintained this speed through the dusk so that when Duntov took over on the 61st lap it was quite dark. He did four laps, then became overdue, and after a few minutes his voice came through with the sad news that he was stopped on Mulsanne with a seized engine. The car had covered 560 miles at an average speed of 98 mph, but this was no consolation for an early retirement."

Zora had a slightly different account. "I exploded with expletives—fucking engine. In the pits, my communication was on the loud speaker for everyone to listen." Whether the GM people responsible for that engine were within earshot of Zora's comments is unknown, but the episode did not reflect well on Zora's relationship with his new employer. Zora later attributed the failure to oil starvation and poor cylinder head design.

Still, those involved, especially the Air Force brass, were struck by Duntov's effort. "We were most impressed that Zora was able to keep that Allard going," said Reade Tilley. "He knew what was going on and how to take care of an engine, and didn't abuse it."

In a postrace memo to Maurice Olley, Duntov attributed the overheating problem to the fact that the cylinder heads were machined to increase the compression ratio, which made them porous enough to allow gases to escape into the cooling system, creating a loss of water.

Zora at the Le Mans esses during the 1953 French classic, before engine problems with his Cadillac V-8 forced an early retirement at the 560-mile mark.

Zora also indicated that the engine of Sydney Allard's number 4 JR had about a 30-horsepower advantage over Zora's number 5 car, thanks to a different camshaft. Despite his expletive when his engine let go, Zora felt the engines showed considerable potential, which could translate into a Le Mans-winning power plant. "I believe that engine-wise both cars were potentially the strongest contenders in the field but due to chassis shortcomings, the circuit speed could not be maintained with minimum safety required."

Duntov went on to suggest that the redesigned chassis was faulty in design and execution from the J2X of the year before, and noted that the cars were bipolar in their steering response. "The reaction to steering was outrunning human reflexes," he wrote. "On acceleration, they reversed their characteristics to understeer and under heavy acceleration were not reacting to the steering wheel at all. On a 120-mph bend, they would run through the complete specter [spectrum], diving toward the inside at the beginning of a bend and as the throttle is applied, would dart to the outside."

Duntov noted that the JR was difficult to drive on the Mulsanne straight but still could be driven at maximum speed, but on the remaining two-thirds of the circuit, the handling was a limiting factor. "The cars which potentially could be the fastest had to be driven with restraint," noted Duntov.

Duntov also noted that racing car development at Le Mans had swung back and forth between an emphasis on maximum speed on the four-mile-long Mulsanne straight to an emphasis on brakes and acceleration. "Presently, I believe the keynote of development should be high-speed handling—the faster cars reaching presently the stage where on over two-thirds of the circuit, speed is a function of handling. These cars have the ability to accelerate to the very fast bends at a much higher speed than these bends can be taken."

Back to Detroit

After the race, Duntov maintained his resolve not to return to Detroit. Instead, he journeyed to Paris and was sitting at a sidewalk cafe along the Champs Élysées in Paris when, by sheer coincidence, a wealthy acquaintance from London named Mickey Foulihan recognized him. When Duntov was still at Allard, Foulihan had recommended a hair dye for Zora, who was self-conscious about his premature graying. After trying out the product Foulihan recommended, Zora's hair turned yellow, and much of it fell out. This was just before the 1952 Le Mans race and the French nick-named him "Le Jeune Blonde." Duntov was 42 years old at that time, but with his blond "do" they were calling him "young man."

When Foulihan ran into Duntov in Paris, Foulihan already knew that Zora had accepted the position with GM and asked what Zora was doing in Paris two days after the race when he should have been back in the States. After Zora explained that he didn't plan to return to Detroit, Foulihan excused himself and walked down the street. Although he was at best a casual acquaintance, for some inexplicable reason he was about to become a pivotal figure in Corvette history. Foulihan came back 15 minutes later holding a Pan-Am airline ticket to Detroit. He handed it to Zora and said, "You've got work to do back there."

TEN

Zora made fast friends with the mechanics at the GM Proving Ground. He was assigned there to work on school bus drivetrains after violating corporate protocols in racing for Allard at Le Mans.

Getting Down to Business

After considerable thought, Zora returned to Detroit determined to make a go of things at General Motors. The powerful allure of what he could potentially do with GM's resources still boggled his imagination. David E. Davis Jr., former editor of both *Car and Driver* and *Automobile* and the former creative director on the Chevrolet advertising account at Campbell-Ewald, described the fascination that car enthusiasts like Duntov had for Chevrolet and, in turn, GM. "We always regarded Chevrolet as the great bitch goddess who mistreated us, humiliated us in public, told lies to our friends behind our backs. But if we could ever hook up with her and wrestle her into the sack, it would be a transcendent moment, the ride of our lives."

Zora had come to Chevrolet hoping to take over the reins of the Corvette program and make a real sports car out of the Corvette. After two months on the job, his mission was far from accomplished. So he would play the game, at least for a while. But there was a bombshell waiting for him upon his return: a transfer away from Olley's R&D group.

The continued tensions between Duntov and Olley had finally reached a breaking point after Le Mans. Olley was still incensed that Zora had gone over Olley's head in requesting Cole's intervention to race at Le Mans.

His new assignment was to work on trucks at the GM Proving Ground in Milford, Michigan, in the far northwestern corner of the Detroit metropolitan area. For Zora, it might as well have been the GM equivalent of Siberia. He would now be cut off from his self-appointed destiny without any connection with the car that prompted his association with the corporation.

Cole rationalized Zora's transfer, saying that Duntov was really a development engineer and perhaps might be happier at the Proving Ground. Duntov was stoic, however, and insisted that his background qualified him to be a design, development and manufacturing engineer. "But if Cole feels that I am development engineer, so be it," said Duntov. Whether Zora would really have stuck around if he had had any other viable options is

Opposite: Zora at a September 1953 Society of Automotive Engineers (SAE) speaking engagement in Lansing, Michigan. He used his knowledge and perspectives on sports cars to his advantage on the SAE speaking circuit. His speeches attracted the attention of people within GM who began to see his potential as GM's resident sports car expert.

debatable. But he was 44 years old and he needed a job, so he stuck it out and took his punishment. If this was management's attempt to break him, he resolved that it wasn't going to work. It was the first of many times he would have to subjugate his personal feelings to the corporate hierarchy in order to achieve a higher, if not more personal, goal.

In agreeing to go to the Proving Ground, Duntov didn't realize he was taking a form of demotion. He didn't find out about it until later, when they tried to promote him from design engineer to assistant staff engineer. "I told them I was already an assistant staff engineer." These incidents also contributed to Zora losing his bonus during his first year with GM. Assigned to work for Maury Rosenberger at the Proving Ground, one of Zora's first tasks was to analyze a driveline vibration on a three-piece shaft belonging to a school bus. Despite the put-down, Zora elected to be patient, keep a low profile and handle the project. "Maybe better things would come," he said.

Overqualified for the task, given his work on Navy submarines, escort vessels and destroyers during World War II, Zora nevertheless quickly sketched up a three-piece driveshaft with different angles of attachment. After he had the new unit built and installed, there wasn't a trace of vibration with the bus either empty or fully loaded.

Speaking Out

Despite his "exiled" status on truck programs at the GM Proving Ground, Duntov acted publicly as if he still had an official role with the Corvette. He had developed a well-honed perspective about sports cars and where they fit in the spectrum of automotive transportation—especially in America, where sports cars were still a relative novelty. When invited to speak before an SAE gathering in Lansing, Michigan, in September 1953 to commemorate the showroom debut of the Corvette, Zora accepted. Senior GM management was no doubt aware of the invitation, which indicated that Zora's "respite" on trucks at the Proving Ground was likely to be temporary.

The Lansing SAE speech was Duntov's first-ever public speaking engagement and he was extremely nervous about the prospect. Ever since blanking out during a high school graduation speech, Zora had been terrified of speaking in public. Later, after returning from Le Mans, he briefed Ed Cole on his experiences in France by reading a memo aloud, but claimed that his tendency to read phonetically caused him to present it poorly.

English was Duntov's fourth language, and initially he felt a little shaky. However, his humor and charm more than made up for any language or speech difficulties. Later, as Duntov became more comfortable speaking,

Detroit News columnist Doc Greene described him affectionately as the "Victor Borge of Engineering."

In his Lansing speech, Duntov laid out the philosophical underpinnings of what he would try to accomplish at GM with the Corvette and other high-performance programs. The bedrock of his thinking was that racing had always been a catalyst for developing passenger cars because it fostered performance, efficiency and reliability. "After World War I," commented Duntov, "sports cars were highly potent machines retaining all the mechanical features of race cars and endowed with comfort comparable to touring cars of the day. But by the mid 1920s, regulations designed to slow down grand prix cars only succeeded in making them more expensive—not any slower. The result was that the sports car as a direct derivative from the racing car ceased to exist. Still, they ran parallel courses."

He described the German and French sports cars of the 1930s as highly potent automobiles that could stand comparison with the best sports cars of the early 1950s. Duntov noted that the BMW might be termed a milestone in sports car development—not so much in terms of performance, comfort or stability per se but in its ease of handling and overall drivability. Unlike a seasoned race car, the BMW could make an average driver look good, a virtue that became increasingly sought after in the development of modern sports cars.

Duntov also noted that sports cars tend to reflect the road systems and national character of their countries of origin. He observed the irony of the fact that England, with all of its rain, showers, drizzle, mist and murk is famous for open-topped sports cars, while France and Italy, with beautiful weather the rule, developed closed sports cars. Zora rationalized the phenomenon by the fact that the road systems are different—the roads in England are narrow and serpentine and most journeys are short—25 to 60 miles would be the length of the average Sunday trip. Furthermore, the narrow British roads demanded the better visibility of an open-topped car. In continental Europe, where many of the primary routes were laid out during the Napoleonic conquests, the roads tend to be straighter. Because the sports car was the fastest way to get from point A to point B, a closed top was preferable to avoid the buffeting that accompanied high speeds. "The performance, apart from being fun, pays off," said Duntov. "On the continent, the sports coupe will carry you on a business trip from a Paris office to a Brussels office [190 miles] faster than a train or plane or from Paris to the Riviera in less than 10 hours [630 miles]."

Duntov discussed the prospects for the Corvette's success in the United States, noting that given our national character, road system and traffic laws, sports cars are not rational purchases in the United States. But,

Zora insisted, there were still plenty of irrational buyers out there. He cited the success story of the MG, the most popular sports car in America. "The MG is inferior in road performance, accommodation and suspension, but superior in controllability."

Duntov reasoned that the MG's appeal was in the intangibles. "The automobile as transportation died with the Model T. The function of the car in the American way of life is far beyond its utilitarian values which are taken for granted. In America, we are selling moods, prestige, standing in the community," he stressed. "That our stylists are able to make a man feel like a million dollars with chrome strips and warts is remarkable, and I must admit that I'd rather drive a fancy Bel Air than a spartan 210 Chevrolet—such is the power of stylists."

Zora was optimistic about the success of an American sports car based on a basic need for individuality. "In our age where the average person is a cog wheel who gets pushed in the subways, elevators, department stores, cafeterias, lives in the same house as the next fellow, has the same style of furniture, wears the same clothing and is told that he is as good but no better than the next fellow, the ownership of a different car provides the means to ascertain his individuality to himself and everybody around."

Zora reasoned that the success of the MG was due to its toy appeal, racing heritage and the fact that it was fun to drive. In contrast, the average American family car tended to obliterate the sensation of driving, making cars like the Corvette that much more desirable. "One of our friends and competitors advertises that their cars do not have to be driven, they drive you!" said Duntov. "Suppose the development continues and one day the car will really drive you by push button, radar or what not controls. The tinted windowpanes of today will be totally black; the suspension will be such that nothing can be felt. What is there to do? Will you travel through Yellowstone Park, in glorious genuine natural colors by television?"

Despite his hunches, Zora was characteristically honest in saying the jury was still out as to whether the Corvette would make it on the American market. He again used the analogy of Henry Ford and the Model T as a metaphor for where the Corvette was in 1953. "If Mr. Ford, prior to his decision to launch the Model T, would have considered statistics instead of his imagination, the world today would have a very different shape. When he took his visionary step, the market for volume sales of the automobile did not exist. He created the market by giving the American public what they wanted at a price they can afford."

Duntov closed by noting that the Corvette was the first American sports car offered to the public and represented Chevrolet's concept of what the American public wanted in a sports car. He described it as either an experiment in ambitious engineering or as a visionary move that will open new markets and make our lives freer. "The automobile started as an instrument of pleasure for a few and became a transportation for all," concluded Duntov. He suggested the same thing could happen with sports cars.

Following Zora's Lansing speech, Walt Mackenzie of Chevrolet public relations thought Duntov could be valuable in attracting a new kind of customer into Chevrolet dealerships. He began soliciting opinions internally regarding the overall marketability of Zora within the corporation.

Not everyone agreed with Duntov's point of view. In a letter to Mackenzie, Bob Ross, a senior account executive on the Chevrolet advertising account at Campbell-Ewald, took issue with Zora's contention that sports cars could only be sold through a racing reputation. "To me that argument is suspect because it's based on European rather than American experience," wrote Ross. "The MGs, Jags, etc. may well have required the stimulus of a racing reputation, but Chevrolet no. Chevrolet is well established with adults. The psychological benefit of the Corvette, to my notion, is that it disproves the company is stodgy, an opinion that prevails here and there with young people."

Ross also took issue with Duntov on whether the high-speed cars of Europe were driven without an increase in injuries and fatalities. "I'd figure that the reason the high-speed jobs have not become highway-scourged is that the average European driver is a bit more stable as a citizen than the average American."

Ross added that the saving grace of the Corvette might be its relatively high cost. "If the Corvette were priced at $500 and distributed in good quantity, it would, I'm guessing, naturally soon be legislated off the highways. Your American cowboys would insist on finding out what it would do and probably all too frequently."

Arvid F. Jouppi, editor of the *General Motors Engineering Journal*, took a kinder view of Zora's speech. "I captured from my study of Mr. Arkus-Duntov's effort, the picture of a well-qualified technical man who has personal knowledge of the entire history of the sport and racing car history. Whatever might be done to the paper must be done in such a way to preserve the writer's *authoritativeness* and *zeal* for his subject."

Jouppi concluded that the major contribution that Duntov could make to Chevrolet's future would be to create a receptive climate for sports cars in the United States. To foster such an environment, Jouppi recommended using Zora as often as possible for the largest technical as well as non-technical audiences he could command. Jouppi also recommended creating a brochure that would leverage Duntov's expertise on sports cars, which would in turn help develop a position for Chevrolet as the authority on the subject, at least on American shores.

Mackenzie took Jouppi's input along with his own gut instincts and began to conceive product demonstrations and engineering exercises that might showcase the talents of Zora Arkus-Duntov for the Chevrolet Motor Division. The result of those brainstorm sessions would soon become evident.

Energizing Chevrolet

Duntov's speeches showed that he was much more than just an engineer. He had a keen marketing mind and a quick grasp of where Chevrolet's problems existed in the marketplace. After only six months on the job, he knew the Chevrolet Division was in deep trouble and that the problems ran much deeper than any inadequacies with the Corvette. He felt that if Chevy were ever going to turn around, it needed to build credibility where it mattered—with the youth market. And so, six months into his tenure at Chevrolet, Duntov wrote the most important memo he had ever produced at GM, a literal road map for what Chevrolet needed to do to energize the company. In his December 16, 1953, memo titled "Thoughts Pertaining to Youth, Hot-Rodders and Chevrolet," Zora drew upon his own background in manufacturing the Ardun overhead valve conversion kits for Ford Flathead engines in the 1940s, to explain that the hot rod movement was growing rapidly. He pointed out that there were a half dozen new publications devoted to hot rods. "From cover to cover, they are full of Fords," wrote Zora. "This is not surprising then that the majority of hot-rodders are eating, sleeping and dreaming modified Fords. They know Ford parts from stem to stern better than Ford people themselves.

"A young man buying a magazine for the first time immediately becomes introduced to Ford," continued Zora. "It is reasonable to assume that when hot-rodders or hot-rod-influenced persons buy transportation, they buy Fords. As they progress in age and income, they graduate from jalopies, to second-hand Fords, then to new Fords."

Duntov suggested that while the new Chevy V-8 then in the pipeline had the potential to attract hot-rodders, Ford had a head start and would continue to dominate the thinking of this group. He noted that one factor that could largely overcome the handicap would be the availability of ready-engineered high-performance parts. While admitting that Chevrolet probably didn't have a lot of credibility with hot-rodders, the existence of the Corvette provided the loophole. "If the special parts are carried as RPO [Regular Production Options] items for the Corvette, they will undoubtedly be recognized by the hot-rodders as the very parts they were looking for to hop up the Chevy," wrote Zora.

It was inevitable that people would race the Corvette, noted Zora, but not with the standard Blue Flame Six; anyone contemplating a serious Corvette racing effort would put a Cadillac V-8 in the car. Zora suggested that even with the new Chevy V-8, racers would still be outclassed by the competition without aid from Chevrolet. "Since we cannot prevent the people from racing Corvettes, maybe it is better to help them to do a good job at it."

The answer for Chevrolet, according to Zora, was to create high-performance parts not only for the engine—camshafts, valves, springs, manifolds, pistons and such—but for the chassis components as well. He noted that the use of light alloys and brake developments—composite drums, discs and such—were on the R&D group agenda already. Zora concluded with, "The thoughts are offered for what they are worth—one man's thinking aloud on the subject."

Zora's thinking had a far-reaching impact, both for Duntov personally and for Chevrolet. Cole agreed with everything Zora suggested—a perfect way to "kick the hell out of the status quo"—and had the power to make it all happen, despite the usual corporate inertia. Chevy, in turn, began to offer a high-performance parts program through its dealers and began to publish a high-performance parts catalog. Special performance package options would soon appear on the Corvette and other Chevrolets. Slowly, word began to get around about what Chevy had available.

But it was the "Thoughts Pertaining to Youth, Hot-Rodders and Chevrolet" memo that laid the groundwork. Indeed, Zora's memo was a major step toward fulfilling the "founding father" role he originally envisioned when he created the Ardun conversion back in the 1940s. The memo was published in its entirety in a *Hot Rod* magazine special 75-year birthday salute to Chevrolet and is appropriately enshrined at the National Corvette Museum in Bowling Green, Kentucky.

Fuel Injection

The "Thoughts on Youth, Hot-Rodders and Chevrolet" memo also had another significant effect—it raised Zora's stock in the eyes of Ed Cole. When Duntov was attempting to explain to a group at the Proving Ground how he achieved this miraculous cure with the school bus driveshaft, he was interrupted by a phone call from Cole. He was summoned directly to Cole's office back at the GM Warren Tech Center and offered a proposition.

"I am about to offer you a job that I would give my right arm to do myself," said Cole. "I want you to help us develop fuel injection." Cole was well aware that fuel injection was the next logical step in extracting more horsepower out of the new 265-cubic-inch V-8 engine that debuted in the 1955 Chevrolet and Corvette.

Fuel injection sprays precise amounts of fuel into the engine's plenum or combustion chamber. Several GM divisions had been working on different types of fuel injection systems since the early 1950s, but Cole pressed hard for his Chevrolet Division to be the first out the gate with the new technology. Better performance and better fuel economy would be the main payoffs, with a side benefit of cleaner exhaust emissions.

GM, however, wouldn't be the first company in the marketplace to offer the technology. Daimler-Benz had introduced fuel injection on its production 300SL in 1954. And it was the Mercedes system that John Dolza, head of the power development engineering staff, had his eye on when he began to develop a system for GM.

Having heard about Zora's experience with engines—including fuel-injected diesels—Dolza approached Cole about using Duntov on the fuel injection development project. Cole agreed and rescued Zora from the school buses at the Proving Ground.

The fuel injection assignment was a major turning point in Zora's GM career. He was now in a position to make his mark on an important piece of new hardware, a technology that had the potential to revolutionize modern engine performance. In Zora's eyes, this mission constituted a high calling, and he was determined to finally show GM and the world what he could do. Success here would constitute the measure of his manhood.

Zora was the Chevrolet representative on the project and was joined by counterparts from the Cadillac and Oldsmobile divisions. His fellow engineers called him "Papa" because of his prematurely gray hair. The team worked together in a campus-like atmosphere at the new GM Tech Center and played Ping-Pong together during their lunches and break periods as a form of relief from the intensity of the work.

Duntov's experience with diesels was in direct cylinder injection, not the constant-flow speed-density manifold injection process GM was developing. The latter was modeled after systems developed in the aircraft industry and was sensitive to the speed of the engine and the density of the intake air. The key challenge inherent in the project was to discover a method to determine how much fuel should be delivered through the injection nozzles at a given time.

One of Zora's first moves was to write to his old friend, Daimler-Benz racing chief Alfred Neubauer. He asked whether Neubauer would be willing to share the plans for the fuel injection system in the 300SL, "providing they are not trade secrets," wrote Zora. There is no record of Neubauer's response.

But it wasn't long before Duntov concluded that the best way to approach the subject was to measure the mass of the air being consumed by the engine as opposed to the Daimler speed density system. Dolza agreed, and the two—working with the Rochester Products Division—began developing a mass flow system that was tested on 1955 Chevy engines.

Duntov then set up his own parallel but separate development group consisting of himself, Fred Frincke and Dan Bedford Jr. They stuck with their mass flow system and carried it through the development process, addressing everything from cold start to warm weather operation and every other conceivable engine operating condition. Dolza also hoped to program a fuel cutoff feature once the driver lifted his foot off of the accelerator in an almost prescient attempt to reduce emissions, but the feature was later scrapped in an effort to simplify the system.

Overall, the early injection systems provided less than spectacular results, showing virtually no difference between fuel injection and carburetion in power output. Further development improved the unit, but not to a significant degree. According to Karl Ludvigsen, subsequent tests with a 1956 Chevy showed that the injected version was 9 percent faster than the carbureted version.

Duntov then began the task of developing a special fuel injection manifold. It consisted of ram pipes to each cylinder united by fore and aft plenum chambers that were fed air by a metering venturi. The final manifold design—nicknamed "the doghouse"—had an upper and a lower section, according to Ludvigsen, "to slow the transmission of heat to the injection nozzles, and to make the engine easier to manufacture and install."

But while the new manifold helped considerably, the frustrations continued in trying to extract significant power gains out of the unit. Duntov brought in racing engine builder Smokey Yunick to assist. One of racing's all-time "characters," Yunick is mostly remembered for his short-brimmed straw cowboy hat, frank opinions and mastery of engines. He remembers Duntov's early disappointments: "Zora was struggling with it and couldn't make heads or tails out of it. He finally figured out what ailed the system: It was a pressure differential. Once you got going fast, it would make the thing go stinkin' rich. But after we got it going good, it was almost as good as two four barrels," added Yunick with characteristic sarcasm.

Zora's contributions helped Chevrolet be first out of the gate with fuel injection, a technology that in the small-block Chevy helped produce one horsepower for every cubic inch of displacement, an American industry first.

Once Chevy's fuel-injected engine was fully developed, it produced one horsepower for every cubic inch of displacement—an American industry first touted heavily in Corvette print advertising. Injection debuted on the 1957 Corvette and became the high-performance mainstay of the Corvette until the advent of big-blocks in the late 1960s.

But while fuel injection made a wonderful bragging point for the Corvette owner—Corvettes with fuel injection were badged accordingly—the reliability of the early units was questionable. Bill Tower, a former GM engineer who went on to build NASCAR racing engines, thinks the early fuel-injected motors got a bad rap. "The problem was always in the distributor system with the points. When the points would kick out, the engine wouldn't start. People thought it was the injector when it was the distributor. A lot of the fuel injection units got thrown away because the distributor was messing up." According to Tower, this necessitated constantly adjusting the points. A fix was later attempted with heavier-duty springs. "But the injectors themselves were very well done," says Tower.

In many high-performance circles, however, the carburetor was still king, and it would take almost three decades before fuel injection became the household word that it is today, thanks largely to the advent of on-board computers and electronic engine management systems. While the original systems seem crude by today's standards, they were all mechanical and were developed without the benefit of modern-day electronics. But it was all-new technology, and Duntov earned three patents for his work on the system, one for the manifold, another for the fuel induction system and a third for a cold enrichment system.

In a Detroit SAE presentation on fuel injection in January 1957 at the Sheraton Cadillac Hotel, Duntov got top billing along with John Dolza, E. A. Kehoe and Donald Stoltman of the Rochester Products Division. Duntov spoke on application development of the system and wrote up his report in a special handout at the show. Certainly, it was major exposure for Duntov and a far cry from his recent "exile" to the Proving Ground.

Despite his patents and his recognition by the SAE, fuel injection was not the career-making vehicle Zora hoped it would be. But his contributions here, which would span several years, bought him some much-needed equity from Cole and gave him a permanent home in high-performance car programs at GM.

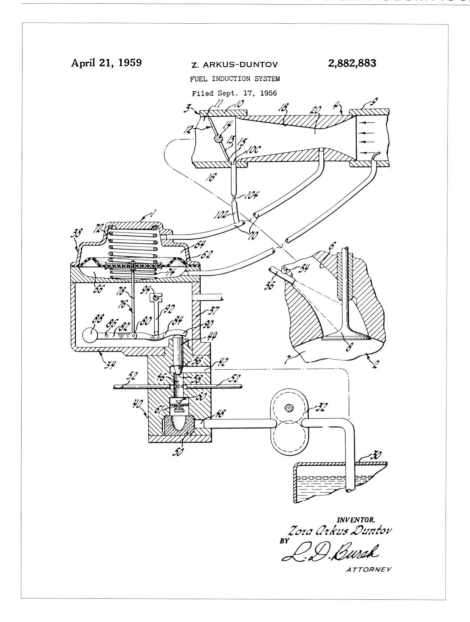

April 21, 1959

Z. ARKUS-DUNTOV

2,882,883

FUEL INDUCTION SYSTEM

Filed Sept. 17, 1956

INVENTOR.
Zora Arkus Duntov
BY
L. D. Burak
ATTORNEY

Duntov earned three U.S. patents for his work on fuel injection, including patents for a manifold, a cold enrichment device and a fuel induction system.

ELEVEN

*Zora's performance in driving Allards in 1952 and 1953 earned him
an invitation to drive at Le Mans for Porsche in 1954.*

Driving the Works Porsches

While Duntov was surviving his first year at General Motors, in the back of his mind was a short conversation he had had with Heinrich Uli Wieselmann following Duntov's effort at Le Mans in 1953. Representing Porsche, Wieselmann, the editor in chief of the well-known German motoring journal *Auto Motor und Sport,* asked if Zora would be interested in driving the silver cars from Stuttgart in the 1954 race.

His two years in a row on a world stage at Le Mans had provided Zora with high visibility in the racing community, and his respectable showing in the high-powered yet unwieldy Allards attracted the attention of Porsche racing manager Huschke von Hanstein. The affable von Hanstein was Porsche's version of Daimler-Benz's Alfred Neubauer. Baron von Hanstein would preside over Porsche's storied racing record in the 1950s and 1960s. Noted for his finely trimmed mustache, beret, thick horn-rimmed glasses and overcoat, "the Baron" was a fixture in the Porsche pits, whether it was at Le Mans, Nürburgring or the Mille Miglia. Von Hanstein also directed Porsche public relations.

Sensitive about approaching Duntov directly, given his status as a GM engineer and a former Allard employee, von Hanstein commissioned Wieselmann to make the connection. His publication *Auto Motor und Sport* was the same magazine for which Zora had written his article about supercharging in 1934. Upon being approached, Zora was naturally interested.

Zora was receptive because, due to a lack of funding, Allard wasn't sure that his team would return to Le Mans. Furthermore, the Porsche opportunity would be a chance to drive for one of racing's up-and-coming teams in the most prestigious endurance race in the world. This was the very prize Duntov had sought when he tested the Mercedes at the Nürburgring several years earlier. It was also what he had hoped the Allard opportunity would lead to during the previous two years. In short, it was Zora's biggest racing opportunity to date.

Opposite: Triumph on victory lane as Zora transports Elfi and other team members to the victory circle at Le Mans in 1954. It was Duntov's first—and biggest—racing win.

But another request to drive for a competitor at Le Mans was sure to raise eyebrows with his superiors at GM. The fact that Zora would consider such a request—despite the rancor caused by his driving for Allard the previous year—was an indication of how central racing was to the choices he made in his life.

Zora would have been more than happy to race for his own employer, but no such driving opportunities then existed at GM. The corporation was still riding the crest of a postwar economy and racing was not part of its business plan; the company was too busy building millions of cars and trucks. In addition, American motor sports was in its relative infancy; it was not the big-time spectator sport it is today. The Indianapolis 500 was the only major event, NASCAR was barely six years old, and road racing was just getting started at places like Watkins Glen, Road America and the Strategic Air Command Air Force bases.

The fact that Cadillac engineers had cooperated with Sydney Allard in 1953 and privateer Briggs Cunningham in 1950 did not represent any GM policy change regarding motor sports. Even if the corporation wanted to go racing, its only competitive engine was the overhead valve Cadillac V-8 being used in Allards. GM lacked any competitive vehicles in its stable, although Zora could see definite possibilities with the Corvette.

But Zora didn't have the time or the authority to develop the Corvette into a competitive racer, given his activities on trucks and later fuel injection. Besides, the Corvette's six-cylinder engine was not up to the task, and the fiberglass Chevy wouldn't receive the small-block V-8 until 1955. By racing for Porsche, Duntov thought he could learn a thing or two that might be helpful in establishing GM's own racing operation.

Zora, still conscious of his less than stellar record behind the wheel, was circumspect in his acceptance of an offer to try out for the Porsche team. In a letter to von Hanstein dated February 16, 1954, Zora wrote, "I am very appreciative of the high opinion you have of me, which I don't think I deserve. I am very glad that you will consider with favor my driving on the Porsche team. Since I first wrote to our common friend, U. Wieselmann, I learned more about the Porsche organization, which makes the prospect of association very positive."

Enter the Spyder

The Porsche effort for 1954 was to feature four 550 Spyders. The 550 was a simple yet elegant mid-engined machine that was to become best known as the car that James Dean drove to his death on a California highway in 1955. Compared to its competitors, the 550s were feathery light, weighing only 1,200 pounds (dry weight without fuel or oil). Three of the entries were powered by 1.5-liter engines and the fourth was powered by a smaller 1.1-liter unit. All were air-cooled, flat fours with twin-overhead camshafts. The combustion chambers were hemispherical—just like Zora's Ardun engine—but contained two spark plugs per cylinder instead of one, an idea that Zora would later employ on a racing Corvette.

In a January 1954 letter to Zora from Porsche's head of finance, Hans Kern, who handled driving contracts, Kern wrote: "We hear you're interested in racing a Porsche at Le Mans. We've seen you drive and you fit the bill." The letter went on to mention that the offer wasn't yet firm and would depend on external factors such as the number of cars entered and the number of drivers under contract.

A follow-up letter to Zora from von Hanstein in February 1954 stated, "We have entered the car according to the regulations, but we have not yet received an answer from the Le Mans manager on how many cars will be accepted. As soon as we get an official reply we would inform you."

Duntov received another follow-up letter from Ferry Porsche himself, the son of founder Ferdinand Porsche, on April 5, 1954. "We are interested in having you on our official Porsche team and therefore want to offer you that starting with our Porsche 1,100 cc," Porsche wrote. Porsche was almost apologetic that he could not offer Duntov one of the more powerful 1,500-cc cars, indicating that these had already been reserved for a couple of Belgian drivers, Johnny Claes and Pierre Stasse. Noted Porsche: "It was only at the beginning of this year that we heard of your interest in driving a Porsche and at this date our plans had already been fixed up."

Despite the gracious invitations, Zora would have to earn the opportunity to drive. The test would be around the Le Mans circuit in a 550 Porsche Spyder with von Hanstein riding shotgun. The car suffered from the terrible oversteer endemic to early rear-engined Porsches, but Duntov impressed von Hanstein during the test with his quick adjustments to handle it. Duntov was invited back for another night testing session with French driver Gustave Olivier and Hans Hermann. Duntov's quick times in those sessions resulted in a formal ride offer from von Hanstein for the 1954 race.

When the Porsche invitation came, Duntov knew he had to be subtler in asking permission from Olley and Cole than he had been the previous year for Allard. He carefully constructed his rationale—a study of Porsche's air-cooled engines as well as other possible technology transfers from the German company. At the time, Porsche was beginning to sell its engineering capabilities aggressively to other automotive concerns. Since then, the company has earned significant revenues through project consultation. In 1953, Porsche was already engaged in negotiations with GM over the sale of Porsche manual transmission synchronizers. GM was also taking a serious look at Porsche suspension configurations, especially the rear swing axles on the 356 Porsche for possible use on an upcoming rear-engine small car, which later became the Corvair. Given the extent of this dialogue, Duntov's request didn't exactly come from out of left field. He further hedged his bet with Olley by arranging a tour of some other automotive-related companies in Europe after the race at Le Mans. Still, he would not receive formal permission from GM management until a few weeks before the race.

Zora accepted the invitation via a special GM teletype message sent out on April 14, 1954. Addressed to Porsche Auto Stuttgart Zuffenhausen Germany, it read: "Your offer drive 1100 Le Mans accepted—Z. Arkus-Duntov, Chevrolet."

In accepting the Porsche ride, Zora hadn't forgotten his old friend Sydney Allard, who was lacking the financial support to race at Le Mans in 1954. Zora dashed off a letter to General LeMay: "As you well know, Sydney Allard, in the jam that he is, could not run at Le Mans this year—that is, if he is not going to get your help. He wrote me about it some time ago, but since I did not hear anything from him lately, I assumed that this scheme was not practical. I had an offer from Porsche for some time to drive their new twin overhead camshaft car at Le Mans, which I accepted by cable yesterday. I was stalling the decision in the hope that Sydney may work something out, for sentimental reasons more than for practical. I have not yet cleared this question with Chevrolet—hope that it will work out OK."

Several weeks before the race, Zora also received an invitation from Ferry Porsche to visit the factory in Stuttgart after the race. Just to make sure he was cleared to go, Zora wrote a quick memo to Ed Cole on June 2, 1954. In explaining to Cole the Porsche visit as well as proposed visits to other European automotive companies, Duntov wrote that Maurice Olley was in favor of it "because of the new things one can learn and some of the processes we are interested in such as direct chrome plating on aluminum, fuel injection, aluminum

Zora was quick to accept the Porsche drive offer for Le Mans even though he didn't have official permission from his GM supervisors.

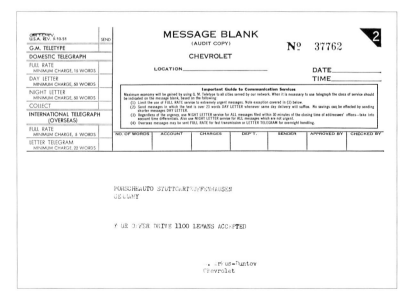

impact extrusion cylinders, pistons, etc." Zora stressed that the GM patent office had no objection to the visit "as long as I keep my mouth shut about our plans."

In order to quickly ascertain Cole's position on the matter, Zora devised a rather blunt single-choice response form for Cole. The options were:

(1) Not in favor of visit

(2) In favor, but on Z.A.D.'s own time and cost

(3) In favor on Chevrolet's time, but on Z.A.D.'s cost

(4) In favor of visit on Chevrolet's time and cost

Cole approved the effort on Chevrolet's time and cost and Zora journeyed back to France several days before the race.

Zora would drive the 72-hp, 1.1-liter 550 Spyder along with Olivier. To distinguish Zora's number 47 car from his teammates' 1.5-liter cars, yellow stripes adorned the rear fenders.

An overall victory against the powerful Jaguars and Ferraris was unlikely, but Porsche's objective was simple: to win the 1.5-liter and 1.1-liter classes. The race plan called for the Hans Hermann/Helmut Polensky car to break up the competition by playing the rabbit and forcing the pace. The other two cars—driven by Stasse/Claes and Richard von Frankenberg/Walter Glockler—would go as fast as they could without breaking. Since Porsche had only one entry in the 1.1-liter class against a number of Italian Oscas, no fixed strategy existed. They'd play it by ear as the race progressed.

In another classic Le Mans start, Duntov used his old track-star speed and agility to sprint to his car and be one of the first underway. He drove about an hour and a half at a fast but even clip when the first pit signal to slow down appeared. Zora ignored it. Later, the sign reappeared from the Porsche pit. Zora reluctantly cut his speed. "I was greatly annoyed," he said, "since further reduction of lap speed would result in increased strain on the car. We were making our time on fast bends and further reduction of speed would bring either lugging in high or screaming in third gear."

Without radio equipment to communicate with the pits, Zora wasn't in a position to argue back. So he followed orders, cutting down on his straight-

Zora got off to a fast start in the race and was signaled to cut down his speed by team officials in the pits. He reluctantly obeyed.

away speed. What he didn't know was that one of the 1.5-liter cars had dropped out after only four laps and von Hanstein decided to run as conservatively as possible. However, after only one and a half hours, his little 550 had lapped all the other 1.1-liter cars at least once.

Driving in a steady rhythm around the 8.3-mile circuit, Zora learned that there were advantages to having less power. He was able to adopt a much smoother driving style compared to his previous experiences in the Allards, with their torquey Cadillac and Chrysler engines. "On the undulated part of the circuit," said Duntov, "the small car simply does not reach the speed at which the slight bends become difficult. With reserve in adhesion, the car is not as closely committed to the predetermined radius and gives the driver considerable leeway."

As the race wore on, rain and wrecks took their toll, but Duntov managed to stay out of trouble. With both Porsches leading their classes by a comfortable margin, Zora was called in for some much-needed sleep. Instead of retiring to a luxury motorhome like drivers do today, Zora and the other Porsche team drivers had to make do with the reclining seat of a Porsche street car, which was placed on the floor of the busy garage area. Contrasting the Porsche experience with Allard the previous two years, Zora said, "Porsche did not give a hoot about the drivers' or anybody else's comfort. But their managing of the race and the pits was excellent."

If the sleeping arrangements for the drivers were limited, those for the mechanics were nonexistent. Porsche assigned two mechanics to each car, one for the engine and one for the chassis. They were required to be ready and available for the entire 24 hours, so they took only catnaps during the race without ever leaving their posts.

When Duntov resumed his second shift, he learned that the second of the three 1.5-liter cars had dropped out. As Duntov took the wheel, Olivier warned him to take it extremely easy on the first lap in order to get acquainted with the location of new wrecks. Said Duntov, "As I cleared the hilltop on approach to the White House (a slight kink on the section of the course opposite the Mulsanne straight), three total wrecks were lining the road—one projecting out on the track right where one wants to be for the correct placing for the White House." Zora later reported his headlights picking up a spinning car after clearing a hilltop. Seconds later he saw three madly spinning cars riding upside down. He managed to avoid them, again taking satisfaction in maintaining control of his car in the midst of chaos on the track. To him it was one of the fundamental appeals of racing.

The race continued uneventfully until near the end of Duntov's third shift when, after one of the torrential outbursts, the engine started to misfire. Then his gearshift lever went limp. Zora stopped on the circuit and began to manipulate the linkage running back from the shifter. "I yanked it until it registered, drove off in reverse, yanked some more and was sputtering in high gear, but in the right direction." Duntov limped back to the pits, where the transmission trouble was corrected. But afterwards his gearbox remained fragile and he was able to use only three gears out of four.

Remarkably, according to Ludvigsen in *Excellence Was Expected*, the misfiring was attributed to cold oil and was treated by covering the oil cooler to warm up the engine. The problem would return.

Later, when Olivier took over, he regained the function of all four gears. By that time, Zora had driven the 1.1-liter Porsche to a remarkable 15-lap lead, and he was finally able to catch some sleep, confident that he had driven his last shift.

Zora's Porsche suffered from gearbox problems as well as a persistent misfire throughout the race. Still, he built up a significant lead in the 1.1-liter class.

With two hours left in the race, however, Zora was abruptly awakened by von Hanstein and told to get ready to drive—a demonstration of von Hanstein's utmost confidence in him. The lead had dwindled to seven laps and the number 47 Porsche, still misfiring, was losing ten seconds per lap to a hard-charging Osca. Zora was more than happy to save the day, although he tried to be prudent in his attitude. "With confidence in the automobile somewhat undermined, I was very apprehensive starting on this last leg," said Zora.

Duntov was told to drive as fast as he could without exerting the car. Then the skies opened and soon a downpour covered the track in some places with several inches of water. This was good news for Zora because it meant that most cars would be in a holding position rather than being able to close in on him. In fact, it was the other way around. Coming to White House, Duntov closed in on a slowish moving cloud of spray. The cloud was generated by the Osca, which had been chasing his Porsche for the class lead. "Apparently the downpour slowed him down more than it did me," said Zora. "I passed with feeling not different from wolf sinking his teeth into prey. I was to see this car once more, but off the road, and this time our lead was not threatened. I had compassion for the man," added Zora, unaccustomed to being in a winning position.

By this time, the original field had dwindled from 59 to about 20 cars. Duntov was amazed at the fact that the crowd of some 200,000 people didn't scatter, despite the torrential rain pounding the circuit. Now he had to protect his lead and stay out of the way of the Ferrari and Jaguar, which were still battling it out for the overall lead.

With some eight minutes to go, Duntov entered what he thought would be the last lap, and he began to contemplate the fact that he might win his class. Driving slowly to time his crossing of the finish line right at the 24-hour mark, he was passed by teammate Stasse in the class-leading 1.5-liter car. Stasse signaled Duntov to line up so they could cross the finish line together, but the pace was too fast and the two cars crossed early. So they took an additional lap. "We didn't regret it," said Zora. "The rain had stopped awhile back and for eight miles the clapping and cheering spectators drowned out the noise of the open exhausts."

Then, after 24 hours and several minutes, the silver Porsches crossed

Top: Zora survived rain and attrition to emerge as the 1.1-liter class winner. He finished 14th overall and 14th in the Index of Performance.

Bottom: Zora beams with pride as he accepts congratulations at the victory ceremony. Elfi (wearing sunglasses) is at left.

the finish line under dark skies and took the checkered flag from a flagman wearing a trench coat and a black beret. Duntov and Olivier won the class and were 14th overall. They also finished 14th in the Index of Performance, a handicapping system to help equalize a wide variety of classes in the race.

Only 18 of 58 cars finished—a record low. The overall winner was the 4.9-liter Ferrari of Froilan Gonzalez and Maurice Trintignant, which prevailed over the Jaguar of Tony Rolt and Duncan Hamilton. Duntov's teammates, Claes and Stasse, won the 1.5-liter class.

As Zora triumphantly drove down pit lane, Elfi, her head wrapped in a silk scarf, jumped onto the front fender of his Porsche and was soon joined by von Hanstein and some of the other Porsche crewmen. Without question, it was the most triumphant moment of Zora's life up to that point. He was ecstatic; his accomplishment at Le Mans would stand in the official results for all time, and no one could ever take that away from him. Later, he coolly dragged on a cigarette on the victory podium, masking the euphoria of what this moment really meant to him. It was Zora's first—and by far his biggest—racing win.

Zora later distributed around GM a series of photographs of the race, many with humorous captions. An image of himself, for example, shows him dragging on a cigarette, his eyes looking up as he puts his helmet on. The caption reads: "Not bad, the blonde in the grandstand." The punch-line was a photo on the following page with Elfi and von Hanstein riding opposite fenders of the silver Porsche. The caption reads: "Now the picture is complete: There is the blonde…you dog!" A lecherous von Hanstein is depicted as saying, "Come here young lady!" Another photo, referencing the fact that an air intake on his car was blocked to cure a misfire, is captioned, "It helped…like aspirin to a dead man." Yet another photo in the series, depicting a victorious Zora driving down pit lane with Elfi and some crew members riding on the fenders, is captioned: "Everybody happy…everybody? Where is the MANAGER?" It was obvious that Zora felt good enough about his accomplishment to show a little humor to his bosses and peers back in Detroit.

Zora's post-race report had a serious side as well, including a technical analysis of the major entries as well as his theories on aerodynamics, particularly as they related to the release of air from the rear of a race car. He sketched out various fastback considerations, making the point that it is best to let air-flow conform to the back of the body for as long as possible. Then it should be cut off abruptly. His theories aligned with the more progressive aerodynamic thinking of the time—another demonstration of his value to Olley—and would later see reality in the long-tailed Porsches that raced at Le Mans through the 1970s and 1980s.

Making Friends at Porsche

During the race, Duntov had noticed that the handling of his car deteriorated as the amount of fuel in the tank decreased. The fuel tank was located over the front wheels. With a full tank, the weight distribution front to rear was 49/51 but when empty, it changed to 45/55. Thinking he knew how to compensate for this phenomenon, Zora told Ferry Porsche that he'd like to discuss this issue during his prearranged visit to the Porsche engineering facility at Zuffenhausen. Zora had an idea about a front stabilizer bar to help cure the oversteering problem.

Upon arrival, he started working with engineers Helmut Bott along with Leopold Schmidt. Porsche at that time didn't have a skid pad—a circular area where a car can be driven in a continuous circle at different speeds or steering angles to evaluate cornering behavior at the limit. Chevrolet, thanks to Maurice Olley, was already employing this technique. At Zuffenhausen, Duntov suggested they find an area wide enough to create a skid pad. Such a surface was found at nearby Malsheim airport. There, Duntov showed Bott a dozen tests GM used to evaluate handling. Bott was impressed with the controlled conditions and measurability of Duntov's methodology. Bott tried different toe-in and rear-wheel camber settings as well as an antiroll torsion bar connecting the front wheels, which also helped reduce oversteer.

Bott and Duntov stayed in close touch even after Zora returned to Detroit. He sent Porsche many sketches of his stabilizer bar design as well as a book on suspension design called *Road Manners*, written by Maurice Olley. "And that book, which they had translated into German, became to them Bible," said Zora.

Duntov kept Olley well apprised of his activities on behalf of Porsche and was eager to credit his boss to the Porsche people whenever possible. "What I learned about suspension, I learned from him," said Zora, appearing to put his earlier clash with Olley behind him. "Prior to that, I did not pay much attention to handling."

But then Zora suggested that his British mentor was old school when it came to measuring handling forces. Olley's approach was to measure centrifugal and gravitational forces on a static car, whereas Zora thought that dynamic tests with a moving car were more relevant. Zora pushed his approach to the Porsche people and it began to pay off.

After several months of development, Bott tested Duntov's stabilizer bar design on a Porsche 356 road car, resulting in marked improvement. Dr. Porsche then asked Bott to begin the same work with the new race car and according to Zora knocked *30 seconds* off its lap time at the 14-mile-long Nürburgring. "Like day and night," said Zora. "And 1955 Porsche, all Porsche, has a front stabilizer."

While Porsche did not publicly advertise that a Chevrolet engineer had helped them solve a major engineering problem, they privately gave Duntov credit and even offered him a new 356 as a goodwill gesture. Duntov politely declined. He had what he really wanted—the visibility and respect of the entire Porsche organization. This led to a close association with Ferry Porsche, Karl Rabe and Professor Albert Prinzing, as well as von Hanstein. Wrote Prinzing in July of 1954: "All of the Porsche people from the lowest mechanics on up love you and won't hesitate to go to you for advice. On Sunday, we'll be racing at the Nürburgring with the new stabilizer. Thanks for the advice. Looks like we'll have the advantage. I'm having the testing department send you the results."

A letter like this from a man of Prinzing's rank was one of the highest compliments Duntov could have received. Albert Prinzing was a childhood friend of Ferry Porsche, and, with his financial background, he played a key role in getting the sports car business going.

In essence, Duntov was now an unofficial member of the Porsche company, and he certainly could have joined the Zuffenhausen firm if he had chosen to do so. But Zora, feeling increasingly conflicted, wasn't ready to do that. While he had cause for concern at GM, given his differences with senior management, he had come to GM for its vast resources. He hadn't begun to tap into the great potential of this industrial giant. At times he may have still felt a sense of rejection from Germany. Now he smelled an opportunity to beat the Germans at their own game in cars of his own design.

At other times, however, he could have been persuaded to join Porsche, had the right position been offered. "There was a time that he wanted to become chief technician for Porsche," said Antole Lapine, a friend and design staff contemporary of Duntov's at GM who later went on to become design director at Porsche. "Ferry would have loved to have the guy on his team—lot of exchange." Interestingly, it was Duntov who tipped off Lapine about a possible career opportunity at Porsche. Lapine took him up on it, leaving GM in 1969. Lapine stayed with the Zuffenhausen firm for 20 years, retiring in 1989.

Even though Duntov elected to stay at GM, he corresponded with Prinzing, Rabe, von Hanstein and Ferry Porsche himself for many years afterward, becoming particularly close with von Hanstein and his wife Ursel. Zora and Elfi spent time with the von Hansteins during Zora's tour of several principal German automotive operations. These were important friendships that put Zora on the map in the world of automotive intellectuals. Gradually he was becoming a member of a very exclusive club, which encouraged him to be bolder in the concepts he presented at GM.

Thanks to his driving performance at Le Mans and engineering contributions on a stabilizer bar for the 356, Duntov garnered acceptance at the highest levels of the Porsche company. Here, during a postrace visit to Germany are (from left) racing director Huschke von Hanstein, Ferry Porsche, his son Gerd and Zora.

A Return to Paris

After the 1954 race, Zora and Elfi spent a few days relaxing in Paris before embarking on a visit to the Citroën works and later Germany. Paris was a wonderful homecoming for the two, as it reminded them of their carefree days in the late 1930s when Elfi danced with the Folies Bergère while Zora was racing to get his career started.

While it was great to go back in time, an incident one particular evening showed that Zora hadn't totally lost his penchant for the fisticuffs that he had displayed back in Russia and Germany. The incident occurred at one of Zora and Elfi's favorite restaurants, the Mediterrané in the Place de l'Odeon. It was one of the finest seafood establishments in Paris, noted for its ecrivisses, the miniature lobsters that Zora feasted on at Le Mans when he was driving for Allard.

When the couple arrived at the restaurant on a beautiful Paris evening, the various entrees were on display over ice for the benefit of passersby. Since it was relatively early, the ecrivisses that Zora ordered were taken right from the street display. He and Elfi also enjoyed the bouillabaisse and were for the most part content with the experience. As they were finishing their dinner, the proprietor came around to ask if they were enjoying their selections.

"Yes, they're good," said Zora, "but they're not *really* good…not quite fresh."

When pressed on this issue by the proprietor, Zora replied, "Everything was fine but the ecrivisses were not quite right."

The proprietor said he regretted the imperfections in the food. Therefore, there would be no charge; the entire meal was complimentary. But Zora left his money for the bill on the table anyway and the proprietor followed him out onto the sidewalk, determined not to accept payment when his customer wasn't satisfied.

"I don't want your money; you didn't enjoy the meal," said the proprietor.

"I pay anyway," insisted Zora, determined to end the situation on his own terms.

After Zora and the proprietor pushed the money back and forth several times, the proprietor suddenly took the wad of bills and inserted it into Elfi's décolletage.

Shocked and more determined than ever, Zora fished around inside Elfi's low-cut dress and pulled the money out and handed it back to the proprietor. But the proprietor, perhaps sensing he was on to a good thing, once again stuffed the money into Elfi's cleavage. Zora shoved the man hard, knocking him onto a parked car on the street. The proprietor lay there for several seconds before gathering his composure, telling Zora, "You are a man of honor!"

They shook hands and went back inside to drink fine champagne and cognac for the rest of the evening. Said Zora, "When we came back a year later, they treated us like royalty." So Zora and Elfi made it a point to stop at Mediterrané to see his esteemed host every time they visited the City of Light.

Touring on GM Time

After a few days in Paris, Zora went to visit the Citroën works to experience a new hydro pneumatically suspended Citroën. A relatively new technology, the Citroen suspension used compressed air and hydraulic fluid to help cushion its occupants, a common practice in today's shock absorbers and ride control systems. GM was considering a similar system.

Duntov took a wild ride in the car with several Citroën marketing guys. As he rode in the back seat, he had no idea what he was in for. "We took off with screaming tires," said Zora, "and after crossing a few intersections I became convinced that I was driven by an 'ex-hell driver' apparently fired from the show for rough driving." Zora also quipped that the scars on the driver's face indicated he might have been used for windshield impact testing.

From the back seat, Zora commented that the Citroën felt like it had no rear axle as they cruised the city streets, but as soon as they got out into the country, Zora was horrified to notice they were closing in at high speed on a rail crossing that was some three feet higher than the road.

 "We became airborne jointly and separately. That is, we took off first with the car as a unit, then we as passengers began our ascent within the car. The roof upholstery failed to slow our ascent appreciably and it was up to the roof itself to prevent our departure to heights unknown. As we descended to the seat again, my portly companions were still glued to the roof, their faces turned toward me with an expression of triumph all over. Apparently, the upward acceleration was holding their jaws shut, but with the beginning of their descent, they both enthusiastically exclaimed, "Did you see it? Our wheels were 12 feet off the ground!"

"In any other car you would be dead now," said the marketing guy.

"He was not fully aware that we had suspicions as to our still being amongst the living," Duntov commented. He said he scarcely noticed driving over broken-up or pot-holed pavement and noted the perfectly level "platform ride" in all conditions. He also observed visible front fender shake but didn't feel anything in the rear.

"The reason for placing me on the right-hand side of the car soon became apparent," said Duntov, "as at about 80 to 85 mph, the car was traveling with the right wheels off the road. They were going over roots, rocks and other irregularities, but nothing was transmitted to the seat of the pants."

Summarizing his impressions, Zora noted that the system had an excellent and level ride with superb wheel control. "The manner in which the car rides is different from any car I have ever driven before," he said.

From Citroën, Zora and Elfi then ventured to Germany to visit a number of high-tech automotive operations, including Daimler-Benz, German piston manufacturer Mahle, and M.A.N., a German firm that manufactured diesel engines. In a memo to Maurice Olley, Zora described Mahle as "the most progressive aluminum processing plant for the German automotive industry. They supply firms as small as Porsche with its nine cars per day output and as large as Volkswagen with over a thousand daily output."

Zora was contemplating the use of lightweight aluminum in engine blocks and cylinder heads and was particularly interested in Mahle's process of chrome-plating aluminum cylinder walls instead of using sleeves, a practice adopted by Porsche. Wrote Zora, "Porsche are the first to use the process in production cars, but now almost 100 percent of air cooled cylinders and many water cooled units have chrome plating as standard equipment." While Zora was fascinated with the process, he never employed chrome plating on cylinder walls at GM, but would go on to use chrome-plated aluminum on other components as a means of reducing the weight of a car while maintaining a stock appearance.

From Mahle, Zora next visited M.A.N., a firm in Nuremberg that had succeeded in the development of the so-called "silent" diesel, which was more efficient and reduced engine noise and idling knock. In the midst of developing fuel injection at GM, Zora saw many parallels between M.A.N.'s efforts with diesels and his own efforts with gasoline engines. "We felt this was a very important development," he wrote Olley in a five-page memo, "since silence means absence of peak or 'needle pressures,' consequently reducing bearing and structural load, and makes possible an engine structure and operation comparable in this respect to a gasoline engine."

Duntov received a demonstration of the system using two 16-ton trucks, one with a standard diesel engine and another utilizing the new combustion process. "There was a marked audible difference between the two trucks," Zora wrote. "The standard diesel had a knocking noise as all diesels, but the new one had a noise level only slightly higher than that of a gasoline engine." Zora also commented on the lack of exhaust smoke with the new process.

Because of the proprietary nature of the technology the company was cautious about sharing details of their process with a GM employee. So Zora—in yet another effort to impress Olley as well as to satisfy his own curiosity—constructed his own theory as to how the system worked, complete with hand-made drawings describing the spray pattern of the fuel injectors and the swirl patterns within the combustion chambers. "The exchange of views of the subject will be greatly appreciated," concluded Zora in his memo to Olley. "The writer is extremely eager for enlightenment, and does not insist that the things are happening the way he thinks they do." Whether Olley ever responded to this memo is not documented.

Zora wrapped up his German trip with a visit to Daimler-Benz, where he saw his old friends Alfred Neubauer and Rudi Uhlenhaut. He spent several evenings at team driver Karl Kling's home, discussing, among other things, the progression of rear-axle technology from the old swing axles of the 1930s to the independent de Dion and finally Mercedes' development of a new "low center axle." The advantages of this axle were lighter weight, "zero" or neutral steering, as described by Kling, and resistance to breakaway. The new axle was a critical component of Mercedes' full-blown racing effort in 1955, which involved assaults on Formula One and Le Mans. "It is interesting," wrote Zora, "that Mercedes, first to introduce the de Dion, is also the first to scrap it, supplanting it by a new superior design."

Zora then moved his discussion to what was happening with Mercedes racing programs. He mentioned the company's experiments in Formula One with all-enveloping bodies, which the rules permitted as an alternative to the traditional open-wheel racer. The following year, Juan Manuel Fangio would drive both the open-wheeled W196 and the closed-bodied W196 on his way to the World Driving Championship.

Much of the established thinking at the time was that the drag reduction such a body would create was in conflict with weight reduction but that the tradeoff was worth it. Duntov felt the real conflict was cooling efficiency with a closed body.

Duntov reasoned that effective cooling of the tires, brakes, engine, oil, transmission and rear end have to be considered and the advisability of the enveloping body then becomes a matter of the outcome of thermal balance of the confined engine and chassis components. Size and horsepower of the engine were contributing factors in cooling as were the types of circuits being raced upon.

Although Zora never used his German connections to secure an actual position, they did play a critical role in his ability to garner respect and visibility beyond the insulated world of GM. Having these kinds of contacts allowed Zora to maintain a broader constituency, which provided him with a sounding board for his ideas among respected peers instead of succumbing to the inbred myopia of a large corporation. Zora's involvement with Porsche and Daimler-Benz allowed him to make his mark both as a driver and an engineer, and it fortified him in taking on an expanded agenda later at GM.

The fact that Zora remained at GM and did not stay in Europe represented a critical juncture, for both Duntov and the Corvette. Had Zora opted to stay in Germany, the Corvette might have become just another footnote in automotive history instead of the most popular sports car in the world. As it was, Zora came back from Europe in 1954 to face a major crisis with the Corvette.

TWELVE

Zora caught his stride at GM in the mid-1950s by conducting performance demonstrations at Pikes Peak and Daytona in vehicles he helped design and engineer.

Driving His Reputation Forward

Zora's "baby" was in trouble. Corvette production in 1954 (3,654 cars) was more than ten times the number of cars built in 1953, yet many of those units were languishing on dealers' lots. Whatever novelty existed for the Corvette in 1953 had already worn off. Serious sports car enthusiasts just couldn't get worked up about a car with a two-speed automatic transmission and a six-cylinder engine. In 1954 the Corvette was still just a pretty face, not significantly different from the car that graced the turntable at the General Motors Motorama at the Waldorf. Zora longed to execute his vision for the car, but the question for him was how.

Despite his wide array of project assignments within GM, Zora didn't have authority over the Corvette. In fact, a dedicated Corvette group didn't exist. Chevy R&D and Chevy Engineering attended to Corvette matters as necessary. There was no chief engineer or anyone who lived and breathed the car on a daily basis.

To Zora, the Corvette's problems spelled opportunity. In the relative absence of people within GM who knew much about sports cars, the existing vacuum would give him a soapbox from which to further promote the themes he had established on the SAE speaking circuit—namely, what makes a sports car and what motivates sports car buyers. In so doing, he could underline his voice of authority on the subject in the hope of gaining a greater engineering influence over the Corvette.

The trigger for Duntov's actions came in the fall of 1954 after an anonymous GM executive buttonholed him and announced with glee that the Corvette was "finished" and no more would be built. Outraged, Zora wrote a memo on October 15, 1954, to Ed Cole and Maurice Olley to try to save the car. "At the time, I really had no standing with Cole," said Duntov, "but I had to adopt a certain path to get my opinion across." He delicately phrased his words, even writing a preamble to his memo: "In this note, I am speaking out of turn. I am giving opinions and suggestions without knowing all the factors. I realize this, but still am offering my thoughts for

Opposite: Zora's first opportunity to make a statement with a GM vehicle occurred behind the wheel of a 1956 Chevrolet on Pikes Peak.

what they are. In order to make the content clear and short, I will not use the polite, apologetic phrasing and say, 'it is' instead of 'it possibly might be'—and I apologize for this now." After this bit of verbal tap dancing, Zora laid it on the line: "By the looks of it, Corvette is on its way out."

Zora suggested that the Corvette failed thus far because it did not meet GM standards for its product. It did not have value for the money. "If the value of a car consists of practical values and emotional appeal," wrote Zora, "the sports car has very little of the first and consequently has to have an exaggerated amount of the second." It was in the performance area where the Corvette fell short, suggested Zora, especially with the six-cylinder engine, where it performed no better than a medium-priced family car. Zora, of course, firmly believed that the more the Corvette performed like a race car the more popular it would be as a street car. It was a belief that would fuel many disagreements in the coming years at GM.

Duntov also criticized GM's inability to have cars on hand in 1953 when demand was high. And once the cars became more available a year later, he was critical of the marketing message, which emphasized the small size of the car instead of the exclusivity. "Were there no virtues to talk about?" asked Zora. He claimed that a condensation of test reports from the motoring press had more glow and enthusiasm than Chevy's own advertising. A flat performance figure, he suggested, doesn't have as much punch as making someone believe that their car can "trim anything on wheels." But with the new V-8 in 1955, Zora predicted Corvette owners would soon feel a sense of superiority, at least when it came to power.

Duntov cited the debut of the Thunderbird, a car in the same class as the Corvette, and warned that if Ford was successful where GM had failed, it might be a major embarrassment to GM. "If it dies, it is admission of failure. Failure of aggressive thinking in the eyes of the organization, failure to develop a salable product in the eyes of the outside world."

He acknowledged that a car line like the Corvette with a sales volume of 3,000 to 10,000 units was bound to be a hindering stepchild in an organization that thought in terms of 1.5 million units. He understood that it was unlikely for Chevrolet to spend major dollars to market a low-volume product. But Zora suggested that there was a larger opportunity here—that the Corvette could have a role in lifting awareness and respect for Chevrolet around the world. "The value must be gauged by effects it may have on overall picture," insisted Zora. This was an important realization, for he had pinpointed the foundations on which the Corvette would enjoy its future success—as a halo vehicle for other Chevrolet products.

Giving Corvette this much more important role, Zora then made the case for what he was really seeking all along—a team within the organization that would eat and sleep Corvette. "I am convinced," wrote Duntov, "that a group with a concentrated objective will not only stand a chance to achieve the desired result, but devise ways and means to make the operation profitable in a direct business sense."

Duntov not only helped save the car with this memo, but also established himself as the "go-to" guy on Corvette matters. Engineering decisions were still the prerogative of Chevrolet Chief Engineer Ed Cole, who was succeeded by Harry Barr in 1956. But Duntov attracted the bulk of the Corvette assignments, such as the application of the small-block V-8 to the Corvette in 1955, the subsequent improvements to that engine and the ongoing development of fuel injection. More important, Zora was developing a growing atmosphere of support for his ideas among senior managers. Without question, Zora had established himself as the authority on sports cars within GM.

Zora the VIP

Zora's growing visibility as a sports car expert was not lost on General Curtis E. LeMay. As the man who had originally encouraged Zora to join GM, LeMay took pride in what Zora was starting to accomplish. Such was LeMay's esteem for Duntov that in 1955 he invited Duntov out to the Strategic Air Command headquarters at Offutt Field in Omaha. The purpose of the visit was to give a talk at the Hobby Shop, where Air Force personnel were building a turbine-powered race car. Clearly, the General saw Zora as someone who had enormous influence on the sports car world and who would make an entertaining speaker for the Air Force personnel at the base.

To transport Zora to Omaha, the Air Force sent a Boeing Stratocruiser to pick him up at Selfridge Air Force Base near Detroit. Duntov was given a full VIP tour of the SAC facility at Offutt, including the command center and even the White House hot line.

During his visit, he and LeMay talked sports cars much of the time. LeMay showed an interest at one time in putting a 1953 Corvette body over one of his Kurtis race cars, but Duntov talked him out of it because of the differences in frame stiffness—the Corvette was actually stiffer and Duntov wasn't sure how the Corvette body would fare on the more flexible Kurtis chassis.

Duntov had also been helping promote sports car racing on SAC bases by speaking to SCCA groups, and in 1953 he actually drove an Allard for LeMay's team in several races on SAC bases—including Turner Air Force Base in Albany, Georgia.

On his return from Omaha Duntov flew shotgun on board a T-33 trainer jet, experiencing g forces he would never encounter in a race car.

Just before landing at Selfridge, he had the pilot buzz his yacht club on Harsen's Island in Lake St. Clair. Zora clearly liked this flying business and talked of getting a pilot's license, but he didn't get around to it until many years later.

As a memento of the trip, LeMay sent Duntov a jet aviator's helmet, which later graced a bookshelf in Zora's study. Duntov even toyed with the idea of joining the Air Force Reserve, but after seeing LeMay in action with his subordinates, Zora changed his mind. Despite his experience in the French Air Force during World War II, he quickly determined he wasn't cut out for the regimentation of the American military. Apparently, GM was bad enough. "There's no contrary word," said Zora. "He [LeMay] says 'go,' and you have to do it. Boom. No conversation. He had fire in tongue. That made me think, the hell with it." If Duntov had enlisted, it probably would have destroyed his friendship with LeMay simply because of proper military protocol.

As it was, they remained close friends and Le May became an avid Corvette enthusiast. During his lifetime he owned several Corvettes as well as a Mercedes 300SL Gullwing. "My idea of utter relaxation," Le May was quoted as writing in his biography, *Iron Eagle*, "was to get in my little Corvette and run along the Potomac parkways for a while and breathe the cool air and feel the power working under my hands and feet, just the way any driver who loves to drive enjoys it."

Witnessing Disaster

Duntov's growing credibility in the world of sports cars was also not lost on Porsche. Zora's efforts to help improve the handling of the Porsche 550 Spyder a year earlier had made him a natural to be invited back by Porsche for the 1955 24 hours of Le Mans. He was slated to drive a 1.1-liter Porsche 550 Spyder along with French driver Auguste Veuillet. This time, no test ride was required.

Porsche had entered six 550s. Four of the Spyders were fitted with 1.5-liter engines and the other two were 1.1-liter cars. Zora was deeply honored to be asked back and when he arrived in France for his fourth consecutive effort at the French 24-hour classic he felt on top of the world.

But the 1955 race was a bittersweet moment for Zora. His participation gave him a front row seat for the most horrific crash in the history of motor racing—a massacre that killed a driver and 80 spectators. The race was about two hours old when the accident occurred, just as the first pit stops were being made at around 6 p.m. Before pulling into his pit in the Jaguar D-Type, Mike Hawthorne had just passed Lance Macklin's Austin-Healey. Macklin swerved to the left to avoid Hawthorne diving into the pits. That put his Austin-Healy into the path of Pierre Levegh's Mercedes, which was closing in at a fast clip. Levegh hit the Austin-Healey's tail, which launched the Mercedes across the track and into a safety barrier. The impact flung the engine and other pieces of the car into the crowd. As the Mercedes burned, sparks from its magnesium wheels shot up into the air like fireworks. The extent of the carnage was difficult to comprehend in the first moments after the disaster. It was only later, as the death toll mounted, that the full horrors became apparent.

Zora came around immediately after the crash and saw the smoke. He was concerned at once about Elfi's well-being because Levegh's car had landed opposite the Mercedes pit, where the Mercedes suite was located. He knew that Elfi often made the rounds to Mercedes and to some of the other teams during the course of a race. He slowed down, but his pit waved him to go on.

Elfi was actually just opposite the Porsche pits when the accident occurred. She saw the whole thing and knew right away that Zora wasn't involved. "I had no idea of the magnitude, but I do remember being stunned." said Elfi. "I remember seeing pieces fly up into the stands. I knew something horrible had happened. I thought 'Oh my God, I wish they would stop that race.' At the time, we had no idea how many people had been killed."

Le Mans organizers were faced with the agonizing decision of whether to let the race continue. They decided to let it go on because rescue work would be seriously impeded if the 200,000 spectators left the circuit while the ambulances were still ferrying casualties to hospitals.

After the accident, Mercedes team manager Alfred Neubauer spoke by telephone with the board of Daimler-Benz back in Stuttgart. Finally, at 2 a.m. it was decided to withdraw the two remaining Mercedes cars out of respect for the victims. At the time, the 300SLR of Stirling Moss and Juan Manuel Fangio was leading the race. The Jaguar D-Type of Mike Hawthorne and Ivor Bueb inherited the win ahead of the Aston Martin of Paul Frère and Peter Collins.

Porsche 550s finished fourth through seventh, with the Polensky/von Frankenberg car winning the 1.5-liter class and finishing first in the Index of Performance. The Seidel/Gendebien car and the Glocker/Juhan car took the next two places. Duntov and Veuillet won the 1.1-liter class and placed

Zora enters the four-mile-long Mulsanne straight in his 1.1-liter Porsche 550 on his way to a second Le Mans class win in 1955. Like the year before, he managed to avoid trouble, which included the worst accident in the history of motor racing after Pierre Levegh's Mercedes careened into the grandstands, killing 80 people. Levegh also died.

Zora and his codriver Auguste Veuillet take the checkered flag to win the 1.1-liter class, placing 13th overall and 10th in the Index of Performance. But it was a bittersweet moment after the earlier tragedy, which caused Daimler-Benz to withdraw completely from motor racing.

13th overall and 10th in the Index of Performance. They covered 2,053.74 miles, and in the process set the fastest lap in class with a 5:20.9 and reached 118 mph on the Mulsanne straight. Their number 49 Porsche was the only car in the class to finish, because the Arnott, Panhard, Cooper and Lotus cars in the class all retired. Everyone was in a a somber mood after the race and few people felt like celebrating.

In the aftermath of the Le Mans tragedy, Mercedes-Benz announced a withdrawal from racing near the end of the season. It was a difficult decision, given Mercedes' stellar record since reentering the sport after World War II, as well as the fact that Fangio had just driven to the world championship for the German team.

Duntov's contributions had helped Porsche solidify its grip on the lower classes and had put the German company into a position to go for the overall win several years later. Wrote Karl Ludvigsen afterward in his definitive history on Porsche, *Excellence Was Expected*: "Porsche had become not only dominant in two classes, but a force to be reckoned with for outright victory."

Zora's accomplishment was written up in the July 1955 edition of *Chevrolet Engineering News*, an internal newsletter. That this company publication would publicize his motor sports achievements—particularly for a competing automaker—indicated an increasing level of acceptance of his racing efforts. It was a far cry from the climate surrounding a similar effort for Allard two years earlier. "It will probably come as something of a surprise to members of the Chevrolet Engineering Department," reported the publication, "to know that one of their number participated in the twenty-four hour road race at Le Mans, France, on the weekend of June 11th and 12th, 1955. This famous test which achieved such widespread and unfortunate publicity in the press because of the tragic accident that took place there, has long been held in about the same high regard as the Indianapolis '500' enjoys in the United States. This year, for the fourth time, Zora Arkus-Duntov, of the Research and Development Group, participated. This year, as in 1954, he won first place in his class, the small sports car class for autos of 1100 cc. displacement."

After the race, there was considerable speculation in the press and elsewhere about the cause of the tragedy and what could be done to prevent similar occurrences from happening in the future. Many attributed the crash to the speed differential among the different classes of cars on the track, with their vastly different engine sizes, which caused closing speeds in excess of 50 mph. The critics maintained that the race would be safer if the slower, lower-displacement cars were banished altogether.

Zora drafted his own opinion about the situation, but whether he ever went public with his views isn't documented. As someone who had driven both small and large cars on the circuit, Zora suggested it would be a mistake to exclude the small cars as a panic gesture. "It comes to mind," wrote Zora, "that if we say the small car we really mean the slow car and such cars can be excluded on the basis of qualification laps. However," he continued, "a damaged car continuing the race becomes a slow car. Such cars can be taken out of the race, but imagine poor Levegh in 1952 being taken out, let's say with five laps to go having a lead of 25 laps on the second place man? This also does not sound right."

Zora then asked the question, what exactly constitutes the danger of simultaneous racing of slow and fast cars on the same circuit? "As I see it," wrote Zora, "the danger looms if the necessity arises for two cars to occupy the same place at the same time."

Duntov then outlined a plan that would provide designated lanes for the slower cars on key areas of the track like Dunlop Bend, the Esses, Tetre Rouge and the Mulsanne straight. There is no record of Zora taking this idea forward, and his idea of designated lanes was never implemented.

Climbing the Hill

Prior to the 1955 Le Mans race, Duntov received a call from Walt Mackenzie of Chevrolet public relations. Mackenzie had been thinking about ways to market Duntov for Chevrolet ever since he had heard Zora's SAE speech a year earlier. Finally, an idea that had been floated by Chevrolet's ad agency, Campbell-Ewald, caught Mackenzie's attention. Code-named "Monte Carlo," the idea was to showcase the performance of the small-block Chevy by entering a 1956 Chevrolet in the Pikes Peak hill climb. It would be quite possible to set a new record in the sedan class, since the existing record, set by a stock Ford roadster, was some 20 years old. When Mackenzie heard the idea, he immediately thought of Duntov and summoned Zora to his office.

Zora's accomplishment for Porsche was heralded in this 1955 edition of Chevrolet Engineering News. *The piece signaled an increasing level of acceptance at GM for Zora's racing efforts.*

As a hot-rodder, Duntov knew all about this hill climb event, the most famous in the U.S. and perhaps in the world. Drivers pitted their skills against the clock in different types of cars, from open-wheeled racers to stock classes. From its start just outside of Colorado Springs, the course rose from 9,402 feet to more than 14,110 feet, well above the tree line. The road was treacherous with no barriers. One mistake could send an errant race car off the road, tumbling thousands of feet.

This was exactly the type of thing Zora had hoped to do at GM. The Chevrolet Division was like a babe in the woods when it came to racing and needed someone like Zora, who not only knew how to set up a car but also how to *drive* it. He could finally compete for GM as he had during the past four years for Allard and Porsche. When MackKenzie asked Zora whether he'd like to be involved, Zora stood up and exclaimed, "Splendid idea! I *have* to be involved."

Duntov was given a leave of absence from the fuel-injection project and traveled to Colorado with Mackenzie and Campbell-Ewald copywriter Barney Clark to find out what they could about this fabled hill climb. It was Duntov's first trip to the mountain. Clark met Zora for the first time at Pikes Peak, and the two took an instant liking to each other. Clark respected Zora's engineering as well as his driving talents.

After checking into the Broadmoor Hotel, Duntov borrowed Clark's station wagon and made the first run up the hill. Clark occupied the passenger seat and Mackenzie sat in back. The tourist traffic was heavy, but Zora darted in and out of it, tossing the poor station wagon from side to side of the road before finally reaching the summit in a cloud of dust. While the trip was no big deal to Zora, the view was much scarier from the passenger seats—so much so that Clark's first ride up Pikes Peak would also be his last. "His eyes were bulging," said Zora, "sitting on the floor as if awaiting impending disaster." Mackenzie was simply quiet but was white as a sheet. Zora, however, was philosophical about the passenger experience. "I think generally a race driver perceives only the road before him at the exclusion of everything else. Therefore I understand how a passenger feels, but I have no choice and drive like race driver."

To help with testing, Duntov sought out Chuck Meyers who had held the Pikes Peak record in a supercharged open-wheel car, winning overall in 1925 and 1931. He recruited a second Pikes Peak expert named Al Rogers, who was also an experienced hill climb driver who had won his class in 1940 and 1948-51. Elfi also joined the group, which made for a contingent of four people on the Chevy team for the three weeks of testing on the mountain. Zora and Elfi set up headquarters at the Broadmoor resort in Colorado Springs and went to work.

A pair of Chevy 210s—a two-door and a four-door—were prepared for the event. The four-door was nicknamed the "Goat," while the two-door was called "McCoy." Both were disguised with special hooded panels, "falsies," around the headlights, a modified grille and taped-over rear taillights, then painted in unflattering black and white striped paint schemes. The disguises were necessary because the official run would be made prior to the introduction of the 1956 Chevrolet. Back then, annual body changes were the norm, and customers rarely got a peak at the new models until they appeared in the showrooms each fall.

Underneath the skin, the cars were surprisingly stock, including their 265-cubic-inch small-block V-8s. Both cars used Corvette mufflers and both featured three-speed manual transmissions with shifters on the column and 4.55 rear ends as opposed to the standard 4.11 units. The 4.55 was later added to the catalog in order to be marketed as a "stock" item. The rear suspensions were also relatively stock since lateral forces were not as significant on the loose gravel of the hill climb course as they would be on a hard pavement. Shocks, however, were beefed up to provide better control over uneven surfaces. Amazingly, the cars were not equipped with roll cages—further testimony to Duntov's courage.

Zora led the team in modifying two 1956 Chevys that he would drive up Pikes Peak in September 1955. While the cars were mostly stock, the bodywork was disguised because the shape of the 1956 models had not yet been revealed to the public.

Chevrolet was concerned about anyone from Ford catching on to the Pikes Peak effort, so Zora was under strict orders not to talk about what he was doing there. If anyone asked, he was just a foreign millionaire who loved to watch the early-morning sunrises from the top of the mountain.

A typical test day started at 2:30 a.m. to allow Zora to make a run at first light before the traffic became heavy. Al Rogers and Elfi stationed themselves up the mountain on a hairpin turn at 11,000 feet. From this position they could signal Zora with their headlights that the road was clear. He would then wait 10 to 20 minutes until there was sufficient light to drive. If for some reason someone was still on the road when Zora was making a run, Rogers would hold the vehicle to prevent a collision. Rogers also made test runs, but Duntov claimed he was always faster up the mountain.

Sometimes Zora took Elfi along as a passenger. Her job was to lean out and look for other traffic above and below their vantage point. She had total confidence in her husband's driving ability.

Elfi accompanied Zora to Pikes Peak and assisted by driving up the mountain road to ward off traffic during test runs.

Driving on the dirt wasn't a totally new experience for Duntov after the hill climbs in Europe and the dirt ovals in the United States. Zora had never before accomplished anything on dirt, but he sensed an opportunity to do something people would remember. He savored the feeling of control on the mountain, and as opposed to the oval tracks, he didn't have to worry about competitors spitting clumps of dirt off their tires. "You can put car in a slide and control with throttle—too much throttle, not enough throttle, like playing violin," he said. The surface of the road, however, was ever changing, ranging from soft dirt to marbles to slick hard pack, depending on weather and altitude.

After the morning runs, Elfi and Zora would go back to the Broadmoor and sleep until early afternoon, then work on the car in the afternoon in preparation for the next day's effort. Some days they would relax and enjoy a Planter's Punch by the swimming pool.

During Duntov's weeks of training, fashion designer Oleg Cassini was at the Broadmoor in the midst of a photo shoot of his newest collection. Zora knew Cassini from New York and conversed with him in French and Russian, letting him in on the real reason Zora was there. They dined together several times in the hotel dining room, feasting on fresh rainbow trout caught in a stream that flowed past the Broadmoor.

During the day, Cassini's models sunned themselves by the pool, and Zora, the star driver of this effort, took full advantage of this fact. For the benefit of the models, he tried to swim a length of the Olympic-sized pool under water, but after half a length he surfaced, gasping for air. He began to reproach himself for his smoking habit, only to realize that he was swimming at a 6,000-foot altitude, breathing air that contained 25 percent less oxygen than at sea level. "Relieved by the solution of this riddle, I light a cigarette and take deep, satisfying draw." The models were unimpressed.

King of the Hill

On Labor Day, September 4, the road was closed to the public for official practice. It gave Zora a chance to compare his car and his driving against other competitors. More than one race car was allowed on the course at a time and Zora came up upon another car that was struggling to stay on the road. "I am glued to his tail until the race car takes a turn wide and I slip under him and emerge with the lead," said Zora. "Nosing ahead of the car with my hardtop Chevrolet, I feel great."

In the paddock area at the bottom of the hill, an Ardun-Ford sprint car was being prepared for the climb. Duntov had to restrain his natural inclination to check out the car and talk to its owner. He didn't want to give away too much about his own effort.

Duntov had to beat a time of 19 minutes, 25.70 seconds over the 12.42-mile climb. As the date drew closer, Zora determined that he could probably run a time of around 18 minutes, 8 seconds, but still didn't know whether that was the best time he could achieve. To ensure that he would run at the fastest possible pace, Zora had a crewman prepare 25 3-by-3-foot boards with arrows pointing up or down in accordance with whether he was ahead or behind his designated pace.

"Before I go to sleep that night," wrote Zora, "I mentally rehearsed the forthcoming Pikes Peak run, but with a difference. Habitually, I mentally drive the track shifting up and down, visualizing the curves and placing myself on the curve and so on. In this case, I visualize only my boards with arrows pointing up and down to visualize my speed."

September 9 was the date for the official competition and Ed Cole, Walt Mackenzie and Barney Clark flew out to see Zora make two runs. The first would be in the four-door Goat and the second, which they hoped would be a faster run, in the two-door McCoy. At 7:17 a.m., Duntov roared away from the starting line in a shower of dust and gravel. He negotiated

Zora did a masterful job of negotiating the dirt and gravel mountain road, while executing graceful powerslides.

the mountain in a rhythm of graceful arching power slides. His skill in driving the relatively stock 1956 Chevy should not be underestimated, given the fact that today's radial tire and suspension technology didn't exist back then. Driving a 1956 Chevy was a handful, and Duntov did a masterful job of keeping the car on the road. He pressed even harder at the top and stormed across the finish line in exactly 17 minutes, 24.05 seconds. Duntov had broken the record by 2 minutes, 0.165 seconds.

At the top, a very animated Duntov was hugged by Elfi and greeted enthusiastically by NASCAR official Bill France and cross-country speed record-setter

Top: Zora gets the checkered flag from Cannonball Baker after negotiating the 12.42-mile Pikes Peak climb in 17 minutes, 24.05 seconds, breaking the previous record by over two minutes.

Bottom: Zora gives Elfi a victory hug, knowing Pikes Peak was his most significant driving accomplishment to date for GM.

Erwin "Cannonball" Baker, who waved the checkered flag. Back then, NASCAR was a fledgling sanctioning body, not the household word it is today.

But Duntov wasn't done. He drove back down the mountain and 50 minutes later, climbed into the two-door hardtop McCoy, hoping to beat his own record as he stormed back up the mountain. But he could only manage a time of 17:41.05. "And I will tell you, after I run two times I was utterly exhausted." After Duntov was finished driving, Al Rogers jumped in and made several runs for the benefit of a movie crew that Clark had hired.

Afterwards the victorious Chevy team celebrated at the Broadmoor. Unlike Zora's class wins at Le Mans for Porsche, Pikes Peak represented Zora's first real driving-engineering triumph for GM, and those present could sense a change in the atmosphere. Walt Mackenzie stood up and announced he was buying a drink for everyone in the house, while Barney Clark offered Zora and Elfi a special bottle of champagne. Even Ed Cole stuck around to toast the team's success.

The Pikes Peak event was Chevy's most comprehensive effort to date in marketing a motorsports triumph, and Zora was at the center of the action. "The Hot One's Even Hotter" was the theme of consumer ads, dealer service brochures and a cover story in the October 1955 *Chevrolet Engineering Digest*, a monthly summary of accomplishments within the bowtie division. Burl Ives even recorded a song about the event while Campbell-Ewald produced a TV commercial featuring action footage from the climb, with Zora talking about the accomplishment.

In agreeing to do the commercial, Zora, mindful of protocol, was careful to make sure he had the approval of Ed Cole and sent him a copy of the proposed script. "I will appreciate your attitude towards this commercial or indications toward another one since the occasions may arise in which I will make some more public uttering," wrote Zora in a memo to Cole dated November 28, 1955. "I like to be sure that what I may say is that what should be said."

The marketing effort provided a good excuse to tout everything from the small-block Chevy V-8 to the "unique outrigger rear springs that give superior cornering qualities." A four-page ad unit heralded: "Here's the Greatest Safety Story of All: 1956 Chevrolet Officially Breaks Pikes Peak Record. Run timed and governed by rigid NASCAR rules."

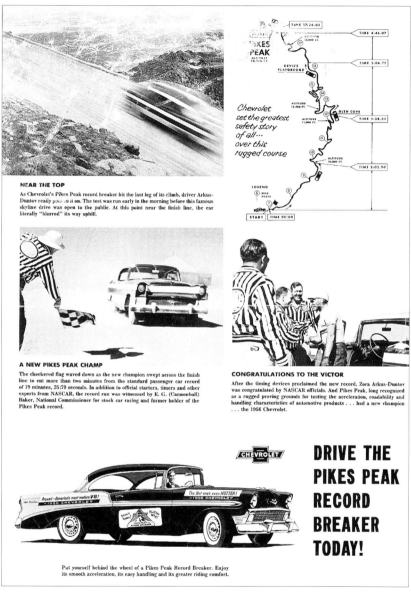

NEAR THE TOP
As Chevrolet's Pikes Peak record breaker hit the last leg of its climb, driver Arkus-Duntov really poured it on. The test was run early in the morning before this famous skyline drive was open to the public. At this point near the finish line, the car literally "blurred" its way uphill.

A NEW PIKES PEAK CHAMP
The checkered flag waved down as the new champion swept across the finish line to cut more than two minutes from the standard passenger car record of 19 minutes, 25.70 seconds. In addition to official starters, timers and other experts from NASCAR, the record run was witnessed by E. G. (Cannonball) Baker, National Commissioner for stock car racing and former holder of the Pikes Peak record.

CONGRATULATIONS TO THE VICTOR
After the timing devices proclaimed the new record, Zora Arkus-Duntov was congratulated by NASCAR officials. And Pikes Peak, long recognized as a rugged proving grounds for testing the acceleration, roadability and handling characteristics of automotive products . . . had a new champion . . . the 1956 Chevrolet.

DRIVE THE PIKES PEAK RECORD BREAKER TODAY!

Put yourself behind the wheel of a Pikes Peak Record Breaker. Enjoy its smooth acceleration, its easy handling and its greater riding comfort.

In one of its first "race win ads," Chevrolet touts its accomplishment at Pikes Peak in this four-page supplement, emphasizing safety rather than speed. Campbell-Ewald also produced TV commercials commemorating the occasion, which featured Zora and folksinger Burl Ives.

The France family at NASCAR also realized they were on the cusp of something big with the Big Three in Detroit. NASCAR heralded the accomplishments in the hopes of getting GM back for more. Bill France even wrote a letter on September 14, 1955, to Chevrolet general manager Thomas Keating that officially certified the attempt. "Congratulations for a new performance record for an American-built, five-passenger sedan," wrote France.

The 150 MPH Corvette

Before he ever made his Pikes Peak run, Zora was already planning his next move. This time he alone would be the instigator. He broached the subject to Ed Cole during the Pikes Peak celebration at the Broadmoor. At the end of the long celebratory dinner, Zora blew a fine billow of cigarette smoke out of the side of his mouth while he held his champagne glass. Then he announced to Cole, "I think we ought to introduce the 1957 Corvette in a spectacular manner. I think we ought to show the world that the Corvette is no longer a dog. Let's show how fast car will really go." "How fast is that?" asked Cole, his eyebrows raised as he held his own glass of champagne. "Oh...maybe...150 miles per hour," replied a confident Duntov.

Later, Duntov admitted that he had pulled this figure out of thin air. The 1957 Corvette wouldn't come close to 150 mph; in fact, the best it could do was around 135 under the best of conditions. But Duntov remembered the paper on high-speed-vehicle dynamics he had written for *The Automobile Engineer* while he was at Allard. He sensed there were things he could do to coax more top end out of a Corvette.

Cole was intrigued, but warned Duntov that his primary assignment was still fuel injection. Nonetheless, Duntov took license and called Corvette body engineer Jim Premo and told him, "Ah, Jim, Cole said you have to do some bodywork on this forthcoming Corvette. Right away."

Duntov then found a 1954 Corvette to hand over to Premo. The body engineer removed the windshield and added an underpan to smooth out the bottom of the car for better aerodynamics. Duntov tuned the exhaust himself and then started making trial runs at GM's new Technical Center in Warren, Michigan, northeast of Detroit. But even with the aerodynamic changes, Duntov was still a long way away from 150 mph. Making matters tougher was the fact that he'd be running on sand, which provided more rolling resistance than pavement.

Zora was still struggling with how to make fuel injection work, but the technology wasn't yet ready for a run of this nature, and he would stick with carburetors. The 1956 Corvette featured an engine upgrade in the form of a Carter four-barrel carburetor setup, which produced 225 horsepower, but Duntov figured that wouldn't be enough and he'd have to get more power out of the engine.

To get the increased output required, Duntov went to work on creating his own camshaft. More than any other component back then, the camshaft was the "brain" of an engine. Today, microprocessors play an equal or greater role in how an engine functions, but in Duntov's day, the camshaft was the primary means of determining the running characteristics of an engine—

how long the valves stayed open and closed and how fast the engine could revolve. The camshaft was everything.

Duntov knew a thing or two about camshafts, both from his own racing days with Talbot engines and from his Ardun overhead valve conversions. He had a configuration in mind that just might work. So he ordered two camshafts built that used the same profile as his Ardun Ford camshaft. The design order was written up on July 31, 1956. In fact, he gave the Ardun specifications, written in metric, to Fred Frincke, who then had them translated into English measurements. The cam had less lift than the factory high-performance cam, but it lifted the valves earlier.

Going into the process, Duntov decided to keep the same valvetrain from the stock small-block because it would be too much to change. "Goal was to increase positive acceleration and decrease negative acceleration." In other words, it opens the valve faster and closes it more gently. This provides higher volumetric efficiency and a better fresh air charge.

Before Zora's new cams were built, he and Elfi headed to the GM Proving Ground in Mesa, Arizona, to begin initial tests with engineer Maury Rosenberger. Duntov's 1954 Corvette test car featured a large fin mounted on the rear deck just aft of the driver for better straight-line stability. In an attempt to reduce drag, he added a tonneau cover over the passenger compartment and reduced the size of the radiator opening with duct tape. Once the new cams arrived, Duntov had them installed and then put the cars on the dynamometer to gauge their horsepower. The dyno showed 240 hp at almost 6,000 rpm.

Duntov now had the necessary punch. During a December 20, 1955, test at the Mesa Proving Ground, Duntov's own test sheets recorded a maximum speed of 156.16 mph with a 2.92:1 rear axle. In subsequent runs, Karl Ludvigsen later reported that Duntov achieved 163 mph at 6,300 rpm at Phoenix with 3.27:1 rear axle gears. He needed the extra horsepower to overcome the higher resistance from the sand he'd be running on at Daytona. At least he would gain some advantage because he would be running at sea level at Daytona versus the 1,500-foot altitude at Mesa.

Now Duntov was ready for Daytona. A work order dated January 4, 1956, stated: "This work order to

Top: In preparation for his Daytona Beach speed run in 1956, Zora began testing versions of a new camshaft in late 1955, which would come to be known as the "Duntov cam." His testing was conducted at the GM Proving Ground in Mesa, Arizona, using a stripped down, V-8-powered 1954 Corvette.

Bottom: Zora was a firm believer in adequate lateral support for the driver. His beach car had a cobbled-up side bolster to hold him into the driver's seat, although he would be running in a straight line at Daytona.

cover time and material to rework car #6901 for maximum speed record run and expenses of transporting the car, personnel to Florida and return." Chevy engineer Frank Burrell, who had accompanied the Allard team to Le Mans in 1953 as a Cadillac engineer, requested the order. The work order specified the following:

Body: 1956 body. Remove windshield, side windows, radio, heater, and top. Install special cover over right hand side of seat and small windshield. Make up headrest and tail fin.

Rear axle: Change to 2.92:1 ratio from #5951 car (1954 mule)

Engine: Remove high power engine from #5951 car. Disassemble engine and inspect for failures. Reseat valves and check valve spring loads. Make necessary repairs to put engine into top condition. This engine to have Duntov camshaft. Front engine mount to be cut away on right side to prevent water leak at water pump.

Transmission: Install close ratio transmission from #5951.

Wheels and tires: Wheels to be standard Corvette. Tires to be standard tires.

Accessories: Install seat belts and brackets. Special tachometer and instruments from #5951 car.

The team arrived in late December to run for a record speed under NASCAR supervision, but bad weather and poor beach conditions caused them to wait it out until January. It also gave them time to make further modifications to the car. "The sand must be a little wet," Zora told Karl Ludvigsen, "hard packed with no tongs of tidewater reaching in, for once you start, you cannot deviate. If you lift foot once, then you will not reach max speed."

Seagulls were also a problem. On several occasions, organizers lulled the gulls off the racecourse by feeding them popcorn farther up the beach.

Finally the combination of wind and sand were favorable, and Duntov took a final drag on his cigarette, strapped on a yellow polo helmet, climbed in and fired up the Corvette. He rammed the shifter into gear and took off down the beach, his tires kicking out large clumps of sand. Duntov had to run as close as possible to the water where the sand was hardest. Once he was a mile and a half down the beach, a wave broke over the course and Bill France himself drove out onto the course, flashing his headlights in an attempt to wave off the run. But Duntov knew that this was it, and kept his foot down. He clocked a two-way average speed of 150.583 mph in the flying mile—an impressive accomplishment for a stock-bodied sports car. The sand at the time was still not ideal, and someone asked Duntov whether he wanted to wait around and try another run. "That's enough," he replied, knowing he had accomplished his mission. Plus he knew he'd be coming back the following month, when Chevy got a chance to face off against arch rival Ford in the newly organized Speed Weeks.

Back in Michigan, Duntov made further modifications to his Corvette. He put on a set of experimental heads with a 10.3:1 compression ratio, increasing its power from 240 hp to 255 hp. He then made a number of test runs at the Milford GM Proving Ground.

In describing these tests, *Sports Illustrated* wrote: "A flash of red catches the eye before the hum of a powerful engine reaches the car. Far down a straightaway on the General Motors vast proving ground near Detroit a sports car streaks onward in the pale afternoon sunlight. The hum becomes a roar as the steel guts of the car yield more speed: 115…120…125. Going flat out as it passes the car is a red blur against the snow-carpeted earth, and the speed soars to 133 mph. Like the Ford Thunderbird, the hot new Corvette is a signal that the giants are stirring."

Keeping the giants' interest alive was NASCAR's Bill France. Even in the mid-1950s, long before there was a Daytona International Speedway (the track was built in 1959), he was gaining renown for throwing a good party. Speed Weeks became a perfect excuse for Detroit auto executives to fly south during the frigid winter months. Henry Ford II would even bring his 100-foot yacht into the harbor.

The engineers liked to hang around the factory garages located in the back of certain dealerships or local race shops like Smokey Yunick's "Best Damn Garage in Town." France, meanwhile, was already learning the fine art of handicapping competitors in order to provide the best possible show for his customers. That formula today has made NASCAR America's most successful auto racing series.

Chevrolet came to Daytona in 1956 with three cars to be driven by three big names—Duntov, John Fitch and Betty Skelton. Fitch was quite possibly America's top active road racer, having just returned from Europe as a Mercedes-Benz team driver. His counterpart, Betty Skelton, didn't have

Top: Despite less than ideal tide conditions at Daytona Beach, Zora puts the power down in a quest to break the 150 mph mark with a Corvette in January 1956.

Bottom: Duntov clocked a two-way average speed of 150.583 mph in the flying mile. In the hearts and minds of car enthusiasts, his effort helped put the Corvette on the map.

Sharing the driving duties for the Corvette team at Daytona in 1956 was aviatrix Betty Skelton, who was working at the time for Chevrolet's ad agency, Campbell-Ewald.

Fitch's driving resume; instead she was an expert at ribbon cuttings. She did it the hard way—in inverted airplanes ten feet off the ground. She held a long list of aviation speed and stunt records and looked like a Hollywood starlet to boot. As such, Campbell-Ewald hired her as a promotional spokesperson for Corvette after doing similar work for Dodge. Her hiring came at the strong recommendation of Bill France.

Skelton represented a different dynamic in Zora's life—that of working with a woman in a professional capacity. Skelton was one of the first female vice presidents at Campbell-Ewald and was also no stranger to Daytona. She had set a stock car flying mile record there in 1954 with Dodge. Still, she had some nervousness at meeting Duntov for the first time. Skelton felt Zora might have a problem with her being preselected for the team without his input. But given Betty's showgirl looks, Duntov found it somewhat easier to be accommodating. He also understood the promotional value of having a woman get involved in the effort. "He was very charming and very gracious," said Skelton.

Still, compared to the aviation community, Skelton regarded the automotive world as behind the times when it came to accepting women. "Being a woman, I knew how difficult it was getting around in car circles and Zora was more accepting than most. It was different in aviation. I was totally accepted there."

Speed Weeks in Daytona

All three of the Corvette entries wore official American livery—white with twin blue racing stripes down the middle. With two high-profile drivers flanking him, Zora was careful not to be outshone. Consequently, he drove the modified-class car, which featured cone-shaped fairings for the headlights and a finned fairing behind the driver's head.

The events consisted of both standing-mile and flying-mile speed runs. Skelton and Fitch in the stock Corvettes were no match for Chuck Daigh's Thunderbird in the standing mile acceleration contest. In an effort to be more competitive, John Fitch put a straight-six engine block from a local junkyard in his trunk to weight it down for extra traction. "There was no restriction at all on that at the time," said Fitch. "But the press made it sound as though I had hidden it there." He placed third, with an average of 86.872 mph against Daigh's winning 88.779 mph. Duntov had the fastest modified sports car in the standing-mile competition, with an 89.753-mph average.

In the production class flying mile, Fitch took top honors, with a run of 145.543 mph. Skelton was next fastest at 137.773 mph. Both were troubled by a strong wind, which also kept Duntov's modified car from equaling his previous mark. He clocked 156 mph on the downwind leg, but the wind slowed him considerably on the return leg and he only averaged 147.300 mph. He wasn't alone. During the official Speed Weeks, only a grand prix Ferrari went faster—by less than one mile per hour.

After Skelton's run, Bill France declared it the fastest a woman had ever driven an automobile. In honor of this distinction, Chevy threw a big party at the Eleanor Village Golf Club with Ed Cole, Walt Mackenzie and others in attendance. One wall of the room featured a giant head shot of Chevy's newest celebrity. Later, to honor her accomplishment, Skelton was given a pearlescent gold 1957 Corvette with a white leather interior that had been done up by Design Staff chief Harley Earl and Bill Mitchell. She used it to pace all of the NASCAR races in 1957.

As part of a story for *Look* magazine, Skelton eventually became the first woman to undergo physical and psychological tests given the seven original Mercury astronauts. Duntov was never jealous of any of the notoriety Skelton achieved; as a tough, free-spirited individual, he knew she was good for the Corvette.

Dreams Come True

Zora's accomplishment on the sand was his biggest to date for GM. From an engineering viewpoint, this was a bigger triumph than Pikes Peak because it was Zora's own technology—the Duntov cam—that made the difference. As a driving accomplishment, the speed records at Daytona paled compared to those at Pikes Peak or Le Mans. Speeding down the beach in

Top: Zora gets ready for his modified-class, flying-mile run at Daytona Speed Weeks in February 1956.

Bottom: Zora managed a one-way run of 156 mph, but due to strong winds, couldn't muster the same speed on the return trip, and averaged only 147.30 mph.

The Corvette team flies in formation at Daytona Beach with the production-class cars of Betty Skelton (right) and John Fitch flanking Zora's modified car.

a straight line was not much of a challenge compared to keeping a 1956 Chevy on the road at 14,000 feet.

But the Daytona effort made a household word out of the Duntov cam, at least among knowledgeable enthusiasts. "The Duntov cam, as it came to be known, was technically an option in 1956, wrote Ludvigsen, "enough to qualify it for production car competition, but it wasn't fitted that year to normal catalogued Corvette engines. Dynamometer tests showed that it gave about 240 hp at 5,800 rpm, with a very fat power curve from 5,000 to 6,000 rpm. Maximum torque was 265 lb-ft at 4,400 rpm."

Overall, enthusiasts hailed the engine for its smoothness and drivability as well as its performance. It had a real-world quality about it as opposed to a fussy racing cam.

"The Duntov cam was not really unique," said Smokey Yunick. "It was just a little better than what we'd call a three-quarter cam. It was extremely durable and increased performance without totally destroying the bottom end. It made for a much smoother running engine with horsepower. It was really a German thing…that goddamn cam, you could drive it on the street."

The significance of the Duntov cam, according to former *Hot Rod* publisher Ray Brock, was that it worked, it was cheap, and you could order it at a Chevy dealer. The Duntov cam was exactly the kind of high performance component that Zora had in mind when he wrote his memo, "Thoughts Pertaining to Youth, Hot-Rodders and Chevrolet." Coupled with his accomplishments with fuel injection and his Pikes Peak run, as well as his efforts to improve the driving character of the Corvette, Zora's dreams were becoming a reality at GM. His decision to come to Detroit—and stay there—suddenly appeared to be a very good one indeed.

THIRTEEN

Zora's first purpose-built race car at General Motors was the Corvette SS, which he designed and engineered. The SS, however, would have a very short racing career.

The Transformation Continues

Hot on the heels of his 1956 Daytona Beach run, Duntov made a number of personal appearances. He was now firmly in control of the Corvette's destiny, even though he didn't have an official title. Thanks to Zora and a small revolving group of engineers—many of whom still had other responsibilities with the company—the evolution of the Corvette was well underway. It received its first major body redesign in 1956. It also benefited from additional power options such as dual four-barrel carburetors and a free-flowing exhaust manifold. These modifications raised power output to 240 hp on the high-performance version, which was a significant leap from the 195-hp V-8 available in 1955. In Zora's view, these changes would force skeptics to take the car more seriously. The chassis tweaks that Zora had recommended back in his first months on the job in 1953 also reached the production line and further enhanced the Corvette's performance credentials.

In a speech before a Society of Automotive Engineers (SAE) group on February 2, 1956, Zora touted the new look and engineering improvements of the 1956 Corvette, but was careful to give credit to everyone who touched the car. "Over the two and a half years involved," he said, "many General Motors engineers added their efforts to making the Corvette a superior car, and most of these men did so in addition to their regular duties."

Zora was most enthusiastic about the chassis changes. His stated objective was to increase high-speed stability and consistency in response to steering wheel input over a wide range of lateral accelerations and speeds. "The Corvette goes where it is pointed without hesitation and stays on track without wind wander or other disturbances," said Duntov. "On turns taken hard, it does not plow or skid, but gets into a drift. If the right amount of power is fed, the drift can be maintained without danger of rear end getting presumptuous and assuming the position of the front."

Zora also talked at length about transmissions. He admitted to a preference for automatic transmissions in racing cars, despite the risk of

Opposite: 1956, Zora was behind the wheel, helping to transform the Corvette from an anemic turntable queen to a respectable sports car.

Zora loved to tout his accomplishments with the Corvette in front of his brethren from the SAE. He used these occasions to become GM's voice of authority on sports cars.

being indicted for blasphemy by sports car cognoscenti. Duntov saw automatics as a means of simplifying the driving task. "Fundamentally a road racing car is a tool designed to enable a human being to cover a circuit of given character in shortest possible time," he said. He described the process involving acceleration, speed, deceleration and changes of direction. Like any good tool, a racing automobile has to be designed for its task and has to suit the faculties and limitations of its users. "It follows that a racing car engineered for the job needs to have at the maximum, three controls. Gas control to accelerate and maintain speed, brake control to decelerate and steering to change directions. Presence of any other elements of control indicates only that for one reason or another, the best tool from the standpoint of mechanical and human engineering is not yet offered in the racing field." In Zora's eyes, this meant an automatic transmission.

Because a suitable automatic transmission for a race car did not yet exist, Zora suggested that racers and sportier drivers should still opt for the four-speed manual with synchromesh. For the record, he observed that many notable race cars, such as MG, E.R.A, Talbot, Delage and Delahaye, were all equipped with preselector transmissions. Duntov would help make an automatic racing transmission part of the engineering agenda at GM. This decision bore fruit several years later as part of the Chaparral racing program.

Overall, Duntov described the 1956 Corvette as a sports car capable of responding to a driver's thoughts—be it accelerating, changing direction, braking or any other maneuver the car could be called upon to execute. "When an automobile responds as continuation of the response of human hand motivated by reflex or thought, then I feel there is a sporting (and very safe) automobile."

Duntov concluded his February speech by speculating on the competition potential of the 1956 Corvette. "As a rally car, the car can be used as it stands," he said. But for circuit racing, special brake linings were necessary—and even those were adequate only for about three hours of racing. Duntov also suggested special shocks to maintain wheel control with tires inflated to higher pressures. With these additions, "a good driver can try against all comers—domestic and foreign—with a reasonable chance of success."

Duntov stressed that he didn't believe that a street machine like the 1956 Corvette could be modified to compete against purebred machines like the Jaguar D-Type or Mercedes-Benz 300SLR. He thought that a racing car should be a single-purpose machine conceived and engineered for racing only and didn't think the Corvette was in that league. Its performance was more befitting a good general-purpose sports car that could be raced successfully by amateurs.

Bound for Sebring

Duntov's opinion that the production Corvette wasn't ready for international racing didn't jibe with Ed Cole's thinking. After Duntov's successes at Pikes Peak and Daytona in 1956, Cole felt the Corvette was ready to compete against the big boys. A few Corvettes had been raced on road courses since 1954 and had shown some promise. Karl Ludvigsen wrote that car owner Bob Rosenthal had brought along a Corvette for his driver, Dr. Richard Thompson, for a race at Andrews Field, near Washington, D.C. Thompson had driven Porsches and Jaguars and had discovered that until the Chevy's brakes failed, the six-cylinder Corvette was as fast as his Jaguar. Ludvigsen also wrote that a Chevy dealer named Addison Austin campaigned a 1955 Corvette at Watkins Glen and other East Coast tracks and finished respectably.

Encouraged by these privateer efforts, Cole committed to run a factory Corvette team at Sebring that same year. But Duntov wouldn't be the man running the show: He had complained a little too loudly to Assistant Chief Engineer Maury Rosenberger and racing great Mauri Rose, the former Indy 500 winner, about the Corvette's brakes being questionable for a 12-hour race. Brakes were the Achilles heel of early racing Corvettes, and philosophical differences flared up between Duntov and his superiors about how to attack the problem. Chevy, Duntov thought, wasn't ready to risk going up against teams like Jaguar and Ferrari. He would rather wait to give the Corvette a chance to look respectable —or better yet, for Chevrolet to develop a purpose-built race car bearing the Corvette name.

"My heart was not in racing street cars," Zora said. But he overstepped his bounds at GM by suggesting in a Cole staff meeting that Chevrolet was endangering the public by doing so. At the time, there were some dwellings very near the Sebring track that were inhabited by low-income families, several of whom were just outside of a fast right-hand bend. Duntov had vivid memories of the horrific Le Mans crash in 1955 and how it helped propel the Mercedes juggernaut out of racing altogether. He didn't want the same thing to happen at Chevy. But Cole didn't see it that way and told Duntov he'd find someone else to run the team.

As a result, Zora would be only a bystander when the Corvette debuted before an international audience. Only weeks after his triumph on the sand at Daytona Beach, it was a significant reversal. The situation contained a certain irony, compared to Zora's later support of racing. At this point Zora was playing the role of conservative, while a senior GM manager—Ed Cole—played the risk taker.

Cole's choice to replace Duntov was John Fitch, who was fresh from Daytona and the sole American from the Mercedes-Benz team. Mercedes was the most prestigious racing operation in the world, and Cole felt Chevrolet had much to learn from such a resource. Fitch, who had first met Cole at Daytona in February, came heavily recommended by Briggs Cunningham, the wealthy sportsman from Connecticut—for whom he had raced in Europe and the United States. Cole was equally impressed and offered Fitch a contract as a consultant after Fitch's beach run at Daytona. He was paid through Campbell-Ewald to avoid any overt factory connections.

While waiting for the weather to break, the team from Chevrolet traveled southwest to Sebring in January 1956. Ever since 1952, a 12-hour sports car race had been held each March on the 5.2-mile road circuit at Sebring, using runways from the former Hendrick Field, a World War II B-17 bomber facility. Set in the swampy scrub pine landscape of central Florida, Sebring was not a sexy location for an international event, but it was America's only venue for endurance sports car racing, and as such Ed Cole wanted to know how Zora's car stacked up against the world's best. Reported Karl Ludvigsen, "In a few test laps, the Corvette, stripped for lightness and softly sprung, showed it could turn impressively quick times." This encouraged Cole to go ahead and approve the entry of four cars. But the clock was ticking fast and the team had roughly two months to prepare.

Race car preparation didn't begin until almost a month later, on February 18. The cars were entered by Dick Doane's Raceway Enterprises, of Dundee, Illinois. Doane, a Chevy dealer, would become known as a front man for factory entries. Fitch was put in charge of hiring drivers and running the daily operations of the team. They set up headquarters in a hangar at the Sebring airport and then began the almost impossible task of whipping four Corvettes into fighting shape within five weeks.

The effort attracted considerable attention in the racing world. According to the British motorsport weekly *Autosport*, in its February 10, 1956, edition, "For the first time, USA's giant General Motors combine is officially taking part in international motor racing. Chevrolet chief engineer Edward N. Cole and designer Zora Duntov have developed a very fast version of the Corvette. Duntov, in an experimental model, exceeded 150 mph at Daytona Beach recently."

The article speculated that the Sebring race was the first stop on a full-blown program culminating with a Chevrolet factory effort at Le Mans. "Chevrolet mean[s] business," the article concluded. It speculated that Chevrolet "intend[s] to use racing as a means of developing and publicizing the Corvette, and to challenge the domination of European cars in the rapidly expanding high-performance and sports car market."

Under normal circumstances Zora would have killed for publicity like this. Yet stories like this were bittersweet, because he wanted Chevrolet to be fully prepared when it stepped onto the world stage, and he knew Chevy wasn't ready. Still, he decided to do what he could to help make a respectable showing but did so long distance from Detroit. Fitch worked from his base in Sebring.

Initially, Fitch only had one car to test—the same 1955 "mule" chassis that Duntov had sorted out for the Daytona Speed Weeks run. The actual race cars didn't arrive until several weeks later. Because the cars were running in a production class, major changes had to be tested and validated by Duntov and his group at Chevy Engineering and then made available on street Corvettes.

"We were testing countless different components," said Fitch. "Things like brake return springs, differential seals, axle seals that didn't dump oil, carburetors that didn't starve in the corners." The task of validating parts brought its own share of frustrations. "The engineers in Detroit were more concerned with supplying the parts for 10,000 Chevrolets a day," said Fitch. Among the engineers at Chevy, none of them had a moment's time for Corvette or Zora. They were swamped. To them, the Corvette racing program was "a flea on an elephant."

As Duntov predicted, brakes were—and would continue to be—a major problem. A number of different drum/shoe combinations were tried, but they did not appear reliable enough to go the distance. The best setup was comprised of Bendix cerametallic linings inside heavily finned iron drums. Cerametallic was a lining surface manufactured out of ceramic mixed with sintered metal. It had better wear properties and more heat resistance than asbestos linings but worked properly only after reaching a minimum operating temperature. The big drums, according to Karl Ludvigsen, also required air-cooling through ducts on the car.

Duntov's concern regarding the brakes stemmed from weight, the enemy of any race car. He knew that heavy-duty drum brakes and cooling ducts added considerable mass that would slow the Corvette down while adding inertia. The Corvette weighed over 3,000 pounds, while the disc brake-equipped Jaguar weighed approximately 2,600 pounds.

Despite his disagreements with Cole, Duntov couldn't bear watching the Corvette's first major motor sports program from Detroit, so he swallowed his pride and traveled to Florida for the final month of testing. He resolved to do his best to make the Corvettes competitive. He worked out of Smokey Yunick's garage in Daytona Beach along with fellow engineers Frank Burrell and Mauri Rose. From Daytona, they would commute to Sebring for the tests. The engines, all built by Yunick, featured Duntov cams and twin carburetors with a special manifold that had 20 percent larger porting. But finding the right carburetor settings for the warm Florida days and the contrasting cool evenings was a challenge.

If the Sebring Corvettes weren't fully sorted out mechanically, at least they made an impressive sight decked out in American racing colors— white with blue racing stripes and blue side coves. The windshields were cut down for better aerodynamics, and small, color-coded lights were installed on the front fenders to make it easier for the crew to identify the cars at night. Three of the cars would run in Class C for production sports cars and one would contest the faster Class B division.

Duntov stayed for the race and watched Fitch's Class B Corvette instantly get into trouble. On the second lap, Fitch's clutch began to slip. In an effort to save it, he said later that he had deliberately slipped it at high revs to heat it up enough to grab, a trick that he had used at Le Mans in 1953. He had to baby the car from then on, but that proved to be the key to survival. Fitch and his co-driver, Walt Hansgen, survived for the next 12 hours and brought their car home ninth overall and first in its class. Ray Crawford and Max Goldman had lost all but top gear in the only production model to go the distance. Still, they finished 15th overall. The two other team cars failed early. As Fitch later told Karl Ludvigsen, Chevy's race performance, "was less than we had hoped, but more than we deserved."

The victory inspired Barney Clark of Campbell-Ewald to write the first Corvette race win ad, titled "The Real McCoy." The

Corvette's class win at the 1956 12-Hours of Sebring was duly noted in this ad, entitled "The Real McCoy," which ran in Hot Rod *and* Road & Track *in July 1956. It was the first ever race-win ad for Corvette.*

THE REAL McCOY

Here is the most remarkable car made in America today — the new Chevrolet Corvette.

Why remarkable?

Because it is *two* cars wrapped up in one sleek skin. One is a luxury car with glove-soft upholstery, wind-up windows, a removable hardtop (with virtually 360° vision), or fabric top, ample *luggage* space, a velvety ride and all the power assists you could want, including power-operated fabric top* and Powerglide transmission*.

The other is a sports car. And we mean the real McCoy, a tough, road-gripping torpedo-on-wheels with the stamina to last through the brutal 12 hours of Sebring, a close-ratio trans-

mission (2.2 low gear, 1.31 second) matched to engine torque characteristics, razor-sharp steering (16 to 1) that puts *command* into your fingertips.

Other people make a luxury car that has much the same dimensions as this. That's not so tough. And the Europeans make some real rugged competition sports cars — and that's *considerably* tougher. But nobody but Chevrolet makes a luxury car that *also* is a genuine 100-proof sports car.

It's a wicked combination to work out, and we didn't hit it overnight. But you'll find, when you take the wheel of a new Corvette, that the result is fantastic — the most heart-lifting blend of all the things you've ever wanted a car to be.

If you find it hard to believe that one car could combine such widely different characteristics we can't blame you. And no amount of talk can tell you half so much as 15 minutes in a Corvette's cockpit — so why don't you let your Chevrolet dealer set up a road test of the most remarkable car made in America today? . . . *Chevrolet Division of General Motors, Detroit 2, Michigan.*

*Powerglide and power-operated fabric top optional at extra cost.

ad showed a gritty action shot of one of the Corvettes during a pit stop at Sebring, where the low-slung 'Vette looked right at home on the racetrack, hence the headline.

As for Duntov, Sebring was another lesson in corporate politics. His earlier stance against running the race had backfired. Despite overwhelming odds, Fitch had managed to cobble up a reasonably successful effort and looked good in doing so. Duntov knew that despite his earlier successes, there were no guarantees for him at GM. He knew he would never be in total control, and he could easily end up being just a small fish in a big pond if he wasn't careful. Next time, he would not err on the side of holding back.

The Racing Goes On—Without Zora

Several weeks later, a similar situation arose on the opposite side of the country. Once again a Corvette would race, and once again Zora would not play a significant role. In fact, he wasn't even present. Zora's available time was being consumed by his working around the clock on fuel injection as well as playing a supporting role at Sebring. As a result, he missed Corvette's first significant West Coast performance.

The event was a road race in Pebble Beach, California, that featured the Corvette racing debut of a dentist named Dick Thompson, who was soon to become a Corvette racing legend. At the time, the Pebble Beach race was not considered to be a significant event: Road racing was an East Coast and Midwest phenomenon. Barney Clark of Campbell-Ewald orchestrated the Pebble Beach effort. But like most early Corvette racing exercises, this race was fraught with uncertainty. Walt Hansgen was originally slated to drive the car at Pebble Beach but called at the last minute to say he was ill but that he was sending an East Coast dentist as a replacement. Clark panicked upon the first sight of Thompson. "There he was," said Clark, "a total preppie, pink striped shirt, Brooks Brothers jacket, looking about 18, rosy-cheeked and so gentle and deferential he made Mr. Rogers look like Dirty Harry." Thompson had most recently been driving Porsche 356s, but even though he had very limited action in Corvettes, he managed to qualify near the top of the field.

Clark described the Corvette's carburetors as "the size of hot tubs," and at the start Thompson buried the throttle, causing his Corvette to simply go "chug." There it sat, drowned in gas, while the rest of the field passed him. Thompson somehow got the car going again and miraculously managed to come around at the end of the first lap leading the field.

"You talk about pure, unbelievable, exultant joy," Clark told *Corvette Quarterly* in 1988. "That was the day, the hour, the second that Corvette became a genuine first-rank sports car. That thing came bellowing past like a rhino in heat, vacuuming up pavement behind it and I realized I had horribly misjudged Dr. D. Under that mild preppy exterior lurked Attila the Hun, and heaven help anyone who was ahead of him."

As Zora predicted, brake problems eventually got the best of Thompson, and Rudy Cleye's factory-assisted Mercedes 300SL Gullwing slipped into first. But Thompson had achieved the moral victory, finishing second overall and winning his class. He went on to win the C Production National Championship in 1956—not a bad beginning for this upstart American sports car.

Weeks later, at another West Coast function, Zora was at a reception in a hotel suite with Barney Clark and Thompson. Zora was toasting their Pebble Beach victory with a martini when in walked *Hot Rod* magazine's technical editor, Racer Brown, and Petersen Publications staff photographer, Bob D'Olivo. Brown came right out and asked Duntov to supply them with a Corvette that they could race in West Coast events, such as

Top: Thanks to support from Chevrolet, Dr. Dick Thompson, a Washington, D.C., dentist, garnered a class win at Pebble Beach in 1956 and went on to rack up Corvette racing wins on both coasts for years to come.

Bottom: Dick Thompson takes another checkered flag in this Corvette, which Duntov had originally prepared for Racer Brown and Bob D'Olivo of Petersen Publications.

Pomona, Del Mar and Riverside. Duntov blew smoke up at the ceiling, sipped his sweating martini and promised nothing.

The Chevy zone office called Brown after a few weeks to ask where he wanted the Corvette delivered. Duntov intended for Dick Thompson to drive this car in West Coast events so he wouldn't have to tow his other car across the country. When Thompson wasn't using it, Brown and D'Olivo were welcome to race it. For Zora, it was a good investment. In the hands of Thompson, Brown and Petersen ad salesman Bill Pollack, the car was virtually unbeatable and helped solidify Corvette's performance reputation in California.

Lessons learned during the 1956 racing season led Zora to create a special option package for Corvette customers in 1957. Known as RPO (regular production option) 684, it consisted of heavier front springs, an extra leaf in the rear springs, a larger front anti-roll bar, a tighter steering ratio, a limited slip differential and ventilated cast-iron brake drums with cerametallic linings. It cost $725. Combined with the availability of fuel injection that year, RPO 684 elevated the Corvette into a formidable sports car.

A Serious Setback

Zora's growing momentum in the world of sports cars slowed after an incident at the GM Proving Ground at Milford in April 1956. It happened while he was testing a Corvette.

Zora took very seriously his role in continuing to develop Corvette street cars. He was intimately involved in all phases of the process— even sorting out mechanical changes himself on the test track. Zora was a master at squeezing every ounce of performance out of his Corvettes, but to do so, he often put himself at considerable risk.

One Saturday he was called in to test one of Maury Rosenberger's cars, which had a handling problem. It was a last-minute request, and this particular Corvette was not equipped with seatbelts, nor was Zora wearing a helmet.

At the time, Corvette seats provided so little lateral support that Duntov would have a large mechanic sit in the passenger seat for the express purpose of bracing Zora in the driver's seat. After a few laps the safety officials at Milford, who insisted that for high-speed tests of this kind that only the driver be in the car, called in Zora and his passenger. Zora went driving off alone and on his first lap, after sliding out of the driver's seat, he lost control of the car. He tried vainly to regain control, but the Corvette jumped a ditch and in the process Zora jammed his head into the roof of the car, which broke his back.

Zora couldn't move afterwards and was fearful that he had been paralyzed. He was rushed to a local hospital, where he regained movement. He was later transferred to a better facility closer to his home. After being in the hospital for several weeks, he was put into a body cast that ran from his armpits to below his waist. The cast was enormously heavy, and Duntov threatened to have GM design staff construct a lighter one, but his doctors later agreed to use some lighter materials. He wore the cast through the summer of 1956 and had it removed just before Labor Day, when the doctors replaced it with a back brace.

While he was recovering from his injuries, he was under doctor's orders to stay away from the office, but since it was a critical period for the development of fuel injection, Ed Cole asked if Zora could work one hour a day. Zora agreed, but this led to greater amounts of time at the office and soon he was toiling all day. Because he couldn't wear pants with the cast, he wore a Scottish tartan kilt instead. Zora didn't care about the potential embarrassment. He had become a hot commodity, more engaged in his work than ever before, and he was determined that no physical injury would slow him down. A sea change was happening at GM, and Zora was at its forefront. He was not about to be caught on the sidelines.

Building a Real Race Car

Duntov had an unwitting ally in his quest for a purpose-built race car—Harley Earl, the father of the Corvette. The ostentatious designer was an avid racing fan and wanted to see his creation mixing it up on the racetrack with the best of the European race cars. Earl had earlier put together a racing Corvette—the SR-2 (Sebring Racer)—for his son Jerry. Designed by Robert Cumberford, the car looked flashy with its rear deck fin and a front end that had been extended by ten inches. It also represented one of the first racing applications of fuel injection. The car featured brake-cooling ducts that ran through the middle of the doors.

But the SR-2 was heavier than a production Corvette and suffered from the same braking problems. Still, stock car driver Buck Baker drove it to finish second place at the 1957 Daytona Speed Weeks in the flying mile at 152.86 mph, and Pete Lovely and Paul O'Shea finished 16th at Sebring. Dick Thompson raced it later that year at Road America, but, as Karl Ludvigsen recounted, it proved to be a better show car than a racer. Several SR-2s were built; one went to Bill Mitchell and another cosmetic street version was built for GM boss Harlow Curtice.

Given the SR-2 experience, Earl knew GM was going to have to up the ante, so he acquired a Jaguar D-Type racer from Jack Ensley of Indianapolis. Ensley had raced this D-Type at Sebring, and had won third place co-driving with Bob Sweikert. Earl brought the Jag into Design Staff and suggested installing a modified Chevy small-block V-8 in the car, knowing all along that this would simply prod Chevy Engineering into building its own car. He was right.

When Duntov heard about the idea, he objected, seeing a host of engineering problems in what Earl was proposing. He didn't know that Earl was playing him like a fiddle. Duntov, of course, wanted to design and build a purpose-built racer himself—not race a Jaguar with a Chevy engine in it. But such a project would have to be properly timed and sold to the right people. As it turned out, the timing was right. Ed Cole wanted to win Le Mans as much as Duntov did, and Cole indicated that he would consider any viable proposal brought forward by Duntov. So Zora put together a design for the car, and when Cole took the plan forward, the car received the blessing of top management.

As opposed to a year earlier at Sebring, there was no question as to who would lead the effort—it would be Zora Arkus-Duntov. This is what Duntov had wanted all along—a purpose-built race car. It was exactly the kind of thing he had hoped to be able to do at GM when he joined the company in 1953. Unlike his earlier experiences with the Arkus race car, his Indy Talbot or the Allard, he could now draw upon the vast resources of the largest company on earth. Impressed with Zora's knowledge and perspective on sports cars and happy with the progress he was making on fuel injection, Cole supported Zora's request.

There were, however, fewer than six months to build and test a car before Sebring came around again. Not deterred by the tight deadline, Duntov created a mini-skunk works in a walled-off area of the Chevrolet Engineering Center. There he worked in close proximity with handpicked people who were in a position to throw themselves totally into the project. Zora was now playing maestro. He looked like a professor, with his close-cropped white hair, crisp button-down shirts and black horned-rim glasses. Duntov diligently worked the arena, cigarette dangling from his lips, while keeping his people pumped up and focused. For months, the team lived amid the mock-ups and the drawings. As the car took shape, parts were laid out symmetrically on the table. Later, a frame and a body became the center of the action.

Meanwhile, over at Design Staff, a body shape was emerging under the direction of Bob McLean. The shape retained a fresh American appearance, with plenty of Corvette cues like side coves and a toothed grille, plus some D-Type Jaguar and Mercedes 300SL features thrown in. Plans called for the race car body to be made out of magnesium—which was lighter than fiberglass. A fiberglass body was used for the test mule.

Extensive testing was conducted with the body to reduce forces that would hamper the performance or stability of the car. During wind tunnel tests at the GM Technical Center, the car's body was coated with tufts of yarns, which helped identify a high-pressure area near its tail. For a time, Duntov considered a reverse-flow process to cool the rear brake, as opposed to the typical use of ducting from the front of the car such as that used in the 1956 Sebring race cars. Since the body program was behind schedule, Duntov actually considered running the car without a body at all.

Underneath the skin, the car was built with weight savings in mind. Power came from a fuel-injected 283-cubic inch Corvette engine with aluminum cylinder heads. Thanks to this and some other aluminum componentry, the entire engine weighed only 450 pounds—some 80 pounds less than the production Corvette engine.

Top: Duntov and his team worked in this mini-skunk works in a walled-off area inside the Chevrolet Engineering Center.

Bottom: Duntov and body engineer Jim Premo inspect the suspension of the SS, which featured a relatively sophisticated de Dion rear axle that attached the rear wheels to a transverse rigid member.

The most important component of any race car is the frame, and Duntov had little time to make critical decisions. While the Jaguar D-Type had a monocoque or unibody frame, Duntov went with a tubular space frame because of timing considerations. According to Karl Ludvigsen, a good example of how to do it already existed in the Mercedes 300SL road car, and so Duntov obtained one and used it as a basis for the SS. The SS frame was carefully welded out of chrome molybdenum steel tubing and weighed only 180 pounds.

The SS featured a de Dion rear axle, which affixed the rear wheels to a transverse rigid member. Here, because of limited time, Duntov elected to go with the tried and true de Dion instead of a pure independent setup. While brakes were always a concern, Duntov once again went with the cerametallic linings and finned drum units, because a suitable disc braking system wasn't available. The brake drums were from Chrysler. The system featured two vacuum servos, one of which operated the front brakes modulated by pedal pressure. The rear servo was connected by a vacuum system designed to react to the amount of pedal pressure and front brake force while adjusting the rear braking to that pressure. Duntov added yet another twist with a special driver-adjustable switch consisting of mercury inside a glass tube, which would move under deceleration to further control the amount of rear braking applied. Despite the high-tech nature of the system, time did not permit proper development, a fact that would have later repercussions.

While Duntov was working around the clock in building the SS at the GM Tech Center in Detroit, John Fitch was once again managing the racing team, which included an SS mule, the SS race car and four other production Corvettes. The mule benefited from over 2,000 miles of testing and showed immense promise as a race car. Thanks to the space frame, the potent small-block V-8 and the de Dion rear suspension, the SS was beginning to look like a winning combination. During testing, two of the greatest drivers in motor racing history tested the SS mule, and both walked away impressed.

Juan Manuel Fangio and Stirling Moss both drove the SS during a Friday practice session before Saturday's race. Fangio quickly shaved two seconds off his best time from the previous year, set in a Ferrari. Rumor was that Fangio had signed a contract to drive the SS at Sebring pending his approval of the car, but was released when it was uncertain whether the SS would be ready on time. Fitch denies this. Moss for his part remarked that the SS mule was one of the finest cars he had ever driven. He was also pursued by Chevrolet to drive the SS but was already committed, so a contract was inked with Carroll Shelby. But Shelby also dropped out and joined the Argentinean on the Maserati team when it looked as if the SS wouldn't arrive. Finally Fitch signed his old teammate from the Mercedes team, Italian Piero Taruffi.

Duntov almost certainly would have made a concerted effort to drive himself had it not been for his broken back a year earlier and the greater priority of getting the SS ready to run. For a while, it appeared that Zora might be able to drive if a second car could be completed on time for the race. But it was not to be, according to Zora, after Mauri Rose and the head of GM research, N. H. McCuen, crashed another mule at the Proving Ground. That put to an end to any hopes Zora entertained about driving. It appeared that Duntov's days as a driver, at least in major races, were over. His position at GM just wouldn't permit him to devote the time necessary to do both racing and engineering, and engineering the cars was more important than driving them.

Duntov was 48 years old in 1957, a relative senior citizen out on the racetrack, but he was still quite capable of driving. He had certainly demonstrated his endurance driving skills in winning his class two years earlier at Le Mans in the Porsche. And he still managed to log some 2,000 miles testing the SS. Still, many of his contemporaries questioned his talent. Mauri Rose had already doubted his ability behind the wheel, and Fitch was only slightly kinder. "I had ways of appraising his driving ability," said Fitch. "I saw him on the road at Le Mans in his Porsche, but I was in something much faster. I don't know of any lap times or anything that were comparable to anyone I did know."

Jim Rathmann took a somewhat more philosophical view: "From what I've seen of the guy he was brave and had plenty of guts. But when you're driving race cars you've got to do it every week. Zora didn't drive enough to get really good. You have to make a living. He didn't have the time to go out and run like the rest of the guys." Rathmann described Duntov's raw determination behind the wheel. During a test session at the GM Arizona Proving Ground, Duntov was out on the track with Rathmann testing modified 348 engines. Recalls Rathmann, "Zora and I agreed that we would run up to 4,000 rpm and then punch it. I went up to 4000 and he passed me flat out, so I caught him and started banging the side of him. But he wouldn't shut it off. He would never back off."

Still, not driving was a bitter pill for Zora to swallow. The SS represented his most comprehensive effort yet to build a car that could win on the world's endurance circuits. Luckily, Zora was too busy preparing the car to dwell on the issue.

The SS at Sebring

The SS race car finally arrived at Sebring the day before the race. During the trip down, mechanics had been tending to last-minute details in the truck, not the least of which was the appearance of the car, a stunning shade of metallic blue. Undeniably pretty, the car was far from ready to race. The SS was immediately moved into a hangar, where mechanics once again swarmed over it trying to get it ready in a matter of hours. To hear the SS's raucous V-8 explode to life in the cavernous walls of the hangar brought smiles to the giddy observers. It was a new day at Chevrolet.

Unfortunately, neither Fitch nor Duntov had time to enjoy the moment. The race car's magnesium body proved to be a heat conductor instead of an insulator and turned the cockpit into a toaster oven. For the race, mechanics cut away the lower body panels near the exhausts, which was where most of the heat radiated from, and insulation was also packed inside the cockpit in the vain hope of keeping the driver comfortable. The mechanics also installed new brakes, and Fitch went out for a practice run with Zora riding shotgun. According to Zora, Fitch was nervous and applied the brakes hard before they were sufficiently warmed up. The resulting spin flat-spotted a tire.

Fitch started the race and managed to hold sixth place for several laps despite flat-spotting another tire due to unpredictable brakes. Still, the car ran comfortably with the other cars and even pulled away from the D Jaguars on the straights. But things started to disintegrate quickly after

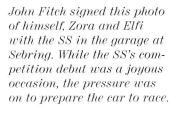

John Fitch signed this photo of himself, Zora and Elfi with the SS in the garage at Sebring. While the SS's competition debut was a joyous occasion, the pressure was on to prepare the car to race.

the SS rolled into the pits with a dead engine. The problem was a faulty coil connection that resulted in a 15-minute pit stop. Fitch then had to replace the coil out on the circuit. Things got worse later when the rear suspension began chattering uncontrollably over bumps, with the tires actually rubbing against the tops of the fenders.

Undrivable and overheated, the Corvette SS was officially retired by Piero Taruffi after its twenty-third lap. In the end the culprit was a rubber bushing at the chassis end of one of the lower rods that provided the de Dion tube with lateral location. Said Duntov later: "It was doomed to fail. If the fitter was not familiar with the installation procedure for these bushings, he could split them during the assembly of the joint. This one had been split in just this way and thus became a built-in focal point for failure. The design itself was not to blame." Zora later told writer Don Sherman, "If a suspension bushing had not failed, the heat from the engine and exhaust would have soon fried the driver. It was then that I switched my mental gears to mid-engine to get rid of this huge heat generator in front of the car."

Zora takes the Corvette SS for a test run at Sebring prior to the race in 1957. His responsibilities in preparing the SS for competition precluded him from actually driving in the race.

After Sebring, Duntov felt good enough about the potential of the SS to proceed with the construction of cars for Le Mans. Knowing the heat conductivity problems with magnesium, Duntov planned to go back to a fiberglass body. While it was rumored that Briggs Cunningham had been hired to conduct the Le Mans effort, no offer was made, but Cunningham would surface again in 1960 in conjunction with another Corvette Le Mans racing effort. Entries for three Corvettes for the 1957 24 hours of Le Mans had been requested and granted before the Sebring race through the offices of a certain "M. St. Giles," the alias being the name of the district in Brussels where Zora was born.

The AMA Ban

The SS would never make it to Le Mans. Zora received a phone call while vacationing in Florida after Sebring advising him that the Automobile Manufacturers Association was discouraging major auto manufacturers from racing. In the late 1950s safety was a big topic among politicians. The sentiment in Washington was that auto racing sent all the wrong messages to impressionable youth. Top GM management was quick to accept the new policy, and by June 1957 word was passed down at GM to terminate all Chevy's racing agreements and activities. Early in May, Duntov was ordered to scrap every fragment of the SS project except for the race car itself. At that time, three chassis frames existed, as well as the actual racecar, the mule and many other components.

Duntov was stunned. The rug had been pulled right out from under him after only one race with a very promising sports racer. Even Ed Cole appeared helpless to do anything about it. Would it be worth staying at General Motors under these circumstances?

Duntov could still have taken a position at Porsche in Germany, but he had tasted enough success at GM during the previous three years and wasn't ready to abandon all his efforts. The SS was just one program and he sensed there would be others. He trusted Ed Cole. Duntov had developed a strong sense of ownership with the Corvette and felt there was much he could still do.

After two years of managing Chevrolet's Sebring effort, Fitch was more embittered than Duntov. When asked to compare his experience at GM with that at Mercedes, Fitch didn't mince words: "I was initially quite excited to think of all GM's capability being devoted to road racing. However, it didn't pan out because they had no background and no real corporate interest. Ed Cole was the prime mover and he brought everyone else along. But there wasn't much support or real substance beyond that. Getting the Corvettes ready for the first Sebring burst the bubble completely. It was pretty negative."

Fitch may have been overly critical, considering that the SS was literally thrown together in a matter of months and yet broke the track record at Sebring by two seconds its first time out. Sure, it wasn't developed sufficiently to finish its only race, but automotive historians could only wonder what might have been if GM had not pulled out of racing. Fitch himself admitted that the basic chassis of the SS was a good one. "If we had enough time, we could have made a very good race car out of it."

The SS would not be relegated forever to a museum. Zora rolled it out again in 1959 at the opening of the Daytona International Speedway. He lapped the two-and-a-half-mile banked track at 155 mph. The SS showed even greater speed at the GM Desert Proving Ground at Mesa, Arizona, where it lapped a high-speed test loop at 183 mph. These runs contributed to the mystique of the SS and added fuel to speculation over what the car might have done had GM not pulled the plug. Without question, the car added substance to the growing legacy of Zora Arkus-Duntov.

FOURTEEN

Zora was becoming increasingly comfortable with American life in the mid-1950s, living in the suburbs and commuting to work in a Corvette.

Growing Roots

I n late 1957, for the first time in his life and almost five years after he joined General Motors, Zora was establishing roots, both professionally and personally. He received his first title that year, becoming director of high performance for Chevrolet. He had accomplished enough during his tenure at GM to warrant consideration for this special new position, which was designed to leverage his growing visibility as a performance expert.

On the surface, the position appeared to be more like a public relations job than a post with any real engineering clout. Chevrolet Engineering at that time was subdivided into multiple groups, which often competed with each other for resources and budgets. As Duntov explained many years later, key decisions were still routed through top managers such as Harry Barr and Ed Cole.

It was, however, Zora's first management position at GM, and with it came a stronger sense of connection to the company. Zora was determined to make something out of his role, regardless of how much power he actually possessed. Rather than acting solely on the agendas of others, he could now establish his own. He could finally begin to use GM resources to pursue his own visions.

The position involved developing components and engines for racing applications as well as working on high-performance street applications like the Corvette. Ever since 1955, when stock car racer Herb Thomas drove a Chevy to its first NASCAR win at Darlington, Cole had been looking for ways to encourage more stock car racing teams to run Chevys. Zora had already begun to assist in this effort.

Initially, Duntov had only one man assigned to him, a chassis expert named Harold Krieger, who was joined later by an engine man, Dick Keinath. Although Zora had not selected the men, his mission would be to shape them and free their minds to think creatively. In time these two men were exposed to a leader who brought a perspective to his job unlike anyone

Opposite: Things were looking up for Zora in 1957, as he parlayed his earlier successes to gain a new job title—director of high performance for Chevrolet.

they had ever worked with before. Previously, they might have been exposed to the kind of career automotive engineer who starts out designing door latches and moves on to window mechanisms. Zora was different; he was a visionary who spoke an entirely different language. His performance perspective was eye-opening for his subordinates, not many of whom had started out as enthusiasts.

A Different Kind of Manager

Initially, Zora was reserved and businesslike in his demeanor. To his subordinates, he often seemed aloof, and his thick Russian accent and fractured English sometimes made him difficult to understand. "He was still not speaking English well," said Keinath. "We would have to figure out what he was saying."

Duntov, as it turned out, had a lot to say. He regarded himself as a born educator, and whenever he worked with people, he tried to educate them as well as get the job done. He often held court with his tiny group in free-form discussions in his glass-walled office at the GM Tech Center in Warren. Topics were usually how to get more power out of an engine or how to solve a suspension problem. Typically, Duntov could be seen with a cigarette dangling from his mouth as he worked with his slide rule.

Zora gave his team a long leash and encouraged them to work through problems and think around obstacles. "He had as many ideas as I had," said Keinath. "He worked on valve designs, manifold designs, ports, dams, different things. What impressed me the most was that he knew engines, chassis, brakes and body. He was like a Maurice Olley except that he was more versatile."

Rather than work on assignments that came from the top down, Zora's group began to create its own agendas and would try to sell them through the corporation. "He would come up with things that I never heard of before: new induction systems and the like," said Dick Keinath. "It was only after I had been with Zora that I realized that we were the innovators right within the corporation," he added. "We ended up doing the planning, development or proposals between Harold Krieger and Duntov and myself. Previously, I was used to management telling us what to do, but with Zora it was just the reverse. Our little three-man group began to feel like we were the engine and chassis group for the whole corporation."

Both Keinath and Harold Krieger always felt challenged by Duntov, and both spent many long hours trying to outthink him. After everyone had gone home for the day, Keinath and Krieger would sit in an office late into the evening and trade ideas. "We'd sit around and ask where we could make things better," said Keinath. "It was always after 5 p.m. because we couldn't get anything creative done during the day; we did our best thinking after hours."

Duntov took an active interest in everything his group was doing. Unlike most managers of his day, he would go up to the drafting room regularly to check work in progress, such as a cylinder head design or part of an engine. He regularly visited the dynamometer cell and watched and listened as his engines were being tested. According to Larry Drake, who later joined the group, Duntov felt that engines had a personality, and he wanted to stay acquainted with them. "He would often say to me, 'Larry, it's trying to tell us something,'" said Drake.

Duntov also ordered flow tests for tuning intake and exhaust port designs long before it became a standard procedure. He would take a proposed intake port design and have it mocked up out of wood or plastic and bolt it together. The machinists would put a valve in it and set it on a carburetor flow device, which would suck the air through it with the valve at different lift positions as they recorded flow and vacuum rates. Changes were made with clay in an attempt to maximize flow.

Later, in trying to induce more swirl into the intake ports of a particular engine to promote more complete combustion, Zora ordered an intake port made out of clear plastic. Zora then lit a cigarette and blew smoke through it to see if he could detect a swirl. Today such things are done by computer, but in the mid-1950s everything was done by seat-of-the-pants procedures.

Establishing a Racing Presence

A major assignment on the racing front was to create competitive engines for Chevrolet, and as early as late 1956, Zora began efforts to ensure the competitiveness of the small-block Chevy working with outside engine builders like Smokey Yunick in Daytona Beach. But it was difficult for Zora's small group in Detroit to provide the level of interaction with the race teams that was needed for them to stay competitive.

To support the effort at a location closer to the action, GM organized the Southern Engineering and Development Company (SEDCO) in Atlanta in fall 1956. Florida-based racer Jim Rathmann, who would go on to win the Indy 500 in 1960, was hired as the general manager of SEDCO. He reported to Vince Piggins. But it was Zora's group that would provide the engineering know-how to keep Chevrolet competitive.

"Ed Cole called me up and asked me if I could run the racing operation," said Rathmann. "I was racing Olds and Chevys at the time. I turned him down three times and he said if I took the job, then I'd qualify for a Chevy franchise. He then promised if Chevy won the championship, he'd help me get a franchise. I asked him who he wanted to be champion. He told me Buck Baker. Well, Baker won and I got my Chevy franchise."

Once SEDCO was set up, Cole ordered five cars through the sales department along with heavy-duty equipment and sold them to SEDCO for a nominal sum. Cole had a list of teams to which he wanted Chevy to supply cars and engines.

"Approach was, if you want to race, we have a car for you," said Duntov. Chevrolet began supporting three different series, including the Grand National, the Convertible Circuit and Short Track Circuits, as well as the Daytona Beach speed runs for the Pure Oil Manufacturer Trophy. Drivers in the Chevy stable included some of NASCAR's top names at the time, including Curtis Turner, Joe Weatherly, Junior Johnson, Rex White, Ned Jarrett, Buck Baker and Jim Reed. SEDCO also supported Corvette racers, such as Paul Goldsmith, Jim Jeffords and Dick Thompson.

Just when the program was beginning to show some promise, however, SEDCO was disbanded, due to GM's conformance with the AMA racing ban in 1957. Rather than being scrapped, much of the equipment was given away to racing teams. According to Paul Van Valkenburgh in his inside account of Chevrolet motor sports, titled *Chevrolet—Racing?*, everyone was paid off, and SEDCO simply disappeared.

Performance out the Back Door

After the AMA racing ban, Duntov, Piggins and Rathmann conspired to find some means of staying in racing. "We were concerned that if we dropped out, even for one year, we were out of it," said Rathmann. With this in mind, they approached Ed Cole about establishing a front organization. Cole approved, and the Advanced Marine Corporation was born. It would be based in Miami and Jim Rathmann would again be the manager.

While Advanced Marine produced some marine engine components, including a Corvette marine engine called the Terminator, its primary business was supplying NASCAR teams with the latest technology from Zora's engine group in Detroit.

At the top of their agenda was implementing a switch to a larger displacement engine, since the small block was beginning to lose its edge against Chrysler and Ford. An all-new engine was in the pipeline. The new power plant, the 348, was intended as a truck block, and Cole wanted to use it as Chevrolet's competitive torchbearer. Despite the corporate ban, Zora was charged with making the new 348 into a competitive engine. He worked in secret with Keinath and Rathmann at Advanced Marine.

GM documents show payments of over $100,000 to Rathmann over a three-year period, from 1958 to 1960. Build orders sent to Detroit from

Advanced Marine included valve springs, intake and exhaust valves, Moraine 400 bearings and crankshafts. All such requests were sent directly to the Chevrolet Engineering Center, "Attention: Z. A. Duntov."

Making the 348 competitive proved to be a challenging project for all involved. Rathmann himself minced no words when it came to the 348, declaring: "That thing was a hunk of junk. We did everything possible to make that thing work, even getting drag racer Bruce Crower involved."

Keinath was softer in his sentiments but was equally frustrated. "It was a real challenge to make the W-engine into a real engine," said Keinath. "We were spoiled by the small-block. It would instantly respond more quickly to our inputs as engineers. The camshaft timing [and] combustion chamber were so compatible."

Occasionally, Zora conducted secret meetings with top race teams. During the summer of 1958, Maury Rosenberger of Chevy Engineering summoned Duntov to the oval at Trenton, New Jersey. Duntov did as he was told and was sitting up in the stands wearing his Ray Bans while dragging on a cigarette when a man approached him and asked for a light.

"You are Zora Duntov?" the man asked.

"Yes," replied Duntov.

"I will be leaving shortly," the stranger continued. "Please wait a few minutes and then follow me."

Duntov followed the man's instructions and soon climbed into the back seat of a car for a clandestine meeting with Buck Baker. Baker had been using the Chevy 348-cubic-inch engine without success and wanted to know what he had to do to make it competitive.

"He cry on my breast, saying 'this is breaking, that is breaking,'" Zora recounted almost 30 years later.

Zora went back to Detroit, started aggressive dynamometer tests on the 348 and encouraged Keinath to become more aggressive. Keinath designed a new camshaft for the engine and began experimenting with hydraulic lifters. It had never been done before on a Chevy racing engine and even Duntov was skeptical. "But it worked and he admitted he was wrong," said Keinath.

Thanks to Duntov's efforts—along with support from Harold Krieger and Dick Keinath—Chevys started winning again on the stock car circuit. Chevys finished first, second and third at the all-new Daytona International Speedway in 1959 in two different races, and Junior Johnson won the 1960 Daytona 500 in a Chevy.

From the 348 W engine, the group went on to develop the 409, which built a reputation among street drag racers as an engine to be reckoned with. The Beach Boys even wrote a popular song about it called "She's Real Fine, My 409."

While Zora was open to working with outsiders like Rathmann on the stock car scene, he was more selective about whom he was willing to work with in road racing. When a race driver named Carroll Shelby approached Ed Cole in 1959 about racing special aluminum-bodied Corvettes in Europe, Zora helped nix the program. He hadn't forgotten about 1956, when Cole had brought in John Fitch to run the Corvette racing effort at Sebring. Zora didn't want Shelby—who had won Le Mans that year driving an Aston Martin with Roy Salvadori—to do the same thing in Europe.

Despite Zora's opposition, Shelby and a fellow Texan, Gary Laughlin, commissioned Italian coachbuilder Scaglietti to build three aluminum-bodied cars that bore no resemblance to a Corvette. Shelby claimed these cars were almost a thousand pounds lighter than a standard Corvette. A race car and two street cars were built, but they were never raced. Interestingly, Shelby then took a similar concept to Ford, which resulted in marrying the British AC Ace body and chassis with Ford 260 and 289 V8 engines—thereby creating the AC Cobra. The Cobra would prove to be the nemesis of the Corvette—and Zora—in the years to come.

The Think Tank Within GM

Over time, Zora's group grew in size and stature. Zora was living his dream now, in control of a small group of men who were capable of writing a few chapters of automotive history—under his leadership, of course. His group would become a test lab for aggressive new engine configurations and the bold use of new materials like aluminum. Car enthusiasm was contagious around Zora and many in his group soon became disciples who would go on to influence other programs.

One of the first engines the group created under Duntov was a three-valve overhead cam configuration built on the small block. It featured two intake ports and one exhaust port, since there wasn't room for a fourth valve due to the location of the head bolts on the small block. Zora wasn't greatly concerned about having two exhaust valves, according to Fred Frincke, who joined the group in 1959, because he felt the piston would push out the exhaust gases anyway.

Based on his Talbot and Ardun experiences, hemi heads were also high up on Zora's agenda. Frincke noted that the team designed a hemi-head configuration for the small block. Zora wanted to go further, however, and design a cylinder head that would incorporate a hemi splayed-valve configuration with a fully machined combustion chamber. The exhaust valve was offset to bring the spark plug in from the side instead of running it through the rocker cover.

"That's the way we did it," Fincke told interviewer Pete Lyons in 1989. "We designed a sphere intersecting a cone and located the intake valve to the right of the sphere while the exhaust valve was offset to the left. The spark plug was inserted from the outboard side. It seemed to work out pretty good."

Duntov also directed his group to design interchangeable cylinder heads that could work with either pushrods or overhead cams. Eventually the group also experimented with different cam-drive systems including belt- and gear-driven cams. The group went on to build a 327 cubic inch overhead-cam small block and later an overhead-cam 427.

These were largely free-form exercises since the team was not necessarily designing engines for particular cars. Many of the components were improvised, since at the time Zora was simply trying to determine what worked without worrying about manufacturing considerations. But with a high-volume manufacturer like GM, production costs and manufacturing considerations and potential sales volumes would become key determinants in whether these grand ideas ever reached the street. In his zeal to do great things, he often didn't pay enough attention to real world realities, a fact that would come back to haunt him.

While willing to promote an open dialogue, Zora, a man of immense pride, would draw the line if a subordinate challenged him too vigorously. "If someone disagreed with Duntov too persistently," said Fincke, "he'd get very irritated and would say, 'You're making me mad.'"

"Zora was like a Baptist preacher," said Gib Hufstader, a chassis and brake man in the group. "He was so zealous, no one could argue with him. All these other managers would try to present facts and reality. Zora presented pure passion."

"He was 100 percent honest," said Denny Davis, who joined the group in 1959. "I had no problem dealing with him because of his honesty. But if you got into an argument with him, and he was right, he'd chew your gut. I got into an argument with him once and he said he'd bet me a week's coffee he was right. Well, as it turned out, he was right, so I owed him coffee for a week."

While Duntov had very strong opinions on the approaches his group used to tackle engineering problems, the group members managed to occasionally work their own agendas. Davis, for example, designed a hydraulic, self-adjusting cam to cure a valve-lashing problem. "I just didn't advertise this to him," said Davis. "I would do an assortment of options on programs I worked on."

Similarly, Keinath took a 283 small block and bored it out into a 302 to put into a Corvette. "Zora asked me why," said Keinath, "and I replied because we can do it and the 348 big-block W engine wouldn't fit in a Corvette. He questioned whether I could do it without more clearance between bores. But he finally let me do it and I ran it in the lab and it was a great car. After I installed it in the Corvette, Duntov drove it first and loved it. It became the 327 in 1962."

Keinath then turned his attention to solving the litany of problems associated with the 348/409 block. According to former *Hot Rod* editor Ray Brock, the engines were suitable for drag racing and short tracks, but the engine could not stand up to the competition on the faster ovals such as Daytona, Darlington and Milwaukee.

That inspired Keinath, now working under Don MacPherson, to design an all-new engine in fall 1962 that overcame all the original limitations of the original 348 truck block. It started off as a 409, the limit of displacement NASCAR allowed Chevrolet, but later became a 427 after a NASCAR rules change. The new engine was called the Mark II, also known as the "porcupine engine" because of its splayed valves, which protruded at unequal angles like the quills of a porcupine. It was similar to a concept that Zora had used on his hemispherical Ardun cylinder heads.

Keinath had created a masterpiece, which powered Junior Johnson and Johnny Rutherford to convincing wins in the 100-mile Daytona 500 qualifying races in 1963. His new racing motor was quickly dubbed by the press as the "mystery engine." It was easy to understand why. "We were 10 miles per hour faster than anybody else," said Keinath. During the actual Daytona 500, Johnson was running away from the field before dropping a valve on the backstraight which allowed Tiny Lund's Ford to emerge in the winner's circle. But Keinath and Chevrolet had made a statement. "After we won the qualifying races, all hell broke lose and we had to walk around in dark glasses and hats, since we weren't supposed to be here," said Keinath.

After Johnson's Daytona qualifying win, the engine quickly disappeared after being challenged by competitors. "We had to convince NASCAR that this engine was a production engine," said Keinath. "Ford knew it wasn't and so did Chrysler. The rules said that if it was a true production engine, it would have to be available for sale to Ford and Chrysler. Well, Ford bought one and they got one of my best engines."

No one in top management at GM knew anything about the program. "But everyone else with Chevy from general manager Bunkie Knudsen on down knew that we had it," added Keinath. Once top management became aware of this made-for-racing powerplant, it quietly went the way of other race-related projects, another victim of the AMA ban.

Still, the "Mystery Engine" became an example of what GM was really capable of and as Ray Brock recounted in the May 1963 edition of *Hot Rod*, the technology behind it was transferred into the 396 cubic inch V-8 that would later debut in the 1965 Corvette, the first big-block engine in the history of the car.

Most importantly, however, was the fact that the Mark II engine was a technology born out of the creative climate that Duntov had established in his early group. As the world was about to find out, there was much more where that came from.

Living the American Dream

Zora's transition into the culture of GM had a social counterpart—that of his adaptation to life in a large American industrial city. As a Russian native who had been pushed westward, Zora had been relatively homeless much of his life, without roots and therefore without attachment. Life at GM in the relative stability of a large Midwestern city offered a chance to establish some roots—perhaps a shot at the American dream—even though Detroit represented a stark contrast to Zora's past residences in cosmopolitan Berlin, Paris, London and New York. No longer in the land of ballet and bistros, Zora and Elfi found themselves in a white-collar social stratum of country clubs, dinner parties, banquets and barbecues. It was a long way from the streets of St. Petersburg with their torch-bearing revolutionaries or the avenues of Berlin, where Nazis had goose-stepped.

Although Zora spent his first months in Detroit at the Park Shelton Hotel (despite Olley's recommendation of the Abington), he wasted no time in finding a place in the suburbs. It happened after an acquaintance from within the auto industry invited him for a boat ride on Lake St. Clair, the large body of water connecting Lake Huron with Lake Erie via the Detroit River. Duntov accepted, commenting on how much he and Elfi would enjoy living on the lake. Zora had always been attracted to water, having lived on or near it in St. Petersburg, Paris and New York.

Hearing of Zora's yearnings, the acquaintance then offered to let Zora sublet his place on the lake while he wintered in Florida. The second floor of the unit, located over an enclosed boatwell, would be exclusively Zora and Elfi's. Zora commented that it would have been an ideal place through which to smuggle Canadian whiskey, a pastime of certain lake residents during Prohibition.

Zora and Elfi moved in later that summer, after Elfi joined him following an extended stay with her parents in London. Having been a vagabond most of his life, Zora had little use for some of the furnishings in the home, despite their potential value to someone else, such as an old grand piano in the living room. After Duntov commented that he didn't like the piano, the owner casually told him to throw it in the lake, so Zora took him literally: he grabbed an ax and hacked the piano into pieces, which he tossed into the water like so much junk. Horrified by Zora's action, Elfi recalled that she managed to save the ivory keys before Zora could toss them in as well.

Within a year or two, Zora and Elfi outgrew their unit and moved to a larger, French-style farmhouse on the lakefront in Grosse Pointe Shores. The house was set amid lush wooded property, which the Duntovs used to host many social gatherings with an ever-growing list of friends.

A large antique bathtub on legs, which Elfi used as a large flowerpot, dominated the front yard. Once, during a party the son of a noted Detroit auto executive got drunk and passed out amid the flowers in the tub.

Top: Elfi poses with her 1955 Corvette in her backyard along Lake St. Clair, near Detroit. Slowly but surely, she and Zora were growing deep roots in America.

Bottom: Zora made sure that Elfi had one of the first V-8 Corvettes, a 1955 in a special silver color.

When Zora discovered him still out cold the next morning, he decided to have a little fun by placing a burning candle in the sleeping man's hands, which raised the eyebrows of the drivers passing by.

Zora loved practical jokes. One of his favorites involved a fake mongoose that a racer named Jack Smith had sent to him. Smith had hoped to obtain a Chevy race car through Duntov, only to lose out on the deal because of the AMA ban. Zora called Smith personally to offer his apologies. Smith was so charmed by Zora that he sent him the fake mongoose as a gesture of good humor. "Mail man arrive one day with box with grille," said Zora. Inside was the mongoose mounted on a spring, which would fly across the room when the cage was opened. Zora used the animal for years afterward to startle unsuspecting visitors to his household.

Hopped-up pilot or prototype Corvettes that Zora was in the process of sorting out frequently occupied the driveway at Elfi and Zora's lakeshore house. During the early years, Zora bought Elfi a Harvest Gold 1955 Corvette with a dark green top. Later that year, he exchanged that car for a V-8 Corvette in a non production color—silver with a black racing stripe. Elfi became a fixture in the car as she drove up and down Lakeshore Drive on summer days with the top down.

Clubs were also an important component of society life in Detroit. Much of executive life centered around the many country clubs in nearby Oakland County. Duntov was never much for golf, so he and Elfi joined a boat/tennis club known as the "Old Club," located on Harsen's Island near the northern tip of Lake St. Clair.

Zora didn't allow himself very many personal luxuries but his boat was an exception. Ever since his youthful days exploring the waterways of St. Petersburg, he longed for the freedom and mobility a boat could provide, so he bought himself an Owens cabin cruiser and dutifully named it "Sea Witch" after Elfi.

Several years later, he replaced it with the "Sea Elf," a Chris-Craft wooden-hulled beauty. Zora only smiled whenever he was asked whether Elfi had inspired the names of both boats. Zora eventually installed twin Chevy big-blocks in the "Sea Elf," making it one of the fastest cruisers on Lake St. Clair. Zora took responsibility for the mechanics and upkeep of the boat while Elfi handled interior decoration.

When he wasn't at a race or a Corvette function, Zora would typically begin his summer weekends with a Friday night boat ride to the Old Club. He and Elfi would mix a Bloody Mary on the boat and take off, flying across the lake at full throttle.

Once docked at the Old Club, they'd enjoy a weekend of sun, friendships, a little tennis and evening cocktail parties by the pool. Costumed theme parties were popular, and Zora and Elfi once won a contest for a shipwreck party where he dressed as a pirate and she was attired in a slinky fishnet-style dress. Both would spend long days sunbathing off the back of their boat. Often they didn't return home until Monday morning. Elfi would stay and clean up the boat while Zora went back to work.

When they weren't out on the boat, Zora and Elfi enjoyed the amenities of Detroit. They were regulars at Baker's Keyboard Lounge, one of Detroit's oldest jazz clubs, as well as the London Chop House, which ranked among Detroit's finest restaurants. Introduced to the Chop House by *Detroit News* columnist Doc Greene, Zora soon became close friends with the proprietor, Les Gruber. Whenever the Duntovs hosted a party, they would purchase their wine directly from

The "Sea Elf" was a Chris-Craft wooden-hull boat powered by twin big-block Chevy engines.

Zora smoked most of his life and handled a cigarette with considerable aplomb. He also appreciated a good dry martini.

the Chop House, since good retail wine establishments were rare in Detroit. Elfi later reminisced that their parties combined GM corporate types with an eclectic mix of entertainers and dancers from around the country.

When socializing, Zora liked a good dry martini served "up," and would often stop for one on the way home at one of the many establishments that surrounded the GM Building. Elfi would often have another drink waiting for him when he got home, following Zora's carefully honed recipe, which called for Beefeaters gin and microscopic amounts of vermouth. "Zora couldn't boil water, but he could make a hell of a good martini," mused his former next-door neighbor, Lyle Tuck. He mixed the ingredients with cracked ice in a little white teapot and poured the elixir into a frosted martini glass. No olive.

With martinis went cigarettes. Zora was a lifelong smoker, starting back in Germany and continuing well into his 80s. He smoked Chesterfields back in Paris but later switched to unfiltered Camels and Pall Malls in New York and Detroit. He was an elegant smoker and frequently used a silver cigarette case, especially when going out for the evening. He sometimes used a cigarette as a tactical device, accurately targeting narrow billows of smoke at adversaries. Late in his 70s he developed a bad smoker's cough, but when he made up his mind to quit, he did it cold turkey without ever lighting up again.

At home, Elfi was a devoted partner who prepared meals, picked out Zora's clothes and even balanced the checkbook. She was a world-class cook, capable of everything from four-star soups to roast duck, and Zora ate better at home than he could at many of the finer restaurants. When he did go out, he often reverted to more simple dishes, such as a hamburger or shrimp or lobster. At buffet-style dinner parties, Elfi would get a plate of food for Zora before taking care of herself, much to the chagrin of the other women at the parties.

Duntov was a fine dresser, also thanks to his wife. She selected many of the elements of Duntov's European-style wardrobe, which featured smartly tailored tweed sports coats and slacks. Duntov occasionally wore an ascot, but Elfi was careful not to let Zora get too carried away with the fashion extremes of the times. They would sometimes lose their few inhibitions at parties and shock their conservative Detroit contemporaries by

Elfi's wearing her short skirts and Zora's donning his expressive sport coats and open-collared shirts, but Zora usually wore tasteful and slightly understated clothes.

Harking back to when she sewed gloves during wartime, Elfi was a terrific seamstress as well and created many of her own outfits, which usually looked like they came off exclusive racks at Saks Fifth Avenue or Bloomingdale's. She also expressed herself through painting, ceramics and metal work, often creating pieces of art based on Zora's accomplishments behind the wheel.

Indeed, America was becoming a comfortable place for Zora and Elfi. For the first time in their lives, they began to feel wanted and accepted. They were no longer resigned to being wandering vagabonds while fleeing the Germans or chasing job opportunities.

Spokesman Duntov

Zora's increasing comfort in America extended to his role as the ambassador for the Corvette on the speaking circuit. He brought his message to new audiences, including a group of advertising executives in New York. In an October 9, 1958, speech before the Madison Avenue Sports Car Driving and Chowder Society, Duntov linked performance not only with speed but also with safety.

In reacting to the safety lobby, which was largely responsible for the AMA ban on racing activities by manufacturers, Zora quipped, "Isn't it strange that speed is a generally recognized virtue in virtually any form of transportation but the automobile?" Yet in a purely engineering discussion, Duntov noted, "We have no choice but to label the speed of transportation as a virtue." He mentioned the astronomical growth in air travel during the 1950s at the expense of slower railroads and buses.

Zora did not define automotive speed in any literal, absolute sense; instead he took a broader view in terms of a yearly average speed computed over all kinds of roads and conditions under which a normal passenger car has to perform. "Within that framework, we can say that all factors in automobile design which contribute to the speed of transportation are performance factors," asserted Zora, citing windshield wipers and washers, headlights, brakes and tires. "Indeed" he concluded, "performance is not only synonymous with the speed of transportation, but also with safety."

"Of course, an automobile cannot perform by itself," said Duntov. "It lacks a brain, no matter how cleverly built, and this will remain so for years to come. So, when we speak of the performance of an automobile, we are actually speaking of the performance of a human being by means of an automobile. Within the frame of this concept, it becomes evident that the integration of the human being and the machine will be a very important factor in the realization of performance."

Zora, who was always drawn to race cars for their unsurpassed feeling of control and superiority over the environment, felt that it was critical for engineers and designers to properly integrate humans into the machines they drove. Throughout his career, Zora was an advocate for supportive seats and excellent visibility. His biggest disputes with the stylists at GM Design Staff were over letting so-called aesthetics get in the way of function.

It was somewhat ironic then, when Duntov showed a sneak peek at the 1959 Chevrolet —perhaps the most controversial Chevy design ever with its rear decklid accented by large fins that appeared to lie on their side to form eyebrows over the Chevy's wide teardrop taillights. Anticipating a negative reaction, Zora, in an uncharacteristic move, began to defend the stylists, saying, "Gentleman, I can hear exclamations, even the cry of outrage. Fins again!

"I must stand up under the fence of the stylists," Duntov continued. "It must be realized that stylists strive to achieve only one thing, and that is, visual appeal, visual effect, in the very same way a painter would strive to achieve the same thing. It makes as much sense to reproach the stylists as to reproach functionalism, or lack of observation of functionalism, as it stands to reproach Rembrandt because his women cannot perform as nursemaids."

The late 1950s represented the zenith of flamboyant, chrome-laden designs. While Zora expressed the long view in his speeches, he would soon grow to resent the sheer power that Design Staff held within the corporation, especially as it related to future Corvette designs.

The 1958–1960 Corvette itself fell victim to the chrome revolution, with the addition of a larger chromed-tooth grille, dual headlights with long chrome strips atop the front fenders, chrome adornments on the car's side coves and, in the case of the 1958 model, twin chromed spears over the trunk lid. Despite its gussied-up appearance, the Corvette was relatively restrained compared to other cars of the time.

Zora then talked about the engineering changes in the 1959 Chevy and stressed the range of horsepower available in the Chevy small-block V-8—185 horsepower to 290 horsepower in the same engine with the same bore and stroke. The only difference, he explained, lay in the fuel system and the camshaft. Zora stressed that brute power does not necessarily mean good performance. "The performance factor we will be concerned with will be the power transmitted to the wheels, and this will be determined by the engine and transmission combinations."

Zora then noted a significant technology transfer from racing the Corvette—the use of cerametallic brakes, which became an option on 1959 Corvettes as well as on police- package-base Chevrolets. Zora never cared for the weight that such systems added to his racing Corvettes, but the linings themselves worked well. "If they can stop a behemoth like the Corvette at Sebring, and after the race are ready to run another Sebring, that is proof of their function," said Zora.

"Since we became acquainted with the material and developed those brakes, we relentlessly tried to find a material which would combine anti-fade characteristics of cerametallic without their drawbacks of erraticness at low temperature." Duntov told the Chowder Society in New York that the new brakes were practically free from unpredictability and were fade-free under all driving conditions.

Zora always saw cars as extensions of himself, which explained his desire to race cars that he built himself. It also helped explain his preference for automobiles that had race car performance levels, even if creature comforts were nonexistent. He felt that the sharper one's reflexes behind the wheel, the more that man could become one with the machine and the more fulfilling and safer the driving experience would be.

After his 1956 Proving Ground accident, vehicle safety was an important theme in Zora's speeches, and he began to address the performance and safety limitations of average passenger car designs that could benefit from a performance-based philosophy. Before an audience of police officials in Michigan, Zora discussed the challenge of making safe yet fast pursuit vehicles out of regular production cars.

He was particularly sensitive to the issue of flat, unsupportive seats common in passenger cars of the day—seats that did not hold the driver properly in place—the very cause of the Proving Ground accident that had broken his back. "Since the conventional passenger car seat does not offer any lateral support, the driver tends to maintain his relative position by holding tightly onto the steering wheel, and could slide out of the driver's seat altogether." said Zora. "The seat belt is only partially effective since it holds the lower part of the body only. A little torso rest attached to the regular backed seat can go a long way toward contributing to precision control."

Zora also commented about the total lack of road feel in the power steering systems of the day and expressed the opinion that higher-effort manual steering was preferable to power steering. While admitting that some power steering systems were better than others, he felt that power steering fell short when compared to manual steering.

Turning to brakes, Zora commented that a consistent action is of paramount importance. Here again, the police officer cannot afford the high level of attention required to apply his brakes carefully. He should be able to apply the brake without locking up any of the wheels or risking loss of control because of lock-up.

"Only a rolling wheel has a sense of direction," said Zora, "and the moment the wheel is locked, it has no preference as to which way to go." The car with four locked wheels is at the mercy of natural forces and is totally out of control. Zora stated that from a stability viewpoint, it is preferable that the front brakes lock before the rear brakes, because if the front brakes lock first, the car will continue to travel in the same direction, whereas if the rears lock first, the car will tend to break away and swap ends.

Today, of course, we live in an era of supportive seats, antilock brakes, stability control systems and a number of other safety-related technologies that help a driver avoid an accident altogether. But Duntov was one of the first to actively put these technologies into the vocabularies of the media and other automotive opinion leaders. He also showed first hand that he had much more to offer the automotive world than just ways to make the Corvette go faster. The bigger question, however, was whether anyone at GM was listening.

FIFTEEN

Duntov tests the Chevrolet Engineering Research Vehicle (CERV I) at the GM Proving Ground in 1959. At the time, the vehicle was the most provocative performance machine yet created by GM.

The Mid-Engined Advocate

Throughout his lifetime, racing was Zora's core, his center. It was the need that drove all his other life choices. Given its importance, over the years Zora had developed a purist philosophy about automotive engineering, seeking drivetrain configurations that provided the best combination of power, weight distribution and visibility.

One of Zora's core beliefs was that the engine be located in the middle of the car, just ahead of the rear axle. It was an extension of his belief that sports and racing cars ought to be extensions of the human body. They should allow the driver the ultimate in movement and control— to be able to accelerate, change directions and stop in ways that were unimaginable back when Zora was a young boy in horse-and-buggy Russia.

To Zora, having this kind of mobility was the ultimate mastery of one's environment. It provided the ecstasy of taking life out to the very edge and the *control* of brushing close to danger and death and being able to walk away unscathed.

The Pragmatic View of a Mid-Engined Car

In a more practical sense, locating the engine close to the center of the car, thought Zora, is the ideal configuration for weight distribution. With weight more evenly distributed at all four wheels, handling improves. And without an engine in front of the driver, forward visibility is better.

But while these were desirable advantages for single-purpose racers, this configuration creates a number of drawbacks for production cars. A mid-engine cuts down on available space in the passenger compartment and reduces capacity. Engine cooling is compromised because of awkward radiator locations. And with the engine located just inches behind the cockpit, noise is a problem.

Despite these drawbacks, Zora felt that sports car buyers would tolerate a certain level of inconvenience if the performance tradeoffs were strong enough and the driver—if no one else—could be well-enough

Opposite: Duntov stands for this official GM portrait with CERV I. The vehicle encompassed many of the engineering agendas Duntov held dear.

integrated into the machine. After all, a sports car was never supposed to be a practical means of transportation. The rules are different. And in certain cases, sports car enthusiasts may regard the negatives as pluses—elements of a car's character and personality. They add to a car's not-for-everyone appeal.

By pushing dramatic new configurations for his sports cars, Zora saw the opportunity to personally define the dreams of car enthusiasts on a worldwide basis, and to help establish General Motors as a performance leader as well as a volume leader. Once again, Zora put aside the reality that most of GM was more preoccupied with volume than with performance figures. Despite the best efforts of Ed Cole and the staff of R&D, GM just didn't see itself as another Ferrari or Porsche. Yet Duntov maintained there was room enough to be both. In his eyes, GM could be a well-respected manufacturer of high-performance specialty cars and a high-volume provider of reliable transportation. Being both meant GM could create economies of scale. It could offer many more combinations of engines and drivetrains simply because the tooling costs could be amortized over many other car lines. And given its incredible resources, why shouldn't GM make the best performance cars in the world? To Zora, such a vision fit former GM Chairman Alfred P. Sloan's original notion of "a car for every purse and purpose."

The door was wide open in the 1959-1960 time period for GM to exert leadership in this area. Few manufacturers had even ventured into midship designs. It wasn't until the mid-1960s that the Lamborghini Miura debuted, followed by the de Tomaso/Ford Pantera and Ferrari 512 Boxer during the late 1960s and early 1970s.

A decade before those cars hit the market, Duntov was dreaming about one. He still remembered how the Germans dominated motor racing in the 1930s with the Mercedes and Auto Union grand prix cars. The Auto Union, with its engine mounted behind the driver, made an indelible impression on him. His experience in driving the 550 Porsches at Le Mans further embedded the advantages of mid-engined machines in Duntov's mind. He imagined taking everything the Germans had done to date and adding to it with better aerodynamics and lighter materials.

The climate for Zora's thinking was reasonably favorable at the time. Zora's bosses were aggressively pursuing new configurations for passenger cars in the mid-1950s, and Duntov played a role in a radically different chassis/drivetrain concept that Ed Cole had in mind for both Chevrolet mainstream passenger cars as well as the next-generation Corvette. The concept, called the "Q Chevrolet," had the engine placed in the front, but the transmission was located in the rear. The transaxle featured an integrated starter motor. The brakes were mounted inboard to reduce unsprung weight. According to Karl Ludvigsen, Zora was assigned to develop a Corvette version of the Q Chevrolet chassis. In designing the Q Corvette, Duntov made it very compact, with a much lower center of gravity than any previous Corvette. To permit the lowest possible placement of the engine, a dry sump or separate lubrication system was specified, which eliminated the oil pan.

While the layout provided subtle improvements, Duntov didn't think the transaxle shifted enough weight to the rear of the car to create any real performance advantages— "Like moving spare tire to rear of car," he said. The concept for the Corvette version of the car was later scrapped after Cole canceled the Q Chevrolet project.

Rather than accept defeat, Duntov pushed to do an all-new mid-engined car. Some of the Q car components still existed, and Duntov reasoned that he could make better use of them by placing the engine in back, ahead of the rear wheels. Cole approved, so Duntov and his team began to lay out Zora's new vision. However, fewer suspension and drivetrain components were available from the Q Chevrolet than Duntov had anticipated, and he and the GM Design Staff could never agree on how such a car should look. Duntov liked a short hood for better forward visibility, while Design Staff, particularly Bill Mitchell, favored a long-hooded look. These factors conspired to prevent the construction of a running prototype.

CERV I

It was then that Zora decided to head in a radically different direction. He wanted to gamble and build a car that had no chance for production, yet a machine that would surely create more controversy than anything GM had ever built. It would be the culmination of all his dreams, the successor to the great Auto Union car—a single-seat, open-wheel racer that would be more advanced than anything then gracing the racetracks.

Thinking back to the Auto Union, Duntov wanted to dispel the myth that a high-powered yet tail-heavy car was inherently dangerous. "If you have an automobile powered like lawn mower," said Duntov, "low performance—it doesn't matter if you build the car tail-heavy or front-heavy. When you build high-performance automobile, it begins to matter. I establish as a guide 40/60 max."

He knew full well that GM had cancelled all racing activities after the 1957 Sebring race, and he knew he'd have to sell Cole on the project using a different approach, so he carefully constructed a rationale based on things the corporation might learn in developing daring new powertrain configurations, especially with the new rear-engined Corvair currently in the pipeline.

Even though the official AMA racing ban was still on, Duntov was anxious to flex some muscle, to show the world that even though GM wasn't racing, it could be very competitive had the company chosen to manufacture racing cars. His new car would be a testbed showcase for all the best race car theory of the late 1950s in terms of both powertrain and aerodynamics and the use of lightweight materials.

The vehicle, known internally as the "R" car, was powered by a Chevy small-block V-8. It was the most exotic small-block yet devised. Its lightweight aluminum core was made of a high-silicone alloy that required no cylinder liners. The block weighed *90 pounds* less than its cast-iron counterpart. Other components were made of lightweight magnesium. The engine was otherwise similar to the stock 315-horsepower Corvette V-8 of 1960, with the same Duntov cam, solid lifters and stock crankshaft, bearings, rods, pinions and rings. But breathing refinements allowed it to put out 353 horsepower at 6,200 rpm.

According to internal GM documents, other power plants were tested in the car as well. Some seven different engine combinations were installed in the car, including cast-iron and aluminum-block versions in displacements of 283 and 327 cubic inches. Both cast-iron and ported and polished aluminum heads were employed as well as supercharged and turbocharged variations later on.

Larry Shinoda and Tony Lapine designed the body for the vehicle under studio head Ed Wayne. With only two layers of fiberglass, the body weighed only 80 pounds. Its design allowed the car to squat at speed for even better aerodynamics. According to Duntov, even the angle of the radiators contributed to higher downforce at speed, which was a fairly novel concept at the time. The complete dry weight of the machine (without gasoline or other fluids) was a meager 1,450 pounds.

The machine also featured one of the first uses of a fuel cell in a race car. Designed by U.S. Rubber at Duntov's urging, the cell was conceived to reduce the possibility of a fuel-fed fire. The rubber bladder was created to aircraft specifications with baffles and a foam core. It was built to withstand rigorous tests, including a parachute drop with a full tank from a high altitude.

Duntov again showed that he was ahead of his time. After the fatalities in the 1964 Indy 500, in which Eddie Sachs and Dave McDonald were killed in a fiery crash on the second lap, the United States Auto Club

The "Hillclimber" undergoes testing at the GM wind tunnel. The body was as sleek as anything that existed in racing at the time. It was designed to Zora's specifications by Larry Shinoda and Tony Lapine of GM Design Staff.

accepted Duntov's recommendation that Indy cars require a fuel cell. A similar unit would eventually be standard equipment in the 1975 Corvette.

The vehicle's transmission, a four-speed manual from the Corvette, was located in front of the differential. The differential featured a Halibrand casing with Chevrolet gears. While Duntov would have preferred disc brakes, the technology wasn't there yet, so he went with a set of all-aluminum drums mounted inboard and flanking the differential. Like the Corvette SS, the car featured the same variable braking control mechanism activated by a mercury switch.

As a forerunner of the 1963 Corvette Sting Ray, the rear suspension was independent and used the axle shaft as an upper link. "In passenger car and racing car, aim is identical," said Zora. "If you can find one piece to do what two pieces are supposed to do, that is good solution."

Duntov's first application of the car was to be another record run up Pikes Peak, much like the run he had taken in the 1956 Chevrolet. With 60 percent of its weight over the rear wheels, the car was ideally suited for hill climbs and, according to Karl Ludvigsen, it was quickly nicknamed the "Hillclimber" at Chevrolet.

In September 1960, the Hillclimber was ready for its test on Pikes Peak. Accompanying Zora to the mountain was Harold Krieger, two R&D mechanics and Al Rogers and Chuck Myers, who had assisted with the effort in 1956. The car was flown to Denver and Chuck Myers borrowed a trailer to tow the Hillclimber with the truck he provided. A film crew came out to Colorado to help document the occasion. They caught some dramatic footage of Zora deftly driving up the mountain. The crew also mounted a camera on the rear of the car to create one of the first uses of an onboard racing camera.

Duntov had experimented with dirt track tires for the run but actually obtained the best traction with conventional low-profile passenger car tires. He used Firestone Town and Country tires, which were manufactured in a special soft compound. Pressures as low as 16 psi were used. They were later checked on a concrete straight for stability in short bursts of up to 150 mph.

Because of snow at the top of the mountain, Zora was not able to make the run all the way to the top, as he had in 1956. Instead, he concentrated on a particular mile-and-a-half segment of the road that began at the 10,000-foot mark. He was comparing his time against another open-

CERV I featured aluminum drum brakes mounted inboard and used the rear axle shafts as an upper link. It also featured a brake proportioning system that allowed the driver to adjust the amount of braking force, front to rear.

Zora makes one of 60 runs up Pikes Peak in September 1960. His times later proved to be very competitive despite poor conditions.

wheel car driven by Jerry Unser. Zora's best time on a .9-mile section was 46.5 seconds. He was disappointed in that time, thinking that Unser had recorded a 44-second time on that stretch of road. But Zora later discovered he was closer than he thought: Unser's actual time on the segment was 45.8 seconds.

All told, Duntov made some 60 runs, including ones with a 283-cubic-inch aluminum engine, but he didn't savor the experience because of the dry and marbly condition of the road. "A short snow squall made the track moist and I could place the car as I wanted. On the other 59 runs I was placing it for the first corner and from then skated through all subsequent [corners] as best I could. More rear tire is a must."

Zora had hoped to make some additional runs in an attempt to beat Unser's times but never got the chance because Firestone, which funded the Pikes Peak effort, had something else in mind. Zora took the racer to nearby Continental Divide Raceway where Firestone conducted race tire tests on the road course. A number of different diameters and widths of tires were tested. At the time, racing tires were going through a major metamorphosis toward wider and lower profiles, and much of Firestone's early development occurred on Zora's white and blue racer. It was a relatively high-powered car for its time, and the challenge was getting enough rubber on the road to handle the accelerating and cornering forces. The Hillclimber thus became an important link in the creation of the modern racing tire, but as a rival for a Formula One car, Zora admitted his machine was still no match.

"We believe we know the reasons for deficiencies and the way to correct them," wrote Zora in a December 1960 internal summary memo. "Tests at Proving Ground and at above mentioned race tracks [Continental Divide and Riverside] brought the deficiencies out and taught us valuable lessons. And it will be seen subsequently, these lessons will be valid and important for better design of 1963 Corvette, or for that matter, any vehicle where the transmission of power to the ground arises as a problem."

The Hillclimber had other potential uses. Duntov would have loved to take it to Indianapolis, but its engine would have needed to be destroked to conform to the 205-cubic-inch limit for stockblocks then in force at the Brickyard. Had it been eligible, however, the car would have caused a stir, because Indy was still the province of the front-engined roadsters, and Jack Brabham's revolutionary rear-engined Cooper-Climax didn't appear until 1961. Two years later, Jim Clark won the 500 in a rear-engined Lotus

Ford. Indy would never be the same, and Duntov saw it all coming in the late 1950s.

Up to this point, the existence of CERV I was largely secret, although speculative articles were beginning to leak out in the enthusiast press. A September 1960 article in *Competition Press* stated: "Rumors of a grand prix car from General Motors have now been confirmed (by a reliable but anonymous source) and the car will appear testing soon. Little is known about the car at this point, but it is certain that the full-race Chevrolet [Corvette V-8] is mounted in the rear as per current Formula One international practice."

The article suggested that Chevrolet was more concerned with proving the speed and reliability of rear-engined cars than in entering racing. "The Chevrolet Corvair, along with Porsche, Volkswagen, Renault and Fiat, are still fighting the battle to overcome what's left of buyer resistance to rear-engined passenger vehicles."

CERV I Meets the World

In November 1960 Zora rolled out his creation on an international stage during the United States Grand Prix at Riverside, California. This event put Duntov firmly on the map in the international racing community. Here, with the full backing of GM management, including Walt Mackenzie and Ed Cole, Zora demonstrated that GM had a thing or two to offer the performance world. His audience included the cream of the crop of grand prix drivers, including Dan Gurney, Jack Brabham and Stirling Moss.

The presence of all these GM executives at the grand prix naturally led to intense speculation in the press regarding GM's racing intentions. For this reason Mackenzie coined the name "Chevrolet Engineering Research Vehicle I" (CERV I) to avoid any overt connection to racing. The acronym didn't stop the inevitable buzz on the part of the press. And Zora was recognized front and center as the brains behind the effort. Wrote Bill Olmsted in the *Riverside Press Telegram*:

> A beautifully designed blue-white machine, unlisted in the program and minus a race number, is causing the greatest discussion and/or speculation in the American racing world. The car is currently stationed near the pit area of the Riverside International Raceway, site of today's grand prix of the United States for single seaters. Zora Arkus-Duntov, the genius of General Motors and designer-engineer-promoter of Chevrolet's astoundingly successful Corvette, tuned up at the raceway Tuesday with a mystery machine which has since been given a handsome blue and white

coating. Under the capable hands of Riverside's Dan Gurney, the car toured around the track in three seconds less time than Dan's record track time. Yesterday, with the Maestro Duntov himself behind the wheel, the CERV I (an unlovely name for a handsome machine) [was] out on a three-lap exhibition with times just eight seconds slower than Gurney's earlier lap.

The press writeups on the car were crafted to avoid the inference that GM was involved in racing. Even the track announcer's commentary was carefully scripted. Despite being an open-wheel race car, special pains were taken to keep CERV I separated from the "future Corvette" category in order to avoid hurting Corvette sales. Still, the masses were convinced this was a grand prix machine, the AMA ban on racing was about to be lifted and GM was going racing again. When the California race fans saw the blue and white racer from GM, they were sure.

Zora didn't alter that perception when he took some demonstration laps on Sunday before the race. He ran two laps at a steady 2:08. At this time, the lap record for Formula One was 1:54.9, set by Stirling Moss. Then Moss took it around, shaving about five seconds off Duntov's time. Drivers Jack Brabham, Carroll Shelby, Chuck Daigh, and Jim Jeffords also sat in the car just to get a feel of the cockpit.

Duntov added fuel to the fire by commenting to the press at Riverside about how motor sports involvement provides marketing credibility for a manufacturer. "Europeans can't be sold with slick advertising or cute slogans," said Duntov. "They must see results. One of the best advertising devices in Europe is racing. If the Ferrari continually wins, the European reasons that it must be the better car."

Certainly, GM had marketing in mind in bringing the car to Riverside. According to a post-event report written by Walt Mackenzie, the objective of the trip to Riverside was "to demonstrate Chevrolet's progressive engineering attitude, and prove to the many who feel that mighty General Motors is apathetic and aloof that we are doing what we can in an area in which many sales-influencing people in this country are keenly interested."

The memo noted the frustration of racing fans with the Big Three's conformity to the AMA racing ban and that race fans were blaming the manufacturers. "They don't understand that we are the victims and they resent us for it," wrote Mackenzie.

A bragging point for the benefit of the media was the fact that CERV I's 283-cubic-inch, 353-hp engine weighed only 350 pounds, thus producing one horsepower per pound, a claim that fit nicely with the one-horsepower-per-cubic-inch claim that accompanied the 1957 fuel-injected motor in the Corvette.

Mackenzie also commented about Duntov's great reputation with this international racing set: "They recognize him as the principal engineer who is keeping the torch of international competition burning, until the day comes when U.S. cars and teams will compete freely, as do the various European countries."

The Riverside appearance garnered considerable publicity in car enthusiast publications. It resulted in a long story in *Esquire* magazine that featured a large color photo of Ed Cole behind the wheel of CERV I. The article documented the transformation of the Corvette from its anemic roots at the original Motorama to a respectable sports car on the world stage, thanks largely to Cole and Duntov. Although Zora would have loved to be the man in the picture, he was happy to share some of the limelight with Cole, if for no other reason than as a means of continuing Cole's support.

In an internal report to his bosses at GM, Zora concluded, "As an engineering tool, it gave us early reading on the functional performance of the 1963 Corvette suspension. It already gave us an indication as to how to bias our engine performance as we are heading toward higher power-weight ratios. Possibly, it indicates [the] type of tire our high performance 1963 Corvette would need. Since we are going to have two 4-speed transmissions in the Corvette line, we have indication that a close-ratio, optional transmission should possibly get closer. As we continue to run the car, we probably will learn more."

In concluding his memo, Zora proposed to continue the program the way they had started it. "That is, I will do the driving, except if the substitution of a top notcher will produce specific results I cannot obtain. I know that you would all rather see me in the easy chair, but I think my driving is good for the product, good for the public image of Corvette and high-performance line and image of our aggressive, young (at least in spirit) engineering staff, and good for me."

After Riverside, Duntov felt the opportunity to expand CERV I's performance credentials and began to experiment with subtle bodywork changes and more horsepower. He wanted to conduct some high-speed runs in which he expected to average over 200 mph. To this end, he fitted a supercharger and later, according to Karl Ludvigsen, twin turbochargers that produced a whopping 500 hp. Duntov said the engine was so strong that it lifted the front wheels completely off the ground under acceleration. The bodywork modifications consisted of a new nose that eliminated the original twin side nostrils and a fairing covering the tops of the front suspension A-arms. A bullet-shaped headrest on the original car was also

Zora debriefs his crew between 1962 CERV I runs at Daytona International Speedway, where he lapped the track at over 167 mph. CERV I would later reach over 206 mph at the GM Proving Ground.

eliminated. With these changes, Duntov made one last speed run at the GM Proving Ground at Milford, Michigan, where he lapped the five-mile-long banked loop at an average speed of 206 mph. He did so not with the forced induction motor but with a normally aspirated, bored and stroked 377-cubic-inch V-8.

CERV I was Zora's first and only open-wheeled car. It was pure Zora. It was without question the most ambitious performance car yet conceived at GM. It could have been the foundation for an ambitious Indy car or Formula One racing program. Instead, it became an orphan, a curiosity piece that again showed what GM—and Duntov—were capable of. While it provided tremendous publicity for GM and visibility for Zora, it was only a tease.

Still, the lessons of CERV I would find plenty of applications elsewhere, and Zora was by no means ready to close the book when it came to designing mid-engined prototypes. CERV I underlined Zora's status in the enthusiast press as a bona fide superstar, someone cut from a different cloth than others at GM. It also clearly demonstrated that he would be perfectly at home working for Porsche, Jaguar or Ferrari. Who knows what he might be capable of?

Another Chance to Race

While CERV I focused considerable limelight on Zora as an engineer, his days as a driver were coming to a close. He had not raced since winning his class at Le Mans in 1955, but he kept a current USAC license for the "Champion" division, which he maintained until 1970. Throughout the years, he had always listed a false birthdate on the form—12/25/19 instead of 12/25/09.

Zora's lack of real experience was demonstrated after he had an opportunity to strap on a helmet to drive a Camoradi Maserati Formula One 250F car owned by Lucky Casner at Lime Rock in 1959. The occasion was a Formula Libre race, and Zora happened to be at the track conducting tire tests for Corvette when he received an offer to drive in the race.

According to Larry Shinoda, during the evening prior to qualifying, Zora had dinner with Larry, Dick Thompson, crew chief Dean Bedford and Tony Lapine. Over dinner, Zora made a toast proclaiming, "Driver must have good steak and proper wine for dinner before driving race car." He ate the steak and savored the wine and went to bed that night.

"The next day, Dick Thompson came to us in the pits and said, 'You guys have to come and see this!' We all jumped into his Saab, and rode to the backstretch of the track.

"We were just outside of the steep hill leading to the backstraight and could hear the Maserati approaching. Then we saw it coming over the rise and could see the large lettering 'Camoradi,' then 'Camoradi' on the other side. Zora was really busy. We all laughed and started to leave.

"Then we heard the Maserati again, this time with new driver Chuck Daigh. He crested the rise in one smooth action and then down the backstretch. Back in the pits, Zora was walking slowly and looking dejected. Dick Thompson said, 'Hey Zora, how did it go?' Zora answered, 'Steak did not help.'" Zora ran the same car for the Camoradi team the following year at Meadowdale but crashed during the race.

Despite his poor showings, Duntov had yet another opportunity to drive in the Indianapolis 500 in 1960. This time it would be in a car owned by his old engine builder, Smokey Yunick, in a machine called the "City of Daytona Beach Special." In his syndicated newspaper column, "Inside Auto Racing," Don O'Reilly wrote: "Auto racing is generally considered a sport for younger men, especially the grueling contest each Memorial Day at the Indianapolis Motor Speedway. This year, however, we may see a former European road racer, many times retired and now past the half century mark in age, make an attempt at the 500 mile."

A driving test was required because it had been more than three years since Duntov had raced at the Speedway. In preparation, he had managed to run a few practice laps the previous August at the Brickyard, driving Jim Rathmann's Hopkins Simoniz Special. But Zora never took the driving test.

Corvette at Le Mans

More than likely, Duntov's absence from the Brickyard was due to a more important engagement over in France. There, a private team was preparing to race a team of 1960 Corvettes in the 24 hours at Le Mans. This would be the Corvette's first appearance at the 24-hour classic. Given Duntov's history at Le Mans, it was an event he refused to miss even though he wasn't leading the charge—at least as far as the public could see.

That distinction went to team leader Briggs Cunningham. A Le Mans veteran, Cunningham raised many eyebrows in France during the 1950 race when he entered two Cadillacs, one with a standard sedan body and the second, which the French dubbed *Le Monstre*, with coachwork designed by a Grumman aerospace engineer. The two cars finished the race in respectable tenth and eleventh places overall.

Several years later, Cunningham built and raced his own cars, which were brusque and powerful thanks to wide bulbous bodies and Chrysler Firepower V-8 engines. In this sense, he was not dissimilar to Zora's old employer, Sydney Allard, but, unlike Allard, Cunningham was a rich man. Besides being a sports car racer and manufacturer, Cunningham was also well known in yacht racing circles, having successfully defended the America's Cup in 1958 against the British off Newport, Rhode Island.

Cunningham planned to run three 1960 production Corvettes in the race, taking advantage of a new rule that allowed larger-displacement, production-based cars to compete. The cars were essentially the same ones Zora opposed running at Sebring three years earlier and were not capable of an all-out win.

By now, however, Duntov had many new ideas that could be applied toward a state-of-the art race car that could win LeMans convincingly. Unfortunately, GM policy kept his ideas in the garage.

Zora's role would be as an advisor for the team and perhaps a backup driver. Cunningham felt that by inviting Duntov, he could tap into his expertise while also getting sufficient parts and equipment from GM to see the effort through.

For Cunningham, this was a scaled-down campaign after many years of running his own purpose-built racers. As with prior Cunningham race efforts, Alfred Momo in Long Island was to prepare the cars. Duntov and Frank Burrell from Chevy Engineering would then assist in setting them up. The engines were not exotic. They used standard iron versions of the cylinder heads with big valves and improved porting, which would appear as the 315-hp engine in 1961 Corvettes. In preparation, the team had run the Corvettes for a 24-hour test session at Bridgehampton in pouring rain several months before the race. At the time, Zora had wanted to see if aluminum heads would last 24 hours. He discovered they would not. He went back to the stock cast-iron heads just two weeks before the team left for France.

Cunningham entered three Corvettes and coordinated his efforts with Lucky Casner's Camoradi team, which entered a single Corvette. In Cunningham's traditional livery of white with blue racing stripes, the cars looked very similar to the Sebring team cars from 1956 and 1957. They ran with hardtops bolted on and their rear windows modified to accommodate fuel filler caps.

Technologically, Zora felt that Le Mans was less suitable for the Corvette than other tracks, such as Sebring, due to the effect of top speed attained on the eight-mile long Mulsanne straight. "Air resistance of Corvette is stag-gering," stated Duntov, "and top speed is therefore weakest link in the chain of performance factors. When we are considering lap speeds in excess of 100 mph, average air resistance governs acceleration more than weight."

Zora noted, however, that the race was twice as long as Sebring, so one might assume that there would be roughly half as many finishers. If the Corvette could finish tenth at Sebring, Zora reasoned it might finish fifth at Le Mans.

Because Le Mans has few slow corners and many high-speed bends, Zora set the Corvettes up for maximum speed on the bends but made them forgiving enough to be able to recover in the event of a driver error. In essence, Zora wanted an almost neutral transitional behavior with a shade of under-steer. He achieved these characteristics by adding an additional front sta-bilizer bar while making use of different levels of hardness of rubber on the stabilizer links. Zora also experimented with tire inflation to find the opti-mal combination of tire pressure on each corner of the car.

The team flew over to France with one Corvette for Le Mans trials in April and tested the car on the course with the gasoline they were sup-posed to get for the big event in June. During the test, the team discov-ered problems with the flexible cable that operated the fuel injection unit. The cables kept breaking in practice, and the team ran out of spares. Then General Curtis LeMay came to the team's rescue. He had some more cables flown directly from Detroit to Paris by an Air Force plane, and delivered them to the team with a day to spare.

Zora and crew set up for a 1960 test session at Le Mans.

Zora was included in the roster of team drivers on the entry form, but somehow Ed Cole got hold of this information and made Cunningham promise that Zora would not be allowed to drive. Since Zora's stock was still very high in the eyes of Cole, it was a likely indication of how important Duntov was to the corporation. It is not known how Cunningham managed to break this infor-mation to Zora during the race weekend, but many years later in a retirement tribute letter to Duntov, Cunningham came clean and explained his promise to Cole.

On race day, the four white Corvettes with blue stripes were lined up together on the grid, making an impressive showing for Corvette's inaugural European race, but the

Top: The starting grid at Le Mans 1960 featured four Corvettes privately entered by Briggs Cunningham, with plenty of support from Zora Arkus-Duntov.

Bottom: At Zora's direction, the crew applies dry ice around the engine of the John Fitch/Bob Grossman Corvette to help solve a cooling problem. The car eventually finished eighth overall.

skies were threatening at the 4 p.m. start. The Corvettes all got away cleanly, but the first car dropped out after only 32 laps, spinning and crashing during a violent thunderstorm. The second Corvette, driven by Dick Thompson and Fred Windridge, found its way into a ditch along Tertre Rouge and lost much of its bodywork. It later succumbed to low oil problems, as water and oil were only permitted to be added during 25-lap intervals.

The surviving Corvette, driven by John Fitch and Bob Grossman, ran as high as seventh overall but had cooling problems, which the team attacked by packing the outside of the engine with dry ice. Fitch managed to bring their car home in eighth position overall, covering 280 laps and averaging 97.92 mph for the daylong race. The Corvettes were a crowd favorite, streaking down the Mulsanne straight amid the towering trees, their baritone exhaust notes contrasting with the 12-cylinder Ferraris. It was a respectable showing, which served to revive Duntov's dream of returning to Le Mans with a serious race car.

Zora's Real Vision for Le Mans

Going to Le Mans with a truly competitive, purpose-built car was easier said than done. Even though GM was still in the midst of a ban on motor racing, Duntov felt that if he kept pressing the issue, he could appeal to the vanity of men like Ed Cole and Harry Barr, and somehow get GM to soften its antiracing policy. Ford and Chrysler were doing so, and Duntov reckoned it was only a matter of time before GM would do the same thing. No corporate policy was going to stop Zora from developing some provocative machines that might just change the minds of upper management.

Duntov began to think of a successor to CERV I that could serve his purposes. A Le Mans machine would require full bodywork, so Duntov began working with Larry Shinoda of Design Staff on a sports racing concept. In a memo to Chevy Chief Engineer Harry Barr on January 3, 1962, Duntov suggested the use of such a car in world championship endurance events, such as Le Mans and Sebring, which were open to prototype and experimental cars up to 240 CID displacement. Duntov felt that Chevy's money would be well spent going the prototype route, since the prototype cars would relegate the production-based GT cars to secondary status. "Since no production numbers are required," wrote Duntov, "we will see traditional European and American vehicles based on passenger car engines."

Duntov proposed a prototype weighing about 1,500 pounds and powered by a 400-hp aluminum block Chevy V-8 with overhead camshafts. He recommended the aggressive use of light metals—titanium, magnesium and aluminum—whenever compatible with the overall objective. The engine would be located ahead of the rear axle, and the chassis would be a space frame or semi-space frame. Duntov suggested a turbine or Wankel engine in this regard and was leaning toward the latter. "The Wankel engine is relatively new and is potentially a future powerplant for passenger automobiles," wrote Duntov. GM would later embrace Wankel technology in a big way, but at the time Curtiss Wright held the licensing rights, and there were many unknowns about the engine.

Plans were drawn up for the prototype, which included a manually controlled power-shifted transmission and an engine featuring three-valve cylinder heads. But this car was never built due to renewed corporate pressure not to build cars that might go against the spirit of the racing ban. Duntov shelved the project, but it was far from forgotten.

Corvair Controversy

While Duntov was pushing for more provocative, risk-taking machines, one actually did go into production. Unfortunately for him, it wasn't the Corvette but the rear-engined, air-cooled Corvair. Duntov found himself an unwitting participant in the controversy over the Corvair and the charges by safety advocates—most notably attorney Ralph Nader—that the car was prone to oversteering, which could result in rollovers during sharp cornering.

The Corvair was Ed Cole's baby. It was Chevrolet's first compact car and had many sports car attributes. While it invited comparisons to the Volkswagen Beetle, it was a far more advanced effort—more on a par with the Porsche 356. But the Corvair became a public relations nightmare for GM and ignited Nader's career.

The major point of controversy with the Corvair was its semi-trailing, swing-axle rear suspension, which critics charged made the Corvair unstable at high lateral gs. The problem was exacerbated by the general feeling of confidence the driver felt, up to the point where the car would suddenly let go. The rear wheels would actually tuck under during hard cornering.

Duntov knew all along that swing axles were a liability without mitigating hardware such as a front stabilizer bar. Because the Corvair had a wider rear track than the Volkswagen, however, he felt it might get by.

According to Duntov, what the Corvair really needed was an independent rear suspension. Duntov had designed one into CERV I in 1958, during the time the Corvair was being developed. But independent rear suspensions were exotic stuff in the late 1950s and were found only on certain European cars. The Corvette wouldn't get an independent rear suspension until 1963.

Besides availability, there was a cost issue. An independent rear suspension would have cost an additional $15 per car, which was a lot of money on a program where pennies were counted in terms of keeping costs down. The addition of a front stabilizer bar as well as a rear balance beam, which could have helped the problem, was also nixed because of cost.

The Corvair went into testing with a basic swing axle, coil spring rear suspension. As problems surfaced, Duntov was asked to evaluate the problem by then Chevy Chief Engineer Harry Barr. Duntov did some calculations and discovered that the relatively high degree of wheel travel (four inches up and six inches down) was a potential problem. Duntov wrote a four-page analysis for Barr in which he determined that the car could overturn at a relatively low lateral g level on the skid pad. He heard nothing afterward, and the Corvair was put into production.

Shortly thereafter, Duntov was asked by Barr to develop a racing Corvair, which made Duntov even more aware of the rear axle problem. The development cars were chewing up their rear tires badly. Duntov decided to limit the rear wheel travel by means of a rebound strap, which limited the degree the rear wheels could tuck under. He also added a front stabilizer bar and began to campaign the Corvair at Sebring and Daytona with the Rodriguez brothers—Pedro and Ricardo—and Ed Hugus doing the driving. But it was fan belts, not the rear axle, that did them in while racing against Ford Falcons driven by Joe Weatherly and Curtis Turner. The fan belt design on the Corvair followed a serpentine route, having to bend four times over 540 degrees versus the usual 360.

Duntov was eventually called in several times to testify as an expert witness amid a plethora of lawsuits against GM over the Corvair. While the plaintiff attorneys kept harping on the fact that the car oversteered, Duntov unwittingly made their case by saying that the car actually would overturn under certain conditions. During his testimony it came out that the heavy-duty Corvair he was working on was inherently more stable. The attorneys tried to pin down just what Duntov did working on the Corvair.

He mentioned the rebound strap, a negative camber setting for the rear wheels as well as the front stabilizer bar. According to Duntov, the rebound strap never made it into production because it affected ride quality.

Several GM engineers, including Frank Winchell, Gib Hufstader and Duntov himself experienced the overturning phenomenon first hand. Duntov was down in Daytona at a test session for the Corvair. He was about to go out and try a new suspension setting when he got a phone call from Detroit. Since he was already belted in and ready to go, he decided to call back after his lapping session. He then went out and promptly rolled the car. Fortunately, he was not injured. He later found out that the call was to warn him not to go out because at Milford a faulty test part had just been discovered that could cause the car to roll over.

The Corvair was updated and redesigned for the 1965 model year, providing the opportunity to fix the rear suspension. This time, the parts were already on the shelf—saved from the 1963 Corvette independent unit. The rear suspension was modified for use on the Corvair, and GM management, wary of all the negative publicity they had endured on the program, elected to use it despite the cost implications. It worked beautifully, and the new suspension went into production in 1965. "And then, 1965 Corvair was flawless," said Duntov.

But it was too late. In his book, *Unsafe at Any Speed*, Ralph Nader wrote, "The 1965 Corvair came out with a more fundamental change in the form of a link-type suspension with dual control arms. These improvements represented new company policy, but not engineering innovations. They draw on well-developed knowledge that went back to GM's empirical work during the Thirties and extending to the experimental rear-engined race car developed after World War II by Chevrolet's key suspension engineer Zora Arkus-Duntov."

Nader was more than a decade off in referring to CERV I as a post-World War II creation, but it more conveniently fit his argument that the solution had been on the shelf at GM for over ten years.

Regardless, the Corvair had endured so much negative publicity that despite the appeal of the 1965 model, it languished in dealer showrooms, loved only by its small cadre of die-hard fans hooked by its fresh looks and sports car handling. Ed Cole's baby and one of GM's most innovative cars ever died a quiet death in 1969. It was a crushing loss for maestro Cole.

Duntov maintained it was low profit margins, not Ralph Nader, that killed the Corvair. Compared to the Ford Falcon, which had a traditional front-engine, rear-drive arrangement, the Corvair, with its air-cooled aluminum engine and transaxle, was expensive to produce. Chevy then developed its own more traditional compact car, the Chevy II, which later became the Nova. Interestingly enough, the Corvair never lost a court case, and its safety was fully vindicated by a research and testing report from the National Highway Traffic Safety Administration in 1972.

Cole defended his car to the end, and even agreed to debate Nader on television on the "Phil Donahue Show." Top management thought this was a no-win situation and nixed the idea. Later, after he retired in 1974, Cole did debate Nader. Against tough anti-GM sentiment going in, Cole handled himself well enough that the debate was deemed a draw.

SIXTEEN

While the Sting Ray represented the zenith of Zora's engineering talents as applied to a street product, it was not the car he wanted to build.

Struggle over the Sting Ray

Zora's quest to make his mark at General Motors would extend, inevitably, to creating his own Corvette. Despite the lack of any real authority, he had already exerted a major influence on the existing car. Little by little, his project assignments for Maurice Olley, Ed Cole and Harry Barr had yielded a Corvette that Zora proudly deemed "a dog no longer." With added power the 1961 and 1962 models represented significant performance increases, thanks to a standard 250-hp 327, and as much as 360 hp on tap via a fuel-injected version. Despite more guts and a new duck-tailed rear end, the basic chassis and layout remained unchanged from 1953, including an unsophisticated solid rear axle. In Zora's eyes, the rear axle represented a severe limitation to the Corvette's performance potential.

Duntov knew the Corvette needed an all-new design, and he had one in mind—a machine that represented everything he had learned about engineering in his 50-plus years. Based on his experiences with the Q Corvette and CERV I, he saw the opportunity to build a rear mid-engined machine that would rank among the world's finest sports cars at any price.

Design Wars

The keys to the Corvette kingdom at GM were not so easily obtained, however. The Corvette had also aroused the passion of Harley Earl's successors at Design Staff, who had their own ideas about a fitting successor to Mr. Earl's original Corvette. Design Staff enjoyed a preeminent position within the corporation. Thanks to Earl's expressive postwar designs, appearance had become more important than engineering. During the 1950s and 1960s Design's sizzle often obscured warmed-over underpinnings.

"Styling was pretty cocky—we didn't listen to anyone else about what we ought to be doing," said former Design Staff chief Chuck Jordan. "We did what we thought was right for the times." Indeed, a race to control the

Opposite: Zora discovered firsthand that control over the look and configuration of Corvettes was a very elusive thing at GM in the 1960s.

future direction of the Corvette was shaping up between Chevy Engineering and Design Staff, and Zora was squarely on the front lines.

His opponent would be Bill Mitchell, Earl's successor as vice president of Design Staff. Like Earl, Mitchell was an iconoclast. Fiercely independent and opinionated, he lived and breathed fast machinery, be it jet airplanes, motorcycles or automobiles. He was a commanding presence with his large round face, long sideburns and bald crown. A native Pennsylvanian, Mitchell had worked in the 1930s as a commercial illustrator for an advertising agency in New York City. In New York, he sketched cars as a hobby, often using classics he'd see in Park Avenue showrooms for inspiration. After seeing some of his work, Harley Earl offered him a job with GM in Detroit. When Earl retired on December 1, 1958, Mitchell was named his successor.

"Bill Mitchell was a product of Harley Earl," said Dave Holls, who worked with Mitchell in the 1960s and went on to become director of Corporate Design under Chuck Jordan. "Bill could have never done what he did without Earl's successful batting average for the corporation. Nobody ever called him anything but 'Mr. Earl,' he had so many winners. He was a complete dictator."

Mitchell already had a design theme in mind for the next-generation Corvette. Back in 1957 Mitchell created a clay model styling theme for the Q Corvette. According to Karl Ludvigsen, he was inspired by a series of Pininfarina and Boano bodies built on Italian Abarths. He was particularly influenced by one record-speed car that he had seen at the Turin Motor Show in 1957. The car had a wedge shape characterized by a sharp crease around its perimeter. Bulges were incorporated above the wheel wells to accommodate the tires within the relatively flat-top shape of the car.

Zora and Bill Mitchell didn't often see eye-to-eye during their respective GM careers, but neither was shy about getting in each other's face. Here, they square off at Daytona in the early 1960s.

Mitchell was so taken by the Abarth car that he brought photos of it back from Italy and showed them to his key designers, who included Chuck Pohlmann, Tony Lapine, Pete Brock and Bob Veryzer. According to Ludvigsen, he challenged each of them to try his own variation of the Abarth as a possible candidate to become the Q Corvette.

Mitchell's team took this basic look and added a fastback roofline and an extreme wedge-shaped front end. For its time, the Q Corvette was a stunning new direction for Chevrolet's sports car. However, management considered it too costly to produce, thanks to its novel powertrain and rear-mounted transmission, and it was cancelled in 1958.

In 1959, Mitchell, by then head of GM Design Staff, had the opportunity to revive and expand upon the Q theme by creating a special race car body. The body was designed by Chuck Pohlmann and Peter Brock under Mitchell's direction and was engineered to fit over the chassis of Zora's original SS mule car, which had been mothballed since GM pulled the racing plug in 1957. Mitchell decided to race the car to test the public reaction to this revolutionary new design theme. When it was all done, its sleek design suggested a graceful yet evil sea creature. Mitchell named it the Sting Ray, even though it was a shark that inspired it.

Duntov was nervous about the whole project for several reasons. Because of the corporate ban on racing, he had no control over the effort. This was strictly a private project staffed by volunteer engineers and Design Staff personnel such as Larry Shinoda. Secondly, as a race car, the Sting Ray wasn't any more advanced than the original SS and suffered from many of the same problems, including bad brakes. Aerodynamically, it might have been worse than the SS, with the body actually providing lift rather than downforce. Since the car's underpinnings were still Duntov's own design and he didn't want a project he had no connection with to come back and haunt him, he tried to prevent Mitchell from obtaining the SS mule. More fundamentally, he didn't want Mitchell running a project—officially or unofficially—with the name Corvette attached to it. Duntov was unsuccessful. As a GM vice president, Mitchell simply had too much clout.

Zora's fears were justified not because the Sting Ray would be an embarrassment on the track for GM but because of the momentum its success would create. The Sting Ray racer proved what a good car the SS actually was. It was not only competitive, it was a winner. The car propelled Dick Thompson to the C-Modified National Championship in 1959. Thompson drove the same car to the same championship in 1960 before Mitchell retired the car so he could display it on the auto show circuit.

Buoyed by wild public enthusiasm for the design, Mitchell had Larry Shinoda execute the adaptation of the Sting Ray into a production Corvette. This move set the mold for the second-generation Corvette to become a front-engined car, a fact that had Duntov fuming. He never liked the long-hooded look of the Sting Ray racer because it interfered with forward visibility. He had been frustrated with the efforts of Mitchell and his designers in trying to design a body for a mid-engined car back in the late 1950s. Both Tony Lapine and Larry Shinoda were assigned by Mitchell to work with Duntov on some early concepts, but their direction from Mitchell was to maintain the long hood. According to Duntov, the end result provided

Bill Mitchell took the Corvette SS mule chassis and built this wedge-shaped body for it. It became the Sting Ray racer, which helped set the design direction for the second-generation Corvette, much to Zora's chagrin.

no indication that they were creating a mid-engined car. "I thought that external design should reflect what car is." Accordingly, Duntov thought Mitchell's idea of car design was frozen in 1937 with the long hood of the Mercedes SS or the Duesenberg J.

But the reaction to the Sting Ray racer—from the public and from GM management—was so positive that it set the direction for the next Corvette and perhaps several generations to follow.

The working prototype for the production Corvette was called the XP-720, which bore an immediate resemblance to the Sting Ray racer. Making matters worse for Zora was another design element added to the XP-720 that would become the trademark of the Sting Ray—a tapered fastback hardtop. The design featured a windsplit that ran down the center of the car from the windshield to the rear deck in an uninterrupted line.

The Battle of the Split Window

Mitchell borrowed the split-window concept from Harley Earl's 1956 Golden Rocket showcar, which was built along the whimsical rocket/aviation theme expressed in vehicles like the GM XP-500 and Firebird show cars. Mitchell's execution, to be sure, was far more aesthetically pleasing, but it still necessitated dividing the back window, which obscured rear visibility. When it was first designed, the split was narrower than in the actual production version. The engineers widened the window so they could get more structure into the glass seals. No matter how wide or narrow the split, for Zora such an intrusion into the driving function was an issue worthy of war.

Venturing over into the inner sanctum of GM Design Staff to air his displeasure, Duntov challenged Mitchell directly. He was on sacred ground. Never before had an engineer, especially one with such little authority on such a low-volume car line, had the audacity to blow smoke into the face of a king like Bill Mitchell. Duntov was out to shift the balance between styling and engineering back toward engineering, but he was one man on a limited-volume car line without a mandate from his superiors. He had his work cut out for him.

Duntov recalled looking at an early prototype of the XP-720 in the GM styling dome with Bill Mitchell. "We are sitting there and Bill was squinting at car and said, 'Ah, look at it. You see the blood, the blood streaming out of the mouth of the car—like big fish.'"

Blood was about to be spilled over the issue of the split window. "My blood," said Zora in a 1992 *Corvette Quarterly* interview with David Barry. Duntov hated the split window for the same reason he hated the long hood—it obstructed the driver's view.

Zora strenuously objected to Bill Mitchell's use of a split window on the 1963 Corvette because it obscured rear visibility. But he lost the battle, at least for one year.

Dave Holls once said that Duntov visiting Design Staff "was like a Lutheran visiting the Vatican." He was in a foreign place. Mitchell was aghast at the idea of an engineer challenging him on Mitchell's own turf, and as a result there were some serious words, even shouting. "Mitchell got very red-faced during these discussions," recalled Chuck Jordan, who witnessed many of the arguments. "Mitchell would say 'I'm the designer and you're the engineer and engineering never sold a godamn thing,'" said Larry Shinoda, also present at the discussions. "Knowing it pissed him off, Mitchell would call Duntov 'Zorro,' or sometimes just a 'fucking white Russian.' Zora in turn called Mitchell 'a red-faced baboon.'"

Mitchell used whatever leverage he felt he could get away with, and even suggested that he could pull the plug on independent rear suspension or other engineering innovations Duntov had in mind for the car. Whether Mitchell had the kind of corporate muscle to control the engineering content of the car was something Zora didn't want to find out, so he took the matter to Ed Cole. The Chevy general manager decided to compromise and let Mitchell have his split window, at least for the first year.

Duntov had taken his strongest stand on an issue since he had joined the corporation—and had lost. For him it was another rude lesson in corporate politics. He earned the longer-term victory, however, and the split disappeared after the 1963 model year. What factors ultimately resulted in the decision are not documented, but Duntov's opposition, combined with scornful reviews from the enthusiast media, may have been enough to kill the split window. Ironically, cost issues may have contributed to its demise as well, since it was cheaper to manufacture and install one rear window rather than two for the fastback.

Despite the corporate bloodshed over the split window, the impact of the Sting Ray on the world market was nothing short of remarkable. The car literally stopped people in their tracks. "When that car came out, I said to myself that I can't believe I can buy this car and drive it," said Jordan. "It was literally like driving a show car."

Most historians agree that the Sting Ray was the best Corvette design ever, the standard by which any new design is measured. If you look back at Corvette history and ask people what was the best Corvette ever, they'll say the 1963 Corvette coupe.

Not everyone in Design Staff was convinced that the Sting Ray was perfect. "I always thought the Sting Ray had too many phony scoops, especially compared to the beautiful E-Type Jaguar," said Dave Holls. "Mitchell told me to 'stop worrying about that fucking Jaguar.' He told me that Harley Earl taught him there should be entertainment everywhere you look around the car."

Much to Zora's satisfaction, many 1963 Corvette owners removed the split window and replaced it with a solid piece of glass.

Zora: Persona Non Grata

"After the big pissing contest, Zora was sort of banned from styling," said Larry Shinoda. "When Zora did the Grand Sport (a special racing version of the Sting Ray), and he needed my help, he really couldn't ask. I would bootleg stuff out the back door. I had this foamcore case with all the contraband stuff for Zora. I kept that thing for years. Gib Hufstader and the guys ended up designing a lot of the pieces on the Grand Sport. Still, there was a kind of begrudging admiration between Mitchell and Duntov."

"I question whether Mitchell ever officially pulled his pass," said Jordan. "We admitted he had some valid opinions, but we didn't want him to tell us how to design. We loved the guy [Zora] and he'd come in and say these funny things, with that accent. But the only time we hated him was when he didn't support what we wanted. As mad as Mitchell got, he admired what Zora did, especially when it came to race cars. The only reason why Mitchell put up with Zora was that he respected racing and the people who knew about it. Zora was not some marketing guy telling him what to do. Mitchell was more tolerant of Zora than anyone."

Still, many in Design Staff felt that legend has built up Zora too high. "The design of that car—good, bad, mediocre—had an awful lot to do with the success of that car," asserted Chuck Jordan. "It's a two-pronged deal. Design Staff was as responsible for the success of the Corvette as Zora was."

Zora and Mitchell also clashed over Zora's suggestion that Chevrolets needed something more distinctive than a bowtie logo as an ornament on the vehicles. "Mercedes has a star and everybody knows what Mercedes is," said Duntov. Zora took it upon himself to initiate some sketches with Ned Nickles, one of Mitchell's more talented designers, who had designed the Corvair, among other things. Mitchell was outraged when he discovered that one of his own guys was working on a project initiated by Duntov. Nickles finished the drawings but after being threatened by Mitchell never presented them. He later gave them to Duntov.

The split window and the logo battle weren't the only ones Duntov had to fight during the gestation of the Sting Ray. Cole also seriously considered offering a four-passenger Corvette much like the Thunderbird, which became a four-seater in 1958. The concept had actually been executed as an attractive four-passenger hardtop known as the Corvette Impala show car back in 1956. Cole, who always kept a wary eye on Thunderbird sales, revived the four-passenger Corvette debate in 1962. The T-Bird had consistently beaten the Corvette in sales since it debuted in 1955 and took an even bigger lead after adopting a four-passenger configuration. While Cole never pushed to abandon the two-seater Corvette, he wanted a hedge against getting slammed by the Thunderbird in the sales department.

Duntov thought such a move would be disastrous. He called it "the ugly duckling." In his view a four-seat design would destroy the performance image of the car and, more important, would destroy the performance halo it had brought to all Chevrolet products. Joe Pike, the affable Chevy sales promotion manager who was also the editor of *Corvette News*, the Corvette owner magazine published for Chevrolet, joined Duntov in his opposition. The cause for the four-seater Corvette faded after GM chairman Jack Gordon sat in the back seat of the prototype at Design Staff. He got stuck when the seat mechanism broke. According to Larry Shinoda, "He stormed off and that was the end of the four-passenger Corvette." Cole claimed he never really ruled out the idea and often used it as a good-natured jibe against Duntov and Pike. But Duntov had managed to preserve the Corvette as a two-seat sports car.

On top of his other concerns regarding the 1963 Corvette, Duntov didn't care for the Sting Ray name. In a September 7, 1962, letter to Joe Callahan of *Automotive News*, Duntov wrote, "I am favoring the name Corvette much more than the Sting Ray. This, of course, is a personal preference for me. Although an entirely new car, it is aimed at the same objective as our past Corvette in later stages of its life. I have nothing against fish in general. Actually, I passionately fish for bass in Lake St. Clair, but

I sometimes have difficulty swallowing the association of Corvette with a fish not noted for its attractiveness of appearance nor nobility of character. But, I repeat, it is my personal preference and not more than that."

Sting Ray Beneath the Skin

While the Sting Ray received the most attention for its styling, the engineering beneath the skin represented a sea change for the Corvette. While it wasn't the mid-engined Corvette Zora wanted, the engineer had resolved to make the best possible front-engined car. Zora had several things in mind: a much stiffer frame with a better front suspension and an independent rear suspension.

According to Karl Ludvigsen, Duntov was able to devise a cost-effective front suspension system using existing Chevy passenger car components. The right and left lower control arms were swapped from their normal positions on a full-sized Chevy. Pressed steel wishbones and a ball-jointed upright was also employed. These parts had already been validated and were ready to use.

Saving money on the front components gave Duntov and his engineers more latitude to develop an independent rear suspension. The geometry for this unit came directly from the CERV I and used a double-jointed driveshaft as an active component of the suspension. Trailing radius rods took the brake and propulsion loads. The differential was bolted to the chassis, which improved handling and reduced unsprung weight.

The rear suspension also featured a transverse leaf spring, because there was no room for the more traditional coil springs except behind the rear axle. It is a feature that is still used, although today's springs are made out of fiberglass. Duntov saw it as a less than elegant solution but one that did its job very well.

In a Society of Automotive Engineers (SAE) speech in September 1962, Zora described the tradeoffs that had to go into the design of the Sting Ray:

> The Corvette must compete with all other sports cars in a market that represents only one percent of total US sales. Regardless of its size, however, this small segment of the market is very demanding and very vocal. Because of the high standards set by sports car buyers, the Corvette has matured greatly in the last 10 years. It has become a mechanically sophisticated automobile, but making it so has been a difficult engineering assignment.

Duntov described the dual mission of making the Corvette respectable as a specialized performance vehicle while using as many high-volume Chevrolet parts on the Corvette as possible to keep it economically feasible.

"With little or no travail, we feel we have been successful on both counts, The new front suspension, for example, contributes greatly to the vehicle's handling excellence and ride, and yet it has about 60 parts that are used in other Chevrolet products. This is also true of other systems such as steering and braking."

One unique aspect of Zora's suspension configurations was the use of an intentionally high roll center, which limited the amount of body roll on the car. "The advantages to this arrangement," wrote Zora, "are higher resistance to roll for a given ride rate, and lower increase of possible camber; that is, lower loss of cornering power." Zora claimed he first made use of a higher roll center in 1957 with the Corvette SS.

Using a higher roll center created a certain degree of steering wheel fight at certain speeds with particular tires. After experiencing this phenomenon at the Proving Ground, Chief Engineer Harry Barr exclaimed that he would "be damned" if he allowed this car to be built. So Zora fashioned a steering damper, but it would only fit on engines with a four-quart oil pan instead of a five-quart pan because of space considerations.

The finished Sting Ray weighed about the same as its predecessor—much to Duntov's chagrin. But a number of the improvements on the 1963 added weight, such as a 20-gallon fuel tank, larger brakes and a frame that was significantly stiffer than its predecessor. Duntov had also managed to reduce unsprung weight in the front and rear suspension, which served to improve ride and handling.

Spawning the Mako Shark

When it came to early evaluations of the Sting Ray prototypes, Duntov maintained tight control over who was able to drive them. According to Ludvigsen, among those *not* on the list to drive a car was Bill Mitchell, and Mitchell's ego was big enough for him not to stand pat. So he built his own car, inspired by a shark he caught on vacation off Bimini. The new car was based on a 1962 chassis and was a successor to the XP-700 show car that first showcased the duck-tailed look. Mitchell's new car, the XP-755 (later called the Mako Shark), featured the Sting Ray look but had a more overt shark theme, with gills on the front quarter panels and graded coloration ranging from a white underbody to a dark iridescent blue on the hood and rear deck.

A shark had to have a bite, however. The Mako's engine bay would house everything from a supercharged 327-cubic-inch engine to a 427cid Mark IV aluminum-block V-8. Mitchell's Mako became one of the most popular and memorable of all the Corvette show cars.

Sting Ray Meets the Public

The new Corvette Sting Ray was a smash hit when it debuted in September 1962. With its traffic-stopping looks and sophisticated suspension, the Corvette was now in a new league and commanded round-the-world respect. Demand was high, with long waiting periods at the showroom. Deals were as hard to come by as the cars. The new Sting Ray graced the covers of every major automotive publication in the United States and Canada.

Besides rave reviews for the design, Duntov's independent rear suspension garnered high marks as well. Wrote *Road & Track* in its October 1962 issue:

> The tendency of the rear wheels to spin freely on acceleration and for the rear end to come sliding around rather quickly during hard cornering was always there. Chevrolet engineers had done a good job with what they had on hand, but there just wasn't enough with which to work. The production-component live rear axle could hop and dance like an Apache with a hot foot.

> Now with the advent of full independent rear suspension described in the previous pages, the Corvette's handling characteristics are considerably different. In a word, the new Sting Ray sticks! Whether you slam the car through an S-bend at 85 or pop the clutch at 5000 rpm at the drag strip, the result is the same—great gripping gobs of traction.

> One thing the designers thought of this time around—the driver. Not only is the steering wheel adjustable for reach (3 in. in and out) so you can drive Italian style, but the seats are comfortable and give enough legroom. Instruments are all new and better placed, with twin 6-in speedometer and tachometer directly in front of the steering wheel. Our only complaint about the interior was in the coupe, where all we could see in the rear view mirror was that silly bar splitting the rear window down the middle.

In November 1962, *Sports Car Graphic* was liberal in its praise for Zora's unique independent rear suspension: "Of course, the big news is the suspension, the rear in particular. It's been obvious for years that Independent Rear Suspension would eventually come to Detroit, but the type used by Corvette proved a real shocker for us, as we never expected anything as 'wild' in the ultra-modern sense. We queried Duntov at length as to 'why' he arrived at this design conclusion. His answer amounted to this. There are two basic purposes for using an independent rear—improved unsprung weight and improved rear wheel geometry. He felt the design used best achieved these motives while embodying the all-important requirements of a production component—low cost, reliability, serviceability, and relative simplicity. The more you study this design, the more you realize how well it fulfills these requirements."

The car helped to establish Duntov as one of the auto industry's most innovative engineers. Wrote Kenneth Rudeen in the October 1, 1962, issue of *Sports Illustrated*:

Until now the Corvette has been a development of the original, rather non-descript auto that began life as a General Motors showcar in 1953. It was at first, neither brisk nor nimble. Then Chevy began to pump sports car life into it. These infusions may be traced to Duntov, a former racing driver, who alone among thousands of industry engineers represents a direct link with European road-racing tradition.

In another speech before the SAE on October 8, 1962, Zora showed good humor in acknowledging the tribulations of bringing a car like the Corvette to market. In the opening of his speech—in which he acknowledged the countless numbers of meetings between various groups within GM—Zora deadpanned, "We all get together and discuss things, what is wrong and how to make it right, and then we are standing around the mockup where we see that the fuel line is attached to exhaust pipe. Democratic process, every voice is heard and although our chief engineer [Jim Premo] doesn't have a loud voice, but his voice carries far. But sometimes he makes errors in judgment. One big red error is to let me speak tonight."

Zora took the audience back to 1953 and pointed out the changes in the car since then. He admitted that the original Corvettes really didn't offer value for the money, which is why they didn't sell very well. The challenge, noted Zora, was to appeal to the market's need for transportation while providing pride of ownership and a fun-to-drive quotient. Zora suggested the new Corvette needed to excel at all three, including upgrading its reputation as a competition vehicle.

Making the challenge more difficult was the fact that a two-seat sports car is by definition a low-volume vehicle by GM standards. "Consequently, the public, which is not aware of our problem, is demanding for their money the high quality which is quite difficult to provide for the money."

Zora stayed away from any temptation to go public with his misgivings over the powertrain configuration, wedge-shaped body or split window.

The Sting Ray was offered in both a coupe and a convertible body style and sold virtually equal numbers of each—10,594 coupes and 10, 919 convertibles during the 1963 model year. After ten years, the Corvette—thanks in large part to Zora—was making money for GM.

SEVENTEEN

Still operating under the constraints of GM's adherence to the Automobile Manufacturers Association's ban on factory racing, Zora had to devise novel ways to go racing with the Sting Ray.

Taking It to the Track

Having created the closest thing to a complete Corvette he could call his own in the 1963 Sting Ray, Duntov now dedicated himself to making the best possible race car out of it. Even though he was no longer driving, racing was still the standard by which he measured himself. It was the only forum where the performance of one car could be benchmarked against another—on neutral ground before the whole the world. Furthermore, Zora knew that even though the Sting Ray was likely to be a sales success based on its engineering improvements and its provocative looks, it still had to establish a winning record on international racetracks in order to be accepted by serious sports car buyers.

For Zora, the idea of beating the Europeans at their own game in cars of his design had high appeal. It was what had kept him in America when he had a chance to move back to Germany in the 1950s. While he had warm feelings for people like Daimler-Benz's Alfred Neubauer and Porsche's Huschke von Hanstein, Zora was at heart a competitor, and this was his chance to show them what he could do with the resources of the world's largest corporation behind him. Perhaps he also wanted to kick a little sand in the Germans' faces for so rudely running him off the continent during the war.

Letting the Customers Do the Racing

The problem was that a ban on factory participation in racing still existed. While other manufacturers, such as Ford, were starting to defy the AMA ban and venture back into racing, General Motors held firm to its antiracing policy. So Duntov decided to develop a product his customers could race instead. To that end, he sold Ed Cole on the idea of creating a special model fully equipped with high-performance options. The resulting package was called the Z06, which consisted of stiffer spring rates, a larger front anti-roll bar and larger/stiffer rear shocks, a Positraction rear axle and a 36-gallon fuel tank. Its brakes featured sintered metallic lin-

Opposite: In developing the Sting Ray as a viable race car, Zora sorts out a Z06 mule car at Daytona in 1962.

The Z06 test mule Zora drove at Daytona featured a body that looked like a cross between a 1962 and a 1963 Corvette.

ings, a dual circuit master cylinder and a vacuum brake booster. The engine was a 360-hp version of the 327-cubic-inch small-block. The total option price was $1,818, and the person who checked the Z06 order box emerged with a race-ready package.

Duntov did much of the development work on the Z06 package himself, recounted Karl Ludvigsen. Using a special blue mule car with a modified 1962 body, Duntov drove it during test sessions at Daytona and Sebring. The body looked like a hybrid between a 1962 Corvette and a Sting Ray. He was gearing up for an event in Riverside in September 1962, where he would find out first-hand whether his car could hold its own against Ford's new torch carrier in sports car racing, the Cobra.

Several days before the race, four production Z06 coupes were driven from the Corvette plant at St. Louis to Riverside, California. There, Bob Bondurant, Jerry Grant, Dave McDonald and Doug Hooper—all in Z06s—took on the lone Ford Cobra, driven by Bill Krause. Krause ran away from the Corvettes until he lost a rear wheel, a malady that also struck Dave McDonald. Doug Hooper, driving a Mickey Thompson-prepared Z06, inherited the lead and went on to win. It was a satisfying victory, but according to Zora, "the writing was on the wall."

Even before the race began, Zora knew his Z06 Corvettes didn't have the right stuff to keep up with the Cobras over the long haul. The Corvette, which weighed over 1,100 pounds more than Krause's Cobra, still suffered from the same brake problems that had plagued it years earlier at Sebring. The Corvette would have to get lean and mean to be competitive with the Cobra.

In a memo to Chevy chief engineer Harry Barr in April of that year, Duntov wrote, "In 1963, Corvette will have slightly better but basically the same relative position. In intervening years, Corvette licked Jaguar, Mercedes and in 1963, it will lick Ferraris of the type as sold and raced by amateurs. It will place itself better than before in international races, but it cannot win overall against prototypes and it cannot win Grand Turismo category (unless by default) against factory-entered cars. The inability to win races against prototypes or racing GTs will have little or no effect on sales of Corvette proper because it will be the hottest machine a person could buy and use on the street."

Duntov explained that Chevy could lighten the high-performance Corvette without affecting the cost of other models and without impairing its utility as a general-purpose machine by lightening optional items. Duntov suggested that changing to aluminum cylinder heads, flywheel and exhaust manifold as well as installing a special lighter rear axle and bi-metallic brake drums could save some 124 pounds.

In the same memo to Barr, Duntov put into perspective the importance of winning, using the argument of American pride: "I feel that a vast section of the population, interested in sports car racing or not, is aware that there is sports car racing, that there is the only American sports car, the Corvette, and that this American car always gets beaten by foreign products," wrote Duntov. "As a national characteristic, Americans do not like to be second best, be it a space race or an auto race. Both are not individual, but rather national contests. They involve technological ability of the national industry and with this, becomes a matter of personal pride. If [John] Glenn's orbit make all of us 'grow an inch taller,' Corvette defeats in sports car racing make loads of people feel a quarter of an inch smaller, and the younger part of the population possibly more than that.

"I feel that a winning car would enable this vast group to grow quarter inch taller and Chevrolet will have a new mass of grateful customers for all our products—cars, trucks and second-hand vehicles."

Building the Grand Sport

Fortunately, Duntov had a supporter in this view. Bunkie Knudsen, who had replaced Ed Cole as Chevrolet general manager in 1961, came from the Pontiac Division, where he had presided over the resurrection of a sleepy "grandmother's car" unit into the third best-seller in the industry. His formula: sporty performance cars and racing.

Fueled by Knudsen's support and his need to breed an American winner, Zora brainstormed a machine that would get the job done against the Cobras. He was well aware of the continuing existence of the AMA ban and thus chose his words carefully in laying down his rationale.

In a February 13, 1963, memo to Harry Barr and others in the engineering department, Duntov urged his colleagues to distinguish between engineering cars for performance versus outright racing: "Neither the resolution [AMA] nor the basic policy equates performance with racing; neither is there any attempt in this resolution to dictate or direct the characteristics of the vehicles we produce."

GM's basic intent should be to engineer a product for the street, noted Duntov. He described how stock car racing helped make a respectable street engine out of the 348. "I don't know who but the blind and deaf, can deny that performance image appeals to a large sector of the population and helps us sell our product.

"It follows, therefore, that if we apply our efforts to engineering high performance product and do that to such excellency that it will be suitable to accomplish the desired effect in competitive events, we will achieve the aims of our management without transgression against the letter of the sport of AMA resolution or against basic GM policy."

Duntov regarded the Corvette as different from a typical Chevrolet passenger car: It could go fast, stop quickly, and negotiate corners at high speeds, unlike the typical Chevrolet. He saw the Corvette's use in sports car racing as more in line with the character of the product. While admitting that engineering the Corvette strictly for racing was a violation of the letter of the AMA resolution, Duntov reasoned that GM had an obligation to make sure that its vehicles operated safely when raced by its customers. "It follows, therefore, that chassis developments must continue, that behavior under racing conditions must be observed, interpreted and weaknesses corrected. The above, I feel, is an obligation."

With his justification tucked safely inside his lapel pocket, Duntov approached Knudsen about formal approval for a "Light Corvette" program. Of course, GM corporate policy still prohibited any division from direct factory participation in racing. So to get around the letter of the AMA agreement, Duntov reasoned that Chevrolet ought to create the hardware that would enable others to race the Corvette. His plan called for Chevy to build 125 light Corvettes for FIA homologation and then sell those cars to amateur drivers.

The timing was right. The governing body of world motor sport, the Fédération Internationale de l'automobile (FIA) had recently created a Grand Touring class of production-based cars in hopes of attracting more manufacturers' interest in road racing around the world. Knudsen thus gave the program an enthusiastic thumbs-up.

The "Light Corvette," which would later be known as the Grand Sport, was initiated with the construction of six prototypes. With a goal of shedding more than 1,000 pounds off the weight of the production car, Duntov and his team, which included Walt Zetye and Harold Krieger, went to work. Through judicious use of lightweight materials, they turned the heavy street Corvette into a well-toned athlete. The engine was to be an all-new variation of the small-block V-8, displacing 377 cubic inches. It featured an aluminum block, Duntov's favored hemispherical heads and two spark plugs per cylinder. The engine featured a cross-ram intake manifold with fuel delivery via four 58-mm Weber carburetors. On the test bench, the combination produced a whopping 550 hp at 6,400 rpm with maximum torque of 500 pound feet at 5,200 rpm. Overall, Zora felt the engine offered the best combination of high horsepower and low weight then available.

The body was made of paper-thin hand-laid fiberglass, and the windows were all Plexiglas, with the exception of the windshield. There was no split window. The birdcage structure of the production car was replaced with one hand-fabricated from aluminum. To save even more weight, the production car's electric headlight motors were removed, and the headlights were set in a fixed position under Plexiglas covers that conformed with the wedge-shaped front end. Compared to modern race cars, the Grand Sport had a relatively stock instrument panel and even had carpeting. It was still a machine one could imagine driving on the street.

Duntov knew he had to solve the chronic problem of inadequate brakes on racing Corvettes once and for all. A disc brake system was a must, and he would lead the way. According to Lowell C. Paddock in his book *Corvette Grand Sport*, Duntov assigned project engineer Ashod Torosian to work with Dunlop and Girling on a disc brake system for the Grand Sport and eventually went with Girling. The company then developed a three-piston caliper that squeezed against solid rotors that were 11-1/4 inches in diameter and 3/4 of an inch thick. These proved inadequate in early testing during which the rotors glowed red hot. Eventually, a one-inch-thick ventilated rotor was adopted. The fruits of this effort would lead to disc brakes being standard on the 1965 Corvette, an American industry first.

The first mule car was completed in November of 1962 and immediately taken to Sebring for testing with Dick Thompson and Masten Gregory. In December Corvette development engineer Bob Clift was one of the first to drive the Grand Sport during a Sebring test session. First reports were gratifying, given the fact that the engine used was not the twin-plug 377 but rather a fuel-injected 327 with some special lightweight components. Optimism soared over what might be accomplished with the more powerful engine in place.

Aerodynamically, less optimism was warranted, as the nose of the Grand Sport lifted under acceleration to the degree that the body fully extended the rebound straps on the front suspension, a force almost equal to the weight of the car. Consequently, the steering was significantly lighter and less responsive. Zora used a large air outlet on the hood to try to relieve some of this pressure, but most photos of the Grand Sport in action show the rear end hunkered down at speed—as if the car had a heavy load in the trunk.

Nonetheless, the Grand Sports were fast cars that had the potential to do well against the Cobras. Additional testing was conducted at Waterford Hills, just north of Detroit. Zora himself would attend these sessions whenever and wherever possible. The stakes were higher than just developing the race cars, because all parts were being evaluated as possible production options to qualify for SCCA competition.

By late December 1962, it appeared that the Grand Sport program was on a roll. There was talk about a street version of the Grand Sport to be built at a special facility near Chevy headquarters in Warren. The New Year would not bring glad tidings, however. Frederick Donner's office on the fourteenth floor of the GM building had heard about the tests at Sebring and had placed a strict interpretation on GM's adherence to the AMA racing ban. On January 5, Duntov was forced to call his troops and cancel the scheduled January tests. The plug had been pulled again. Enough parts had been fabricated to build five complete cars, but no more would be built, and the twin-plug 377 engine was stillborn.

Duntov was incredulous once again. He thought his rationale of letting customers race the Grand Sport was a sound means of getting around the letter of the AMA ban. Now another opportunity for GM to make a statement on the racetracks of the world had been quashed.

The beginning of the 1963 racing season was a painful one for Zora as he watched the Shelby Cobras destroy everything in sight. The overweight Z06 Corvettes were left to carry the torch for Chevrolet. They suffered an embarrassing defeat at Riverside at the hands of Ken Miles and Dave McDonald—who had defected from Corvette—in their Cobras. Enough was enough.

Duntov's disgust turned to anger and ultimately determination. Knowing he had Ed Cole's moral—if not formal—support, Duntov decided to defy the ban. Too much of his time and attention had been invested to let the whole Grand Sport program go to waste. His orders from upstairs were not to build any more cars, but there was nothing said about the cars that had already been built. So Duntov loaned the Grand Sports to trusted teams who would not divulge their secrets.

The list was short: Illinois Chevy dealer Dick Doane and Gulf Oil research executive Grady Davis. Two white Grand Sports were lent out, both with 360-hp fuel-injected engines displacing 327 cubic inches. These stroked 327s were a far cry from the more powerful 377 engines that were designed for these cars, but they proved to be test beds for the cooling and drivetrain requirements of the 396-cubic-inch engine, which would eventually be offered in the 1965 1/2 Corvettes. Because they were not official production cars, they ran against sports racers in the SCCA C-modified class. The Grady Davis car driven by Dick Thompson finished as high as third in its class that year.

But Duntov wasn't happy with the results. He thought that the engines weren't powerful enough to give the drivetrain and brakes a proper test.

So risking the ire of the Fourteenth Floor—which to date had ignored his outlaw program—he went even farther out on a limb and called the Davis car back into Chevy and installed a new twin-inlet Rochester fuel injection system. With more power under the hood, Dick Thompson then registered the Grand Sport's first racing win at an SCCA national event at Watkins Glen in late August 1963.

Dick Doane ran his Grand Sport in only two races in 1963—at Meadowdale where he drove to a sixth-place finish, and at Road America, where he led for many laps before succumbing to a blown engine.

Although the Grand Sports didn't distinguish themselves, Duntov was encouraged by their performance. The cars were being raced and he still hadn't been called on the carpet by management. So, he reasoned, maybe he could get away with one last push at the final race of the year, at Speed Week in Nassau.

The question was how to pull it off. Duntov knew he'd have to find a third party to run the effort but wanted someone with the money and professionalism befitting a quasi-factory effort. He found it from an unlikely source: a 22-year-old heir to a Houston oil fortune named John Mecom Jr. With movie star looks and remarkable maturity, Mecom had already distinguished himself earlier in the 1963 racing season running a Cooper-based Xerex Special built originally by Roy Gane for Roger Penske. The team, headquartered in a huge garage at Houston International Airport, had the winningest record in the SCCA nationals that year. Mecom had the money to hire the very best drivers. In addition to Roger Penske, he had hired Augie Pabst and A. J. Foyt. In short, he had the resources and organization that Duntov needed to try to rub some dirt in the faces of Carroll Shelby and his fleet of Cobra drivers.

His battle plan ready, Duntov called all the Grand Sports back to Warren, including the Davis and Doane cars. Additional modifications were made to three of them for the assault on Nassau. If Ed Cole knew about this effort, he remained silent. The temptation to beat the Cobras just once was too great.

For a company loudly proclaiming it wasn't involved in racing, some of the best resources of GM went into making a competitive Corvette race car. Duntov started with new, single-plug 377-cubic-inch aluminum-block V-8s fitted with aluminum heads. But rather than deal with a fussy fuel injection system, Duntov elected to go with four twin-throat 58-mm Weber carburetors. The resulting output was 435 foot pounds of torque at 4,000 rpm and 485 hp at 6,000 rpm.

Working with Goodyear, Duntov elected to use a new lower-profile racing tire, which necessitated going to an 11-inch-wide rim. To make room

The Grand Sport may have looked like the new Stingray, but it was purpose-built from the ground up. And its purpose was to beat the Cobra.

for the wider tires, the Grand Sport's fenders were flared out and the rear fascia was drilled with a continuous line of holes. New hood panels sported two forward-facing grilled air inlets.

The cars, painted in the "Cadillac blue" colors of Mecom Motorsports, were trucked from Detroit to Don Allen Chevrolet in Miami for final prep. But rather than transport them by truck to the port of Miami, Bob Clift recalls that he and several others drove the raucous, thundering race cars through the streets of Miami to the docks.

Clift, Gib Hufstader and other members of Duntov's staff were under strict orders not to get involved in any physical assistance with the team; they were there only to provide advice. If anybody asked, they were to say they were "on vacation." Hufstader remembers that "Chris Economaki [the editor of *National Speed Sport News* and an ABC sports broadcaster] was our worst enemy. We wanted to keep a low profile at the race track and tried our best to stay away from the interviews and the reporters." Duntov said his own presence at the races was rather commonplace, so much so that many times he was reported as being at events even when he was not there.

Once the cars arrived in Nassau, there was still plenty of work to be done. "The cars suffered from chronic axle problems which were failing after about 50 test miles," said Clift, "so we took them out to Nassau's new airport and ran them back and forth on a long access road that was lined with crocodiles. The goal was to warm the cars up and put a load on the teeth. "This was before we had oil additives which help prevent the metal from fusing together. We would vary the speed—we wanted to get a gradually increasing load while keeping the oil cool." Meanwhile, Hufstader devised a differential cooler designed to cool the rear axles by 10 to 15 degrees. It was mounted under a shroud on the rear deck of the cars.

The Corvettes got a thorough going-over by arch rival Carroll Shelby as they were being unloaded off the docks. Shelby said he wasn't surprised to see the quasi-factory Chevrolet effort at Nassau. "We knew they were building them," said Shelby. "We knew everything they were doing. That's the reason we put a 427 in the car instead of a 289. That was the first time we ran a 427 in competition."

What did Shelby think of the Grand Sport as a race car? "It was all right. It certainly was light enough. The 377 didn't have as much horsepower as our 427 Ford, but the problem with the Grand Sport was that they didn't have any wind tunnel testing—those front wheels kept lifting off the ground."

While the Grand Sports looked very impressive with their fastback rooflines, muscular fender flares and fat racing rubber tires, they still suffered from the aerodynamic problems endemic to the Sting Ray. The front ends would visibly lift under power, and large hood vents were ineffective in reducing the lift. Another problem was fuel starvation with the big Weber carburetors during high g cornering.

Still, it was the fastest race car Dick Thompson had ever driven. "The car was so light, yet powerful and for the first time, I could go through the corners with the Porsches," said Thompson. "And it had real brakes! Augie Pabst was driving a Lola, but I didn't have any problem with him until my differential began to overheat. The front end was always light, but if you backed off slightly on the throttle, it would come back down. At least the Nassau course, laid out on the old airport runways, was a little slower so it didn't affect us that much."

The Grand Sports soon proved they were for real, winning a five-lap qualifying race that preceded the December 1 Tourist Trophy event for GTs and prototypes. Along with Pabst in the Chevy Lola, the two Grand Sports driven by Dick Thompson and Jim Hall soundly beat the Cobras and a Ferrari GTO to get the front-row grid positions. The Lola won the subsequent 99-mile Tourist Trophy, after the Corvettes both retired with rear end trouble.

The Mecom team had one more shot at the Governor's Cup on December 6. The team's fixes were effective and all three Grand Sports showed well. Penske's car finished an outstanding third, on the same lap as Foyt's winning Chevy Scarab and the runner-up Ferrari 250P. Augie Pabst was fourth and Dick Thompson, slowed by difficulties, was sixth. Shelby placed his best Cobra no better than eighth.

In the longest and most important race of Speed Week, the 252-mile Nassau Trophy contest on December 8, the Grand Sports finished fourth (Thompson) and eighth (Cannon), despite a series of pit stops to have the hoods taped down. The best Ford-powered finisher was a Cobra in seventh place.

Duntov was almost giddy afterwards, which was evident in a risky internal memo to E .J. Premo dated December 16, 1963:

Top: Zora confers with his most successful driver, Dr. Dick Thompson, in the paddock at Nassau. Thompson later remarked that the Grand Sport was the fastest race car he had ever driven.

Bottom: The Mecom team cars owned the front of the grid at Nassau with the two Grand Sports in the center flanked by teammate Augie Pabst in a Lola.

At Nassau in 1963, Augie Pabst (left), Zora and Roger Penske share in the satisfaction of knowing that in the Grand Sport, they finally had a car capable of beating the Cobras.

The superiority of Chevrolet-powered specials over Ford-powered specials and all comers was clearly demonstrated. The superiority of Light Corvettes over Ford Cobras and all other GT and GT prototypes and high performance level of Corvette was also asserted.

The whole week was a red letter week for Chevrolet and a black one for Ford.

In the last battle of the season in the war between Chevrolet and Ford, the winner and again champion was Chevrolet. Cobras manned by drivers as Dan Gurney and Bob Holbert were completely outclassed by Corvettes. The Cobras as well as Cooper Fords did not show the reliability that they have demonstrated throughout the season—they were blowing engines almost as soon as they would be put into the chassis.

Since the news of Corvette participating was known to Ford four or more weeks in advance, I surmise that all their efforts were made to increase engine output. Whatever they achieved was not enough to approach Corvettes but too much for their engines to take.

The Corvette success at Nassau—combined with the fact that his managers had not censured him—caused Duntov to believe that his success may have caused a quiet change in GM policy. If he could run with a quasi-factory effort and get away with it at Nassau, why not at Sebring or Le Mans? Duntov proposed finishing the two remaining cars and providing Mecom and Grady Davis each with two cars and Jim Hall with one car.

Duntov rated the cars' prospects at Daytona, Sebring and Le Mans. "At Daytona, since the cars can run only in 250 miles free-for-all race and not in 2,000 kilometers race, which is reserved for GT only [not prototypes] their chances against modified are slim. However, the Daytona bank is very punishing and they may finish better than the paper form suggests." For Daytona, Duntov thought that he might be able to reduce frontal area by cutting the coupes down into roadsters with small windshields, so he had cars 001 and 002 cut down in January of 1964 at the GM Tech Center in Warren.

Back to Outlaw Status

For Le Mans, Duntov suggested that while aerodynamic drag could work against the Corvettes, the smoother French track might be easier on the cars than the airport runways at Sebring. But it would all be a pipe dream, as word of the Grand Sports' success at Nassau finally got the attention of the Fourteenth Floor. Bunkie Knudsen was called in and given a stern warning that Duntov and company were to have no further association with the Mecom racing team. Yet Duntov was not singled out for any disciplinary action, despite disobeying direct company orders. Clearly, he had guardian angels, such as Ed Cole and Bunkie Knudsen, who not only protected him but also quietly cheered him on.

After Nassau, instead of Duntov being required to call the cars in and destroy them, the Grand Sports were turned over to privateers such as Delmo Johnson, John Mecom and Jim Hall. Putting cars into the hands of his customers was exactly what Duntov originally envisioned with the original Grand Sport program, except for the fact that he wanted to build a hundred cars—not five.

Duntov was forced to cease any close ties to the program. Still, he occasionally slipped parts and engines into the hands of participants, but never again did he play the kind of role he had with the Mecom team in 1963.

Eventually the other three Grand Sports were released as well, including two roadsters. The cars remained a big part of the American road-racing scene through 1966, but they were faced with increasingly sophisticated mid-engined Chaparrals, McLarens, Ferraris and Lolas, and the Grand Sports' influence waned. The final major race for a Grand Sport was the 1967 Daytona 24-hour, where Jim White, Tony Denman and Bob Brown ran the car against an impressive field of Ford GTs and Ferraris but dropped out after 72 laps.

As much attention as the Grand Sport project generated during those years between 1963 and 1966, looking back, Duntov had bittersweet memories about the entire program. It paled compared to his earlier hopes to build a purpose-built, four-wheel-drive race car based on the CERV II to go head to head with Ford and Ferrari at Le Mans. Duntov later described it as "a quick and dirty sledgehammer project, of which I am not particularly proud."

But history may have proved him wrong. As an engineering accomplishment, the Grand Sport program was remarkable. It was an amazingly effective public relations exercise, and the cars showed incredible potential despite an alarming lack of development. The Grand Sport program garnered as much publicity as it did because of Duntov's relentless effort to keep jouncing against GM's corporate policies. Since the car looked so streetable, it may have also tickled the Walter Mitty fantasies of many Corvette fanatics. The Grand Sport may not have earned Duntov any political gold stars on the Fourteenth Floor, but what he did achieve constituted an indelible contribution to Corvette's racing pedigree.

CERV II in the Wings

At the same time the Grand Sport program was underway, Duntov was scheming about a far more ambitious project. Encouraged by Bunkie Knudsen's overall support for racing as a means to sell more products, Duntov dusted off his CERV II plans. He wanted to be ready in the event that GM's policy ever changed.

This time, he had a few new tricks up his sleeve. He was now thinking about a prototype/race car featuring four-wheel drive and an automatic transmission in a full-bodied, mid-engined layout. While Knudsen never had official clearance to build a vehicle like this, he wanted a plan to be able to go up against Ford, which had since decided to go full-bore into a "Total Performance" racing program that included Indianapolis and Le Mans. Ford's Le Mans hopes at that time rested on the Ford GT40, based on a British Lola sports car chassis. CERV II once again skated on the edges of what Chevrolet could do under the AMA racing ban, but at least on paper it provided a formidable challenger in the Chevy stable.

Duntov's interest in four-wheel drive was no major surprise. He had written a paper in 1937 called "Analysis of Four Wheel Drive for Racing Cars" and had been a close observer of what Auto Union and Mercedes were doing in this area before the war. He was intrigued by the benefits of all four tires biting the pavement even if it meant carrying extra weight for the components necessary to drive four wheels instead of two. Furthermore, a projected 550 horsepower from the engine was far more than could be utilized with the racing tires of the period, according to Paul Van Valkenburgh, an engineer who worked for Winchell in the 1960s. Thus Duntov concluded that four-wheel drive was mandatory.

While four-wheel drive had the advantage of added traction and stability, Duntov had to devise a means of distributing torque between the front and rear wheels. He elected to go with separate transmissions and torque converters for each end of the engine, reasoning that a pair of transmissions would be lighter than one large transmission plus clutch, transfer case and driveshaft. It was an all-new principle, and Duntov earned a patent on it

Duntov had more in mind than just basic four-wheel drive, however. He calibrated the torque converters to take advantage of weight transfer to pump more torque to the car's rear wheels under hard acceleration and less torque once it was moving at high speed. Duntov also wanted the flexibility of multiple drive ratios, which would alter the bottom and top-end driving characteristics. He achieved this by equipping both axles with compact two-speed gearboxes. Controlled by a single cockpit lever, they gave a direct drive and a 1.5:1 reduction.

Power was provided by an all-aluminum 377-cubic-inch V-8 similar to the Grand Sport engines. The only difference was the use of a Hilborn constant-flow fuel injection system instead of the Webers used at Nassau. During testing at the GM Proving Ground at Milford, Duntov achieved a zero to 60 run in 2.8 seconds as well as a top speed of 214.01 mph on the test track.

Wind tunnel studies had been performed on a sports racer prototype called the XP-817, and the results fairly helped define the final shape of CERV II. Tony Lapine and Larry Shinoda designed the body. Scale models of both a roadster and a coupe were tested, with the coupe intended for Le Mans. However, it was the roadster that was built for testing and development. Although it was a low-drag design, they soon discovered it wasn't stable at racing speed. "Because lifting forces were so high, I felt like I was in a wheelbarrow and a giant hand picked me up at 150 mph," said Duntov. So he devised one of racing's first uses of a retractable spoiler, called a "cow tongue" spoiler, which popped out of the rear deck just aft of the engine. "For a straight high-speed run, we didn't need it," said Duntov, succinctly attributing the decision to "additional drag."

CERV II also made use of some of the most advanced race tires in existence at the time, which were developed by Firestone. They were wide and low profile in a 9.5 x 15 size for all four corners, and were mounted to 8.5-inch Kelsey Hayes magnesium wheels.

Top: CERV II featured four-wheel drive and an automatic transmission and torque converter for each end of the car.

Bottom: Zora takes some demonstration laps in CERV II. Had the opportunity presented itself, he would have used this car to go up against the international racing community at Le Mans.

The Fight for Funding

Quite simply, CERV II represented everything Zora wanted in a Le Mans-bound race car. But now he had to sell the corporation on racing the car. That process would involve overcoming the competition—literally and figuratively—within the company. Duntov found himself in a three-way internal battle for resources against Vince Piggins, who managed an engine group supporting NASCAR racing, and Frank Winchell, who was involved in the development of the Corvair as well as supporting GM's clandestine association with Chaparral Cars in Midland, Texas.

Although the three departments never competed in the real world because the projects never went head to head, they did contend for resources and money. This was especially true between the Corvette group and R&D,

which had a bigger budget and more facilities, thanks to its involvement with higher-volume cars, such as the Corvair.

Having different approaches to their jobs, Winchell and Duntov in particular were antagonists. Winchell may have been a better fit in a large corporation like GM. While extremely competitive, he didn't mind keeping a low profile, as opposed to Duntov, who enjoyed basking in the limelight even if it meant irritating senior GM managers like Ed Cole. "Frank was opposed to exposure," said Van Valkenburgh. "He wanted Chevy R&D to be invisible, whereas Zora was the opposite—he wanted to be a public figure. Frank felt that the more visible he himself was, the less he could get away with. Winchell was totally hands-on and self-taught. He didn't even have an engineering degree. He went to work for economic reasons. Everybody worked for Frank; nobody worked with him. He was strong-willed, assertive," Van Valkenburgh concluded.

Winchell cultivated the relationship with Chaparral and appointed one of his most promising young engineers, Jim Musser, to be the chief liaison. In this mutually beneficial relationship, Chevrolet gained the use of the Chaparral shops and test track in the arid scrubland outside of Midland, Texas. Chaparral, in turn, received lots of hardware to play with from Chevrolet—everything from engines, transmissions, suspension pieces, and so on. It was all in the interest of research and development.

Winchell first began to venture into prototype territory when he teamed up with Bill Mitchell on a Corvair-based project. Mitchell wanted a sports car based on the Corvair, and Winchell was working on various configurations with the Corvair driveline package mounted ahead of the rear axle. Musser was given the job of engineering Chevrolet's first monocoque chassis, and Larry Shinoda did the body. The result was the very slick-looking Monza GT or XP-777. The Monza GT caught the attention of Jim Hall, who invited Winchell and his staff down to Midland to look at a mid-engine V-8 fiberglass chassis he was working on called the Chaparral 2.

The Chaparral 2 developed into the GS2 (Grand Sport 2), which bore comparison to Duntov's CERV II. Like CERV II, the GS2 had an automatic transmission designed by Winchell but had two-wheel drive instead of four. The GS2 name was borrowed from Duntov's modified Grand Sport Corvettes and, according to Van Valkenburgh, Winchell may have thought it necessary to one-up Duntov.

The GS2 was built at Winchell's shop and then trucked down to Midland, where it could be tested in absolute secrecy. The car was a beauty—a sports racer with an aluminum-block 327-cubic-inch engine and a single-speed automatic transmission. It was a forerunner of the many generations of Chaparral sports racers that took American road racing by storm in the mid- to late-1960s. Chaparral was a leader in its aerodynamic research. Hall developed spoilers and articulating wings that kept his cars glued to the ground on high-speed turns as well as in tight corners.

Naturally, CERV II, the GS2 and the men who created them drew comparisons to one another. Each man was critical of the other's efforts. Winchell was a powertrain guy who did not look kindly on Duntov's twin-torque converter arrangement; Winchell thought it was too complicated for a race car. Duntov, on the other hand, was an engine/suspension guy and thought that Winchell didn't understand the relationship between the track (the distance between each set of wheels) and the center of gravity; he felt that Winchell's cars were too narrow.

Duntov admitted that Winchell could irritate him, especially when not giving adequate credit to Duntov for the engines that he provided Winchell's group. But when push came to shove, Duntov ultimately acknowledged that Winchell had some good engineering approaches, and the two were ultimately in a position to learn from each other. The steering knuckles used on the Grand Sport Corvette, for example, were from Chaparral.

Considerable budgets went into Winchell's programs and at times Duntov was envious. For the key decision-makers in the corporation, directing more money into Winchell's programs was their way of controlling Duntov's zeal for high-profile activities. Duntov found it impossible to lie low, and Winchell excelled at doing so. If GM was going to go racing, they much preferred to fly under the radar with Winchell and Chaparral. Furthermore, Rattlesnake Raceway afforded much more secrecy for testing than the GM Tech Center.

Eventually, the cars were tested against each other. In March 1964, CERV II was brought down to Midland and tested against the GS2, but teething problems with the two-speed box driving the front wheels and problems with the disc brakes caused CERV II to suffer in comparison to the simpler R&D car.

As a result, CERV II never saw the kind of limelight on international racetracks that Zora envisioned for the car. In the summer of 1964, the edict came down from Bunkie Knudsen that CERV II would not be used to compete against Ford at Le Mans. Instead, the Chevy torch would be carried by Chaparral. (A Chaparral 2F competed at Le Mans in 1967 and showed enough speed to have its overhead wing banned by the organizers the following year. During the race the car, driven by Phil Hill and Mike Spence, succumbed to automatic transmission problems.) Not being chosen to represent GM at Le Mans was yet another bitter blow to Duntov, who lost a chance to race his most advanced car to date. To add insult to injury, he had been outmaneuvered by one of his bigger rivals within the halls of GM.

Several years later, the cars were matched again for tire tests, with CERV II being equipped with the aluminum version of the fabled L88 big-block. Again it went up against a modified GS2B. The R&D group was also anxious to test four-wheel drive against suction traction as the best way to make a race car go quickly around a corner. Chaparral at the time was working the 2J, which used two motorized fans at the rear of the car and a rear wheel enclosed by a full skirt. The object was to create a low-pressure situation under the car, thereby vacuuming the car to the pavement.

By the time CERV II was brought back to Rattlesnake it was several years old. "I was doing the computer simulations in 1968 for suction traction with the Can-Am race series in mind," said Van Valkenburgh. At the time, the Can-Am was the SCCA's top professional racing series. The cars were wide, low sports racers with no limits on engine displacement or aerodynamic devices. As such, the Can-Am was a racing engineer's dream series. "I was also looking at four-wheel drive as an alternative to suction traction and was therefore interested in looking at CERV II again. My thinking, however, was that suction traction was far more effective than 4WD."

During the tests, the GS2B with a 327 engine outdid Zora's car by a substantial margin, according to Larry Shinoda, who was there for the tests. "It was several hundred pounds lighter," said Shinoda. That killed any hopes of resurrecting Zora's CERV II program. "Zora took it pretty bitterly," said Shinoda. "He felt that the guys who were running the tests may have sabotaged his car."

CERV II was as close as Duntov would come to a competition-bred, mid-engined racer. But the car never saw a track, due to GM's "no factory racing" policy, combined with what may have amounted to a "not-invented-here" sentiment at Chevrolet R&D. It underscored Duntov's limited political power within the corporation. The fact that both the GS2B and CERV II were developed behind separate firewalls within GM emphasized the engineering capability within the company as well as the political lines of demarcation. If the company could have sanctioned a way for Duntov and Winchell to work together, the results might have been formidable.

Despite the fact that CERV II never raced, it would not result in a technological dead end: It provided yet another important link in Duntov's ongoing quest to build a production mid-engined Corvette. Many of the design features of CERV II, particularly four-wheel drive, would later surface in other mid-engined machines that Duntov would use to tantalize the automotive community. But hope was fading that these ideas would ever see the production line.

EIGHTEEN

*Zora holds court with his key engine men and their exotic creations, which did much
to establish GM's performance capability—even if they never saw a production line.
Pictured around Duntov left to right are Cal Wade, Fred Frincke and Denny Davis.*

The Corporate Robin Hood

During the late 1950s and early 1960s, Duntov exerted an effective if unofficial command of a small but extremely dedicated group of engineers. Unlike the Corvette program today, which contains hundreds of engineers, designers, packaging experts, structural experts and safety technicians, it was a simpler world back then. "In early days, just seven," said Duntov. But those seven had the pleasure of working with a man who dwelled in a corporate Sherwood Forest and was not particularly mindful of budgets or protocol.

The Instigator

To be successful, Duntov exercised a highly engaging management style that motivated his subordinates to do things they wouldn't ordinarily consider. "Zora managed by love," said Roy Sjoberg, a former Corvette Development Manager under Duntov who later became chief engineer of the Viper at Chrysler Corporation. "He didn't understand Harvard, MIT, Sloan programs, he just managed by emotion. He got your emotions involved and once your emotions were involved, your commitment goes on ad infinitum. CERV I and CERV II were all done by volunteers. Zora just said, 'We go do this thing, yes?' And we always said, 'God yes, we've got to go do it.'

"Then Zora would say, 'I have no expense account, we have to share costs.' And we're all going, 'Yeah, Zora, we understand.' He managed by love. As a manager, once you have it, you don't have to look over your shoulder at all. These guys will follow you to hell's half acre."

Creativity was the hallmark of how Duntov's group functioned. One of Duntov's strengths was answering a challenge or recognizing a need—something that could be made to improve performance, efficiency or cornering. "People respond to an intensity I have," Duntov once said when asked why he was able to get so much accomplished with so little corporate sanction and such a miniscule budget.

Opposite: Corporate life at GM involved endless meetings, but those that involved Duntov resulted in actionable decisions that often ignored corporate policy, budgets or rules.

Duntov's management style was straightforward; he had no political agenda. He made his vision clear—the pursuit of daring, cutting-edge technology, be it a race car, a prototype car or a production car. He stuck to his beliefs, and was not worried about creating a career path. Duntov had the position he wanted. Because he was governed by his inner voice and not by external standards, he often clashed with the Fourteenth Floor at General Motors over his preoccupation with thinly disguised racecars. GM still prided itself on being America's number one source for cars and trucks, not for another Ferrari or Porsche.

Yet for Zora, his inner voice was more real than any rule the corporation made, according to Dr. Ron Westrum, a professor of sociology and interdisciplinary technology at Eastern Michigan University. Duntov saw organizational boundaries as merely a convenience of management—and if they got in the way, he'd break the rules. He had seen whole societies being tossed aside during his life; therefore, he vowed he wouldn't be a slave to a few corporate standards that often appeared arbitrary.

In managing his team, he enforced high-performance goals and strategic thinking. According to Westrum, Duntov fit the pattern of a technological maestro functioning in a large-scale operation. "They ask the critical questions, know the issues and don't compromise," said Westrum. "They may not be the best engineers but they understand how the whole thing is going to work. Duntov was more of a systems thinker. He really needed to see how things fit together."

Life on the Fringe

Duntov had few levels of authority in his group; instead, there were large amounts of personal responsibility with everyone involved who was familiar with the overall task. This approach was directly counter to the traditional top to bottom organizational structure within GM. Some high-level managers saw Zora as a freak who knew nothing about the way "we do things in the big corporation." According to Westrum, this was a common occurrence in large bureaucratic structures where management's favored course of action is often codified into doctrines and expressed through the organization's structure, which is set up to react to events occurring in an expected way. "This makes them slow to react to changing environments and high technology because the very features that make them predictable also make them highly vulnerable," said Westrum.

Consequently, organizations like GM are likely to botch tasks that require rapid information flow, innovation and critiquing. "The reason is use of ideas from the organization's periphery threatens the status of the organization's center," said Westrum. "Rather than tolerate new or critical ideas, whatever their value, they will be sacrificed to protect the organization's structure and statuses." Zora's emphasis on performance was definitely seen as peripheral thinking, which was easily dismissed by managers more preoccupied with volume and market share.

Yet the fact that the Corvette was a low-volume car line that was out of the mainstream did create advantages. GM management often turned a blind eye to the activities of Duntov and his merry men. For those managers, it was better in many cases not to know what was going on for fear of accountability to the Fourteenth Floor. Ignorance was more blissful and usually safer. "We often intentionally looked the other way, " said Paul King, who later became director of engineering for Chevrolet. "We had our hands full on production cars and we weren't spending a lot of time with Corvette or racing."

Consequently, Zora and his team had a window of opportunity to build race cars and exotic concept Corvettes that had little or no chance of ever going into production. Roy Sjoberg called this phenomenon "intrapreurialism," and Duntov was a master practitioner. "He was able to do entrepreneurial activities inside of GM, not with their consent, but by default," said Sjoberg. "That's what I learned from him. Don't ask for a 'yes'; if they don't say no, do it. It's much easier to apologize later than ask for permission."

Maintaining an entrepreneurial spirit often meant finding creative methods to finance his programs, sometimes piggybacking his plans onto other departments' budgets. "Normally in a business, if it's not in your budget, you don't work on it," said Walt Zetye, a chassis engineer who later became Duntov's right-hand man. "We always tried to get some other group to do our testing for us, if we didn't have a budget."

Zora was often mischievous about his wayward ideas, always looking for a way to do things, sometimes without the other departments' knowledge. He became adept at understanding the bureaucracy's financial limitations and working the system. Some have suggested Zora had someone in the finance department who coached him. It also didn't hurt that supporters like Ed Cole—when called upon—could usually get the accountants off his back whenever Zora got into a jam.

Duntov's racing background, which was unusual for a GM employee, had caused a stir when he first came to the company. "I had seen him working around R&D and on some other projects," said Zetye. "I heard he had worked at Porsche and was a racing driver. I had a good feeling about him. As we went on, it became like a father-son relationship. As he got more confident in me, he accepted my designs and we got along quite well."

Duntov demanded accountability from every member of his group. "He would be talking to me in group meetings about camshafts and I would get good questions from him," said engineer Denny Davis. "He would go from me to the guy next to him and talk about suspension, brakes, clutches, you name it. He knew what in the hell was going on and could talk intelligently about everything."

Larry Drake's job was to test Zora's engine ideas. Given GM's anti-racing policy, Drake expected the position would give him little to do. He was wrong. "Between eras of CERV and exhaust emissions, we did more to develop engines, horsepower per cubic inch, than ever before or since." Drake recalled that policy shifts made for a very frustrating situation. One day every dyno would be humming for 24 hours, and the next day all the engines would be sitting in the halls and nothing would be happening. "However, due to Zora's persistence during that period of fickle program approval, we worked on many things," said Drake. Such projects included Weber carburetors, six different variations of fuel injection, production FI, tuned intake and exhausts, at least two dozen camshafts, aluminum heads and blocks. The list was remarkable for a company that wasn't partici-pating in racing.

Whenever Duntov had the opportunity to test a Corvette SS, CERV or Grand Sport it was a source of pride to the people who worked in Chevy Engineering. Knowing this, Zora loved to fire up an irascible race motor and repeatedly stab the throttle, the garage walls echoing the blast from the motor's crackling exhausts. It was a sound of energy, of vitality, that something was happening—something hot. Zora translated this enthusi-asm to the Tech Center test loop. Normally the province of staid sedans, the Tech Center was suddenly GM's own Fiorano, the Ferrari test track. Housewives hanging laundry in the stillness of their Warren backyards near the Tech Center were suddenly rattled by the distant thunder of race cars in heat. GM was alive and well.

"Zora was driven by more horsepower, more rpm, better handling, another speed record—that was his adrenaline," said Herb Fishel, now head of GM's Motorsports Technology Group. "For him it was a matter of how to get this done. CERV II and all of these unusual engine combina-tions evolved because Zora was driven by that. His heart and his interest were in the right places for the right reasons."

Fishel knew about Duntov from reading *Hot Rod* while growing up in North Carolina. "I flew up to Detroit in March 1963 for a job interview fresh out of North Carolina State and they offered me a job. They asked me if there's anything I'd like to do on the first day. I said I'd like to meet Zora Duntov. I was getting ready to leave and sure enough he was in his office. I met him and they could have hired me for nothing."

Delegating the Details

If Zora had a protégé, one individual to whom he was closest during his tenure at GM, it was Walt Zetye. The affable Zetye predated Zora at GM, having joined the corporation in 1946, where he was assigned to work on suspension and steering design under the supervision of Maurice Olley. He also helped define the 1953 Corvette, designing the front suspension, steering, driveline and frame concept.

Throughout the 1950s, Zetye worked in chassis, front suspension and steering systems for Chevrolet passenger cars and was involved with the Q Chevrolet in 1958 under Bob Schilling. In 1959, Zetye was assigned to work with Zora, where he designed many of the underpinnings of the 1963 Corvette. He held a co-patent with Zora on the design of the 1963 Corvette rear suspension.

Walt spent a lot of time on ride trips with Zora, and after a time, he even began to dress like Zora, with his expressive sport coats and open-collared shirts. Zetye also served as a buffer between Zora and the rest of the staff, especially at times when Zora was upset about something.

Zora's interest in Zetye derived not only from Zetye's engineering talents and loyalty but also from the fact that, like Zora, he was someone who had many outside interests beyond GM. Zetye maintained friendships throughout the United States, Mexico and Europe and was involved with Dr. Aldo Gucci and his associates in the fashion world. In April 1976, Zetye even modeled some of Gucci's fashions at a charity event in Chicago.

Zora counted on men like Zetye and Gib Hufstader in part because of his own often poor management of the details necessary to execute projects. Zora craved the big idea, but would become impatient with the finer points involved in executing and perfecting that idea. This was certainly true during his Ardun engine days, and the pattern carried forward into his GM career.

Zora saw his role differently. His mission was to put provocative ideas into the system and let others work out the execution of those concepts. Consequently, assembly and quality issues got the short end of Duntov's time. He delegated many of these responsibilities to his staff. Corvettes were never well known for having fine assembly quality, and Duntov didn't pay as much attention to plant affairs as he could have, according to Gib Hufstader. "They didn't like him that much at the plant and felt that he was too aloof, too distant, or too demanding. I don't think he had much patience for the process of building a car at an assembly plant. He really didn't have much interest."

He also didn't have much control. Body, electrical and engineering staff on loan from other platforms often worked on the Corvette in their spare time, originally handling the heat and air conditioning systems. Exacerbating the problem was the fact that Zora didn't care for these disciplines because he saw them as nonessential to going fast. Chassis, suspension and powertrain were critical components of a sports or racing car; a body without squeaks and rattles was not.

Still, Zora realized that the body and electrical people had a job to do and he didn't get in their way. "Zora was no more or less responsive than other executives I worked under, but he would not hamper progress on something," said body engineer Bob Vogelei, who joined the group in 1963. "If I didn't hear anything from him I knew it was safe to proceed."

Duntov hated paperwork. He wasn't particularly well organized and had people like Vogelei and Zetye handle much of it. But when Duntov did sit down to write, he did it well. He was a terrific customer relations correspondent and would take the time to personally respond to every customer letter he received. He gave special attention to young students working on term papers or letters from aspiring Corvette owners. When replying to these would-be Corvette drivers, he would conclude with the line, "I sincerely hope that your dream of owning a Corvette comes true."

A 1972 letter from John Bradshaw of Burlingame, California, typified the kind of esteem in which the enthusiast public held Duntov:

> I realize that you must be an extremely busy man, and not have much extra time, so I will get to my main point: In the many articles I have read about you and how you have carefully controlled the direction that the car progressed in, I learned that often you have had to "battle it out" so to speak with the stylists and so-called "bean counters." I do not think that the public realizes that to achieve the present day model, that much work and effort had to be expended in an attempt to produce an excellent GT.

> I wanted to thank you for so well preserving the Corvette, so that it is the great automobile that it is today.

As always, Zora took the time to reply to Bradshaw personally, writing: "Letters such as yours are indeed rare and lift our spirits, particularly during a time when there are so many automotive critics and others who appear on occasion to be opposed to our designs."

That Zora was able to build cars like the Corvette SS and CERV I from his peripheral position on the organization chart suggests comparisons with other American design leaders who defied the odds to do great things. Examples include Clarence "Kelly" Johnson, at Lockheed Aircraft, who developed everything from the P-38 fighter to the high-flying U-2 and hypersonic SR-71 spy planes; and Bill McLean, who developed the Sidewinder air-to-air missile in the early 1950s. Both Johnson and McLean were confident in navigating their teams around the organizational obstacles—financial and otherwise—that got in the way of their great ideas.

Engineer Irv Culver coined the term "skunk works" to describe Johnson's semi-clandestine department within Lockheed Aircraft. Johnson's skunk works was able to achieve amazing breakthroughs in very short periods of time, often under budget. McLean, meanwhile, developed an enormously effective weapon, the Sidewinder missile, of the utmost simplicity, with about two dozen moving parts and fourteen radio tubes. Sidewinder used an off-the-shelf rocket motor. In similar fashion, Duntov often had to make do with Chevrolet passenger car parts that were available on the shelf, such as what he used in fashioning the front suspension of the Sting Ray in order to have enough money to create an independent rear unit. Otherwise, the money just wasn't there to design, validate and manufacture custom parts for the Corvette.

McLean had a style not unlike Duntov's, according to Dr. Ron Westrum. "He'd walk into an engineering department and commandeer whatever he needed. He'd recruit a team of people, often without compensating the affected parties. For these people, the project is supremely important; organizational politics doesn't matter. They are driven by the goal, are often insubordinate, and they hope posterity will legitimize them."

A Life Outside GM

Duntov's ability to survive at GM could also be credited to his own balance as an individual. He was a man with a tremendous appetite for living. He'd seen danger early and often in his life, but instead of becoming bitter and withdrawn, he came out swinging and had an insatiable hunger to take things to the edge. In many ways, he was like a Hollywood star: He was bound not by convention but simply by his own actualization as an engineer, race driver and risk taker.

Duntov's multiple interests outside of the corporation—his friendships and social outlets —kept him well rounded and emotionally healthy compared to many of his peers, who put their entire identity into a corporate hierarchy that they could not control. These things allowed Duntov to tolerate the alien culture of GM and not be driven insane by politics or programs that survived or died according to executive whim. With all the things he had seen and done, the corporate push-pull was irritating and frustrating, to be sure, but ultimately to Zora it was not life-threatening.

When and where he could, Zora struck out against the conformity that was so ingrained in the Detroit automotive culture. In his July 1996 column in *Automobile* magazine, David E. Davis Jr. described a Christmas party hosted by Karl Ludvigsen, then with public relations for GM Design Staff. "Lots of GM executives were there with their wives and it was all very dark suit, very stiff. Suddenly there was a loud roar as Zora and Elfi arrived in some outrageous secret-engined Corvette, both of them looking as though they thought the party was in Palm Beach. They entered Ludvigsen's house like a spreading brushfire— Zora in raw silk trousers and espadrilles and an open shirt and a silk scarf with ginger blossoms on it, and Elfi done up as a bouquet containing all the temptations of the flesh. In five minutes, everybody in the house wanted to go home and change their clothes."

Ed Cole himself would occasionally socialize with the Duntovs, especially during the years following his divorce from his wife Esther and before his marriage to Dollie Cole.

Duntov used his boat to entertain many celebrity guests and racing drivers, among them astronaut Alan Shepard and race driver Jim Rathmann. The 1960 Indy winner had his own Chevy dealership in Melbourne, Florida, and was responsible for putting six of the seven original Mercury astronauts into Corvettes on a promotional basis. The only one who didn't partake was John Glenn, who preferred a Chevy station wagon. Shepard visited Duntov at the GM Tech Center when he picked up his Corvette and later was photographed in front of the GM styling dome for *Corvette News*, the official Corvette owner publication. Later Shepard went water-skiing behind Zora's boat.

While Zora was rich in friendships, he also had a couple of soulmates. One of these was Anatole C. Lapine, a Latvian-born designer who worked in the Chevrolet studios at GM before going on to Porsche as their director of design in 1969. The two met in Bill Mitchell's studio in 1956, prior to GM's decision to build the Corvette SS. Harley Earl had just acquired Jack Ensley's D-Type Jaguar and was considering the possibility of dropping a Chevy V-8 into it.

The group was discussing alternatives to the Jaguar monocoque frame and Lapine brought up the Mercedes 300SL. "I mentioned Mercedes (I had apprenticed with Daimler in Hamburg)," said Lapine. "Zora, who was speak-

Zora and Elfi were often the life of a party and were part of social circles far beyond GM. An expressive couple, they did on occasion enjoy shaking up their GM contemporaries.

ing with his thick Russian accent, says to hear me mention Mercedes didn't surprise him since he thought I had a German accent.

"Then I shocked him by addressing him in Russian. His eyes lit up and he grabbed me by the biceps, saying, 'We must drink tonight! Come to my house in Grosse Pointe.' That night, we drank vodka, ate herring and never lost sight of each other after that."

Nurturing Friendships

Friendships like Lapine's became more important to Zora in the absence of an immediate family. Zora's father Jacques had died alone in Paris in 1956 after surviving a Nazi concentration camp in World War II. Jacques never took another wife, a fact that haunted Zora and Yura, who had earlier discouraged him from marrying a woman he was seeing because she lacked an education. Meanwhile, Zora's mother Rachel and stepfather Josef had moved to Florida. There, Rachel was being treated for mental illness in a sanitarium. Zora visited her there occasionally, but in her compromised state, she could no longer play the strong role she had in Zora's earlier life, and Zora rarely talked about her.

Designer Tony Lapine (with Duntov) became one of Zora's closest associates within GM.

Zora remained extremely close to his brother Yura, even though they no longer lived in the same city. Yura continued to live in New York after Zora moved to Detroit to join GM. Yura had gone to work for Curtiss Wright in the 1950s but in 1960 he made a major career shift, leaving engineering to join the Dreyfus Fund as advisor and investment officer. By 1965, he was a vice president in charge of research at the Dreyfus Fund, which eventually developed assets of over $1 billion, making it one of the ten largest mutual funds in the United States. As an investment officer, Yura was responsible to over 300,000 stockholders to make the best possible use of their investment funds. He became as visible in the financial community as Zora was in the automotive world.

Zora visited Yura in New York often, and the two silver-haired sophisticates would prowl Manhattan together just like in the Ardun days. Yura would often meet up with Zora at the races, especially at places like Nassau. Yura also attracted a number of high-roller friends, among them John DeLorean after he left General Motors and Nicola Bulgari of the Italian jewelry family. Bulgari was a devotee of GM cars, particularly Buicks and Corvettes. When Bulgari ordered a 1971 Corvette, Yura asked Zora to expedite the order and ensure that Bulgari got "a really good car."

During race weekends Zora often hooked up with his brother Yura—and his female companions—at places like Nassau.

In the 1960s, while Zora was soaking up attention in the automotive enthusiast magazines of America, Yura was establishing his own reputation in financial journals. In 1966, Yura left Dreyfus to head Equity Growth Fund of America, but the move did nothing to slow the growth of his career. *Finance* magazine referred to Yura as the "Urbane Economist" in a January 1968 feature story. "His accent and gracious manner mark him as a man with an international background. His conversation is witty and he leans toward the ironic. Yura Arkus-Duntov's silvered, well-tailored appearance suggests a writer or a film critic rather than an economist-engineer."

Like Zora, Yura shared an affection for beautiful women. He had married a stunning actress named Brooke Byron in 1945. She came to New York from a pig farm in Kentucky and started off in modeling jobs, then graduated to B movies and eventually television soap operas. Their marriage, however, was short-lived. Yura went back to his bachelor lifestyle and could always be spotted with a beautiful woman in tow. Later, he married Daphne Bagley, who left her husband, a German count, after being knocked off her feet by the suave Russian.

Zora and Yura would usually talk by telephone—in Russian—at least once a week on Sundays and would try to get together whenever possible.

Zora's Roving Eyes

By now, Elfi had resigned herself to Zora's dalliances, knowing it was too late to try to change him. But occasionally she raised hell. Once Lapine met with Zora the day after he and Elfi had had a fight. As Lapine told the story, it seems a young woman Zora was seeing had put a Corvette in a ditch and then had called him at home at 3 a.m. Elfi was irate and was not speaking to Zora when he and Lapine headed out early the next morning to go fishing in Zora's boat. "It was God-awful," said Lapine. "The sun was beating down, we were hungry with no breakfast and he was bothered by this serious problem at home. Feeling guilty, he tried to get the Detroit Coast Guard station to connect him with the house on the ship-to-shore. He was successful, but then they started arguing, Zora cursing in Russian and Elfi in German and French. Then the Coast Guard cut into the conversation and told him to stand by, thinking he was a foreign freighter. Zora screamed into his mike, 'I don't have foreign frequency....I am pleasure barge!'"

Knowing Duntov's proclivities, Arnie Brown, an engineer who worked with Duntov on the Corvette and who later was at Opel, told of a creative approach he had used with Zora to get time off for a dental appointment:

"I went into Zora's office one morning and asked for the next morning off.

"Zora says, 'That's nice….Can I find out why?'

"'I'm going to dentist.'

"Zora says, 'In this country, dentists make appointments on Saturday. I suggest you try that next time.'"

Several months later, Brown tried again.

"I went into Zora's office and asked for the next morning off.

"'Dentist?' asks Zora."

Brown closed the door. "'This is very personal. Her husband is out of town.'

"Zora smiles understandingly and says, 'Then by all means take the day off, and take a second day off for me.'"

Brown did as he was told—he went straight to the dentist.

Brown related the time that Duntov was in Rome with some other GM officials and was to meet GM's top executive from Italy. "We were sitting in the lobby and finally the GM executive comes out with his wife in tow. She is breathtaking—a combination of Gina Lolabrigida, Sophia Loren all rolled into one. Legs, cheekbones, the whole package. This vision of loveliness leaves Zora completely unbalanced. He is not attentive, not answering questions, not participating in the conversation whatsoever.

"All of a sudden, I feel Zora's hand on my knee. 'Arnie, can you come out with me; I have to tell you something very personal.'"

Out in the hallway, Zora leaned into Arnie's ear and said, "Arnie, must have this woman."

When they got back out to the table, Arnie's wife asked him what Zora wanted. He replied, "It was very personal."

When Duntov had a stroke in 1969, Walter Keating, the son of former Chevrolet general manager Thomas Keating, visited Zora at Henry Ford Hospital in Detroit. "There was Zora in his room and he couldn't talk," said Keating. "With her back to Zora, Elfi said, 'Walt, Zora has a girlfriend and I would like you to find her so she can cheer Zora up.' Zora, fully alert, but unable to speak, was waving wildly no, no, no. He recognized the ploy on Elfi's part to flush the girlfriend out."

When in the doghouse, Zora would sketch himself on a little card in an apologetic pose while holding some flowers in front of Elfi. No words were necessary—the little stick figures said it all.

External Support

In his travels, Duntov crossed paths with many celebrities: actors, racers, athletes and successful businessmen. Among them was actor Steve McQueen, whom Duntov met on the race circuit. The two men continued to share their interests with each other through letters. Duntov turned McQueen onto Corvettes, while McQueen helped rekindle Duntov's interest in motorcycles. In a letter to McQueen written November 4, 1966, Duntov vowed to take McQueen up on his offer to go riding the next time he was in L.A. Duntov closed the letter with, "Well I run out of bits of advice, but have a request—kiss your terrific wife on my behalf, or on a second thought kiss her hand on my behalf. It has more decorum and besides you won't be reaching for your shotgun next time I am around."

Zora maintained personal correspondence with many well-known racers, including Stirling Moss, Phil Hill, A. J. Foyt and Paul Frère. Whenever he was in New York, Duntov frequented Le Chanteclair, the bistro owned and operated by former grand prix driver René Dreyfus. Located on 51st Street at Lexington in midtown Manhattan, the establishment was a major draw for celebrities from around the world, particularly those in automotive endeavors. Former CBS news anchor Walter Cronkite, who was a big road racing enthusiast, was a regular.

Zora also continued to communicate regularly with those he worked with in previous jobs and project work—Allard, Neubauer, Porsche, Chinetti, and others. He also maintained a strong loyalty to Maurice Olley, despite any friction that existed earlier in his career. The two exchanged correspondence throughout their lives, and Duntov looked after his former boss later, when Olley suffered financial setbacks and was living in destitution in a Detroit motel. Zora always respected the man and vowed he would never abandon a friend.

NINETEEN

By the late 1960s, Zora found himself increasingly isolated from corporate protectors like Ed Cole and was cut off from the real decision-making regarding future Corvettes.

Sharks in the Water

In 1965, Zora had been with General Motors for 12 years—far longer than in any other position he had ever held. While he had been the catalyst behind a wholesale makeover of Chevrolet's performance reputation, he found himself in the identical situation he had been in during the critical decision phase of the 1963 Corvette—still without any real power in the organization. The awareness of his dozen years at GM only served to underscore his exasperation at not having more control. Had he been more politically minded, he might have ascended to a level of real power but would have done so at the cost of leaving behind many of the hands-on projects he loved.

This was the dilemma Ed Cole faced. Cole traded the ability to be a hands-on guy for the chance to have a larger influence in the corporation. And Zora's successes at GM could always be traced back to Cole. He had always been Duntov's trump card, his secret weapon. But over time, the two grew farther apart on the organizational chart, with Cole advancing from Chevy's chief engineer to general manager in 1956, then group vice president of all car and truck divisions in 1961, executive vice president of all GM central staffs in 1965 and finally president of the corporation in 1967. Each promotion took Cole farther away from the hands-on engineering he loved and made it more difficult to support Duntov in his endeavors.

While Duntov always represented the kind of talent Cole wanted on his team, the immense corporate pressures Cole faced often strained their relationship. In Cole's roles at Chevrolet, and later at the corporate level, market share and profit were always critical, yet many of Zora's activities were not geared toward an instant return on investment. Furthermore, Cole's bosses could not be seen as openly supporting racing and were adamant about adhering to the AMA ban on motor sports. Cole's boss, GM Chairman James Roche, had been burned badly during the Nader Corvair investigation and was bending over backwards to promote safe cars at GM. "Roche took it as a religious mission that we would do everything we could to support safety," said Alvie L. Smith of the GM corporate public relations department. Smith served as Cole's personal speechwriter during much of his tenure. GM's utter market dominance at the time made it a target for a possible antitrust breakup, and senior management didn't care to rock the boat.

So while the engineer in Cole supported Zora's performance activities, the corporate citizen in Cole didn't. The result was a constant push/pull, with Duntov feeling off balance much of his career, not knowing whether he had management's support.

Furthermore, there were plenty of people in the chain of command who would try to block Zora's access to Cole. Zora recalled that when Jim Premo succeeded Harry Barr as Chevrolet chief engineer in 1963, he warned Duntov to stop contacting Cole or using Chevy general manager Bunkie Knudsen to get to Cole. But knowing how important Cole was to him, Zora had no intention of cutting that connection. Fortunately for Zora, Premo was largely preoccupied with Chevrolet's core business and didn't have the ability to enforce his edict.

Politically on the Outside

Over time, Duntov was able to carve out considerable influence, but that influence was outside the corporation. His highly publicized concept cars and race cars enabled him to single-handedly personify the energy and character of GM in the car enthusiast community. Senior managers still commanded attention in the mainstream media, such as when Cole graced the cover of an October 1959 issue of *Time* in a feature story about the Corvair. However, it was Duntov who became the hero of enthusiast magazines like *Hot Rod, Motor Life, Road & Track* and *Sports Car Graphic*.

Zora didn't help his cause internally, as he sometimes exhibited poor judgment and unfortunate timing. "Zora was always in some kind of trouble," said former GM engineer and executive Alex Mair. Keeping Duntov reined in became a constant challenge for upper management, especially as his projects became more visible within the corporation.

In the winter 1992 issue of *Corvette Quarterly*, former *Automobile* magazine publisher David E. Davis Jr., who crossed paths with Duntov both as editor of *Car and Driver* in the 1960s and later as creative director for Chevrolet advertising at Campbell-Ewald, recalled an incident when Duntov took him for a few laps in a Sting Ray with a prototype 396 engine. "We hopped in and drove faster and faster around the test track loop. Each time around the hairpin, he was getting a little more ragged. He finally came sailing in, the car pushed and we went straight off and landed in the weeds about 100 feet from the end of the track. Every single seam was full of grass and dirt. The two of us are sitting in reverent silence. He restarted the engine, put it in gear, turned to me and said, 'Best I think not to discuss with management.'"

On another occasion in the late 1960s GM Chairman Frederic G. Donner was taking a tour of the test track facility in his limousine. Automatic gates controlled the track and permission was required by radio in order to be allowed onto the loop. Duntov was driving a very low-slung prototype Corvette. He hated having to wait for permission to get on the track, so he roared right under the gate, cutting right in front of Donner's limousine and out onto the track. Upon seeing such a flagrant violation of the safety rules, Donner screamed, "Fire that man," to his associates in the limo, among them Alex Mair. "Next thing you know Cole and I were down in the boardroom trying to save Duntov's job," said Mair.

These factors seriously undermined any influence Duntov might have had as critical decisions were being made on a third-generation Corvette to succeed the Sting Ray. On Corvette matters, Duntov still worked through Jim Premo, who would then take recommendations on Corvette matters to the Chevrolet general manager and on up through the corporation. But other factions in the company had Premo's ear, and Duntov often found himself in competition with Design Staff or Frank Winchell's R&D group regarding major product decisions, which were often subject to budgets and politics.

The configuration of a new Corvette was especially contentious, with the winner being the group that could capture the most sizzle for the least amount of money. Under those circumstances, Duntov's group, with its penchant for risky engineering, was far from being in the driver's seat. As Cole ascended within the corporation, Duntov increasingly found himself on the outside looking in. Furthermore, the rest of the company was getting wise to Duntov's creative financing schemes, which further restricted his operational freedom.

It was Frank Winchell who got out in front of Duntov in the race to build the next Corvette. He had been the man behind the Corvair program and had in similar fashion produced a rear-engined prototype, the XP-819. Instead of an air-cooled flat four, the XP-819 featured a water-cooled V-8 mounted behind the rear axle. Its handling was unpredictable, however,

Zora became the living embodiment of Chevrolet performance in car enthusiast magazines. Here he sits with his brood of exotic engines for a December 1967 cover of Hot Rod.

thanks to the rearward weight bias, which created severe oversteer in transitional situations despite the use of extra-wide rear tires. Consequently, the XP-819 was never regarded as a serious Corvette alternative.

Nonetheless, Duntov responded with his own design in 1965—another mid-engined layout with radiators mounted in the rear. He employed many of the same design themes that went into the stillborn Q Corvette project from the late 1950s. Having learned a lesson from his previous efforts in working with Bill Mitchell, Zora tried to maintain total control of the effort. To that end, he commissioned his own scale model mock-ups of the body, which were attractively proportioned, and positioned the cockpit in the middle of the car with a short hood and buttresses flowing off the C-pillar. Despite Zora's best intentions, however, this mid-engine design fared no better than the others. The official reason was the heavy tooling costs of a required transaxle. But the fact remained that Duntov didn't have the political muscle to push a program like this through. Besides, Corvettes were selling well in excess of 20,000 units per year—high for a sports car—and there was a growing reluctance at GM to change a successful formula.

Further hindering Zora was the Bill Mitchell factor. Design Staff still wielded a strong influence within the corporation on all vehicle lines. While Corvettes experienced far more subtle changes from year to year, Design Staff still played the most influential role in the shape and configuration of new Corvettes. Furthermore, Mitchell could execute expressive shapes that didn't require expensive tooling changes. Maintaining the front-engine/rear-drive configuration favored Mitchell's preference for long hoods and short rear decks. Clearly, Mitchell would be no friend of Zora's mid-engine dreams.

Design Staff's Pet Shark

Back in mid-1964, Mitchell began to develop a successor to the Sting Ray and once again went back to the lines of a shark for inspiration. It was called the Mako Shark II. Its shape suggested a cross between a Sting Ray and the Batmobile. Low slung, with high, exaggerated fenders, the Mako II had a haunting look to it. The rear deck featured a mysterious, louvered rear window, a feature that never made it to production but which spawned an aftermarket trend. The louvered window design was later used on John DeLorean's DMC sports car in the early 1980s. Rather than a hood, the Mako's entire hood/fender assembly tilted forward in Jaguar XKE fashion. It was an unquestionable showstopper with its retractable rear bumper and spoilers—a novelty even in race cars of the time—and a 007-style revolving license plate. An early mock-up contained an aircraft-style steering wheel with a cockpit-adjustable steering ratio.

When the first mock-up appeared in April 1965 and began to grace the auto show circuit, Zora was concerned that the car's popularity with the public would make it a favorite to become the next Corvette, much as the Sting Ray racer did with the 1963 Corvette. His concerns were justified, but there was a bigger issue that would transcend styling considerations in determining the configuration of the car.

Independently of Zora, senior GM management had approved a plan, likely endorsed by Jim Premo, that carried over the same chassis from the 1963 Corvette, a cost-cutting move that saved GM millions. It also guaranteed that the third-generation Corvette would be a front-engined machine with a long hood and short rear deck.

The Mako Shark II contained many of the design elements that Duntov detested, including a long hood and arching fenders that intruded into the driver's line of sight.

For his part, Mitchell had made the decision about the next Corvette relatively easy for senior management. He had created another head-turning design that would divert attention from the car's warmed-over underpinnings. Zora had once again been left out in the cold.

The defeat was even more stinging than losing the mid-engined battle in 1963. Zora's hopes for GM being ready to go to a mid-engine configuration were much higher this time around, since his original idea had been given more time to take root. Now his quest took a step backwards. The new-generation Corvette would be little more than a 1963 model with a new body and interior. Zora could not imagine a worse scenario.

Without another card to play, all he could do was to make the best car he could out of the new Corvette. But as the months wore on, he was unable to bottle up his sentiments. He eventually put them in black and white for everyone in the corporation to see. It would almost cost him his job.

Zora Seeks an Influence

While Mitchell's Mako Shark II might have made an arresting show car, Zora felt its shape limited its function as a driving machine. The design retained Mitchell's long-hood, short-deck look, which Zora detested. Making matters worse in Zora's eyes were the car's high, exaggerated fenders, which intruded into the driver's sight lines. During a prototype ride and drive at the GM Proving Ground, Duntov criticized this feature directly to Chevy general manager Pete Estes. "I had him drive and then asked him how well he could see," said Zora. "He mentioned high fender blocking

Zora took his case against the design of the Mako Shark II directly to Chevrolet general manager Pete Estes, who then ordered Design Staff to tone down the design for production purposes.

vision to left and right, like tunnel. Feeling of oppression. We finish the ride and I followed up with a letter saying that maybe the design will be appealing to some people, but universally it will be not accepted. Therefore I propose to eliminate this car. And the reply I got was that the car was cancelled."

But the car wasn't really cancelled; it was just delayed for a year, from 1967 to 1968. To help ease Duntov's pain, Mitchell called him and agreed to reduce the fender height. The ploy seemed to work. "He now looking at me as member of styling group," said Duntov. So Mitchell directed Larry Shinoda to modify the clay model, flattening out the fenders and making some other adjustments. Estes approved the changes and the new shape of the 1968 Corvette was set.

The new street design maintained the overall flare of its Mako II predecessor. The coupe models featured a steel structure behind the passenger compartment that allowed for removable T-tops. As opposed to a fastback roofline with louvers, the production version rear window was flat and upright, and housed within the flying buttress roofline. Overall the car appeared lower and wider than the 1963-1967 Corvette, with large fender wells to accommodate the new generation of wider performance tires being used on muscle cars of the era. The standard wheel rims were now seven inches wide, which increased cornering capability and lateral acceleration limits on the skid pad. The wider rubber caused more ride harshness, but since stability was so dramatically increased, Duntov felt the tradeoff was worth it.

Duntov Vents

Despite Duntov's influence in improving the basic car, he was still burning from the decision to go with an unambitious makeover of the 1963 Corvette. In a March 21, 1967, memo to Alex Mair, who had just succeeded Jim Premo as Chevrolet chief engineer, Duntov referred to the new Corvette as not the kind of car he would have produced had he been holding all the cards.

In the memo, he warned that the relatively minor chassis and drivetrain changes to the 1968 Corvette would result in less attention being paid to the Corvette by the enthusiast press. "Introduction of the 1968 will make a splash, followed by a round of road tests, but after that with innovations not forthcoming and consequently nothing to write about, Corvette will gradually disappear from the magazine pages."

Duntov then prescribed what needed to be done for the press launch, including extensive chassis work over the coming months to make the car behave with respect to ride and handling, especially when factoring in the car's new seven-inch rims and wider tires. Duntov also indicated that work was needed on the car's carburetor setups and cooling system. "Beyond that point, if the engineering is to remain stagnant, only routine attention in the engine and chassis area will be required," wrote Duntov, further betraying his frustration with the entire process.

"Nothing concrete is planned for 1969," continued Duntov, "and we may expect the reaction similar to the disappointment which greeted the appearance of the Camaro—Chevrolet, formerly an innovator, comes out with a plain and somewhat deficient car."

Duntov pointed out that he felt Corvette's role as a halo car for the Chevrolet Division would slip unless Chevrolet employed more cutting-edge technology. But even without further innovations, Duntov accurately predicted the car would continue to sell just as well as the 1963 car. He warned, however, that if competition were to materialize in the form of a mid-engine sports car from Ford, Corvette would have few takers.

"A large part of a sports car appeal is its resemblance to a race car, the 'Walter Mitty' part of us," wrote Duntov. "Mid-engined Ford will have it. Corvette lost it when the front-engined racers became antiquated. Ford will be progressively modern and new, Corvette outdated, antique and old."

Duntov noted that in addition to having a modern design that would more closely resemble a race car, Ford would have all the rub-off from its victorious racing prototypes, which were then dominating at Le Mans. Yet he felt that Ford was missing the boat by not having a two-passenger sports car available to capitalize on the prestige its racing effort brought to the whole division.

"Watching the racing prototypes win is one thing and having the possibility to buy an exciting sports car from the showroom is another," wrote Duntov. "Ford GT and Chaparrals are very exciting, but hardly anybody dreams of owning them as pleasure cars. The most effective way to capture attention and imagination is by provision of an exciting product people can project themselves as owning.

"Elizabeth Taylor is pretty hot stuff," continued Duntov, "but it is the girl next door who gets the attention—she, in difference to Miss Taylor, is in realm of potential ownership. Maybe Ford realized that they missed that link and will do something about it."

Duntov cited the fact that Ford was showing a prototype of the mid-engine Pantera at the Chicago Auto Show and the time was right for GM to enter the mid-engine market. "They must assume that we, having invested into an all-new body for 1968, are intending to stay with our present car for a number of years to come," he wrote. "Consequently, they know that after the novelty of the 1968 Corvette appearance has worn out, they can move in and get the undivided attention for their all-new modern car."

Knowing that an engineering reorganization might be on the way, Duntov concluded his memo to Mair with a plea to retain the Corvette group to ensure the continuation of innovations as well as adding design responsibility to the group. The latter request was intended as a hedge against the kind of power Design Staff wielded.

With his spiteful comments, Duntov clearly crossed the line in writing the memo to Mair, and Estes began looking for another place to put him. Duntov was given an opportunity to go to Opel in early 1967. The German-based GM division needed engineering help at the time, and Jim Premo had just been named chief engineer of Opel. At Estes' behest, Premo invited Duntov to Germany just as GM was considering the consolidation of Opel, Vauxhall and Holden engineering operations and the position of assistant chief engineer would then be open. The job would involve shuttling between Detroit and Frankfort, but Duntov ultimately declined the offer, thereby possibly passing up a more lucrative career path. He was also considering an offer from Volkswagen at the time but didn't want to leave the Corvette platform.

"If Zora had a weakness," said Karl Ludvigsen, "it was his commitment to the Corvette program which clearly limited his usefulness on larger GM projects. He was political enough to survive at GM but he wasn't diplomatic. He was very good at managing a small team, but would have been very uncomfortable with a large engineering operation."

Engineering Shake-up

After turning down the Opel opportunity, things went from bad to worse. Estes followed up with the rumored reorganization of the engineering department, which served to commonize engineering processes across all Chevrolet car lines. Duntov's Corvette group, however unofficial, was being disbanded. The question for Estes was what to do with Duntov. He would be a management headache in the new organization, so Estes decided to leverage Duntov's already substantial public appeal for the corporation. Duntov was put in a special public relations position effective April 1, 1967. The job was packaged as a combination of press spokesperson and engineering consultant, much like Rudi Uhlenhaut at Mercedes, but it effectively cut any direct Zora ties to engineering in the Corvette program.

Zora did have an assignment to make modifications to the Camaro, which was scheduled to be the 1967 Indianapolis 500 pace car, but he would no longer be "Mr. Corvette," at least when it came to hands-on engineering. He would be a figurehead only—a guy who attended press shows and dinners and provided quotes for hungry journalists. It took him completely away from what he had come to GM to do.

Before Duntov could react, however, he was out of work for a full two months in May and June of 1967 while he was treated for an enlarged prostate gland. In hindsight, the affliction may have allowed him to cool off rather than giving him an opportunity for a confrontation that might have led to a resignation or dismissal.

During his recovery, Duntov decided to get out of Detroit altogether. He visited a specialist in New York who was recommended by his old New York friend, Julian Hoffman. But because he was anemic from taking sulfa, once Zora got to New York, he waited five weeks before undergoing surgery. .

Zora spent several months in New York in May and June 1967 undergoing treatment for an enlarged prostate.

After considerable soul searching, Duntov returned to work in late June 1967 in his new "PR" position but resisted the temptation to raise hell or quit. For better or for worse, he would go along with the program. One of his first tasks was to travel to Europe to speak to journalists about the new 1968 Corvette. While it was a role he had performed many times, he couldn't get used to the fact that he was now a spokesman, not an engineer.

After several months, he couldn't take it anymore and drafted an angry note to Ed Cole:

> In the week preceding reorganization of April 1, 1967, you enthusiastically announced that removing me from all design responsibilities and placing me on special assignment to you, which you could not very well define, is the challenging change I have been waiting for.
>
> Although I could not see anything but PR related activities for the product, the engineering of which I could not any more contribute, I was swayed by your convincing appearance of sincerity and decided to attempt to make a go of it. When I say go, I mean to make an attempt to contribute to engineering of the product in the areas I am qualified without directing actual design.
>
> My prestige in the outside world and promotional or PR effectiveness apparently looms very large in your eyes as an asset to

Chevrolet—this may be true but let me state one fact—prestige and among some attention I enjoy is based on my contribution to engineering in general and to Chevrolet product in particular. I will retain very little prestige if it will be realized that Corvette is in areas outside of my direct responsibility.

Whether Zora ever sent this note to Cole is not documented. A handwritten draft was found among his papers, but no copy of these words on official Chevrolet engineering letterhead has ever been found.

Chief Engineer at Last

Back in engineering, there is no question that the development of the 1968 Corvette was hampered without Duntov running the show. The car was originally supposed to be a 1967 model but had been delayed due to noise, body and drivetrain-related problems. Problems also surfaced with the car's vacuum-operated hidden windshield wiper doors.

While many of these problems would have existed even with Duntov around, given his preoccupation with strictly performance matters, they were exacerbated with Duntov away from the action. It was proof that Zora had been contributing more than the company realized. As an all-new car, the Corvette needed a dedicated caretaker, yet major issues in the design of the 1968 car were falling through the cracks. Estes and Mair knew they couldn't risk a rash of negative stories about the Corvette with Duntov out of the picture. Duntov had been essentially functioning as a chief engineer all along, even though he hadn't owned the title.

Realizing this, Estes restored Zora as the engineering caretaker of the Corvette. "We in the Corvette group suspected that Cole interceded on Duntov's behalf," said Gib Hufstader. No matter how the appointment came about, Duntov was finally given the formal title he had been lacking for 14 years, the title everyone thought he already had—chief engineer of the Corvette. Duntov was the first individual car line engineer to be named in such a capacity.

Still, the new position didn't provide total autonomy. Various division-wide engineering groups were still charged with work on portions of the car. Duntov, however, now maintained authority—at least on paper—over all aspects of the Corvette, from advanced development to the quality of the finished product.

Looking back on the whole episode, Mair said that while he respected what Duntov was trying to achieve, he was sensitive to the burdens that Duntov's activities imposed on other groups in the company that were doing engines and transmissions. "We were building thousands of cars a day and a handful of Corvettes," said Mair. "People didn't want to have to spend that much time thinking about this very small-volume car. Many of these people thought that Duntov viewed the Corvette as much more important than it really was."

At the time, Chevrolet alone had close to 30 percent of the market, more than the entire GM Corporation has today. Given those kinds of numbers, the Corvette was a relatively small piece of the pie that was produced by a small group of oddballs. "Yet if everyone in Chevrolet operated like Zora did, nothing would have ever gotten done," said Mair.

But Mair and many others felt that despite the more mundane needs of the mighty corporation, there was a need for Zora and his team. He was the renegade over in the corner who'd say "I don't understand" whenever he didn't want to listen. They thought of him as a required nuisance as long as he didn't get too much in the way of the big picture. "Zora was different and we liked him," concluded Mair.

When Zora returned to action in July 1967 following his prostate surgery, he was assigned to prepare the prototypes for the 1968 press preview. The big-block cars were still suffering from overheating problems, so Duntov quickly improvised a solution. According to Ludvigsen in his book *Corvette, America's Star-Spangled Sports Car*, Duntov cut two holes underneath the car's chin, just ahead of the spoiler. He also added a strip to the spoiler to make it twice as deep, thereby increasing the local pressure in that area and encouraging the air to flow up through the holes. Then the spaces around the radiator were sealed off so the air had nowhere to go except through the radiator.

The quick fixes worked. Press day was successful, and the changes Duntov made were adopted immediately for production cars. But overheating would continue to be a problem, especially with the big Mark IV engine. The big blocks required special hoods, one for the Mark IV and another one for the L88 that drew cool air from a high-pressure area at the base of the windshield. According to Ludvigsen, this hood cut the L88's acceleration time by seven seconds in a zero to 140 mph run.

The third-generation body proved to be more aerodynamic than the old one, but only slightly. The L88, for example, was capable of 185 mph with the new body versus 183 in Sting Ray form. Like the 1963 body style, the new body still had the tendency to lift under hard acceleration. Zora played around with spring rates to help mitigate the problem, but the lifting persisted.

Corvette's Checkered Reputation

Duntov was wrong in his prediction that the Corvette would fade from the automotive landscape. If nothing else, he may have underestimated his own natural appeal to magazine editors. Publishers had learned long ago that a Corvette on the cover sold magazines, and Corvettes continued to be a hot topic. But the news wasn't always positive. Despite the buzz in show-rooms, quality bugs and sophisticated hardware from abroad began to erode the Corvette's image among automotive opinion leaders. The worst problem with the press might have been *Car and Driver*'s refusal to road-test a 1968 Corvette, which, according to former editor Steve Smith, was literally falling apart with fewer than 2,000 miles on it. GM's public embarrassment over this issue may have served as a catalyst toward making Duntov chief engineer. Zora had no doubts: Years later he asserted that "Steve Smith article was what nailed it down."

If the Corvette drew mixed early reviews among the enthusiast magazines, it was a clear winner with the public. The Corvette won "Best All Around Car" in the annual *Car and Driver* Magazine Reader's Poll, despite the shoddy quality of the 1968 model. This was an amazing tribute to the appeal of the Corvette as well as to Duntov's ascending reputation in the automotive community. By 1975, the year of Duntov's retirement, the Corvette had won that honor nine out of eleven years.

Even the Corvette's harshest critics succumbed to its raw appeal. In a follow-up to Steve Smith's original piece, for which he had refused to do a road test, *Car and Driver* wrote:

> Chevrolet's Corvette ranks just one notch below immortality on America's list of mechanical achievements—and well it should. Like barbed wire and the cotton gin, it borrows from no one. Every working aspect and every styling feature evolve from Chevrolet's plan to build the ultimate American car. The Corvette is exciting, it's lusty, it stimulates all of the base emotion lurking deep in modern man. It is the Barbarella of the car maker's art.

The press clippings amused Zora. Yes, the Corvette was capable of generating considerable excitement despite its traditional configuration and shoddy quality. But what might have been? What would they be writing instead had Zora been given free rein? He would never know.

Despite his misgivings, Duntov's legend was beginning to grow around the world. He took a 427 Corvette with tall gearing over to Europe and came back with impressive reviews. Journalist/race driver Paul Frère drove the car at Zolder in a back-to-back test against a Porsche and a Mercedes. The Corvette destroyed the other two cars, lapping the Dutch circuit significantly faster. Wrote Frère in *Auto Motor und Sport*:

We found it very flattering that Z. Arkus-Duntov was accompanying the car. He drove it himself in the most expert manner and exposed himself to a critical discussion with the press. The behavior of the new Corvette on curves was surprisingly good, in a different class than the old Sting Ray. The new car does not break away as easily as the old one and is much easier to correct. Z. Arkus-Duntov drove the car more expertly than anybody present and he is surely correct by thinking that one has to learn how to drive this car.

In a GM internal memo dated November 27, 1967, public relations staff member G. W. Wolf Jr. wrote: "In spite of the disagreeable concluding remarks, I find the *Auto Motor und Sport* article the most favorable yet written by this publication on a U.S.-built General Motors vehicle."

The DeLorean Years

Estes was promoted to group vice president of car and truck operations on February 1, 1969, and was replaced by John DeLorean, who was fresh from the Pontiac Division. Only 44 years old, DeLorean was a prodigy—tall, handsome, charismatic and talented. He went on to become the most well-known and unconventional GM executive ever, thanks to his bold thinking, stylish wardrobe and beautiful wives, Kelly Harmon and later Cristina Ferrare.

As a fellow maverick, Duntov had hoped that DeLorean might help him achieve some of his goals for future products. DeLorean had done wonders at Pontiac by finding ways to create a lot of youthful appeal with an aggressive menu of engine options that brought eye-opening performances from run-of-the-mill sedans and mid-sized cars. It was DeLorean who came up with the idea for the Pontiac GTO which became a major impetus for the transformation of Pontiac into a hot seller among the car enthusiast community.

DeLorean seemed to understand car enthusiasts, which gave Duntov hope. To get their relationship going in the right direction, Duntov wrote DeLorean a status quo memo several weeks after DeLorean had taken over the reins at Chevy. In the memo, Duntov analyzed the state of the Corvette for his new boss, underscoring how important the Corvette had become as well as what challenges lay ahead.

"In the late 1950s, production was steadily climbing and by 1962, 12,000 Corvettes were produced," wrote Duntov in his memo to DeLorean. "The all-new 1963 Sting Ray exceeded 20,000 units, and in subsequent years, was crowding 30,000, which is the maximum capacity of suppliers and the assembly plant (9-10-hour day/6-day week)." Duntov explained that prior to the introduction of the 1968 model, the Corvette was the highest unit profit maker in the Chevrolet Division. It became a boon for dealers, with the profit on one Corvette being roughly equivalent to three Impalas. In 1968, some dealers made a practice of charging above the suggested list price and got it. Duntov stressed that while the 1968 car was enthusiastically received, it was a record-breaker in terms of customer complaints and warranty costs. "Manufacturing is aware that the problem exists," wrote Duntov, "and until the problem is solved, the quality picture will continue to be spotty." Zora made no mention of any actions he had in mind to fix the problems at the plant.

Duntov noted that customer demand was running at about the same rate as in 1968. "However, we must assume that the existence of 125,000 Sting Ray owners ready for a change for a new model were a factor in this heavy demand."

While the big-block was still very popular, demand was down slightly from several years earlier. "The 427 cubic inch engines accounted for 43 percent in 1966 and 1967 prior to dropping to the current level of 37 percent. Automatics have been running at an 18 percent level until the introduction of the 3-speed turbo Hydramatic, which climbed to about 20 percent for the last and current year [1969]."

Duntov then provided his own analysis of the driving characteristics of the 1969 Corvette. "When you drive the Corvette, bear in mind that the 300-hp/350 cubic-inch base car is the nicest by Corvette standards. The 350-hp/350 cubic-inch picks up air cleaner noise. The 427 has a higher noise level and a harder ride. The 427 with rocker exhausts [sidepipes] is a noise champion, but our customers love it and a heavy backlog for this option exists." For once, Duntov simply stated the facts and held his tongue. Maybe he was learning from his past actions and wanted to start fresh with the new top manager.

When DeLorean arrived at Chevy in 1969, the Corvette still had significant quality problems. It was badly manufactured, and even with his new title of chief engineer, Duntov had done little or nothing to improve the quality of the car. He didn't know or care enough about plant operations to be able to make the proper recommendations.

But John DeLorean did. According to DeLorean, the basic design of the car wasn't the biggest problem, but he considered the plant somewhat obsolete. Part of the solution was to systematically solve problems at the St. Louis Corvette plant as well as to update the facility itself, making it one of the first plants to use assembly line hydraulic shakers to de-rattle and de-squeak the cars. "St. Louis was one of the worst plants that GM had," said DeLorean. "Nobody wanted the foreman job. They were afraid someone would beat them up and slash their tires." After a year or so, the St Louis Corvette line was up to the highest quality standards within GM.

A Major Setback

While Duntov reestablished control of the Corvette program, he was not out of the woods regarding his health. The first signs of trouble appeared in June 1969, after he had entertained some French visitors at the GM Tech Center. He spoke in French to them but then unintentionally would mix his French and English for several days afterward. He reported this to a doctor, who first thought it might be a brain tumor. Duntov was hospitalized for observation at Henry Ford Hospital in Detroit but insisted on leaving the hospital to attend the wedding of Bunkie Knudsen's daughter in Bloomfield Hills. The doctor finally released Duntov, but told him to be back by 10 that evening and not to drink any alcohol.

The wedding took place outdoors on an unseasonably cool day, and Duntov ignored his doctor's advice by enjoying a glass of champagne at the ceremony. Elfi took him back to the hospital that night, but when he awoke the next morning, he couldn't speak. He was later diagnosed as having had a stroke. Yura flew in from New York to visit and arranged to have some of the Ford family doctors care for Zora, since he was close personal friends with Charlotte Ford, Henry II's daughter.

Fortunately, the damage was limited to his speech. Duntov used a scribble pad to communicate until he could talk again. He underwent months of therapy, with his doctors recommending that he concentrate on speaking only one language. Naturally, he chose English, but for the remainder of his life, his Russian/German accented speech was slow and often unintelligible. He claimed he was thinking in German and then had to translate his thoughts into English.

Chevy chief engineer Don McPherson, who replaced Alex Mair in 1968, appointed Walt Zetye as chief engineer in Duntov's absence. But the irrepressible Zora was back at work before the end of the summer of 1969, working an hour or two a day until he was back on a full schedule. But during his illness he had lost another critical battle in his quest to build a mid-engined Corvette, and time was starting to run out.

TWENTY

Zora goes about the business of making the third-generation Corvette into a formidable competition car. Here he directs the effort of his engineers at a test session in late 1967.

The Back Door Man

After his Corvette engineering connection to the Corvette almost came to an end in 1967, Duntov needed to reassert a grip on his career. His stroke, as well as 15 years of painful confrontations at General Motors had taken their toll but ultimately hadn't destroyed his inner resolve.

It would be several years before Zora would have a chance to design a new Corvette, so he decided to get back to the business of winning races—corporate support or not. But there would be no more bold racing prototypes or factory-direct programs.

This was in stark contrast to the situation at Ford. Zora's counterpart, Roy Lunn, was busy supporting an international Ford racing effort out of Kar Kraft, a factory-supported facility just a few miles away from the Ford headquarters in Dearborn. An Englishman who worked for both A.C. and Aston Martin before joining Ford, Lunn was doing what Duntov always dreamed of doing: Building specialized sports cars—first the Ford GT40 with Lola's Eric Broadley and later the Ford J-car (standing for its class in the FIA's "Appendix J") which was an in-house effort. Not content with class wins, these cars were taking overall victories at the world's most prestigious endurance races such as Sebring and Le Mans.

Back at GM, Duntov had to focus on letting his customers do the development work, using their cars as guinea pigs to improve future street Corvettes. Duntov would provide the parts out the back door. After the parts were used up, they were shipped back to the General Motors Tech Center for analysis. Duntov and his staff made themselves available by telephone to field questions and sometimes showed up at the racetrack.

This backdoor flow of parts and knowledge helped the Corvette become a formidable production racer, both in SCCA production classes and in class competition at Daytona and Sebring. But given the constraints placed on Duntov, Corvettes would never be a true threat to win outright in a major endurance race.

Opposite: Zora tests a third-generation, L88-powered Corvette to help bolster a back door support program for racers. The program allowed Corvette to dominate its classes in SCCA competition throughout the early 1970s.

Still, these Corvette racing programs were something that Corvette customers could directly relate to, unlike the Ford GT which was never intended to be a street machine. The difference was that Zora offered made-for-racing components on street Corvettes, which helped embellish the car's performance image considerably.

The Mighty L88

Perhaps the best example of making racing components available for Corvette street cars was the big-block L88 engine, which was offered as an option beginning in 1967. Featuring a heavy-duty forged crankshaft, connecting rods and pistons, plus aluminum heads, it easily put out 450 hp in showroom form and could be modified to produce much more.

Although the L88 didn't formally debut until April 1, 1967, it was in development for several years prior to that as Zora's men—Denny Davis and Fred Frincke—began to modify the Mark IV big block originally developed by Dick Keinath for Corvette racing applications.

According to Richard Prince writing in *Corvette Quarterly*, the first real world test of the L88 engine was in 1966, when a prototype unit was loaned to Roger Penske for installation in a Corvette he had entered at Sebring. Dick Guldstrand drove the car using production cast-iron heads, because the aluminum heads destined for the L88 were not yet homologated. He won his class anyway.

Formal homologation papers for the L88 were filed in January 1967, and several months later, on April 1, 1967, the L88 made its racing debut at the 12 hours of Sebring. In the hands of Don Yenko and Dave Morgan, the L88 immediately showed what it was made of, powering their blue and white Sunray DX Corvette to a GT class win and a 10th overall finish.

Thanks in part to this victory, the L88 became a regular production option and according to Prince, "it remains the most heralded production engine of our time."

Later that year at Le Mans, Yenko joined Dick Guldstrand and Bob Bondurant to drive a red, white and blue L88 Sting Ray entered by Peyton Cramer of Dana Chevrolet in Southgate, California. Duntov, mindful of his backdoor policy, stayed away from the race, although he sent Gib Hufstader to quietly provide technical assistance. The car had shown amazing speed for its class, exceeding 170 mph on

The restrictions of GM racing policy forced Duntov to offer made-for-racing components on street cars to get around the letter of the law. The most noteworthy example in this regard is the 450-hp L88 engine.

the Mulsanne straight. In qualifying, it knocked 10 seconds off the GT record. During the race, it was leading the GT class at the 12-hour mark before throwing a rod. But its performance was positive enough for Zora to seek ways to encourage more racing teams to run L88s.

In order to foster more international racing of Corvettes, Duntov created a special racing package and had it certified as a Group III touring car by the FIA, the international governing body of motor sports. According to Karl Ludvigsen, Zora then put together a special L88-powered hardtop roadster racing package with a curb weight of only 2,776 pounds and then testified—falsely—that Chevrolet had built 500 of these cars between August 1 and November 1, 1967. Only three machines were actually built. They were handed over to the American International Racing Team to be campaigned in the 1968 Daytona 24-hour endurance race.

The race package L88s were extremely potent race cars, capable of 0 to 60 mph in 4.2 seconds, 0 to 100 mph in 8.0 seconds and 0 to 140 in 17.0 seconds, according to Ludvigsen. The team was backed by actor James Garner, freshly smitten with racing after starring in the 1966 John Frankenheimer film *Grand Prix*. But while fast—reaching over 180 mph on the banking—the cars were not reliable and did not finish the race at Daytona or at Sebring.

Ironically, the noncertified L88s did better at Daytona. Sunray DX sponsored a three-car team led by Pennsylvania Chevrolet dealer Don Yenko, who was teamed with Formula One and Can-Am star Peter Revson. Jerry Grant and Dave Morgan drove a second car, a 1967 coupe, while the third car was a 1968 driven by Chevrolet engineer Jerry Thompson and a kid named Tony J. DeLorenzo.

The Grant/Morgan car once again demonstrated the competitive strength of the L88, winning the GT class and finishing 10th overall. But a litany of mechanical problems caused the other two cars to finish 25th and 27th respectively.

The DeLorenzo/Thompson partnership led to one of the most successful Corvette racing efforts ever in terms of the sheer number of wins. The enterprise actually started back in 1964 when DeLorenzo, the 21-year-old son of the General Motors head of public relations, Tony G. DeLorenzo, was working in a summer job at Chevrolet. At the time, he ordered a black, fuel-injected coupe with all the high-performance options. Since Duntov kept close track of who was ordering high-performance hardware, he immediately called DeLorenzo and asked who was going to drive the car. DeLorenzo lied and said it was his father, but Duntov sensed all along what young DeLorenzo had planned. So Zora personally took the car out on the skid pad and bedded in the tires and brakes.

From then on, Zora made sure that DeLorenzo always received good parts and equipment. But supporting a racing effort from a distance had its share of frustrations for Zora. He wanted to be at the track where he could be part of the effort and make sure the team was using the equipment as intended. However, without his presence at the races, things could go wrong.

After the 1968 Daytona 24-hour race, DeLorenzo wrote a letter to Ed Cole that referenced equipment problems during the race. "Our engine was stronger than anyone there and ran flawlessly for 24-hours. We could hit 6,000 RPM in fourth gear with a 2.73:1 axle—before reaching the end of the backstraight (approx. 180 mph)."

In the letter he complained about the fact that the steering relay rod assemblies were bending badly under heavy brake applications. The culprits were the new, wider 8-1/2-inch wheels the team was using. "No one at Chevrolet was aware of a problem that would be caused by using 8-1/2-inch wheels on the car," wrote DeLorenzo "We managed to reinforce the ones we had, but couldn't really bear down on the brakes for fear of bending a relay rod during the race." They wound up fourth in GT and 24th overall—the other two cars were first and third in GT respectively.

DeLorenzo's letter was forwarded to Duntov by way of Pete Estes. Duntov replied in a heated memo to Estes written on February 27, 1968. "DeLorenzo knows for some time the origin of his large self-inflicted problems. Both the relay rod bending and outboard bearing failures on the left (inside) front wheel were induced by the 2.0 inches offset of the homemade 8-1/2-wide wheels. The 1968 car will accept this width and desire to use wide rims is natural. However, the 2.0-inch offset is excessive and it increased the load on the outboard bearing by 280 percent."

Duntov then adopted a slightly more conciliatory tone. "Although both problems could have been avoided if Tony would follow our advice, we were the real culprits. We neglected the updating of our heavy-duty chassis and our knowledge about the car in this type of operation. Consequently, our advice was based on judgment rather than facts and therefore, was not firm enough to be followed without questions."

After DeLorenzo started following Zora's advice, he went on to become one of the most successful Corvette racers ever. Teamed with Jerry Thompson, the two snapped off an amazing run of 22 straight A-Production victories in their Owens Corning Fiberglass L88 over a two-year period beginning in 1969. It is a record that still stands today. Zora was enormously proud of this effort, especially since it demonstrated the strength of his Corvette group's technical know-how as well as the viability of a solid grass-roots support system.

Racing Sells More Corvettes

Despite the enormous success of the L88, Zora was never a fan of big blocks. He felt they unbalanced the car. He preferred powerful, smaller displacement engines, which didn't carry a weight penalty.

Zora didn't argue with the success the Corvettes were having in the more powerful A-Production classes, but B-Production class didn't allow the larger displacement engines and Zora wanted Corvettes to win in both classes. He was also concerned about the debut of factory-backed American Motors AMX's into B Production, so he pushed for a small-block capable of putting out greater horsepower and torque. That engine became the mechanical lifter LT1, which put out 370 horsepower at 6,000 rpm and 380 pound-feet of torque at 4,000 rpm.

The LT1 engine would become the centerpiece of a ZR-1 option package for SCCA B-Production racers (not to be confused with the Lotus-designed 32-valve V-8-powered Corvette that appeared in 1989). The original LT1 featured a cold-air induction hood, heavy-duty brakes and chassis components. It was a delightfully balanced sports car.

"The ZR-1 was my white hope for ecstasy in racing," said Zora years later. It was scheduled to debut in 1969, but was delayed a year until 1970. Hopeful that the LT1 would make inroads on the racetrack, Duntov vigorously disagreed with this decision. He was concerned about handing the class over to AMC. "They will make mincemeat of our small-engine Corvettes," he warned GM's W .J. Dettloff in a 1969 memo. "American Motors advertising not only does not pull any punches, but wears brass knuckles and they will do a good job of hurting Corvette prestige," concluded Duntov. But his efforts to have the package released that year were unsuccessful and the LT1 did not come out until 1970.

All told, the ZR-1 was not a major success in the marketplace, largely because it was a $1,000 option that required a number of other heavy-duty options. Only 53 units were built over a three-year period.

Zora's underground efforts helped make the Corvette a fixture at the races, and created a long string of successes that far surpassed any of his previous racing accomplishments. It solidified Corvette's performance reputation and may have done more to sell Corvettes than did the Ford racing cars that bore no likeness to what was available in the showrooms.

Sales of the third-generation Corvettes trended sharply upward from its predecessor as Chevrolet's sports car became a bigger marketplace success in 1968 and 1969, A record number—28,566 units—were sold in 1968, followed by a whopping 38,762 units in 1969. That incredible peak volume was due to Chevrolet general manger John DeLorean's decision to extend production into the winter of 1969-1970 to make up ground on order backlogs that resulted from a two-month strike earlier in the year. These numbers helped push the total number of Corvettes built to a quarter million. The Corvette achieved that milestone on November 7, 1969, a fact that made Zora Arkus-Duntov very proud despite any misgivings about the configuration of the car itself.

Corvette and the Tire Wars

Like his relationship with DeLorenzo and Thompson, Zora also was the key man behind the scenes in the success of John Greenwood in the early to mid-1970s. Young and impetuous, Greenwood had a checkered reputation—part goof ball, part Attila the Hun. This image was accentuated by his brutal yet successful driving style that left many competitors in the dust. He attacked projects with incredible energy and sometimes got in over his head. But he managed to stay at the top of professional racing for eight consecutive years in Trans-Am and International Motor Sport Association Camel GT competition.

A former drag racer from the Detroit suburb of Birmingham, Michigan, Greenwood started building Corvettes for SCCA A-Production classes and won the A national championship in 1970. He showed up for the national championship runoffs that year with a giant American flag screaming red, white and blue across the hood of his Corvette. The paint scheme was so eye-catching and so appropriate for an American sports car that it became his signature. His success caught the attention of Gib Hufstader in the Corvette group, who introduced Greenwood to Duntov. Before long, Greenwood was testing half shafts, driveshafts and other driveline components for the Corvette group. In working with Greenwood, Zora saw a chance to step up his efforts in something beyond SCCA competition and perhaps go back to Le Mans.

Zora and privateer racer John Greenwood in the early Seventies. Greenwood represented Zora's best opportunity to go back to Le Mans.

Soon Duntov stopped peddling parts out the back door and started attending many of the events Greenwood ran. He saw an opportunity in Greenwood to go racing again. As opposed to funding the operation himself, the money would come from outside of GM. Race car sponsorships, especially in sports car racing, were still relatively rare in the early 1970s, but Zora and Greenwood caught wind of B.F. Goodrich's goal of creating an international motorsports program around the company's T/A line of street radial tires. The tire maker wished to conduct a high-profile program for marketing purposes and Zora smelled a way he could go back to Le Mans without violating GM corporate policy.

Duntov followed up directly with BFG president Gerard Alexander, who had offered to develop a high-speed radial tire for street Corvettes. That meeting resulted in a multi-year endurance-racing contract. In 1971, Greenwood used the 12 hours of Sebring to warm up for Le Mans. Partnered by comedian Dick Smothers, Greenwood won the GT class and finished seventh overall.

The following year, the team went to Le Mans. As luck would have it, Zora's backdoor support system resulted in five privately run Corvettes at Le Mans that year—two for Greenwood, one for Dave Heinz and Bob Johnson and two entered by Frenchman Henri Greder, one of which was driven by French rally driver Marie Beaumont. Greder had been running a Corvette in a variety of European events including Nürburgring and Le Mans. In 1971 Beaumont had contested Le Mans in a Corvette, but had retired at half distance.

The BFG effort with street radials stirred things up at archrival Goodyear, which was developing its own radial racing tire. In early 1972, Goodyear approached several teams about using the tires in the upcoming Daytona endurance race, which for that year was to last for only 6 hours instead of the usual 24 because of a gasoline shortage.

Among the teams Goodyear approached was that of Dave Heinz and Bob Johnson who were running a very strong Corvette with a rebel flag motif. Goodyear had made an enticing offer for the team earlier that season at Daytona: Test Goodyear's new radial tires at Daytona and if they won, Goodyear would sponsor them for the rest of the year. The team accepted Goodyear's offer, raced at Daytona with unmarked tires and won. They beat Greenwood in the process and repeated their performance at Sebring. That prompted Goodyear to suggest they run at Le Mans.

However, there were two problems with a Le Mans effort. First, their race car was not eligible to run at Le Mans in its current configuration. Secondly, it was past the deadline for filing new entries that year. Both challenges would be overcome.

Le Mans rules required a semi-stock interior with roll-up windows. The rebel Corvette was a tube-framed car with a fully gutted interior and plastic side windows. The car's confederate flag paint job didn't wash well with the organizers either. So the team started over. They bought a junked Corvette convertible in Miami for $600 and built a new car over a six-week span using cobbled together parts. Gib Hufstader created a special rear end with the long gearing necessary for the four-mile Mulsanne straight. The engine was a box stock L88

French driver Marie-Claude Beaumont (left) and her boss, French team owner/driver Henri Greder, flank Zora outside a dealership near Le Mans in 1972. Zora was in France to provide low-profile technical support for privateer teams running Corvettes at Le Mans.

with a lowered compression ratio to be able to handle lower octane French gasoline.

While the team took care of the car, Goodyear's racing director Leo Mehl took care of the entry situation, approaching Luigi Chinetti who was running all of Ferrari's GT factory racing efforts—using Goodyear rubber—under the banner of the North American Racing Team (NART). Mehl asked Chinetti to enter the Corvette as a reserve entry. Although Chinetti had agreed, it became a moot point before the race, however, when Chinetti withdrew his team cars after a technical argument with the organizers over his Ferraris' engine size. That left all of the NART team pit slots, paddock area and even a garage facility at a Volkswagen dealership in Le Mans available for use by the Corvette team.

Duntov traveled to Le Mans for the race and was able to see his old friend Chinetti, who hung around despite withdrawing his Ferraris. They both had the opportunity to watch the red Corvette, painted in Ferrari team colors, become the first Corvette to ever finish Le Mans. During the race, it rained 18 out of the 24 hours. Although Johnson crashed the car during practice, it was repaired in time for the race. But the fuel cell was pushed forward during the accident and it took longer to fill the tank. The car also suffered an electrical problem early in the race, but still the Heinz and Johnson car managed to finish 15th overall, being clocked at over 212 mph on Mulsanne. After the race, Chinetti presented Duntov with an honorary silver plaque that had his name engraved above the Ferrari logo of the North American Racing Team. For many years, it graced a china cabinet in the Duntov household.

Although the Heinz and Johnson car was the only Corvette to go the distance at Le Mans in 1972, it was not the only Corvette to contest the French classic that year. The Greenwood cars led their class for hours in the race before succumbing to crankshaft problems. Greenwood admits his cars always did much better in the sprint races than at endurance venues like Daytona and Le Mans. Crankshaft failures at Daytona and Le Mans took out both cars in 1972, and they never lasted longer than eight hours. Zora felt that Greenwood often overreached himself in a desire to win races, that his aggressive big-block engines—some of which were bored out to 500 cubic inches—tended to put too much stress on the car's other components.

Although they may not have lasted the distance, Greenwood's machines were fast. Greenwood took the GT pole position in qualifying at Le Mans, which was all the more amazing, considering he was running on street rubber. During the race, Greenwood developed a rhythm and just let the car drift out of each corner. In the rain, the street radials provided no disadvantage at all.

After his BFG partnership expired in 1973, Greenwood entered the Trans-Am series where he won races at Road America and Edmonton and garnered enough points to clinch the 1973 manufacturer's title for Chevrolet.

Beyond the Enduros

In 1974, Duntov stepped up his effort with Greenwood, collaborating with Gib Hufstader on a "silhouette racer." This purpose-built race car maintained a visual connection to a street Corvette, yet contained a dramatic wedge shape with wide fender flares that smoothly blended into the door lines. It was also fitted with a front air dam, which kept air from entering underneath the car. It came to be known as the "widebody." Underneath the skin was a tube-frame chassis designed by noted race car builder Bob Riley.

Duntov worked out the basic specs of the car with Greenwood and then had Design Staff develop a body shape. "Zora paid attention to every aspect of the design and even tried to get some downforce out from the leading edge of the wide fender surfaces," said Greenwood. The body was actually built by Gary Pratt and his Protofab fabricating company in suburban Detroit. The widebody pieces were recorded as GM part numbers with the hopes of homologating such parts for use at Le Mans.

The widebody sat above a completely revised suspension, massive four-piston ventilated discs, and a new tubular rollcage, which played a major part in adding rigidity to the chassis structure. All this made it the most sophisticated racing Corvette yet. Unfortunately, that sophistication was shadowed by reliability problems. Although the car was tremendously fast, it never won anything.

"We always ran a pretty severe wedge," said Greenwood. "We created a tunnel effect and could enter the banking at Daytona at 221 mph. Those were pretty huge cars to be able to run that kind of speed. We had a splitter on the front of the car that kept air from flowing underneath the chassis.

"Duntov came right out with a design that worked and we never did develop anything that ran better, even though we tried a lot of different things," said Greenwood. "We did come up with a pretty good rear wing and some spoiler end caps."

The Greenwood association was the last harrah for Zora in big-time motor sports. Looking back, once again he felt a sense of pride tinged with disappointment—disappointment over what might have been, especially compared to what rivals at Ford, Porsche, Jaguar and Ferrari had accomplished during the same time. Nonetheless, he overcame tremendous odds— at great danger to his own career—to create a racing pedigree for the Corvette that still stands today.

TWENTY-ONE

*Zora had failed thus far in his career to sell the corporation
on a mid-engined design—and time was running out before
his mandatory retirement in 1975.*

CORVETTE PROTOTYPE

One Last Stand

Duntov was nothing if not persistent. Despite his proposals being shut down for a mid-engined Corvette in 1963 and 1968, Zora never lost hope. Now that he was chief engineer, he knew he had one last shot to make something happen in the early 1970s before he arrived at mandatory retirement age in 1975.

Two obstacles were working against Zora: opposition from Design Staff and the lack of proper mid-engine powertrain components. It was the same old story—tooling costs would run into millions to supply the necessary automatic and manual transaxles. Henceforth, if Duntov were to achieve his goals, he'd have to design a powertrain system using available parts.

Raiding the Parts Bin

Zora's efforts centered on an experimental car known as XP-882. In conceiving this car, he'd had a wide range of General Motors drivetrain components to choose from. He found that hardware from the front-wheel-drive Oldsmobile Toronado might be just what he needed. But there was a problem: using these components would place the engine higher than Duntov wanted it to be. It also limited him to an automatic transmission version of the car because a manual shift wasn't available on the Toronado.

But Zora had a solution. He turned the engine sideways and mounted it transversely, locating the transmission on the side of the engine facing the passenger compartment and the differential on the other side. To connect the two, he ran the drive shafts through a tube in the center of the engine's oil pan. The differential case was then firmly affixed to the oil pan. Final drive gears were centrally located between the wheels in an aluminum housing. To add 4WD later would be a simple matter of adding a shaft to the bevel gears down through the center of the car to another differential. He earned a patent for this arrangement, which was granted in May 1971.

Opposite: Zora with XP-882 at a 1970 auto show. This provocative machine represented one of his last and greatest hopes to build a production mid-engined Corvette.

While transversely mounted engines are commonplace today, this was a relatively early application. The Lamborghini Miura and Ferrari's Dino 206/246 were among the few other cars on the market with this configuration. But the Miura had a unit transaxle with a gear transfer drive at the left end of the engine and the transaxle entirely behind the engine.

Zora needed a simpler approach while striving for more compactness. His solution created a wheelbase that was only 95.5 inches. By fully utilizing the lateral space around the engine, he created more longitudinal space, which allowed for a trunk. Clearly, Zora was working hard to chip away at the traditional objections to a mid-engine machine.

The finished XP-882 was low, wide and aggressive, with a roofline a full ten inches lower than the pre-1963 Corvette. The car was designed in a coupe version only. It looked like a street-going competitor to the Ford GT40, while maintaining a distinct Corvette resemblance with its sharp, chiseled edges and a new, louvered fastback roofline. The XP-882 weighed about 3,000 pounds, with a 44/56 front-to-rear weight distribution. The gas tank was located between the front wheels with a filler cap in the center of the front deck. The radiator was located up front as well.

Concentric coil-shock units suspended the car at all four wheels, with a wishbone suspension and power rack and pinion steering at the front. In back, the independent rear suspension used the axle shafts as stressed members.

Although four-wheel drive was part of Zora's plan all along, it was not used in the original prototype of the XP-882. In an article published in *Vette* magazine, Duntov wrote: "At the onset when the midship Corvette was authorized in 1968, I told the design group that we would plan the car with 4WD in mind at all times, but to keep mum about it. I felt that it was too much to ask upper management to have the foresight that 4WD for high performance sports cars was a necessary, coming thing. But the capability for 4WD was built into the chassis from the beginning. It was many months before I succeeded in convincing management that this was the way to go. The universal objection was over the complicated driveline."

The XP-882 took the world by surprise at the 1970 New York Auto Show. General Motors had not planned to show the car, but given the fact that Ford Motor Company was showing the mid-engined Pantera (built by de Tomaso in Italy), and American Motors was showing the AMX/3, Bill Mitchell and Alex Mair had second thoughts. Urged on by Duntov, they elected to unveil the XP-882 in New York. In the rush to display the car, they didn't even have time to create a name—it was called "Corvette prototype."

But the "Corvette prototype" caused a sensation and completely upstaged the Pantera and the AMX/3. Suddenly Duntov's mid-engine machine had momentum. Duntov proceeded with the development of a manual transmission in addition to the Turbo Hydramatic automatic. Plans were put in place to offer the car with a 400-cubic-inch version of the small-block V-8.

Then the usual concerns began to creep in. While the XP-882 was a beautiful machine that would have been a fitting successor to the 1968 Corvette, there were worries at Chevrolet that the car would be expensive to build, would offer no significant increase in performance and would be sold with only an automatic transmission. At the time, Chevy general manager John DeLorean was still considering the idea of a metal-bodied Corvette on the Camaro platform. A mid-engined machine would have been a much more expensive proposition.

Wrapping It in Aluminum

Duntov kept the heat on. In 1974, he was so anxious to sell the world on a mid-engined Corvette that he was willing to forgo one of Corvette's most exclusive features since 1953: the fiberglass body. In its place would be a shining aluminum body designed by Reynolds Aluminum. Reynolds was anxious to showcase the possibility of aluminum automobile bodies and saw the mid-engined Corvette as a natural. A mathematical model was built which determined the necessary thickness of the aluminum skin.

Duntov received assurances that Reynolds would provide an aluminum body and structure identical to that of a steel car. The car, crafted in a small prototype shop in Detroit called Creative Engineering, wound up weighing 400 pounds less than an equivalent steel body. This finished car, called the "Reynolds Aluminum Corvette," was a beauty. Its GM name was XP-895.

XP-895 was a mid-engined machine featuring an aluminum body produced by Reynolds Aluminum, but it fared no better than Zora's other mid-engine concepts in reaching the production line.

Anticipating the usual cost objections from the bean counters, Duntov ordered a feasibility study for what it would require to manufacture a similar car for production with an eye toward profitability. He determined that two shifts could produce 40,000 units a year out of the Corvette St. Louis plant. (In 1972, 27,000 Corvettes had been built.) To be conservative, the figure of 30,000 units was used for tooling and profitability calculations. While GM estimated the total tooling costs to be $80 million (including $5 million for a new paint facility), Duntov's own estimates were $40 to $50 million, including the tooling for four-wheel drive.

Duntov also explored potential servicing costs for a mid-engined car and determined they would be less costly than a conventional Corvette of the day. As an example, Duntov cited in *Vette* what would be required to remove the engine and transmission of the third-generation Corvette (1968) versus his mid-engine car. For the former, the job required removing the engine mount and transmission mounts, radiator and shroud,

cross-member (automatic), distributor and then a careful detachment of the engine and transmission from the frame. The mid-engined car required only the removal of the engine mount and suspension attachment.

Given this convincing data, along with the extremely enthusiastic public reception for the XP-882 and the XP-895, it appeared for a time that a mid-engined Corvette was inevitable—whether its body was made out of aluminum or fiberglass. Adding to the momentum was some unexpected support from Ed Cole that surfaced in the midst of a totally unrelated matter involving Duntov.

Bonus Bombshell

In Duntov's mind, the scars from his demotion from the Corvette program in 1967 hadn't fully healed. He still had a love/hate affair with the corporation that employed him. One of the sticking points for Duntov was his financial compensation from GM. Duntov felt he was underpaid for most of his career at the company and suggested it was largely due to politics. One traditional way of making mavericks like Duntov conform was to hit them where it hurts—in the wallet.

Bonuses were, and still are, a major part of the compensation package at companies like GM. The company can easily match or exceed an annual salary on the executive level. Duntov felt that despite his popularity among fellow engineers and hourly workers, he was stepping on the toes of a large number of his bosses, which precipitated less of a bonus than he deserved. "They have power of setting my salary and bonus and they can pinch me when they can," said Duntov. It happened early in his career under Maurice Olley, and, according to Zora, it continued to happen over the years.

Zora had finally had enough and spitefully suggested that if GM couldn't afford to pay him a better bonus, maybe they needed the money more than he did. In other words, he said no to what he considered a paltry bonus. The refusal caused consternation throughout the halls of GM, and the matter was referred to Alex Mair, general manager John DeLorean, Pete Estes and eventually Ed Cole. "They were giving him something like $20,000," said DeLorean. "I told Cole he should get $100,000, and I wanted to award it to Zora immediately. What he does gets more visibility for GM in the enthusiast press than everyone else at GM put together. If you were going to pay for the advertising and exposure he created, you'd have to pay $5 million. He's worth all of that."

But Cole didn't see it that way. He called Duntov demanding to know what was going on. After a heated conversation, Cole suggested that Duntov resign. Duntov refused. He liked his work and the people of GM. He felt he had been cheated systematically, but in his mind resignation was out of the question.

Duntov stayed on but felt a considerable rift between him and Cole. In addition, the two had had no contact for several months. But when Duntov heard that his pet project, the XP-882, was not likely to make it into production, he decided to make his case directly to Cole—rift or no rift.

New Lease on Life

Duntov called Cole's secretary for an appointment. To his surprise, the secretary said Zora could come over any time. Duntov took that as an olive branch, so he met with Cole but also took the opportunity to bring along an armful of blueprints and engineering sketches for a mid-engined Corvette. Cole was surprisingly receptive not only because he valued having Zora around, but also because he shared a similar agenda.

Cole had purchased the rights to the Wankel rotary engine and was now seeking a way to get the public excited about this radical new powerplant. A mid-engine Corvette would provide the perfect display case for a rotary engine. Duntov and Cole agreed to create yet another new show car based on the XP-882. But Cole wasn't thinking in terms of just low-volume, mid-engined sports cars. He was really trying to sell America on the Wankel engine as a viable powerplant for high-volume small cars like the Vega. During the course of the meeting, Zora let Cole know that he had decided to accept his bonus. Suddenly, the ice had melted.

Invented in Germany during the mid-1950s by Felix Wankel, the rotary engine was a radical concept in internal combustion engines, and it showed immense promise. It was small and powerful and had fewer moving parts than a piston engine and thus had potentially lower manufacturing costs. Cole was sky-high on the possibilities. He had bought the rights from NSU/Curtiss Wright to use the engine. While the Corvette provided one obvious application, Cole saw the rotary being used in a variety of high-volume Chevrolet vehicles. The foremost among them were the Vega and the Monza, the latter of which grew out of the Vega platform according to GM designer Jerry Palmer. Cole even ordered the platform modified in order to accept the rotary (the centerline of the rotary engine was higher than a reciprocating engine) at a cost of millions of dollars.

After Cole and Zora had patched things up, Cole approached Bill Mitchell with the idea of freshening the look of XP-882 to better showcase the new engine. The new machine would come to be known as the Aerovette. Under Mitchell's guidance, the Aerovette became a sleeker version of XP-882, with an even cleaner almond shape (.325 drag coefficient) and a smooth, flat fastback roofline with a window. The Aerovette showcased a special

The Corvette Aerovette provided an attractive display for GM's rotary engine technology.

four-rotor version of the Wankel. Gull-wing doors, inspired by the Mercedes 300SL, were another prominent feature. Duntov loved the look of the Aerovette. "In my mind, it was the best body that Bill Mitchell ever designed."

The Aerovette's four-rotor engine consisted of a pair of two-rotor units connected together and mounted transversely, just like the original V-8. *Car and Driver* described the Aerovette as "more like a set of Siamese twins than a single 4-rotor engine." According to Gib Hufstader, "It was more than a case of hooking two 2-rotor engines together. We had to handle cooling jackets, oil channels, common sump and oil pump. We tested it on dynos and it was putting out between 360 and 370 hp. It became the largest automotive rotary engine ever built."

The car's potential performance was incredible. *Car and Driver* quoted Zora as stating that "this Wankel car is faster 0-100 mph than [a] 454."

The plan was to show the Aerovette plus a two-rotor concept car with a body constructed by Pininfarina at the 1973 Paris and London motor shows. All the GM executives from around the world were going to be there, and Cole saw the occasion as a terrific opportunity to get the organization on board. The potential international press attention was also enticing.

But by the time the show cars were built and ready to display, problems with the Wankel engine were tainting its attractiveness to GM. Poor fuel economy, leaking seals and a tendency to run hot were all factors that decreased its desirability as a high-volume engine. Despite the initial promise of lower costs, a Wankel engine cost about $250 more to build than a V-8, which was a huge differential. With the engine's many problems, suddenly the linkage of the rotary engine with the Corvette wasn't so attractive.

A Victim of His Own Success

Furthermore, there was still a strong undercurrent of opinion within GM to keep the Corvette as it was. Zora had first-hand evidence of this at the London Motor Show when then-Chairman Richard C. Gerstenberg addressed the mid-engined issue directly with Duntov. Wrote Zora, "Mr. Gerstenberg said like a father to a dim-witted child, 'We build Corvettes in numbers crowding 40,000 a year and still cannot satisfy the demand, why do you insist that we abandon this successful design and barge head-on into a new design?'" Gerstenberg suggested a more cautious approach, indicating that if the market got soft, he would reconsider his position on mid-engined Corvettes.

Duntov later wrote in *Vette,* "The words of Mr. Gerstenberg fell like a sledgehammer on my head. What about technical leadership for Chevrolet? What about performance leadership and my desire to produce a ne plus ultra American sports car? I felt I was betraying the people in the Corvette group, the Chevrolet people of Design Staff and Corvette people at large by withholding the introduction of the ultimate Corvette."

Zora then blamed his own acceptance of the rotary engine as a factor in the failure of the mid-engine concept. "I reproached myself for tying the Corvette with the rotary engine's thermodynamic inefficiencies. How to tell Mr. Gerstenberg that we liked reciprocating engines and that the rotary engine was an abortion enforced by Mr. Cole! No, I couldn't do that. I entered into an agreement with Cole, fair and square, so I had to bear the responsibility for the unholy alliance with the rotary engine."

While the Aerovette project was shelved, speculation continued to run rampant that Chevrolet would offer a mid-engine Corvette. The question was not whether but when.

A cover story in the February 1977 issue of *Road & Track* predicted that for the 1980 model year, Chevrolet would offer a more conservative version of the Aerovette sans the Wankel engine and the gull-wing doors.

The *Road & Track* article speculated that it was about time Chevrolet came out with the real thing after years of teasing the public with a succession of mid-engined show cars. The article cited the sales intrusion being made by cars like the Pontiac Trans Am following the emasculation of the Corvette due to new fuel economy standards and emission controls. Suddenly the Trans Am's performance was not that different from the performance of the Corvette—at a far more attractive price. In 1977, the base price of a Corvette was $8,647.65, and it was easy to bump the sticker up to $11,000 after checking the option sheet. The Trans Am could be had for many thousands less. Given the narrowing of the gap, it was time for the Corvette to once again reassert its position as a technological flagship for GM.

But the pundits were wrong. Corvette sales were clipping along at record numbers in the 1970s, and Chevrolet had no intention of tampering with a solid sales winner. Ironically, Corvette was a victim of its own success. The more profitable it became, the less daring it needed to be in terms of engineering and technology, and its role as a halo car diminished.

Climate Change

The year 1973 represented a sea change in American performance cars, and it was not a positive shift. A well-orchestrated supply pinch by the newly formed Oil Producing Export Countries (OPEC) resulted in shortages at the pump, and gasoline prices almost doubled. The oil crisis, coupled with increasing government standards for pollution controls, triggered one of the most profound changes ever in the American auto industry—a swing toward horsepower-robbing emissions devices and a major push towards higher fuel economy. High-horsepower, fuel-chugging engines such as those found in the Corvette were suddenly the targets of government bureaucrats and legislators alike.

The 1973 energy crisis brought on a major deproliferation in Corvette power combinations. The big-blocks, as well as the solid-lifter LT1s, were victims. Prior to 1973, Corvette had as many as five different engine combinations available, but by 1975 there was only one engine upgrade—a 205-horsepower version of the 350-cubic-inch small-block instead of the standard 165-horsepower version. According to Zora, the extremely high cost of getting a particular engine certified was the limiting factor behind the reduced number of drivetrain choices.

But while the mid-1970s might have been the low point, there was hope on the horizon. The 1975 model year brought the debut of Ed Cole's catalytic converter, which, combined with modern engine electronics and sophisticated fuel-injection systems, helped make performance cars possible again. The dual exhausts were routed to a single converter, then split for dual exit. The 1975 models also featured a high-energy ignition system that replaced the old transistorized ignitions. It included the Corvette's first no-points distributor.

The 1975 car also had an unadvertised new feature, a fuel cell gas tank. The Corvette's gas tank was located at the tail of the car, which made the Corvette more susceptible to fuel tank fires resulting from rear-end collisions. Litigation resulted and GM had been quietly settling these cases rather than letting them go to trial. Zora felt that the only thing to do to continue the Corvette's configuration was to come up with a fuel system that didn't leak fuel as a result of a barrier hit at 40 mph. So he took a page from CERV I and II and developed a racing-type bladder fuel cell for the Corvette. The cell itself was produced by Goodyear and earned Duntov one of his many patents.

During his remaining years at Chevrolet before his retirement in 1975, Duntov had explored a number of major technological enhancements for the third-generation Corvette. These included the use of a transverse fiberglass leaf spring (eventually adopted in 1982), antilock brakes (offered in 1985), a Bosch fuel injection system and the use of an aluminum body for the Corvette.

Clearly, Duntov helped set the agenda for automobile technology we take for granted today yet in his mind he never realized the ultimate Corvette, the car that would embody everything he knew as an engineer.

As Duntov's career wound down in 1973-1974, he made peace with Ed Cole despite the fact that Cole was up to his eyeballs in crisis management. Cole's baby, the Corvair, finally died in 1969, a market failure after years of negative publicity, and a motor mount that Cole had designed was subject to a massive recall. The Vega was having problems and Cole faced a host of challenges regarding emissions and engines. These and other problems may have prevented him from reaching the very top spot—as chairman of the board of GM. Unquestionably, the troubles of the last few years had taken a toll on Ed Cole, who in 1974 told *Newsweek* that after 44 years at GM, the fun of the car business was gone. He retired at the mandatory age of 65 on September 29, 1974.

While many historians have characterized Cole as a staunch defender of the Corvette, his support, according to Duntov, came not because he was a sports car enthusiast, but because he understood the halo effect a car like the Corvette could have on the rest of his Chevy Division. "His interest was not Corvette at all, but passenger car," said Duntov. "That's where the profits were and he did not relate to Corvette per se." Duntov may have been overly critical on that score, however, considering how often Cole went to bat for Duntov over the years as well as how much Cole enjoyed driving Corvettes.

After Cole retired, he and Zora kept in touch. The two had an increasing fondness for aviation. Cole was an avid flyer and had flown a Beechcraft Bonanza for many years prior to ascending to the presidency of GM. He often flew to major races like the Daytona 500 and enjoyed flying down to Florida to watch space launches from Cape Canaveral. However, in 1965, GM issued a policy statement forbidding its top executives from flying their own planes.

But after retirement, Cole bought a British twin-engine Beagle from race driver Jim Rathmann that Cole used to fly himself to meetings around the country. Cole also shared with Duntov his idea of producing a super-freighter airplane for a firm called International Husky that could carry automotive components around the world. Cadillac would eventually employ Cole's vision with its two-seat Allante, and flew bodies designed and manufactured at Pininfarina in Italy to Detroit for final assembly.

Early in 1977, Cole and an associate bought a portion of Checker Motors, the taxicab manufacturer in Kalamazoo, Michigan. Cole became chairman and chief executive officer—a position that appeared to reenergize him. He had plans to revamp the company's aging product line and had approached Duntov about the possibility of joining the company. Those plans were never realized. After Cole left Pontiac Airport for a meeting in Kalamazoo on the morning of May 2, 1977, he encountered foggy rain on his way and crashed into a cornfield. Ed Cole was dead at the age of 67.

Although Zora kept his feelings largely to himself, he was deeply saddened by the news of Cole's death. Despite their often-rocky relationship, Duntov knew well that Cole—far more than any other individual—was the man who had made his success possible.

TWENTY-TWO

Zora Arkus-Duntov
Retirement Dinner

January 13, 1975

Mr. Don McPherson — Master of Ceremonies

ZORA'S EARLY DAYS

PIKES PEAK ADVENTURES

CORVETTE DESIGN   *— Mr. Bill Mitchell*

ENGINE DEVELOPMENT   *— Mr. Larry Drake*

SOUND OF CORVETTES   *— Mr. Ron Martoia*

CORVETTE ENGINEERING — Mr. Walt Zetye

1958 SEBRING RACE   *— Mr. Jack Rausch*

HURST PERFORMANCE PRODUCTS — Miss Linda Vaughn

FAMOUS QUOTES

GIFT PRESENTATIONS

*Zora reached GM's mandatory retirement age in 1975 and merited
one of GM's biggest send-offs ever for a nonexecutive.*

Bowing Out

A ge is a subject he doesn't talk about much. He's close on 60 and it's weighing on him. But it doesn't stop him. Seemingly, nothing can. You see it when he drives. A few laps at the photographer's insistence—just to finish off. Never mind that it's just to use a roll of Tri-X. It's done right. Wide open throttle until the last millisecond—brake late—brake hard—on the power early. Not a twitch in the line. Just a taste of tire smoke filters through the cockpit. Hell. Zora Arkus-Duntov will still blow the doors off 98 percent of the people who buy his cars. And that bodes well for next year's cars.

This description of Duntov in the pages of *Car and Driver* in 1970 summarized what Duntov had become, at least in the eyes of enthusiasts and the enthusiast press. Zora couldn't bask in the glory, however. The job of chief engineer on any car line was becoming more complicated in the early 1970s as the industry changed at a prodigious rate. Given government regulation over safety, fuel economy and emissions, plus quality concerns inspired by better-built foreign competitors, the American automotive industry was faced with daunting challenges.

Suddenly the issues that mattered to Duntov were not as relevant in this major climatic shift. Some felt that with his high-performance agenda, Zora was not inclined or equipped to handle the myriad details of building a modern car. Some thought that he was becoming an anachronism.

Not that it mattered. Zora would turn 65, General Motor's mandatory retirement age, on December 25, 1974. Zora wasn't ready to retire, but the car that had been his life was about to become somebody else's.

A Successor Not of His Choosing

Senior management had already picked Duntov's successor, an enterprising young engineer named Dave McLellan, then 40. With his longish sandy

Opposite: Zora knew how to squeeze every ounce of performance out of the cars he built, but time was catching up with him in the early 1970s, and in a new era of emission controls and quality concerns, performance was no longer in fashion.

hair (like Zora, McLellan would go prematurely white), stylish glasses and natty appearance, McLellan not only looked like a car guy, he was one. His passion was Porsches, and he had been president of a Detroit area Porsche club and the owner of several 356s as well as a 911 he picked up at the factory in Germany.

A native of Munising, on Michigan's Upper Peninsula, McLellan graduated from Wayne State University in Detroit with a degree in mechanical engineering. After graduation, he went to work at GM's Milford Proving Ground and worked his way into the Chevrolet Engineering Center, where he held a succession of engineering jobs and developed the chassis for the Camaro Z-28. He later participated in a project promoted by John DeLorean that explored building the Camaro, Nova and possibly even the Corvette on the same chassis.

In April 1972 he was promoted to assistant staff engineer of Chevrolet's passenger car programs. After a year in this position, he took a leave of absence to go to MIT for a year as an Alfred P. Sloan Fellow to earn his master's degree in management. This was a sort of finishing school for promising young managers. Armed with these credentials, McLellan was promoted to staff engineer in July 1974, which made him a logical successor to Duntov in the eyes of GM management.

But McLellan didn't have Duntov's exotic European pedigree and was not Duntov's choice as a successor. Duntov would have preferred Walt Zetye, who had served as Duntov's principal lieutenant during his later years at GM and who shared Duntov's agendas. But Duntov wasn't consulted in the decision.

By the time Duntov was ready to retire, the Corvette was in dire need of quality upgrades. Performance was a lost cause thanks to emissions controls, and while Ed Cole's catalytic converter would eventually help turn that around, the emphasis was on workmanship, safety and creature comforts. McLellan was equipped to deal with these issues —and Zora wasn't.

But if Duntov had to retire, this was the perfect time to do it, because the Corvette—as well as the entire performance car market—was at its lowest ebb in 1975. All of the engine combinations were gone, having been replaced by a standard 165-hp version and one optional engine of 205 hp.

"The world of performance was in a vertical dive in 1973/1974," according to Gib Hufstader. "All of us felt the sense of the absolute uselessness of performance engines. The purge was on V-8s. Everything was going to be V-6. It was such a big job to certify an engine for emissions that we didn't have time for all the performance versions. We'd go into meetings and the engine guys didn't know how they were going to make the emission standards."

McLellan would have a style vastly different from that of his predecessor; he was much quieter and less flamboyant. An automotive intellectual, he shared Duntov's desire to make the Corvette into a technological masterpiece but was also mindful of the equity the Corvette established as a front-engined, V-8 sports car. He cited Porsche's experiments in deviating from its rear-engined, air-cooled roots to front-engined, water-cooled cars such as the 924, 944 and 928, which did not enjoy the market success of the 911. "After so many years, the mold was set," said McLellan. "The only true Porsche accepted by the cognoscenti is the 356-911. In contrast, go to any Corvette show and most people ignore the mid-engined prototypes. Their definition of a Corvette is a front-engined car with a long hood and rear drive."

McLellan was also a realist. He felt that Zora's prototypes were a long way from being production cars. Many were simply design exercises, dream cars not engineered for real-world suspensions to function beneath the skin or to accommodate real people. "The Aerovette was really a 7/8 size car," said McLellan. "And if Chevy ever decided to mass-produce it, they would have to figure out how to make a convertible out of it."

While Duntov and McLellan overlapped with each other for about six months, the relationship was awkward. While Zora had nothing personal against McLellan, he didn't give him the same nurturing that he would have given his own hand-picked successor.

During McLellan's transition period, he and Duntov were together during a test trip to Pikes Peak. The episode became a symbolic contrast to Zora's earlier heroic exploits on the mountain. According to McLellan, Zora drove a white 1975 Corvette up to the top. At the summit Zora was under the impression that he was out of gas. So he decided to coast down without the engine running and engaged the engine when necessary to facilitate braking. In this mode, raw gas and air were congregating inside the catalytic converter so that when he got to the bottom, the heat buildup in the converter caused the mixture to ignite and eventually consume the car. It was an embarrassing moment for Zora and perhaps a sign that it was time for him to move on.

From the beginning, McLellan knew he'd have to establish his own team, but he did hang onto several of Zora's people, including Gib Hufstader, Dan Crawford, and Walt Zetye. "We knew that Dave might have been pretty sensitive succeeding Zora," said Gib Hufstader. "Consequently, we rarely brought up Zora. It was kind of like that era was over." Despite his sober outlook, McLellan was wary of replacing a legend like Duntov. In 1983 at a Society of Automotive Engineers dinner, McLellan refused to sit at the head table if Zora was also going to be there. As a result, Zora was seated inconspicuously out in the crowd.

Roasting the Russian

Despite any differences of opinion that might have emerged over the years between Duntov's philosophy and the rest of the company, GM was prepared to offer Zora a rousing send-off at his retirement dinner. For a man who never made it to the ranks of senior management, the magnitude of Duntov's party was nothing short of phenomenal. The affair was held on January 13, 1975, at a Warren, Michigan, banquet hall near the GM Tech Center. Hundreds were invited and many more sent letters and cards. The event, organized by Chevy director of engineering Paul King, turned into a major roast of Zora and one of the larger retirement gatherings ever conducted for a GM employee. It was a love-in.

The MC was the new Chevy chief engineer, Don McPherson. Speakers included Ed Cole, Bill Mitchell, Gib Hufstader, race queen Linda Vaughn, Walt Zetye, engine men Fred Frincke and Larry Drake, as well as a number of speakers from key equipment suppliers.

Sharing a laugh at Zora's January 1975 retirement party at the GM Training Center in Warren, Michigan, are from left: Dave McLellan (facing away from camera), Bill Mitchell, Elfi Duntov, Pete Estes, Zora and Ed Cole.

In the smoky ambience of a large banquet room, Ed Cole gave the longest speech and didn't mince his praise for Zora. He raved about Zora's persistence: "You could never turn him off," said Cole. He described walking through the Chevrolet Engineering Center and continuously seeing mystery parts that didn't have any obvious application to a current model. "That's for Mr. Duntov" was the reply he got upon asking who the parts were for.

"Zora managed to bootleg more things through Chevrolet than any other engineer that I've ever known," said Cole. He stated, "That was damn good for Chevrolet, even if it caused chaos in the accounting department after Duntov's cost overruns got charged against other departments' budgets."

Cole acknowledged the unique access Duntov had to his office on the fourteenth floor

after Cole had become president of GM. "Any time he had a little something he'd call my secretary and say, 'Can I have a date with Mr. Cole?' We never talked about it with the general manager of Chevrolet or anybody else. He used to come in kind of unannounced, and we'd kind of connive with one another as to how we could put some of these things across legitimately. Since we had done so much illegitimately before, [referring to their earlier joint efforts to skirt the no-racing policy] we had to kind of turn it into something that was legitimate."

Recognizing the creative stagnation that was taking place in the mid-1970s as the auto industry grappled with dry issues like fuel economy and emissions, Cole stressed that the business needed more Zora Duntovs. "There's not a kid on the street who is not interested in new automobiles, new machinery, new ways of doing things," said Cole. "The technology's here, as far as I'm concerned, and we can excite this business. And this is what's wrong, I believe, with our business today. We don't have anything really to sell.

"Chevrolet should be very thankful for the contribution that he made over the years. I just want to say that I am very happy and was very privileged to have a chance to work with this most incredible man. He knew how to get the job done, and that's what we need today."

Bill Mitchell followed and stayed away from any overt references to their famous run-ins over the 1963 split-window Sting Ray. Instead he acknowledged that guys like Zora made the business exciting. "Zora has given a stimulus to us which is wonderful," said Mitchell. "And I think in all of our days we're going to owe it to you, Zora, we don't want to miss you, and I want you to know you'll always be welcome to come back and put that shot in the arm to us. Because with all the restrictions we have today, we need some romance in the business. And thank God we have the Corvette, and thank God, Zora, you've put into the Corvette what made it go."

Mitchell referenced the fact that the auto business had become over-wrought with restrictions and regulations, which made him appreciate the value of Zora even more. "The biggest thing I want to say," said Mitchell, "is that this has been a hell of a life for us, with all the 'don't do this, don't do that,' backlight troubles, headlight troubles, headroom troubles, crushability, and with all of this. But when Zora comes into our place, everything lights up.

"I think in life, wine, women and song to me make life worth living, and that's what Zora and the Corvette does for a big corporation like General Motors."

On the lighter side, Jim Williams, the head of Chevy public relations, put together a list of "Zora-isms" for the group. They included:

"Not to worry."
"We will solve."
"Arrange car for her."
"I give her car for a week."
"Is not possible."
"Girl return car yesterday."
"Mmmmmm (in doubting, disapproving tone)."
"I will tell you."
"I propose a change."
"Built mid-engine car."
"Go full-throttle."
"What do you mean, car not pass test?"
"To hell!"
"Part is not man enough for the job."
"Design is product of diseased mind." ("product" pronounced
        "pro-DOOKT")
"Is faster than Corvette?"
"Is SLOWER than Corvette."
"From this blind spot comes car I did not see."
"Is hell-bent for election."
"Hundred miles per hour in second gear."
"Then, I smell smoke."
"Is a good story."
"Writer is engineer."
"Probably leak is from Design Staff."
"Can't remember."
"I tell press nothing!"
"Should sleep on that."

An Album of War Stories

At the end of the evening, Duntov received a special album filled with letters from well wishers, among them Karl Ludvigsen, Briggs Cunningham, Walt Mackenzie, *Popular Mechanics* editor Joe Oldham, *Motor Trend* editor Eric Dahlquist, aviatrix Betty Skelton Frankman and Pennsylvania road racers Don Yenko and Donna Mae Mims.

Former *Hot Rod* editor Ray Brock recalled some "wild and wooly" times down in Daytona Beach when Zora was making his speed runs in the mid-1950s: "You were always a sharp engineer. I remember when you came up with a highly scientific method for improving traction on your '55 'Vette on the beach: an old 6-cylinder engine block in the trunk!

"Then there was the SS program, CERV I, hobby-horse injectors and the times you let me sneak looks at some of those experimental engines which we never did see in a production Corvette. Not only has working with you these past 20 years been interesting, it was downright fun. Especially after I deciphered your accent and found out what you were saying."

John Fitch, the driver/manager whom Cole had hired to run the Corvette race program in 1956, described Zora as one of those exciting people who make everything more interesting and more fun. He took the opportunity to nudge Zora about both his philosophy and reputation as a driver and a lover: "Zora has always been convinced in his heart of two things about himself and his life, to his own great personal jeopardy," wrote Fitch. "It's quite miraculous that neither have killed him in the course of a long and spectacular career. One was his conviction that he was the greatest driver in the world and the other that he was the greatest lover of the age. As every ambitious driver knows, the former is only a matter of the vehicle and the rest of us know the latter is a matter of opportunity. Looking back over the years, I think Zora was probably both."

Joe Oldham of Hearst Magazines summed up the feeling of many journalists in his good-natured jab at the retiring legend: "Well, you've really done it to us this time," wrote Oldham. "You've really put us in a giant pickle. What are all of us dumb automotive writers to do at next year's preview? What are we to do all of next year and the year after that? Who will bail us out when we need technical information on Corvette suspension? Who will explain the new features of the '76 Corvette? Who will show us the right line through the ride and handling course? Who will explain the nuances of Corvette engineering?

"Sure, Chevrolet will give your title and office to someone else when you retire this fall. And I'm sure he'll be a very competent person who knows his business. But he will not be Zora Arkus-Duntov, creator of the Ardun cylinder head, godfather of the Corvette, race driver and engineer extraordinaire. You are a legend, Zora, and I am proud to be counted among your friends and acquaintances."

One of the guys who knew Duntov better than anyone else was Walt Mackenzie, who handled public relations for many of Duntov's early racing efforts, including Pikes Peak in 1955 and Daytona in 1956. Mackenzie discussed Zora's "proactive approach" to public relations: "Anytime Zora had something he wanted to see in print, he would usually try me first. If for reasons of policy or for whatever reasons, no results were forthcoming,

'Low profile Zora' would reach up for another peak and out would come an article profusely illustrated.

"I must tell you that when that happened, someone would lay it in front of [GM Chairman] Mr. Donner. He would send it to whoever was then Chevy's General Manager. He, in turn, would send it to John Cutter [GM corporate public relations staff] or call him over across the hall. John would call me and ask me what I knew about it. I would, finally, ask Zora. He would look at me archly, and say, 'Vwhy Vwalter, how would I know about that?'

"Almost every year I had the pleasure of being with Zora at the New York Auto Show," wrote Mackenzie. "Usually we would also both attend the *Car and Driver* formal award dinner, as the Corvette, year after year, won "Sports Car of the Year Award." Zora invariably captivated the gatherings there with his anecdotes. It may not be well known to some, but Zora is one of the best and wittiest speakers to appear on the SAE technical circuit."

Don Yenko wrote about the commotion that would often accompany a Duntov visit to any racetrack. "Unfortunately, Zora, you've been severely hamstrung by your company's 'not *really* racing' policy," wrote Yenko. "Your inimitable charm has worked against you in this case. Your classic European accent…the cosmopolitan charisma…the photogenic shock of white hair…all cause you to be in the working press's dream. Consequently, there's no chance of you surreptitiously attending a race on your own time without the big write-up, 'CHEVROLET BACK IN RACING!'

"But, even with these handicaps, you and your exclusive group of engineer magicians have made the Corvette into the-hardest-to-get, largest-selling-sports-car in the world (and, happily for me), they sell for more *used* than new.

"You've also rationalized a street machine into a very creditable race-car and in a uniquely impartial way. I remember many times at Sebring when we had problems where Zora himself would come to the rescue with new brakes, or gearboxes, or whatever, for *every* Corvette entered. It would have been easier and quicker to just equip the frontrunners (or so we told you) but you would have none of it."

Betty Skelton Frankman, the aviatrix who drove one of Zora's Corvettes during the 1956 speed runs on the beach in Daytona, remained a lifelong friend of Zora and Elfi. "Zora has forgotten more about automobiles than I shall ever know," wrote Frankman. "He has taught more about driving and building automobiles than I shall ever learn. But it is ZORIKA ARKUS-DUNTOV, THE MAN, that most of all makes me honored to be his friend…and very proud, as well as humble, to call him my hero."

TWENTY-THREE

Zora finally bought a Corvette of his own upon retirement—a silver-blue 1974 big-block that he personalized with his initials, ZAD, on the driver's door.

Life After GM

Zora Arkus-Duntov wasn't ready to leave General Motors. His mind was still razor-sharp and brimming with ideas about how to make Corvettes accelerate or go around corners faster. Although he had become an established deity in the automotive world, he wasn't ready to bask in the adulation of the Corvette community or to move to Florida and tee it up at the country club. Zora's soul, his entire foundation, was based on driving or engineering high-performance equipment. Nothing else could satisfy him. Certainly he thought he would have the opportunity to contribute to future performance development at GM as a consultant.

He was mistaken. Dave McLellan, Corvette's new chief engineer, didn't care to work in Zora's shadow any more than he had to. In addition, consulting projects were not forthcoming from other GM divisions. Whether he liked it or not, Zora was no longer wanted in the company where he had made so much history. Fortunately for him, plenty of offers *did* come from outside the corporation.

The DeLorean Challenge

Weeks after his retirement from GM, Zora joined John DeLorean as a consultant on DeLorean's new DMC-12 sports car project. Known for its gull-wing doors and etched stainless steel body, the DMC-12 would be permanently etched in the consciousness of the sports car buying public, but not for the reasons DeLorean would have liked.

A year after he left GM in 1973, DeLorean founded DeLorean Motor Corporation, obtaining $120 million from the British government to build a factory in Dunmurry, Northern Ireland. He augmented the government money with millions from private investors.

The opportunity to join the DeLorean Motor Company (DMC) was irresistible to Zora. It held great promise, because Zora knew that DeLorean had to pursue unconventional approaches to distinguish his vehicle in the sports car market. Zora recognized that teaming up with DeLorean might

Opposite: Zora became involved in a number of Corvette projects bearing his name, the foremost among them being the Duntov Turbo Corvette built by American Custom Industries in Sylvania, Ohio.

provide him with a way to fulfill his mid-engine dream, even if it wasn't for GM. For his part, DeLorean was happy to have a man of Duntov's caliber available to him. "He knew the business, he knew cars," said DeLorean of Duntov. "He knew a lot about sports cars, certainly more than I did or anyone else in the company. He was one of the primary sources of information. His opinion was invaluable. Above all, he was a good and loyal friend."

Such was DeLorean's belief in Duntov that his original notion was to acquire the rights from GM to produce Duntov's stillborn mid-engined prototype designs. This was despite the fact that DeLorean and his superiors had never authorized these cars to be built when he was at GM. But the 1973 energy crisis convinced DeLorean that he had to pursue something lighter than Zora's concepts. He also knew he'd have to adopt a smaller displacement engine. DeLorean wanted Duntov on his team and put Zora on a $1,000-per-month consulting retainer.

Much to Zora's disappointment, he never had a chance to design a car from the ground up for DeLorean. He spent several years on the sidelines as a sounding board, but never was a principal architect of the car. Eventually, he was asked to critique a pre-prototype that had been created by Mike Pocabello, a former engineer at Chaparral Cars who owned Triad, an engineering firm in Troy, Michigan. In his review, dated February 11, 1978, Duntov concluded, "Yes, the car will provide safe and reliable handling and provide road stability under all road conditions." But he reserved final judgment until he could drive the car on the road and the skid pad.

DeLorean himself wasn't sold on Pocabello's design, but instead of giving Duntov a larger role, in 1978 DeLorean brought in Colin Chapman of Lotus. Chapman scrapped everything that had been done previously—largely because the original design did not perform well in simulated tests—and created a backbone-type chassis with front and rear subframes holding the engine and suspension. Chapman also recommended a longitudinal arrangement for the engine, which became a 2.7-liter Renault V-6.

Chapman's entry into the picture pushed Duntov even further to the sidelines. Later, after Duntov was once again asked to critique the car, he did not hide his negative appraisal. He was particularly sensitive to the early media reports as they emerged. He grew increasingly concerned about the car's tendency to oversteer as prototypes were built and tested by the media.

In response to an *AutoWeek* article written in February 1980, Duntov wrote to DeLorean in October of that year:

> If the car has the same drawback now as described in the report, the car will be in trouble. Magazine writers all have access to

the skid pads to wring out the car and the opinion of the writers as you well know is important. What is more disturbing is the idea that the customer is pirouetting on a dry road. If the oversteering was taken care of in the meantime, it is just as well to let me drive the car and put it through the paces as magazine writers would. That will be insurance for you that nothing in the car's behavior will have surprises.

Should the car provide unsatisfactory, then we have urgent work to do. Let's avoid mistakes committed in the design of the pre-1965 Corvair. After six or seven years of valiant fight you stand on the threshold of fulfilling your dream. Let nothing spoil it.

But DeLorean didn't respond and as time went on, Duntov expressed increasing frustration because he was in Detroit, far from the action. In a February 26, 1981, letter to DeLorean, Duntov wrote: "After our conversation on the 24th of this month, it transpired that you did not plan to involve me in the nitty-gritty aspects of your business. My offer to go to Ireland and see that the cars will be all right was met with refusal. Whatever consideration taking part in your mind, no matter how important, the consideration of the first show to the press should take priority."

Duntov made it clear that he wanted to join DMC as an employee, where he could have more control, but DeLorean was aware of the company's many internal problems and wasn't ready to make that move. DeLorean told Zora that he intended to proceed slowly because of Zora's association with the Corvette and his hard-earned equity with Corvette people. But to Duntov, that wasn't an issue. He wanted be an active participant in a real-world project, not a has-been on the Corvette show circuit.

Desperate to become more involved in DeLorean's company, Zora recommended that DeLorean announce that Duntov had joined the company. Instead of hiring Duntov, however, DeLorean offered Zora a higher retainer. DeLorean's offer in April 1981 was to buy ten days of Duntov's time per month, for a total annual compensation of $30,000. The extra money didn't make a lot of difference to Zora—he simply wanted to be the individual who solved the riddle about how to make the car a success. Duntov wrote: "Don't worry about overpaying me or underpaying me, what gets me is a lack of personal communication."

The DeLorean's stainless steel body was designed by Ital Design's Giorgetto Giugiaro, while Duntov, Lotus Cars' Colin Chapman and Mike Pocabello, formerly of Chaparral Cars, contributed to the chassis and drivetrain.

The months dragged on with Duntov doing what he could from Detroit—thousands of miles away from the action in Ireland—with much of his consulting done by letter. Unlike his days at GM, when he could personally test a prototype at a test track just outside his office window, here he was totally cut off from any real knowledge of what was going on.

When early media reports from long-lead press shows were positive, Duntov warned DeLorean not to let those initial reports lull him into a false sense of security. "Before writers lay their hands on the cars for intensive testing including skid pad, urgent work should be done. Maybe different perception of the cars exists between you and me. You look with pride, understandingly [sic], as a parent sees his child, and I am concentrating on the faults and attempt to remedy. I feel urgency to act and your silence is driving me nuts."

If there was an initial complaint about the DMC-12, it was the anemic performance of the car's Renault V-6 engine. Zora strongly recommended building a certain percentage of higher-end turbocharged cars to help create a stronger performance image for the entire line. In a May 30, 1981, letter to DeLorean, Duntov wrote: "The way I see it, we need a turbo to provide a 'flagship' car on which the attention of the public will be centered. Magazine writers are invariably flocking to top-of-the-line cars. With total production of 20,000 cars, one thousand turbocharged cars will be ample enough."

Legend Industries was contacted about providing a turbocharger system, which was tested in several cars in 1981. After driving the turbocharged car at Bridgehampton, New York, Duntov pronounced: "The turbo feels good—like the doctor's orders for the DeLorean." But the turbo never advanced beyond the prototype stage, due to the company's increasing financial problems. Duntov also discussed four-passenger and four-wheel drive versions of the car with DeLorean and his key lieutenants, but these projects never got past the talking stage. Duntov felt that four-wheel drive only made sense with a turbocharged engine.

Zora then turned his attention to the subject of handling. In a June 30, 1981, letter to DeLorean, he wrote: "The DeLorean is short of dramatic. Although *Car and Driver* in its July issue gives a clean bill of health in the handling department, I know it differently. Actual facts will transpire when the magazine writers put the car to standard tests —including skid pad and slalom. On the skid pad, excessive understeer prevents to obtain lateral g of which the car is capable.

"The choice you have to await for the results of magazine tests or take what I am saying as a gospel and recognize urgent necessity of work," concluded Duntov. After the DeLorean finished dead last in a *Car and*

Driver magazine handling comparison with other sports cars, DeLorean agreed with Zora's recommendation in a short letter dated September 21, 1981. Zora reminded DeLorean that a maximum lateral acceleration in the 1.2 g range was a primary objective back in 1974, when the project was conceived.

The fortunes of the DeLorean Motor Company took a turn for the worse in 1982 as sales stalled amid increasingly negative media reports on the car as well as increasing labor problems in Northern Ireland. Duntov, though, made one final attempt to wrest control of the project, and in a letter written on May 2, 1982, he offered to become chief engineer of the company:

> I understand that you are managing to surface above the water. Congratulations. I never gave up the belief that you will win your fight. Coming back to business: Last February or thereabout I figured we had one year to remedy all deficiencies. I was wrong. Six months later or thereabout, the bottom fell out of the DeLorean. What other circumstances lead to that, I don't profess to know, but the car is largely to blame for our inability to fix the shortcomings on time. It is true that all proposals I made were accepted by you, but the long line of communications—Detroit, New York, Irvine and Dunmurry has slowed progress to a crawl. In July, I stopped for one day in Dunmurry, executed the fix of the door—to my knowledge the revision is still not in production.

> The car as perceived by the sporting public is wishy-washy, indifferent animal—no top speed, mediocre figures of lateral acceleration, slow time in slalom and jerky ride. On another spectrum of the market the people don't care about performance, but appreciate style in their transportation. These people shy away from the car as our warranty claims suggest.

> I propose to make me chief engineer. In this capacity, I would have the authority that a consulting engineer does not have. My change of heart—explanation is very simple: As a consultant I wait for things to happen, as chief engineer I take responsibility and see to it that the changes happen fast.

But the end was near for DMC. In October 1982, DeLorean was arrested and charged with fraud, racketeering and attempting to deal 220 pounds of cocaine with a street value of $50 million as a means of financing his ailing company. His prospective "business" partners turned out to be FBI agents, who nabbed him at Los Angeles International Airport in October

1982. The ensuing legal problems effectively ended the DeLorean Motor Company. DeLorean was eventually acquitted of the cocaine charge and later charges of fraud and racketeering, but he was embroiled in litigation for years afterward and didn't settle most of his cases until the early 1990s.

Duntov maintained that he could have helped DeLorean create a real sports car that would have been more accepted by car enthusiasts. But Duntov could only have done that if he were part of the DeLorean organization. He never had that chance, and although he was put on retainer as an outside engineering consultant, he was out of the decision-making loop. When things started to spin out of control, Duntov watched from the sidelines, unable to do anything. Given the company's ultimate downfall, however, the sidelines may have been the best place to be

All told, Zora's first taste of life outside GM was fraught with the same frustrations that haunted him at GM—an inability to sell his ideas where they mattered—at the very top of the company. Zora had less contact—not more—with DeLorean over time, which resulted in an overall lack of control over key decisions. Yet the situation at DeLorean was in many ways worse than at GM, given Duntov's physical separation from the manufacturing operation in Northern Ireland as well as the fact that much of his communication took place by letter. Zora wanted to be the man who made the car succeed. Had it not been for DeLorean's legal difficulties, Zora might have been successful in helping create a respectable performance image for the DMC-12.

Despite it all, Duntov never lost his affection for DeLorean. "Personally, I like him," he said in a 1989 interview. "But he still owes me $12,000."

Life in the Aftermarket

Fortunately, Duntov had many other consulting projects to occupy his time, including Holley Carburetor in Warren, Michigan, which was then a division of Colt Industries. Holley was a large original equipment and aftermarket supplier of carburetors and manifolds. Duntov's visibility with the Corvette and his association with fuel injection at GM made him a natural as a consultant for Holley. The company needed Duntov to help it deal with issues gripping the original equipment and aftermarket manufacturers in the mid-1970s as Holley sought technologies to make performance cars perform as they had in the glory days of the1960s. The agenda included turbocharging, fuel injection, carburetors and special manifolds that could squeeze more power out of smaller displacement engines.

In the mid-1970s, carburetors were still the most common fuel delivery device. Despite Duntov's efforts on fuel injection for GM in the 1950s, the technology had still not become mainstream because of the limitations of mechanical systems. It wasn't until electronic and throttle body systems were developed in the mid- to late 1970s that fuel injection began to make inroads as a high-volume technology. Holley, of course, had built its reputation with high-performance carburetors and manifolds, and did not have a viable fuel injection system. At the time, Holley was trying to develop its own electronic fuel injection, which the company called "Electrosonic Carburetion."

But Holley's version of electronic fuel injection never caught on as an original equipment application, and two years later, the company shifted its attention towards throttle body fuel injection. Despite Duntov's vision, Holley was never a major player on the original equipment front—either with electronic fuel injection or throttle body fuel injection—and subsequently focused most of its attention on the high-performance aftermarket.

One of Duntov's contributions to Holley was a new carburetor/manifold system called "The Z System." According to an advertisement for the product, the Z System featured "a unique resonating channel in the manifold, which balances fuel/air distribution across all eight cylinders, resulting in a new level of efficient performance." Zora himself graced the ads, which showed him standing next to a Camaro Z-28 with a Corvette in the background.

Zora's manifold was designed to solve a common problem called cylinder starvation in a typical V-8 engine. While most manifolds have a divider that creates complete flow separation between the opposing cylinders, there was a challenge to overcome. The cylinders at the end of each bank tend to get "cheated" in terms of air/fuel charge compared to the adjacent cylinder because of the pulsations created from intake valves opening and closing. Duntov set out to find a way to help the "cheated" cylinder receive a full fuel/air charge. He created a connecting or resonating channel, which allowed the opposing cylinders on each end of the engine to borrow fuel and air from the runner of the opposite cylinder. The connecting runner provided not only a source for more fuel/air mixture, but also a more favorable pressure pulse from the opposite bank.

Duntov continued consulting for Holley through the early 1980s, and he correctly predicted that four-

Zora put his vast knowledge of engines to work for Holley Carburetor in the late 1970s. His "Z System Manifold" for V-8 engines balanced fuel/air distribution across all eight cylinders.

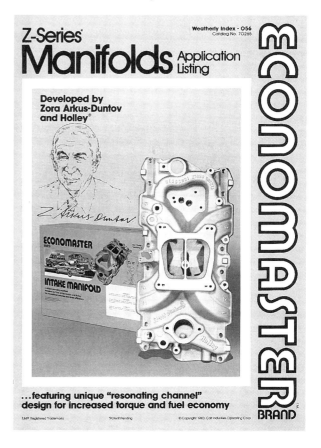

and six–cylinder engines would replace the V-8 as mainstream engines. He urged Holley to come to the market with a range of aftermarket manifolds that could provide more power for these smaller displacement engines. But Duntov still longed to impact an entire vehicle, especially after the demise of the DeLorean. That chance came through an old rival, Malcolm Bricklin.

Back to the Eastern Block

Bricklin was another iconoclast, who made his mark on a number of different endeavors. Besides creating his own sports car, he also founded the Handyman chain, which was similar to Home Depot or Builders Square. By the time he was 21, he was a millionaire.

Bricklin was best known for his Bricklin sports car which, during the 1970s, had briefly challenged the Corvette's status as America's only sports car—even though it was actually built in Canada. Featuring gull-wing doors and a plastic body, the Bricklin was hailed at the time for its energy-absorbing bumpers and other safety features. But it was never a serious sales competitor for the Corvette, and the Bricklin car faded from the scene as its creator turned toward other endeavors.

One of Bricklin's other ventures had been the importation of Subarus into the United States. He later switched to importing the Fiat Spider and X1/9 partnering with Pininfarina and Bertone after Fiat North America withdrew from the United States market in the early 1980s. "We lined up hundreds of dealers, a sales and service and parts operation to keep these cars coming into the states," said Tony Ciminera, a former public relations director for Fiat North America who teamed with Bricklin as vice-president of product development on the project.

While importing Fiats, Bricklin and Ciminera came across a curious little car called the "Jugo." It was made in Yugoslavia by an outfit called Crvena Zastava in the city of Kragujevac. Organized with the assistance of Fiat, the Zastava complex could build a quarter-million vehicles a year. Bricklin and Ciminera were initially unimpressed by the quality of this small car and ultimately commissioned hundreds of improvements. The car was designed to use the Fiat 128 transmission and drivetrain. It didn't take long for them to hatch an idea for how to bring the "Jugo" to America. "We even brought in Henry Kisssinger and his international business consulting firm to help," said Ciminera. We agreed to pay for all of the certification and emissions testing, promising to give the factory the blueprints for exactly how the cars needed to be configured for sale in America. We also asked them to change the 'J' to a 'Y' and call it Yugo."

The two, along with a consortium of others, set up an umbrella company called Global Motors in Upper Saddle River, New Jersey, as well as a subsidiary company called Yugo of America to handle direct distribution. In 1987, the first Yugos hit American shores and were a surprising success, thanks to an aggressive marketing campaign and an astoundingly low $3,999 base sticker price. Suddenly, an all-new car could be had for less than many used cars. But the promised high quality of the vehicles was slow to materialize and service from the Yugo dealerships was questionable. Despite a sparse network of dealers, over 160,000 Yugos were sold in America during a six-year period.

In 1988, Bricklin felt the Yugo needed a performance boost and called Duntov to consult on how to make the Yugo go faster and handle better. Duntov brought Triad Engineering into the picture and began to work over the suspension. They revised the shocks, added a rear sway bar, lowered the rear end and performed some other tweaks. "It was all easily accomplished and the difference in the handling of the car was incredible," said Ciminera.

But Bricklin and Ciminera had something more in mind with a project that was right up Duntov's alley. They felt Yugo would never succeed by taking Toyota and Honda head on; it would do better as a niche brand, anchored by a sleek little four-wheel drive, mid-engined sports car that would sell for under $10,000. Their concept was the TCX-1, a lightweight machine built with many existing international components assembled at a relatively low cost in Yugoslavia.

Styling was deemed critical for the car to be accepted in the American market, so Bricklin recruited Karl Ludvigsen, who had established his own market consulting firm in London, to solicit design treatments for the proposed cars with various design studios. The contract ultimately went to Tom Tjaarda in Turin. Ludvigsen also brought in Mike Loasby, formerly with DeLorean and Aston Martin, to develop a chassis and drivetrain with Duntov. The two teamed up on a novel, yet inexpensive four-wheel-drive solution. They took a Fiat 128 drivetrain, in which the engine was normally mounted transversely, and turned it north-south with the driveshafts pointing fore and aft. These were connected to front and rear differentials, while viscous couplings provided a continually variable torque split. The longitudinal arrangement also provided some flexibility for adding fuel injection, supercharging equipment and emissions devices. They also created a forged aluminum double-wishbone suspension for all four corners.

While the TCX-1 project was underway, Ciminera and Bricklin were considering sponsoring a single-marque series much like the International Race of Champions or the Volkswagen Rabbit Cup to develop a stronger performance image for the Yugo brand. But Duntov sold the others on a the concept of a speed run to go after a handful of records he felt could be attained by a modified Yugo. Zora solicited the help of Corvette endurance racer Kim Baker. Duntov planned to use the Yugo GVX models, which were modified much like a Volkswagen GTI with stiffer shocks and sway bars and a Bosch fuel injection unit. Duntov looked into the FIA record book and came back with a handful of time/distance class records that the Yugo was capable of breaking, including the flying mile and flying kilometer.

Baker then set up the cars, rented the high-speed banked course at Talladega, Alabama, for a week, secured tires from Goodyear and was all set to go when Tony Ciminera received a call from Yugo's vice president of finance. The message was to shut the operation down. A war had broken out in Yugoslavia and the company felt that under the circumstances it would look frivolous to the citizens of Yugoslavia to be staging a speed exhibition featuring a Yugoslavian car. Duntov got the call at his hotel the night before the run. The cars never turned a wheel. "It was one of the most embrassing moments of my life to tell Zora the program was off," said Ciminera. "I thought it might have been the last hurrah for Zora to be able to make a record run." The conflict was the beginning of the end for the Yugo in America and killed any hopes of building the TCX-1.

Putting His Name to Work

During the final 15 years of Zora's life, he was approached by a number of different engineering firms about lending his name to modified Corvettes. One of these was the Duntov Turbo built by American Custom Industries of Sylvania, Ohio. The Duntov Turbo featured a turbocharged Chevy V-8, some chassis improvements, and a very slick, modified Corvette body with fender flares and a modified front end featuring exposed headlights. It was sold through Chevy dealers for approximately $37,500, which was a substantial increase over the price of a regular Corvette. Due to its high price, few cars were sold, and the Duntov Turbo quickly faded from the market.

In 1985, Duntov collaborated with Triad Engineering and Mr. Gasket, a consortium of high-performance aftermarket companies in Berea, Ohio, to create a stainless steel tubular space-framed Corvette. It featured a special thin-wall, metal-casting process (Simul-Cast) developed by Mr. Gasket principal Jim Browning. The space-frame Corvette was shown at the 1985 Specialty Equipment Manufacturers Association (SEMA) annual convention in Las Vegas and was named Grand Sport after its lightweight racing predecessor. Browning claimed that Simul-Cast components were 20 percent lighter than aluminum for a given application. The Mr. Gasket Corvette weighed only 2,500 pounds versus 3,200 pounds or more for a stock Corvette.

In the early 1990s, Duntov was involved in several attempts by Triad to market an ultra high-performance Corvette as an alternative to the factory ZR-1. By then, Triad was specializing in turnkey programs for limited production cars like the GM Cyclone pickup truck and Typhoon utility vehicle. It also developed show cars like the Cadillac Voyage and even the pace cars for the CART PPG Indy Car World Series. The first effort was a big-block Corvette with a 454-cubic-inch engine featuring dual-injector, port fuel injection. Early promotional materials claimed the engine would put out 500 horsepower and 475 to 550 pound-feet of torque with a top speed in excess of 200 mph. The car was to have a power-to-weight ratio of less than 7.5 pounds per horsepower, versus 9.3 pounds per horsepower for the ZR-1.

Duntov—with Triad Engineering—created this stainless-steel, space-frame Corvette while consulting for Jim Browning of Mr. Gasket. It is shown here at the 1985 Specialty Equipment Manufacturers Association (SEMA) show in Las Vegas.

Zora, who was 80 at the time, saw the project as an opportunity to fix all the things that he thought were wrong with the fourth-generation Corvette. The upgrades included more precise steering, a more nimble suspension and the replacement of the digital gauges with analog readouts. Sketches were drawn up, but a prototype was never built. Duntov backed out at the last minute, apparently feeling the financial terms of the agreement were not favorable enough.

In 1992, another effort was made, this time with a four-wheel-drive Corvette. The principals included Duntov, Triad and John Aragona of a firm called Automotive Specialties Corporation. The concept, based again on the fourth-generation car, would be called the "Arkus-Duntov." Plans called for the creation of a special body and the purchase of a four-wheel-drive system from a major original equipment vendor. Target pricing was in the $90,000 to $100,000 range, with a total annual production goal of 1,000 to 1,500 cars. But the project required millions of dollars of investor money and insufficient funding was raised.

Duntov also lent his name to a different type of Corvette, a series of 1:32 scale Corvette models developed by Action Performance Companies, Inc. The series covered the entire production run of Corvettes through the fourth-generation model. The company used Zora extensively in their advertising, which ran in Corvette and other enthusiast magazines.

During the early 1980s, Duntov also took on consulting work for Energy Conversion Devices. The Michigan-based firm, led by an eccentric named Stanford R. Ovshinsky, was hard at work on semiconductor research with an eye towards developing a viable battery system for electric powered vehicles.

In a February 24, 1981, letter to Lionel Robbins, director of marketing and systems applications, Duntov covered his thoughts about replacing belts for auxiliary drive for automotive engines by thermoelectric power. "After giving it some thought, I found it is not practical, but what is practical is to replace the alternator with a thermoelectric power device."

"Some time ago," Zora continued, "GM introduced pulse air to replace the air pump on some of the engines. The move was to save in terms of energy and costs. I feel that thermoelectric power is falling into the same category to make waste heat work for you and the cost factor of thermoelectric versus alternator."

Whether Energy Conversion Devices ever followed up on Duntov's recommendations is not documented. ECD sold off its thermoelectric division several years later, but the firm was still active in the early 2000s developing nickel metal hydride batteries, photovoltaic panels and hydrogen storage systems.

In 1989, Zora finally found a willing buyer for his services at GM. The Buick Motor Division brought him in to consult on the Buick Turbo V-6 engine being developed to race at the Indianapolis 500. The project got started after Zora was invited to visit a Buick Special Products facility in Flint, Michigan, and take a close look at the engine. During his initial visit, Zora observed that while the Buick was well tuned for peak power—a fact borne out by the Buick's high number of pole positions recorded at Indy and other speedways—the engine needed more performance in the middle and upper ranges of rpm. This would make it more responsive in real racing conditions where cars must get back up to speed following pit stops or yellow-flag situations.

Zora then wrote a letter to Buick general manager Ed Mertz offering his services. His offer was accepted, and he was put on a monthly retainer to conduct fuel atomization tests. Duntov conducted flow tests on several Buick V-6s built by engine builder Vince Granatelli using a dynamometer from a local Troy, Michigan, shop. He also traveled to Phoenix International Raceway for on-track testing.

Several months after the project began, Buick switched from a mechanical injection system to an electronic system, with which Zora had no experience. Suddenly, 80-year-old Zora was in no position to help. Advanced electronic controls had finally outpaced the engineer who had been trained in the 1930s.

TWENTY-FOUR

An aviation fan most of his life, Zora sold his boat and bought this Rockwell Commander 112A following his retirement.

Never Say Die

W hile consulting projects provided a certain satisfaction that his engineering skills were still wanted, they weren't nearly enough to sustain Zora's sense of purpose. He still needed to gratify the daredevil within. His mind raced with possibilities for going fast and setting records, and all the while he refused to concede the fact that he was over 80 years old. There was always one more run to be made, one more possibility—and that is what kept him alive and vital. Given the chance, Zora would have much preferred to go out in flames on Turn 4 at Indy than die in a nursing home or hospital bed.

Wings for the Restless

Zora's restlessness led him to sell his Chris-Craft boat so he could pursue an activity he had dreamed about ever since he took the ride on a Junkers Tri-Motor as a student in Berlin: owning and piloting an airplane. He bought a Rockwell Commander 112A, a low-wing, single-engine plane with an orange and white fuselage. He kept it at Detroit City Airport on the east side of Detroit and used it for short recreational flights around Michigan and the Midwest.

Duntov first flew an airplane with a friend in upstate New York back in 1941. "I was convinced I could fly an airplane from watching him, so I took over the controls and climbing through the clouds, I lost orientation," said Zora. His continuing interest in aviation was fueled by his Allard racing days with Curtis LeMay and Francis Griswold of the Strategic Air Command, and his opportunities to fly in Air Force planes.

Unfortunately, Zora's demanding business schedule made getting a pilot's license difficult. But at 59 or 60 years old, he began to ponder life after retirement, when he'd have more time on his hands. So he took a flying lesson while in Arizona at the Desert General Motors Proving Ground. He followed that up with occasional lessons, and then elected to take a two-week

Opposite: Duntov helped celebrate the Corvette's longevity as well as his own as a guest of honor at a ceremony honoring the one-millionth Corvette in August 1992. With him is then-Chevrolet general manager Jim Perkins.

Zora at the controls of his Rockwell Commander plane that he used for short recreational trips around Michigan.

concentrated course in Vero Beach, Florida, that would result in an instrument rating.

After Duntov had been in rigorous training for two weeks, his curriculum called for him to take several 250-mile cross-country solo flights. He got lost for a time on the first flight, veering off the flight path he was supposed to maintain. The second flight took him right into the eye of a major thunderstorm, but somehow he managed to land the plane. The following day, Zora met with his instructor, who admonished Zora for not turning back when he saw the thunderstorm. The real casualty was the instructor, who got fired after the incident for not briefing his student on how to handle his plane in such circumstances. Duntov never finished his flight schooling, but he did finally get his license several years later.

After purchasing the Rockwell, Zora would fly with whoever was brave enough to go up with him, including Elfi. But as the years went on, he had fewer takers. He had constant difficulty communicating with the control tower due to his slow, almost unintelligible speech following his stroke.

A Corvette to Call His Own

While Zora was employed by GM, he never bought a Corvette for himself because he was constantly driving prototypes as part of his job. After his retirement he finally bought a Corvette, a 1974 model with a big-block engine. While the car was originally green, Zora had it painted silver with blue trim and the initials ZAD painted on the door. Zora took to the local freeways and boulevards like he was racing in the Daytona 500. In 1989 he was offered $100,000 for the car from a Corvette collector, Les Bieri. Zora accepted the offer and sold the car to Bieri, who has since donated it to the National Corvette Museum.

Zora also bought a Honda motorcycle in the late 1970s and would often entertain his Grosse Pointe neighbors by popping wheelies in front of his house whenever he had an audience.

A Continuing Need for Speed

Zora felt that despite his age, he could still set new speed records as well as be a competitive race driver. In 1974, he approached motor racing consultant Larry Truesdale—formerly of Goodyear—in an effort to take a refurbished CERV II to Alabama International Motor Speedway in Talladega, and break the closed-course lap record then held by A. J. Foyt in a Coyote Indy car at 217 mph. But nothing ever came of the project.

In 1979, Duntov contacted Jo Hoppen, then motor sports manager for Porsche and Volkswagen, about campaigning a Super Vee open-wheeled race car for a season. Hoppen politely refused. Duntov often talked about going back to Indianapolis and was hopeful someone might offer him a chance to drive the pace car or, better yet, to try to qualify an Indy race car.

Ten years later, Zora still felt he could drive competitively. According to race team owner/driver Tommy Morrison, Zora was upset at not being asked to participate in a 1989 Morrison Motorsports effort to set a number of 24-hour closed-course distance speed records in a pair of Corvettes. In the exercise at Fort Stockton, Texas, two Corvettes driven by eight drivers set twelve FIA international class records and three world records. A red Morrison ZR-1 sponsored by EDS and Mobil 1 shattered that record on the way to a 24-hour average speed of 175.885 mph. The event was extremely dangerous, yet Zora felt he still had the stuff to handle it.

The reality was that Zora's driving days were well behind him. Zora simply could not comprehend that he was physically no longer able to drive a race car. Yet his own denial on this score indicates how important driving was to his identity.

Helping soothe his ego were occasional opportunities to associate with other retired driving greats. One such occasion took place in 1975 at Williamsburg, Virginia, where Zora joined a distinguished group of former Le Mans winners. Included in the group were René Dreyfus, the 1939 French national champion; Carroll Shelby, who won Le Mans in 1959; Phil Hill, who won the race in 1958, 1961 and 1963 and was also America's first world champion; Zora's old crew chief, Luigi Chinetti, who won Le Mans in 1932, 1934 and 1939; Peter DePaolo, who won Le Mans in 1922; and Dan Gurney and A. J. Foyt, who co-drove to a Le Mans victory in 1967. The group was pictured driving miniaturized replicas of the classic race cars of the 1920s and 1930s.

Living Vicariously

If Zora could no longer drive himself, he still sought to maintain the close company of those who could. He and Elfi entertained Porsche star Peter Gregg for several days in August 1974 and they all recounted the many adventures of their lives. The experience prompted Gregg to write: "I think for all three of us, there was a little surprise in just how much we enjoyed each other's company. Truthfully, I have never felt more comfortable visiting anyone, nor have I had a more enjoyable conversation with people only known for a short time."

Zora with road racer Peter Gregg in the mid-1970s. When Zora could no longer drive, he enjoyed the company of many of the big names of the day such as Gregg and Danny Ongais.

Zora also arranged a tour of the General Motors facilities for Gregg in the hopes that he might be able to recruit him into a road-racing program involving the Chevrolet Monza. "The Chevrolet part of my visit was fascinating, too," wrote Gregg in response. "Truthfully, it was a bit depressing that the competition side of Corvette seems over, and depressing a little that Zora is not heading the performance program of the Monza. One of these days, the Monza prototype will arrive for evaluation and I intend to offer my services to Vince Piggins [then Chevrolet's racing director] as a brief test driver. If this car is the winning car of the future, I would like to be involved with it, as a customer primarily." In addition to Gregg, Zora was close friends with Indy car racer Danny Ongais, whom he would look up every year when he attended the Indianapolis 500.

Zora was also a regular at the Daytona 500. He served as the grand marshal of several NASCAR events and was always warmly embraced by the France family, who never forgot what a boost Zora had provided them in the early days of the sport with his Pikes Peak and Daytona Beach runs, which helped put NASCAR on the map.

In 1989 Zora was awarded the Thomas Senter Trophy from the Ford Motor Company for his contributions to Ford performance with his Ardun engine program. The award was presented in August 1990 during the Monterey Historic Races, in which Allard was the featured marque. There Zora was reunited with many of his surviving contacts at Allard as well as with his silver J2 Allard, which he raced at Watkins Glen.

Losing Family

In 1980, another chapter closed in Zora's life. Yura died from kidney cancer; he was 64. His death hit Zora very hard, and for years afterward, Zora proclaimed that his own life was over as a result. Despite their physical distance and Yura's career success in the financial community, Zora still thought of himself as Yura's protector, and now he was deprived of that role. After Yura's death, Zora rarely spoke about him. Much later, Zora admitted, "Loss of Yura for me like 75 percent of my life."

Yura's death left Zora without any immediate family. His mother Rachel and stepfather Josef had died in the mid-1970s. Jacques—Zora's natural father—was still working as an internal combustion engineer in Paris at the time of his death in 1956.

With Yura gone, Zora held on to his remaining friendships. He had maintained close contact with Asia Orley until Asia's death in the late 1970s in St. Croix from injuries sustained in a car accident. While Zora rarely traveled to New York, he kept in touch by phone with Julian Hoffman and Vadim Gonsoff. He also remained very close with Tony Lapine, who was then living in Germany as the director of design for Porsche.

Discarded Monuments

Most of the engines and artifacts of Zora's career at GM no longer exist. Much of the hardware was scrapped because GM did not have the storage capacity to hold onto it, and selling prototype equipment to interested buyers was out of the question, because GM did not wish for nonproduction equipment to get into the hands of the public. While Design Staff saved a number of concept Corvettes, many of the engines and other hardware that Zora and his group had designed did not survive.

At the time of his retirement, Zora enlisted the help of Gib Hufstader to try to save three engines that had been stored on wooden frames at a Chevrolet warehouse in Warren, Michigan "One of them was a three-valve engine," said Hufstader. "So we went over there one day with Zora and started going through the storage tags. We were told they had all been scrapped. I asked where the scrap pile was. I found it and climbed up the pile, but I didn't see anything at first. But then I climbed some more and recognized a single-cam hemi-head engine for CERV II. It was dented here and there. We pulled it out." Hufstader had it restored and then sent it to the Indianapolis Motor Speedway Museum. One of the other engines they were seeking—the twin-plug Grand Sport engine—did not survive.

While GM had managed to save two of Zora's most precious relics— CERV I and CERV II—these were eventually turned over to the Briggs Cunningham Automotive Museum in Costa Mesa, California, in 1972. In the 1980s, however, the Cunningham collection was sold off, and CERV I emerged in private hands, despite GM's best efforts to get it back.

Duntov himself joined the fight, making a 1988 deposition before a Wayne County, Michigan, attorney regarding the history and conditions in which he permitted the turnover of cars like the Corvette SS, CERV I and later CERV II to the Indianapolis Motor Speedway Museum and the Briggs Cunningham Museum respectively.

In his remarks about CERV I, Duntov said: "It recently came to my attention that the CERV I vehicle was scheduled to be auctioned in Monterey, Calif., on August 19, 1988. I was surprised and shocked to learn of this since it violates the agreement and understanding under which General

Motors donated the CERV I and CERV II to the Briggs Cunningham Museum. As I recall, we had a brass plaque affixed to the vehicles that stated, 'Donated by Chevrolet for Educational Purposes.' I observed these vehicles at the museum over the years and got to know Mr. Burgess, the museum's curator. To assist him in maintaining these vehicles, I provided him with blueprints and engineering support. I did not do this so that anyone other than the public could benefit from my efforts.

"If I would have thought that there was even a remote possibility that the CERV I and CERV II could have gotten into private hands, General Motors never would have donated these vehicles to the Briggs Cunningham Museum. We did not intend that individuals would ever profit from the sale of these vehicles and that they would cease to be available for public display and study. Their loss is irreplaceable."

CERV I and CERV II remain in private hands. The loss of rare vehicles like this, which represented a significant chapter in Corvette history, was instrumental in GM providing indirect support for the effort to build a National Corvette Museum in Bowling Green, Kentucky.

Corvette's Patron Saint

For the final 20 years of his life, Zora had another full-time occupation—that of patron saint of the Corvette on the extensive Corvette show circuit. Duntov was the guest of honor at countless parades and concours competitions. He was the headline name at all the major shows, such as Bloomington Gold, Corvettes at Carlisle, the national conventions of the National Corvette Restorers Society (NCRS) and the National Council of Corvette Clubs (NCCC). He would typically sign autographs for hours at a time for awestruck fans, sometimes in the midst of unbearable heat and humidity. But Duntov, usually with Elfi by his side, loved the adoration. A pretty girl in the autograph line would usually energize him, and he would sign every hat, poster, T-shirt or body part that came his way.

Zora was one of the primary guests of honor at the Monterey Historic Races in 1987, where Chevrolet was the honored marque. The event might have been the last assembly of the early legends of Chevrolet performance—including names like Bill Mitchell, Dick Thompson, Roger Penske, Jim Hall, John Fitch—and Duntov was front and center. But the occasion was bittersweet for Zora after he was informed he would not be allowed to drive the Corvette SS around the Laguna Seca track. Instead,

Zora confers with John Fitch from the passenger seat of the Corvette SS at the Monterey Historic Races in 1987.

he rode as a passenger. John Fitch took the wheel. Zora tried to keep a stiff upper lip, but the look on his face betrayed his disappointment.

In the 1990s, Duntov was a must-invite for any major Corvette event. In June 1992, he presided over the groundbreaking ceremonies for the National Corvette Museum in Bowling Green, Kentucky. Wearing his old driver's suit and yellow polo helmet, Zora climbed aboard a bulldozer featuring a giant Corvette cutout glued to its side. Taking a drag from his cigarette, Duntov deftly lowered the blade, revved up the dozer and made a couple of passes over the ground, much to the delight of the assembled Corvette fans and local officials.

"A piece of cake" seems to be Duntov's reaction after breaking ground for the National Corvette Museum in June 1992 from behind the controls of a "Corvette" bulldozer.

Later that summer, Duntov fired up the millionth Corvette for the first time as it was coming down the assembly line at the Bowling Green plant. Duntov was one of several VIPs occupying important positions as the white convertible with red interior neared completion. Duntov also participated in a special millionth Corvette luncheon at the St. Regis Hotel in Detroit across the street from GM headquarters. The guest list included a veritable "who's who" in the history of the Corvette.

Zora's desire for fame was satisfied by his induction into the Automotive Hall of Fame in 1992, where he joined the ranks of automotive immortals like Ettore Bugatti, Enzo Ferrari, Louis Chevrolet and Henry Ford. While his initial induction took place in Midland, Michigan, in September 1991, the institution has since moved to Dearborn, where there is a permanent display devoted to Duntov's accomplishments.

On Labor Day weekend in 1994, Duntov was center stage for perhaps the biggest single-day event in Corvette history, when the National Corvette Museum officially opened its doors in front of an estimated 120,000 people over a four-day period. The highlight of the weekend was the convergence of two gigantic parades of Corvettes from all over the country— one parade from the north and one from the south—that totaled over 5,000 cars. Traffic on nearby I-65 ground to a standstill as the road between Nashville to the south and Louisville to the north was solid Corvettes. Duntov was the celebrity extraordinaire all weekend, and spent much of his time posing for photos with his successors, Dave McLellan and Dave Hill. The event drew extensive news coverage on all of the major news networks.

While he soaked up the limelight, Duntov was sensitive about how Corvette history was being rendered and was quick to correct any mistaken impressions that may have emanated from uneducated speechwriters. He cringed whenever a GM executive referred to the 1953 Corvette as an "instant classic." He knew from painful experience how close the car came to being terminated.

In a letter to Chevrolet's Jim Perkins after the opening of the National Corvette Museum, Zora wrote, "Rewriting history is wrong, regardless of the purpose. To me, one of the great things about Corvette has been its ability to overcome adversity. Fiero could not do that. Allante could not do that. Reatta could not do that. Even Thunderbird could not do that in its original form. Corvette did it over and over again. It's a battle-tested warrior. We diminish the car and the people who kept it going when we obscure that reality."

Zora had very thin skin about anyone challenging his engineering or driving talents or his version of the facts. In July 1980, Duntov sued *Car and Driver* magazine and technical editor Don Sherman over a statement in an April 1979 column written by Sherman, suggesting that the Corvette rear suspension from 1963 on was "ill conceived." At the time, Sherman was commenting about a television commercial for the Audi Fox, which claimed the Fox was faster through a slalom course than a Corvette. Los Angeles consumer advocate David Horowitz challenged Audi's assertion and reenacted the matchup for his TV show, which showed the Corvette to be faster than the Audi. This prompted Sherman to write in his column about the relative differences between light front-wheel drive cars and heavy rear-wheel drive machines like the Corvette:

> The Audi has front wheel drive, which means the two wheels carry more than 60 percent of both driving and steering responsibilities. The natural results are understeer in all circumstances and very predictable, easy-to-manage handling. The Corvette, on the other hand, spreads its weight evenly about four wheels, with the back ones doing the driving. The steering wheel controls only the front pair of tires, but the Corvette does in fact steer through all four wheels. This secret advantage in the hands of an accomplished driver can be very effectively used to humiliate Audis. Four wheel steering is what long hook and ladder trucks use to swing around sharp corners. In a car, it can produce steering response quick enough to give most drivers headaches. In the Corvette, this characteristic happens to be an unwanted side effect of an ill-conceived independent rear suspension layout: cornering forces cause rubber bushings to deflect in such a way that the rear wheels steer away from the center of the turn. As a result, each twitch of the steering produces a

double twitch through the chassis: the front wheels turn in immediately and then a split second later the rear wheels steer out slightly
to help change the car's heading.

While Duntov was never mentioned by name in Sherman's column,
Duntov claimed he was well known enough to be recognized as the creator of the Corvette's rear suspension and claimed Sherman's statement
caused damage from a loss of reputation as well potential consulting opportunities. Duntov thus pressed forward with his lawsuit. Depositions were
taken, but after a change of venue, the suit was eventually dismissed in
March 1983 on a legal technicality.

Zora also questioned *Road & Track* about a story that appeared in
the March 1989 issue about the new Nissan 300ZX. The article pointed
out the novelty of an angled upper control arm on the front suspension
and the advantages of this configuration in keeping the tire at a proper
angle to the road in both hard cornering and straight ahead motoring.
"Neat, eh?" Zora wrote. "Except 1963 Corvette came with suspension geometry designed to do just that. The years between 1963 and 1989 represent
26 long years required by Nissan to find a solution that was incorporated
in the '63 Corvette."

Duntov remained hypersensitive to the importance attached to Harley
Earl and Bill Mitchell in the Corvette history, despite his own experience
in confronting the very real power the men exhibited in determining the
shape and configuration of Corvettes. Zora's continuing resentment led to
a tiff with former Chevrolet studio head Clare MacKichan of Design Staff.
In a presentation at a 1989 National Corvette Restorers Society convention in Bend, Oregon, MacKichan apparently hadn't named Zora high enough
on the list as one of the most important people in Corvette history.

Zora also took exception to an account of the grand opening of the
National Corvette Museum by Robert Cumberford, published in *Automobile*
magazine Cumberford, himself a former member of Design Staff, suggested that the museum displays contained "just a touch more 'Father of
the Corvette,' veneration of Arkus-Duntov than is strictly justified by the
facts." The article referred to Zora's rift with MacKichan, which Zora later
vigorously denied in a harsh letter to editor/publisher David E. Davis Jr.

Still Knocking on GM's Door

Despite indifference on GM's part, Duntov continued to volunteer his services as a consultant well into the 1990s. Not knowing where else to go, he
became a regular visitor to Jim Perkins' office. As far as Perkins was concerned, these were courtesy visits. He tried to use Duntov as a resource,

if only out of respect and admiration, even though Zora's specific input was unlikely to be transferred to the Corvette platform group.

For his part, Duntov never quite understood that Perkins had little control over the configuration of future Corvettes. That was now the responsibility of the Corvette engineering group, a totally separate entity from Chevrolet ever since the late 1970s. "I sat with Zora for hours," said Perkins, "and had him work me over because he didn't understand that I didn't have the same latitude during my tenure as Chevy general manager [1989 to 1996] as Ed Cole did. It was tough for him to understand the differences in GM from Cole's day."

But Zora never gave up hope. In a 1992 letter to Perkins, Duntov proposed that all engineering expenditures connected to the current car be eliminated. Instead, he suggested a midship all-wheel-drive sports car with favorable mass distribution on the order of the 45/55 midship design and torque split accordingly with viscous coupling. He referred to the fact that his patented driveline from the Aerovette, which ran through the oil pan, had since been adopted in the then-new 1991 Acura Legend LS after Duntov's 17-year patent expired.

Several years later, Duntov visited Perkins at Chevrolet just as final plans for the fifth-generation Corvette were to be locked down. It was clear before the meeting that the ship had already sailed as far as the chassis and drivetrain of the new car were concerned. It would be front-engine, rear-drive, just like its predecessors. "He came to my office and a shouting match almost developed," said Perkins. "He, of course, thought mid-engine was the way to go and had hand-drawn plans for the C5 with a midship engine. He began to get angry and I said, 'You don't understand.' Then he stood up and stated, 'Then I build the son of a bitch myself.'

"He wouldn't speak to me for a while," added Perkins. "But a month or six weeks later, he came back with a proposal to run with some backers who were going to do a car. Who was I to say he was too old? That to me was the spirit and the heart and the soul of the man...."

It was also a strong indication that 20 years after retiring from GM, Zora was still trying to control the direction of future Corvettes. He also continued to be frustrated by his lack of success in doing so— just as he was when the second- and third-generation Corvettes were being developed. As much as he had accomplished, it seemed to Zora that there was something very unfinished about his life.

Not that Duntov was totally ignored. While the fifth-generation Corvette that debuted in 1997 was undergoing its final stages of development, chief engineer Dave Hill invited Duntov to spend a day at the North American Vehicle Launch center and see firsthand how the Corvette was developed.

Duntov appeared interested and seemed genuinely impressed by both the solid structure of the chassis and the much-improved forward visibility compared to the previous model. Unfortunately, circumstances never allowed Duntov to drive a running prototype of a fifth-generation Corvette.

Zora did, however, receive an invitation to drive a Dodge Viper several years earlier. His old cohort, Roy Sjoberg—with the blessing of Chrysler engineering director François Castaing—invited Duntov out to the Chrysler Proving Ground at Chelsea, Michigan, to drive this new Corvette competitor. After Zora's drive, many of the Viper development engineers sought his autograph. In order not to embarrass GM, no one in Chrysler leaked that Zora had visited.

Zora and Elfi

Zora and Elfi grew closer together during his twilight years. They were seldom seen apart as they traveled to Corvette functions, auto shows and other speaking engagements. They were still a handsome couple with a deep and mature love for each other. Still, Zora never lost his wandering eye, even well into his 80s. At age 84, he and Elfi took a cruise with Carroll Shelby and his new bride Lena, who later died tragically in a car accident. Lena was tall, Scandinavian, blonde and beautiful. Shelby, meanwhile, had suffered through a series of health problems in recent years and had recently undergone a heart transplant.

Zora couldn't keep his eyes off Lena that first night at dinner on the boat. Finally, he leaned over and whispered into Shelby's ear, "Maybe time for Zora to get new heart." "He never hit on her, but he lusted for her," said Shelby. "He lusted for all of the young girls on the cruise. He never lost that sparkle in his eye. If you don't have that spark, you might as well head for Forest Lawn…."

Zora and Elfi at a historic racing event at Steamboat Springs, Colorado, in 1990. They were a fixture at many Corvette shows and races, where they signed autographs and acted as good will ambassadors for the Corvette.

The Final Goal

Zora still had plenty of spark; there were many things he still wanted to do and he still had a driving need to stay in control. Since his attempted speed records with sports cars weren't panning out, he decided to do it with an airplane—a Bede Aircraft BD-5 single-seat special. His plan was to fly it to a piston-powered speed record of 235 mph at the Experimental Aircraft Association annual Fly-In at Oshkosh, Wisconsin.

Zora had sold his Rockwell Commander when he bought the BD-5. The problem was that the

Zora goes about modifying his BD-5 airplane with which he hoped to break a piston-powered speed record in 1996.

BD-5, with its tiny fuselage, narrow, swept wingspan and rear propeller, was a very unstable airplane and had a high mortality rate "This airplane had one of the worst safety records of any kit plane," said Gib Hufstader. Some 30 people had died flying the stubby-winged craft, including the very Alabama man who sold a plane to Zora. He had crashed a second BD-5 just like the one he sold to Duntov.

"But flying this plane was his dream and I was not going to be the one to discourage him," said Hufstader. "It kept him interested and happy."

Making things even trickier for Duntov was a modification that placed the pilot 17 inches further forward than normal to allow for a more powerful engine. It made the airplane even less stable. Duntov originally planned to use a small displacement engine out of a race car but then elected to install a turbocharged three-cylinder Suzuki engine from a Geo Metro. He enlisted the support of Jim Perkins and Jon Moss (Chevrolet's in-house hot-rod and concept car builder) to obtain the necessary parts. As he accumulated the necessary pieces he stockpiled them in the study of his home. Duntov housed the BD-5 at a hanger at Detroit City Airport and began the process of modifying the airplane for his run. But the modifications took longer than anticipated. Zora meanwhile tried to arrange for sponsorship of his effort, approaching among others Geo, the now-defunct import car division of Chevrolet.

But potential sponsors were more concerned with the downside if something should go wrong and shied away from the effort. Zora, his health deteriorating, confided to some close associates that he was worried whether he had enough strength to fly the airplane. It was then that Hufstader began to intentionally "misplace" some parts in order to slow down the effort and eventually prevent Zora from making the run.

There was another, more sinister obstacle that would prevent Zora from going for the record. During the construction phase, Duntov's health began to take a serious turn for the worse. Although he had quit smoking several years earlier, he suffered from a heavy smoker's cough. He was diagnosed with lung cancer in the summer of 1995. He did not undergo any radiation or chemotherapy for his condition because of his advanced age. He became increasingly depressed about his health and used the airplane project as a way to keep his mind on something positive.

But things deteriorated further in the spring of 1996, when Zora began to use an oxygen tank to breathe. During the early morning hours of Sunday, April 21, 1996, Elfi discovered Zora unconscious in the spare bedroom of the house where the oxygen tank was located. She called 911 and EMS workers rushed him to St. Johns Hospital in Grosse Pointe. About eight hours later Zora Arkus-Duntov died at the age of 86.

Word spread rapidly about Zora's death via the Internet and telephones. His obituary made the *New York Times, Los Angeles Times, Detroit News/Free Press, Washington Post* and *Chicago Tribune*, and his life was the subject of a nationally syndicated column by political commentator George Will, who wrote: "If you seek Arkus-Duntov's monument, look around, at that 'vette coming on in the passing lane."

The Duntov wake was not a morbid affair, but rather a celebration of his incredible life. It drew hundreds of admirers and associates from the automotive industry. The parking lot of the A. J. Peters Funeral Home in Grosse Pointe was the final destination of a motor parade of brightly colored 'Vettes of all vintages. In a manner Zora would have approved of, Corvette designer John Cafaro modified Duntov's silver casket with side gill decals from a 1965 Corvette and Corvette logos front and rear. Zora was later cremated, with his ashes going to a special display at the National Corvette Museum.

Two months after the wake, a special ceremony was held at the National Corvette Museum. It was a postmortem roast and tribute to a great man. Speakers included National Corvette Museum president Dan Gale, *Automobile* magazine publisher David E. Davis Jr., Chevrolet general manger Jim Perkins, former race queen Linda Vaughn, former *Hot Rod* magazine editor Ray Brock, Corvette engineer Gib Hufstader, Chevrolet public relations director Ralph Kramer, and many others.

That day, the museum was decorated with posters from Mid American Designs, a large Corvette parts and accessory house in Effingham, Illinois. Showing an image of Zora from the grand opening of the museum, the copy read: "One man can make a difference. Zora Arkus-Duntov was that man."

EPILOGUE

From the beginning of his life until the very end, Zora never lost his desire to run free—and fast.

Epilogue

T he National Corvette Museum is now a fixture along I-65 in Kentucky, just down the road from the Corvette manufacturing plant. On most days, traffic is a steady thrum of trucks, buses and cars making the long haul from the Gulf Coast region to points north, such as Chicago and Indianapolis.

Here, deep in the heart of America, is the final resting place of Zora Arkus-Duntov. His ashes are interred in a special exhibit about his life. A life-sized white plaster figure of Zora stands next to the display, holding a Duntov camshaft. Framed photographs, mementos and diplomas surround the exhibit, and a grainy black and white video tells the story of Zora doing something extraordinary with the machines he loved.

The display tells the story of a man—the consummate outsider—who sought control in a storm-tossed, alien world by seeking to physically master that world. That mastery came by designing, engineering and driving machines that represented the ultimate form of freedom and mobility. To press the laws of physics while experiencing the exhilaration of speed was—to Zora—the ultimate form of control, the very thing he had craved as a youth in Russia.

His coming to General Motors was a precipitous moment not only for the corporation, but for the survival of the Corvette, which surely would have gone the way of so many other forgotten nameplates had it not been for Zora's persistence and determination. Yet his life at GM was bittersweet, rich with accomplishment yet rife with the realization that he could have done more if he had been able to capture more ownership of the Corvette engineering program and Chevrolet's motor sports efforts. But that control was elusive. For Zora, the price to be paid for true authority—just as in many corporations—was walking away from the hands-on activities he loved. It was a bargain he was unwilling to make.

While his legacy is already cast in concrete within the automotive community, the larger question is what we can take from his life. Was he a

Opposite: Zora's ashes are interred at the National Corvette Museum in Bowling Green, Kentucky, in a special display devoted to his life.

swashbuckler from a bygone era, or could his essence have applications in the business world today? He came from an age when individual heroism and decisive behavior had much more relevance than in today's system-driven world. Yet without question, Duntov represented one end of the spectrum: Any large organization populated entirely by his likeness would be a disaster.

But the smartest companies have found ways to harness the energy and creativity of their mavericks without disrupting the rest of the organization. Former Chrysler President Robert A. Lutz, who has since joined GM as Vice Chairman, attributed Chrysler's success in the 1990s to a delicate balance of right- and left-brain types, with the right-brain "car guys" being permitted to create products that appealed to their own instincts—not to clinics and focus groups. People like Zora are a necessary component of a vital, energetic organization. It's no coincidence that Duntov worked at GM during its heyday.

Still, Duntov types by their very nature create challenges. They must work within organizations populated by people with very different motivations, not all of which align with the vision of the maverick. "The fact that people like Duntov are different and more creative and see things that others don't makes them unpopular from the get-go," noted Lutz. "Duntov was surrounded by people who derived a great deal of comfort out of working for a very large company. One of the things they enjoy is that things are stable and predictable. Therefore there is a resentment of and a resistance to people who are running around saying this is not running as good as it should and I've got a great idea."

Dave Cole, president of the Center for Automotive Research at the Altarum Institute in Ann Arbor, Michigan, and formerly of the University of Michigan's Office for the Study of Automotive Transportation, says large companies need to create places outside of the traditional restraints for the more creative types to function. "A Lockheed skunk works or the old Chevy Research & Development were ideal grounds for this," said Cole. "The latter was a big toy shop. It was staffed by a bunch of renegades, including Duntov. Since my dad [Ed Cole] was a renegade himself, this is where his alter ego resided inside of Chevrolet. They were doing all kinds of leading edge things. He spent a great deal of time there with the engines and technicians often with his sleeves rolled up. He loved to be involved in new and exciting projects. This was his 'toy shop.'"

The question today is how the industry can attract future Zoras in an era of systemization where it is becoming increasingly difficult for one man to influence the direction of an entire car. With complicated electronic, fuel, and safety systems, the ability to personify a car, as did Zora Duntov, Enzo

Ferrari and Ettore Bugatti, is almost impossible. Most of the true mavericks have headed toward the highly entrepreneurial information technology sector. Will technology help the automotive innovators to come full circle? Time will tell.

Meanwhile, Zora Arkus-Duntov stands as one of the most famous men in the history of the American auto industry. Perhaps his best monuments are the Corvettes—over 1.2 million of them—that roam the highways of America. All of their drivers—whether they know it or not—can thank Zora Arkus-Duntov for the performance pedigree they carry with them.

Notes

The following abbreviations are used throughout:

ZADM: Zora Arkus-Duntov memoirs.

ZAD-PL: Zora Arkus-Duntov interview by
                 Pete Lyons.

EAD: Elfi Arkus-Duntov interview by author.

KL-CASSSC: Karl Ludvigsen, *Corvette: America's
                 Star-Spangled Sports Car*, an
                 Automobile Quarterly Library Series
                 Book, Princeton Publishing, Princeton,
                 NJ, (1973).

All other interviews cited were conducted by the author unless otherwise specified.

Chapter One

Pg. 3. Ice story, ZADM.

Pg. 4. "Instinctively applying lesson learned..." ZAD-PL, (June 6, 1989).

Pg. 4. Conditions in Russia leading up to revolution, Richard Pipes, Alfred A. Knopf, *Concise History of the Russian Revolution*, New York, (1995) p. 23.

Pg. 4. Background on Jacques Arkus, ZADM.

Pg. 5. Background on Rachel Kogan, ZADM.

Pg. 5. Background on Rachel Kogan's family, Tamara Milman interview, (Nov 11, 1997).

Pg. 5. Origins of Zora's name, ZAD-PL, (June 16, 1989).

Pg. 5. Zora's two birthdays, ZAD-PL, (June 16, 1989).

Pg. 5. Parents settling back into St. Petersburg, ZAD-PL, (June 16, 1989).

Pg. 6. Anti Semitism in Russia, Richard Pipes, Alfred A. Knopf, *Concise History of the Russian Revolution*, New York, (1995): 260-261.

Pg. 6. Tradition brought family together for Passover, Tamara Milman interview, (Nov 11, 1997).

Pg. 6. Jews migrate back to large cities, Richard Pipes, Alfred A. Knopf, *Concise History of the Russian Revolution*, New York, (1995): 260-261.

Pg. 7. "Dear God, let that night..." ZAD-PL, (June 23, 1989).

Pg. 7. Swimming boast, ZADM.

Pg. 8. Tree climbing story, ZADM.

Pg. 8. Crashing bicycle, ZADM.

Pg. 8. "You are destined to die..." ZAD-PL (June 23, 1989).

Pg. 8. Chinese magician, ZAD-PL, (Aug 28, 1989).

Pg. 9. Pouring water on Uncle Laska , ZADM.

Pg. 10. Drawing pictures, seeing sternwheeler, ZADM.

Pg. 10. Eclipse story, ZADM.

Pg. 11. Streetcars in St. Petersburg, ZAD-PL, (June 16, 1989).

Pg. 11 Runaway streetcar, George Levy, "Zora," *Corvette Quarterly*, (summer 1988): 35-36.

Pg. 11. Putting salt on rails, ZAD-PL, (June 16, 1989).

Pg. 11. Bicycle sprocket, ZADM.

Pg. 12. Operating ferry on Nevka River, ZAD-PL, (June 22, 1989).

Pg. 12. Starting chauffeur's Mercedes, ZAD-PL, (June 16, 1989).

Pg. 12. Birth of Yura, ZAD-PL, (June 16, 1989).

Pg. 13. Hiding Yura in cupboard at school, ZAD-PL (June 21, 1989).

Pg. 13. Zora's closeness to Yura, Daphne Arkus-Duntov interview, (Oct 10, 1999).

Pg. 13. Build up to Revolution, ZAD-PL (Aug 28, 1989).

Pg. 14. February Revolution, ZADM.

Pg. 14. Defending bread rations, ZAD-PL, (June 16, 1989).

Pg. 15. "No, you will not shoot..." David E. Davis, Jr., "American Driver," *Automobile* Magazine, (July 1996).

Pg. 15. Brandishing weapon in the market, ZAD-PL (June 16, 1989).

Pg. 15. Accompanying Rachel on inspection trips, ZAD-PL (June 21, 1989).

Pg. 15. Exposure to cultural arts, ZAD-PL (June 16, 1989).

Pg. 16. Rachel obsession with cleanliness, ZAD-PL, (June 28, 1989).

Pg. 16. Pulling gun on doctor, ZAD-PL, (June 16, 1989).

Pg. 17. Running away from boarding school, ZAD-PL, (June 21, 1989).

Pg. 17. Rachel's high academic expectations, ZAD-PL, (June 21, 1989).

Pg. 18. Jacques' attempts to discipline ZAD-PL, (June 22, 1989).

Pg. 18. Jacques taking Zora to library, ZAD-PL, (Aug 28, 1989).

Pg. 18. "They're working day and night..." ZAD-PL, (June 21, 1989).

Pg. 19. Jacques not accompanying family to Crimea, ZAD-PL, (June 22, 1989).

Pg. 19. Zora sizing up his new stepfather, ZAD-PL, (June 22, 1989).

Pg. 20. Josef Duntov opening hydroelectric plants in Russia, ZAD-PL (June 22, 1989).

Pg. 20. Zora's infatuation with cousin Tamara, Tamara Milman interview, (Nov 11, 1997).

Pg. 21. ZAD building snowmobile, ZAD-PL, (June 23, 1989).

Chapter Two

Pg. 25. Zora being sent for by his parents in Germany, ZAD-PL, (June 21, 1989).

Pg. 26. Stenciling his name on generator, George Levy, "Zora profile," *Corvette Quarterly*, (spring 1988).

Pg. 26. Meeting Bernd Rosemeyer, ZAD-PL (June 16, 1989).

Pg. 26. Rosemeyer riding the "Wall of Death" at Lingen, Peter Stevenson, *Driving Forces*, (2000) p. 107.

Pg. 27. Witnessing his first motorcycle race in Russia, ZAD-PL, (June 16, 1989).

Pg. 27. Zora learning how to race a motorcycle, ZAD-PL, (June 16, 1989).

Pg. 28. Description of Bob automobile, E.P. Dutton, *New Encyclopedia of the Motorcar, 1885 to Present*, New York, (1982) p. 96.

Pg. 28. Zora's first experiences behind the wheel, ZAD-PL, (June 16, 1989).

Pg. 29. Early academic troubles at Darmstadt, ZAD-PL, (June 16, 1989).

Pg. 29. Witnessing servant girls bathe in river, ZAD-PL, (June 21, 1989).

Pg. 30. Meeting Nadia Niernberg, ZAD-PL, (June 21, 1989).

Pg. 30. Relating to Tolstoy novel character, ZADM.

Pg. 30. Sleeping with Jenny, ZAD-PL, (Sept 18 1989).

Pg. 31. Gunplay with student at Darmstadt, ZAD-PL, (Aug 2, 1989).

Pg. 31. First airplane ride, ZAD-PL, (Sept 19, 1989).

Pg. 31. Switching majors from electrical to mechanical engineering, ZAD-PL (Sept 29, 1989).

Pg. 32. Primus tractor, ZAD-PL (Aug 2, 1989).

Pg. 32. Meeting Arnold Zoller, Karl Ludvigsen, "The Origins of Supercharging," *Automobile Quarterly*, (fall-winter 1970).

Pg. 33. Designing supercharger for 12-cylinder, 2-cycle engine, Zora's resume.

Pg. 33. Working for Elo, ZAD-PL, (June 23, 1989).

Pg. 34. As a sprinter, EAD, (Feb 22, 1997).

Pg. 34. Getting knocked out in boxing match, EAD, (Feb 22, 1997).

Pg. 34. Walking ledge of building in Berlin, ZAD-PL, (Aug 28, 1989).

Pg. 35. Hitler use of racing to develop military technology, Peter Stevenson, *Driving Forces*, (2000) p. 26.

Pg. 35. Alfred Neubauer, Beverly Rae Kimes, *The Star and the Laurel*, (1986) p. 201.

Pg. 36. Rosemeyer's racing success, Peter Stevenson, *Driving Forces*, (2000) p. 26.

Pg. 36. Purchasing the Bob automobile, ZAD-PL, (Aug 2, 1989).

Pg. 37. Driving father's Chevrolet, ZAD-PL, (Aug 2, 1989).

Pg. 37. Driving Bugatti, ZAD-PL (Aug 2, 1989).

Pg. 37. Meeting Asia Orley, Asia Orley diary.

Pg. 37. Racing MGs, Asia Orley diary.

Pg. 38. Asia's racing accident, ZADM.

Pg. 38. Racing frustrations, Asia Orley diary.

Pg. 39. Zora's early girlfriends, EAD, (Feb 22, 1997).

Pg. 39. Elfi and Zora's first encounter, EAD, (Feb 22, 1997).

Pg. 39. Elfi family background, EAD, (Feb 22, 1997).

Pg. 40. Early romance, EAD, (Feb 22, 1997).

Pg. 40. Bugatti engine on bed, Zora Arkus-Duntov *Road & Track*, (January1992).

Pg. 40. Elfi's early anxiety, EAD, (Feb 22, 1997).

Pg. 40. Zora standing in front of his window, Tony Lapine, (Oct 27, 1997).

Pg. 41. Courtship in Berlin, EAD, (Feb 22, 1997).

Pg. 41 Harassment by Nazi's, EAD, (Feb 22, 1997).

Pg. 42. Brainstorming the Arkus, ZAD-PL. (Aug 29, 1989).

Pg. 43. Entering Grand Prix Picardie, Asia Orley diary.

Pg. 43. Chronic problems with Arkus, Asia Orley diary.

Chapter Three

Pg. 47. Increasing Nazi presence in Germany, EAD, (March 1, 1997).

Pg. 47. Elfi's parents send her to Paris, EAD, (March 9, 1997).

Pg. 48. Joining Mondiale, ZAD-PL (June 21, 1989).

Pg. 48. Running gear cutting machine, ZAD-PL, (June 21, 1989).

Pg. 48. Early experiences as a manager, ZAD-PL, (June 21, 1989).

Pg. 49. Designing lathe, ZAD-PL, (June 21, 1989).

Pg. 49. Paper on 4WD in racing cars, Zora resume.

Pg. 49. Advantages of 4WD, ZAD-PL, (Aug 2, 1989).

Pg. 50. Meeting Dr. Porsche, ZADM.

Pg. 50. Meeting Ettore Buggati, Zora Arkus-Duntov
         Road & Track, (Jan 1992).

Pg. 51. Elfi joins Follies Bergere, EAD, (March 1, 1997).

Pg. 52. Zora proposes to Elfi, EAD, (March 1, 1997).

Pg. 53. Zora sciatica attack, EAD, (March 1, 1997).

Pg. 53. Zora joins Marchak, ZAD resume.

Pg. 55. Elfi wins lottery, ZAD-PL, (Sept 14, 1989).

Pg. 55. Zora and Elfi's wedding, EAD, (March 1, 1997).

Chapter Four

Pg. 59. Rachel's attempt to get Z to enlist, ZAD-PL,
         (June 22, 1989).

Pg. 60. Zora's early experience in service, (June 22, 1989).

Pg. 60. Zora's attempts to join Yura's unit, Coles Phinizy, "The
         Marque of Zora," *Sports Illustrated*, (Dec 4, 1972).

Pg. 61. Life in Paris before invasion, EAD, (Feb 1997).

Pg. 61. "My dear, I saw Zora..." Letter to Elfi from Zora,
         ZADM.

Pg. 62. Elfi's escape from Paris, EAD, (Feb 1997).

Pg. 63. Potez Aircraft, *Complete Encyclopedia of World
         Aircraft*, Brown Packaging Books Ltd. London, p. 762.

Pg. 63. Potez Aircraft, Walter J. Boyne, *Clash of Wings,
         World War II in the Air*, Touchstone, (1997) p. 50.

Pg. 64. Merignac as bombing target, Coles Phinizy,
         "The Marque of Zora," *Sports Illustrated*,
         (Dec 4, 1972).

Pg. 64. Comparing Potez to a Lockheed P38, Stacy Schiff,
         *Saint Exupéry, A biography of Antoine Saint
         Exupéry*, DaCapo Press, NY, (1994).

Pg. 65. Elfi escape from Paris (continuation), EAD,
         (March 3, 1997).

Pg. 67. Seeking a way out of the country, ZAD-PL,
         (June 29, 1989).

Pg. 68. Eating pigeons, EAD, (March 22, 1997).

Pg. 69. Courting daughter of Spanish consulate, ZAD-PL,
         (Aug 3, 1989).

Pg. 69. Journey to America aboard refugee ship, EAD,
         (March 28, 1997).

Pg. 70. Entering America through Ellis Island, EAD,
         (March 28, 1997).

Chapter Five

Pg. 73. Early attitudes about America, ZAD-PL, (Oct 28, 1989).

Pg. 74. Other Arkus relatives in U.S., EAD, (March 28, 1997).

Pg. 74. Deciphering damper design, ZAD-PL, (Aug 29, 1989).

Pg. 75. General Machinery, Birger Olson letter to George
         Rubissow, (Feb 12, 1941).

Pg. 75. Visiting submarine operations at Brooklyn Navy
         Yard, ZAD-PL, (Aug 28, 1989).

Pg. 75. Patent for polyharmonic damper, ZAD-PL,
         (Aug 29, 1989).

Pg. 76. Buying Elfi fur coat, D. Randy Riggs, "Ardun the Art of
         Zora," *Automobile Quarterly*, (Dec 1996) p. 59.

Pg. 76. Setting up Ardun Mechanical, ZAD-PL, (Aug 28, 1989).

Pg. 76. Changing last name to "Arkus-Duntov," ZAD-PL
         (Aug 28, 1989).

Pg. 77. Protecting Yura, ZAD-PL, (Aug 28, 1989).

Pg. 77. Ardun successes, Ardun advertisement (1943).

Pg. 78. Marking up breather nut, ZAD-PL, (Aug 28, 1989).

Pg. 78. New Ardun location, ZAD-PL, (Aug 29, 1989).

Pg. 78. Jet helicopter, ZAD-PL (Sept 16, 1989).

Pg. 78. Scrapping jet helicopter, ZAD-PL, (Aug 29, 1989).

Pg. 78. Penthouse parties, EAD, (May 20, 1997).

Pg. 79. Vadim Gonsoff, EAD, (May 20, 1997).

Pg. 79. Becoming American citizen, ZAD-PL, (Oct 28, 1989).

Pg. 81. Elfi pregnancy, EAD, (April 6, 1997).

Pg. 81. "For Elfi was major tragedy," ZAD-PL, (Oct 28, 1989).

Pg. 81. Zora's ballerinas, EAD, (April 6, 1997).

Pg. 82. Elfi's new independent life, EAD, (May 20, 1997).

Pg. 83. Zora splits with Luba Restova, EAD, (April 6, 1997).

Chapter Six

Pg. 88. Approaching Ford Motor Company, ZAD-PL,
         (Aug 28, 1989).

Pg. 88. Zora as a draftsman, ZAD-PL, (Aug 28, 1989).

Pg. 89. Ardun hemi heads, ZAD-PL, (Aug 28, 1989).

Pg. 90. Ardun motor specifications, Ardun Mechanical
         Corporation advertising insert, (1947).

Pg. 91. Truck applications for Ardun engine, *New York
         Times*, (Aug 4, 1947).

Pg. 92. Zora on cover of *Iron Age, Iron Age*, (Sept 4, 1947).

Pg. 92. "The Coke bottle shaped lifters..." D. Randy Riggs,
         "Ardun, The Art of Zora," *Automobile Quarterly*,
         (Dec 1996): 57-67.

Pg. 92. "Ardun was a great hot water heater..." Ray Brock
         interview, (April 28, 1989).

Pg. 93. Developing little Ardun as racing engine, ZAD-PL,
         (Aug 28, 1989).

Pg. 94. Veritas background, George Rainbird, *New
         Encyclopedia of Motorcars*, 1885 to Present,
         London (1982) p. 642.

Pg. 94. Asia Orley brokering Veritas deal, ZAD-PL,
         (Aug 28, 1989).

Pg. 95. Background on C&T Automotive, D. Randy Riggs,
         Automobile Quarterly, (Dec 1996): 57-67.

Pg. 96. "City of Burbank" Flying Mile record, Jerry Chesebrough, *Hop Up* magazine, (March 1953).

Pg. 96. Other Ardun speed records, D. Randy Riggs, "Ardun, The Art of Zora," *Automobile Quarterly*, (Dec 1996): 57-67.

Pg. 97. Chinetti and Duntov at Indianapolis, ZAD-PL, (Aug 29, 1989).

Pg. 97. Chinetti's origins in US, Stan Grayson, "The Man Who Raced For Fun," *Automobile Quarterly*, (1975).

Pg. 97. Appeal of Indianapolis to Duntov/Chinetti, ZAD-PL, (Sept 18, 1989).

Pg. 98. Duntov's "swinging door" Talbot, Donald Davidson, Indianapolis Motor Speedway interview, (May 1997).

Pg. 98. "You must pass the driver's test..." Letter from George Rodway, Indianapolis Motor Speedway, (April 29, 1946).

Pg. 99. Appeal of the dirt to Zora, ZAD-PL, (Sept 18, 1989).

Pg. 100. 1946 Pikes Peak entry, official Pikes Peak entry from, (July 31, 1946).

Pg. 100. Response from Pikes Peak organizers, Western Union telegram, (Aug 21, 1946).

Pg. 100. Sponsorship by Cornelius Printing, Donald Davidson, Indianapolis Motor Speedway interview by author, (May 1997).

Pg. 100. "I do not know what to recommend about the Talbot..." Letter from Wilbur Shaw to Zora, (Oct 10, 1947).

Pg. 100. Schell's offer to purchase Talbot, French Cable Company telegram from Harry Schell to Zora, (March 11, 1947).

Pg. 101. Driving Veritas at Monthlery, ZAD-PL, (Sept 13, 1989).

Pg. 102. Elfi's dancing at Copa Cabana, EAD, (March 1997).

Pg. 103. Schell's offer to drive Cisitalia, ZAD-PL, (Sept 18, 1989).

Pg. 104. Driving in hillclimb at Chateau Tierry, ZADM.

Pg. 104. Zora's times at Shelsey Walsh, letter from Midland Automobile Club Archive, Woodbride, Upper Sapey, Worcester, (March 20, 2001).

Pg. 104. Sydney Allard at Shelsey Walsh, Tom Lush, "*Allard, The Inside Story*," Motor Racing Publications, London, (1977) p. 88.

Chapter Seven

Pg. 109. "Known affectionately as the Guv'nor...", David Kinsella, "*Allard*," The Haynes Publishing Group, Sparkford, Somerset, England, (1977) p. 154.

Pg. 110. Adlards Motors background, Tom Lush, "*Allard, The Inside Story*," Motor Racing Publications, London, (1977) p. 12.

Pg. 110. Reliability trials, John Allard interview, (March 2001).

Pg. 110. CLK 5, Tom Lush, "*Allard, The Inside Story*," Motor Racing Publications, London, (1977) p. 18.

Pg. 110. Allard shop description, "Output From Enthusiasm: How a company directed by an active competition driver builds high performance cars at a reasonable price," *The Motor*, (March 10, 1948).

Pg. 111. Zora's swap of Ardun heads for use of Allard, ZAD-PL, (Oct 27, 19899).

Pg. 111. Ardun insert appearing in Watkins Glen program, John Allard interview, (May 4, 2001).

Pg. 112. Controversy over Zora's amateur status, ZAD-PL, (Oct 27, 19899).

Pg. 113. ZAD bringing chocolates to Allard shops, EAD, (May 3, 1997).

Pg. 113. Zora and Yvonne de Carlo, ZAD-PL, (Aug 29, 1989).

Pg. 115. Allard engine options, John Allard interview, (May 4, 2001).

Pg. 115. "Also disappointing were the test-bed findings of the Ardun engine Tom Lush, "*Allard, The Inside Story*," Motor Racing Publications, London, (1977) p. 113.

Pg. 115. "Owners who had previously driven a modified, side-valve engine found the Ardun something of a disappointment..." David Kinsella, "*Allard*," The Haynes Publishing Group, Sparkford, Somerset, England, (1977): 187-188.

Pg. 115. Interchangeability of Chrysler and Cadillac V8 parts, Memo from Zora to S. H. Allard, R. J. Canham regarding interchangeability of Chrysler and Cadillac V8 parts, (Aug 21, 1951).

Pg. 116. Fiberglass Palm Beaches, John Allard interview, (May 4, 2001).

Pg. 116. Zora's practical joking, ZAD-PL, (Oct 27, 1989).

Pg. 116. Relaxing with Sydney Allard and crew after hours, ZAD-PL, (Aug 29, 1989).

Pg. 117. Mercedes W165, Alfred Naubauer, Barrie and Rockliff, *Speed Is My Life*, London, pp. 173-174.

Pg. 117. Zora's Nuburgring test drive, ZAD-PL, (Aug 29, 1989).

Pg. 118. Reactions to postwar Germany, EAD, (May 3, 1997).

Pg. 118. Standing wave phenomenon, ZAD-PL, (Aug 29, 1989).

Pg. 118. Rudi Uhlenhaut background, Beverly Rae Kimes, *The Star and the Laurel*, (1986) p. 262.

Pg. 118. Zora similarities to Uhlenhaut, ZAD-PL, (Aug 29, 1989.)

Pg. 119. "I take this occasion to thank you..." Zora letter to Rudi Uhlenhaut, (Nov 26, 1951).

Pg. 119. "If we can't take you as a driver..." Letter from Alfred Naubauer to Zora, (Oct 16, 1952).

Pg. 119. Suggesting Stirling Moss as Mercedes team driver, ZAD-PL, (Aug 29, 1989).

Pg. 119. "I'm slightly doubtful..." Stirling Moss interview, (Nov 1999).

Pg. 120. Zora's desire to drive for Allard, ZAD-PL, (Aug 29, 1989).

Pg. 120. Offer to drive C-type Jaguar at Goodwood, ZAD-PL, (Aug 29, 1989).

Pg. 121.   Allard team pit to car communication, Tom Lush, *"Allard, The Inside Story,"* Motor Racing Publications, London, (1977) p. 144.

Pg. 121.   Mercedes wins overall at 1952 Le Mans, Beverly Rae Kimes, *The Star and the Laurel,* (1986): 301-304.

Pg. 121.   Allard hospitality at Le Mans, EAD, (May 20, 1997).

Pg. 122.   Zora's paper on high-speed testing, Zora Arkus Duntov, *Automobile Engineer,* (Dec 1952): 535-542.

Pg. 122.   Offer to consult with Pegaso, Chevrolet memo from Zora to Maurice Olley, (July 1, 1953).

Pg. 122.   Memories of Spanish border towns, ZAD-PL, (Oct 27, 1989).

Pg. 123.   Analysis of Pegaso operation, Chevrolet memo from Zora to Maurice Olley, (July 1, 1953).

Pg. 123   Investor offer to buy Allard, ZAD-PL, (Aug 29, 1989).

Pg. 124.   General Le May encouraging Zora to write to Ed Cole, ZAD-PL, (Oct 28, 1989).

Chapter Eight

Pg. 127.   "After almost two years with Allard..." Zora letter to John Cuccio, Studebaker corporation, (Oct 22, 1952).

Pg. 127.   Cuccio's reply, letter from John Cuccio to Zora, (Nov 2, 1952).

Pg. 128.   "I am at your disposal..." Zora letter to James C. Zader, Chrysler Corporation, (Nov 20, 1952).

Pg. 128.   Chrysler reply, letter from A.G. Herreshoff to Zora, (Dec 9, 1952).

Pg. 128.   "The decision on my part to seek an association with a large company is..." Zora letter to A.G. Herreshoff, (Jan 3, 1953).

Pg. 128.   Query letter to Ford Motor Company, Zora letter to Benson Ford, (Nov 20, 1952).

Pg. 128.   Ford's reply, letter from J.J. Tigue to Zora, (Nov 26, 1952).

Pg. 129.   Initial letter to GM's Ed Cole, ZAD-PL (Aug 29, 1989).

Pg. 129.   Cole's reply, letter from E.N. Cole to Zora, (Nov 4, 1952).

Pg. 129.   "To hell with him..." ZAD-PL, (Oct 27, 1989).

Pg. 129.   Possible GM overseas possibility, letter from J. Kjolhede to Zora, (Dec 19, 1952).

Pg. 129.   Zora's response to Kjolhede, ZAD-PL (Oct 27, 1989).

Pg. 129.   "If you are still available, we would consider employment with Chevrolet Engineering..." Maurice Olley letter to Zora, (Jan 5, 1953).

Pg. 129.   "I am still available and interested in employment..." Zora letter to Olley, (Jan 9, 1953).

Pg. 130.   "Thank you for your letter of January 9..." Olley letter to Zora, (Jan 22, 1953).

Pg. 130.   "We are now considering whether our organization..." letter from A.A. Maynard to Zora, (Jan 26, 1953).

Pg. 130.   "I propose to join your company as a development engineer..." letter from Zora to L. England, Jaguar Cars, (Jan 29, 1952).

Pg. 130.   England reply, letter from L. England to Zora, (Jan 3, 1953).

Pg. 130.   Query letter to Fairchild Aviation, letter from Zora to C.M. Wieden, (Jan 7, 1953).

Pg. 131.   Atomic compressor at Fairchild, ZAD-PL (Aug 29, 1989).

Pg. 131.   Fairchild's involvement with nuclear-powered airplane program, Mary Shaw, Fairchild Corporation, interview, (April 23, 2001).

Pg. 131.   Fuel injection seminar in Paris, ZAD-PL, (Sept 14, 1989).

Pg. 131.   Travel restrictions at Fairchild, ZAD-PL, (Oct 28, 1989).

Pg. 131.   Knowledge restrictions at Fairchild, ZAD-PL, (Oct 27, 1989).

Pg. 132.   The American sports car market in the early Fifties, KL-CASSSC, p. 13.

Pg. 133.   History of fiberglass-bodied sports cars, KL-CASSSC, p.14.

Pg. 133.   Willy's Wildfire, KL-CASSSC, p. 15.

Pg. 134.   Bob McLean's layout of 1953 Corvette, KL-CASSSC, pp.18-20.

Pg. 134.   Early GM experiments with fiberglass, KL-CASSSC, p. 16.

Pg. 134.   "I went to Motorama and found the Corvette breathtaking..." Zora letter to Maurice Olley, (Jan 28, 1953).

Pg. 135.   "Should the red tape of an interview arrangement be the reason..." Zora letter to Maurice Olley, (March 17, 1953).

Pg. 135.   GM interview offer in Detroit, letter from Maurice Olley to Zora, (March 24, 1953.)

Pg. 135.   "Please wire the following information..." Western Union telegram from Maurice Olley to Zora, (April 12, 1953).

Pg. 135.   "We should have something definite to report in about a week...." letter from Maurice Olley to Zora, (April 8, 1953).

Pg. 135.   "Since we are practically in mid-April now..." Zora letter to Maurice Olley, (April 12, 1953).

Pg. 135.   Using General LeMay as reference, letter from Zora to Curtis LeMay, (April 12, 1953).

Pg. 136.   "We have made a reservation for you at the Abington Hotel..." letter from Maurice Olley to Zora, (April 24, 1953).

Chapter Nine

Pg. 139.   Background on GM building, Detroit Institute of Arts, *The Legacy of Alfred Kahn,* (1970): 20-21, 100-101.

Pg. 139. "What was good for the country was good for General Motors..." Edward Cray, *Chrome Colossus, General Motors and its Times*, McGraw Hill Book Company, New York, (1980): 6-7.

Pg. 139. Background on Durant, Sloan, Kettering, Lawrence R. Dolph and Dr. Ron Westrum, Maestro Management, white paper by GM consultants (1995).

Pg. 139. "The essential goodness of the company was never questioned..." David Halberstam, *The Fifties*, Fawcett Columbine, New York, (1993) p. 489.

Pg. 140. "Once an executive reached a level of prestige at General Motors...." Maryann Keller, *Rude Awakening: The Rise, Fall and Struggle for Recovery of General Motors*, William Morrow and Company, Inc., New York, (1989) p. 17.

Pg. 141. "General Motors was Republican..." David Halberstam, *The Fifties*, Fawcett Columbine, New York, (1993) p. 489.

Pg. 141. "It's like entering the priesthood..." Brock Yates, *The Decline and Fall of the American Auto Industry*, Empire Books, New York, (1983) p. 80.

Pg. 141. "It was the duty of the rare General Motors employee..." David Halberstam, *The Fifties*, Fawcett Columbine, New York, (1993) p. 488.

Pg. 142. "After World War II, Cole was the great hope of the corporation..." Lawrence Dolph interview, (1995).

Pg. 142. Background on Ed Cole, Karl Ludvigsen, *Automobile Quarterly*, vol. 16 no. 2, pp.147-159.

Pg. 142. "Ed Cole had carte blanche at Chevy to get the place moving..." Alex Mair, interview (Sept 21, 1998).

Pg. 143. Duntov described by GM as being of Belgian extraction, David Halberstam, *The Fifties*, Fawcett Columbine, New York, (1993) p. 489.

Pg. 143. Small block V8 scheduled to arrive in 1955, KL-CASSSC, p. 40.

Pg. 144. "God's gift from heaven..." Commemorative video by Performance Racing Industry, *A Salute to the Wonderful Engineers Who Brought Us the Chevy Small Block*, (Dec 2, 1995).

Pg. 144. Internal opposition to small block, ZAD-PL, (Sept 13, 1989).

Pg. 144. Chevrolet R&D offices, Gib Hufstader interview, (March 5, 2001).

Pg. 144. Zora's relationship with Mauri Rose, ZAD-PL, (Sept 13, 1989).

Pg. 145. Zora's later efforts to help Rose drive Indy pace car, ZAD-PL, (Sept 18, 1989).

Pg. 145. Zora's friendship with Ben Griffith, ZAD-PL, (Sept 13, 1989).

Pg. 145. Griffin's hypoid gear, ZAD-PL, (Sept 13, 1989).

Pg. 145. Maurice Olley background, Maurice Hendry, *Cadillac, The Complete History*, An Automobile Quarterly book, Kutstown, PA (1979) p. 228.

Pg. 145. Quiet, introspective Olley, EAD (Jan 4, 1998).

Pg. 145. Origins of Zora's solution for tail-heavy car, Cameron C. Earl, British Intelligence Objectives Sub Committee, Investigation of German Grand Prix Racing Cars Between 1934 and 1939, (1947): 83-87.

Pg. 146. Olley's negative reaction to Zora's tail-heavy vehicle "fix," ZAD-PL, (Oct 27, 1989).

Pg. 146. Olley later changes attitude, ZAD-PL, (Aug 28, 1989).

Pg. 146. Suspension fixes on early Corvettes, ZAD-PL, (Sept 13, 1989).

Pg. 146. "Consciously he would not build that car..." ZAD-PL, (Sept 27, 1989).

Pg. 147. Exhaust staining problem on early Corvettes, KL-CASSSC, p. 38.

Pg. 147. Two-cycle engine development, ZAD-PL, (Oct 27, 1989).

Pg. 147. Zora's effort to drive for Allard at Le Mans, ZAD-PL, (Aug 28, 1989).

Pg. 148. Origins of SAC racing program, Steven J. Thompson, "Racers on the Runways," *Car and Driver*, (April 1992).

Pg. 148. Early SAC races, Reede Tilley interview by author, (May 30, 1997).

Pg. 150. LeMay forbidden to race by act of Congress, John Allard interview, (May 4, 2001).

Pg. 150. "We thought he was a hell of a guy, a real gentleman racer..." Reede Tilley interview, (May 4, 2001).

Pg. 150. U.S. Air Force assistance for Allard team, Tom Lush, *Allard, The Inside Story*, Motor Racing Publications (1977) p. 153.

Pg. 151. Allard use of pit-to-car two-way radios, ZAD-PL, (Oct 27, 1989).

Pg. 151. Zora's view of 1953 Le Mans race, Chevrolet memo from Zora to Maurice Olley on the 1953 Le Mans Race, (July 1, 1953).

Pg. 152. "Duntov was lapping steadily around 4 minutes, 40 seconds..." Tom Lush, *Allard, The Inside Story*, Motor Racing Publications (1977) p. 155.

Pg. 152. "I exploded with expletives..." ZAD-PL, (Oct 27, 1989).

Pg. 153. Mickey Fouilhan story, ZAD-PL, (Aug 29, 1989).

Chapter Ten

Pg. 157. "We always regarded Chevrolet..." David E. Davis Jr. interview, (March 13, 2001).

Pg. 157. "But if Cole feels that I am development engineer, so be it..." ZAD-PL, (Oct 27, 1989).

Pg. 158. Zora's confusion over his title, ZAD-PL, (Aug 28, 1989).

Pg. 158. Zora developing driveline for school bus, ZAD-PL, (Sept 14, 1989).

Pg. 159. "Victor Borge of engineering" ZAD-PL, (Aug 29, 1989).

Pg. 159. Lansing SAE Speech, Z. Arkus-Duntov, Chevrolet Motor Division, *Sports Car Development*, presented at Society of Automotive Engineers, Michigan Section Meeting, Lansing, Mich., (Sept 1953).

Pg. 161. Bob Ross reaction to Duntov SAE speech, Letter from Bob Ross to Walter MacKenzie, (Jan 1954).

Pg. 161. Arvid Jouppi reaction to Duntov SAE speech, Letter from Arvid F. Jouppi to Walter MacKenzie, (Jan 1954).

Pg. 162. Zora's most famous memo, Zora, "Thoughts Pertaining to Youth, Hot Rodders and Chevrolet," Chevrolet internal memo, (Dec 16, 1953).

Pg. 163. "I am about to offer you a job I would give my right arm to do myself..." ZAD-PL, (Sept 14, 1989).

Pg. 164. Zora rescued from Proving Ground, ZAD-PL, (Oct 29, 1989).

Pg. 164. Contacting Alfred Neubauer, Letter from Zora to Alfred Neubauer, (Feb 12, 1954).

Pg. 165. Dolza's fuel cutoff feature, ZAD-PL, (Sept 14, 1989).

Pg. 165. Disappointing early results, KL-CASSSC, p. 58.

Pg. 165. Zora's "doghouse" manifold, KL-CASSSC, pp. 58-59.

Pg. 165. "Zora was struggling with it..." Smokey Yunick interview, (Jan 21, 1998).

Pg. 166. "The problem was always in the distributor system..." Bill Tower interview (Feb 6, 2001).

Pg. 166. Zora's fuel injection patents, Fuel Induction System; U.S. Patent Office #2,882,883 (April 21, 1959), Manifold; U.S. Patent Office #2,947,293 (August 2, 1960), Cold Enrichment Device U.S. Patent Office # 2,949,102 (Aug 16, 1960).

Pg. 166. Zora's Detroit SAE speech, Z. Arkus-Duntov, General Motors *Fuel Injection System*, SAE Annual Meeting, Detroit, Michigan (Jan 18, 1957).

Chapter Eleven

Pg. 171. Baron Huschke von Hanstein, EAD, (June 7, 1998).

Pg. 171. Von Hanstein background, Richard von Frankenburg, English version by Charles Meisl, *Porsche, The Man and His Cars*, G.T. Foulis @ Co. Ltd., London (1961) p. 189.

Pg. 172. Heinrich Uli Wieselmann, ZAD-PL, (Aug 29, 1989).

Pg. 172. "I am very appreciative of the high opinion you have of me.." letter from Zora to Von Hanstein, (Feb 16, 1954).

Pg. 172. Porsche 550 Spyder, Zora Chevrolet internal memo to Maurice Olley, (Aug 3, 1954).

Pg. 173. "We hear you're interested in racing a Porsche at Le Mans...", Porsche letterhead Memo from Hans Kern to Zora, (Jan 1954).

Pg. 173. "We have entered the car according to the regulations..." Porsche letterhead memo to Zora from Prinzing and von Hanstein, (Feb 23, 1954).

Pg. 173. "We are interested in having you on our official Porsche team..." Porsche letterhead memo to Zora from Ferry Porsche, (April 5, 1954).

Pg. 173. Zora's Porsche test drive, ZAD-PL, (Aug 29, 1989).

Pg. 173. GM technology exchange with Porsche, Chevrolet internal memo from Zora to Maurice Olley (Feb 16, 1954).

Pg. 174. Zora receives approval to race at Le Mans, ZAD-PL, (Aug 29, 1989).

Pg. 174. "Your offer drive 1100 Le Mans accepted..." GM teletype message from Zora to Porsche (April 14, 1954).

Pg. 174. "As you well know, Sydney Allard..." Zora letter to Gen. Curtis E. LeMay, (April 16, 1954).

Pg. 175. Zora's multiple choice response form for Cole, Memo from Zora to Ed Cole, (June 2, 1954).

Pg. 175. Zora's racing 550, Karl Ludvigsen, "Excellence Was Expected," *Automobile Quarterly*, (1976) p. 143.

Pg. 175. Porsche racing strategy, Zora Chevrolet internal memo to Maurice Olley, (Aug 3, 1954).

Pg. 175. Early race action at Le Mans, Zora Chevrolet internal memo to Maurice Olley, (Aug 3, 1954).

Pg. 176. Advantages of driving an underpowered car, ZAD Chevrolet internal memo to Maurice Olley, (Aug 3, 1954).

Pg. 176. Lack of amenities in the Porsche pits, Zora Chevrolet internal memo to Maurice Olley (Aug 3, 1954).

Pg. 176. "As I cleared the hilltop on approach to the White House..." Zora Chevrolet internal memo to Maurice Olley, (Aug 3, 1954).

Pg. 176. Problems with Zora's 550, Zora Chevrolet internal memo to Maurice Olley, (Aug 3, 1954).

Pg. 176. Misfiring engine, Karl Ludvigsen, "Excellence Was Expected," *Automobile Quarterly*, (1976) p. 143.

Pg. 176. "Apparently the downpour slowed him down more than it did me..." Zora Chevrolet internal memo to Maurice Olley, (Aug 3, 1954).

Pg. 178. Taking an extra victory lap, Zora Chevrolet internal memo to Maurice Olley, (Aug 3, 1954).

Pg. 179. Changing weight distribution of the Porsche 550 during the race, ZAD-PL, (Aug 28, 1989).

Pg. 179. Recommending skidpad to Porsche, ZAD-PL, (Aug 29, 1989). Karl Ludvigsen, "Excellence Was Expected," *Automobile Quarterly*, (1976) p. 143.

Pg. 180. "Road Manners by Maurice Olley, ZAD-PL, (Aug 29, 1989). Karl Ludvigsen, "Excellence Was Expected," *Automobile Quarterly*, (1976) p. 143.

Pg. 180. What I learned about suspension, I learned from him..." ZAD-PL, (Aug 29, 1989).

Pg. 180. Zora's belief that Olley was "old school" regarding dynamic handling, ZAD-PL, (Aug 29, 1989).

Pg. 180. "All of the Porsche people from the lowest mechanics on up love you..." Prinzing memo to Zora, (July 1954).

Pg. 181. "Ferry would have loved to have the guy on his team..." Anatole Lapine interview, (Oct 27, 1997).

Pg. 182. Paris restaurant incident, Anatole Lapine interview, (Oct 27, 1997), EAD, (Sept 16, 1998).

Pg. 183. Citroen pneumatic shock test ride, Zora Chevrolet memo to Maurice Olley, (Aug 6, 1954).

Pg. 184. Visit to Mahle, Zora Chevrolet memo to Maurice Olley, (Aug 6, 1954).

Pg. 184. Visit to M.A.N., ZAD Chevrolet memo to Maurice Olley, (Aug 6, 1954).

Pg. 185. Visit to Daimler Benz, ZAD Chevrolet memo to Maurice Olley, (Aug 6, 1954).

Chapter Twelve

Pg. 189. Poor market for Corvette in 1954 KL-CASSSC, p. 40.

Pg. 190. Zora's attempt to save the Corvette, Zora Chevrolet internal memo to Ed Cole and Maurice Olley, (Oct 15, 1954).

Pg. 190. Driving in inaugural SAC race 1953, Letter to LeMay from Zora, (Sept 29, 1953).

Pg. 191. Visit to Offut field, ZAD-PL, (Oct 30, 1989).

Pg. 192. Zora contemplates joining Air Force reserve, ZAD-PL, (Oct 29, 1989).

Pg. 192. LeMay enjoying his Corvette, Steven Thompson, "Racers on the Runways," *Car and Driver* (April 1992).

Pg. 193. 1955 Le Mans tragedy, Karl Ludvigsen, "Excellence Was Expected," *Automobile Quarterly*, (1976) p. 154.

Pg. 193. Elfi's recollection of 1955 crash, EAD, (June 7, 1998).

Pg. 194. Duntov and Veuillet set fast lap in class, Karl Ludvigsen, "Excellence Was Expected, "*Automobile Quarterly*, (1976) p. 154.

Pg. 194. "Porsche had become not only dominant in two classes..." Karl Ludvigsen, "Excellence Was Expected," *Automobile Quarterly*, (1976) p. 154.

Pg. 194. Zora's Porsche drive written up in official Chevy engineering publication, *Chevrolet Engineering News*, (July 1955): 5-6.

Pg. 195. Zora's thoughts on how to avoid a future 1955 tragedy, ZADM.

Pg. 195. The Pikes Peak challenge, ZADM, ZAD-PL, (Sept 14, 1989).

Pg. 196. "Splendid idea! I *have* to be involved." ZADM.

Pg. 196. Zora meets Barney Clark at Pikes Peak, Barney Clark interview, (Nov 13, 1997).

Pg. 196. Zora drives B.Clark and W. MacKenzie up the mountain, ZADM.

Pg. 196. Bringing in Chuck Meyers and Al Rogers, ZADM.

Pg. 197. The"Goat" and the "McCoy," *Chevrolet Engineering News*, (Oct 1955): 14-20.

Pg. 197. Modifications to the cars, ZADM.

Pg. 197. Confidentiality on the mountain, ZADM.

Pg. 197. Testing on the mountain, ZADM.

Pg. 198. Cavorting with Oleg Cassini's models, ZADM.

Pg. 199. Zora's final tests and official run, ZADM.

Pg. 200. Post run publicity, Campbell-Ewald archives, *Chevrolet Engineering Digest*, (Oct 1955).

Pg. 200. Zora requests Cole's permission to appear in TV commercial, Zora memo to Ed Cole, (Nov 28, 1955).

Pg. 201. NASCAR congratulates Chevrolet, Letter from Bill France to Thomas Keating, (Sept 14, 1955).

Pg. 202. Zora proposes Corvette speed record, ZAD-PL, (Sept 14, 1989).

Pg. 202. Seeking ways to get more power out of small-block, KL-CASSSC, p. 44-47.

Pg. 202. Developing the Duntov cam, ZAD-PL, (Sept 14, 1989, Oct 31, 1989).

Pg. 203. Mesa test runs, Test Run sheet, Summary of Corvette Maximum Speed Runs on Desert Proving Ground 5-Mile Circular Track, (Dec 20, 1955).

Pg. 203. Achieving 163 mph at Mesa, KL-CASSSC, p. 47.

Pg. 204. Modifications to beach cars, Chevrolet Engineering Department Build Work Order, (Jan 4, 1956).

Pg. 204. Zora's driving technique in the sand, KL-CASSSC, p. 48.

Pg. 205. Publicity buildup for 1956 Speedweeks, John Fitch and Kenneth Rudeen "Bring on the Hay Bales," *Sports Illustrated*, (Jan 16, 1956).

Pg. 205. NASCAR hospitality at Daytona, Ray Brock interview, (April 22, 1998).

Pg. 206. Betty Skelton's antics in airplanes, Betty Skelton, *Little Stinker*, Cross Press, Winter Haven, Fl., (1977): 75-80.

Pg. 206. "Being a woman, I knew how difficult it was..." Betty Skelton interview, (Jan 24, 1998).

Pg. 206. Fitch uses engine block for better traction, John Fitch interview, (Nov 8, 1997).

Pg. 207. Flying Mile results, Roger Huntington, Sports Cars Illustrated, (July 1956): 50-53.

Pg. 207. Skelton undergoes astronaut tests, Betty Skelton interview, (Jan 24, 1998).

Pg. 208. Duntov cam becomes RPO, KL-CASSSC, p. 48.

Pg. 208. "The Duntov cam was not really unique..." Smokey Yunick interview, (Jan 21, 1998).

Pg. 208. "The significance of the Duntov cam was that it worked..." Ray Brock interview, (April 22, 1998).

Chapter Thirteen

Pg. 211. Changes on 1956 Corvette, Zora SAE speech, (Feb 2, 1956).

Pg. 211. "Over the two and a half years involved..." Zora SAE speech, (Feb 2, 1956).

Pg. 212. Attitudes about automatic transmissions, Zora SAE speech, (Feb 2, 1956).

Pg. 212. "When an automobile responds as continuation of the response of human hand..." Zora SAE speech, (Feb 2, 1956).

Pg. 213. Belief that Corvettes weren't ready for international competition, Zora SAE speech, (Feb 2, 1956).

Pg. 213. First uses of Corvette in competition, KL-CASSSC, p. 49-50.

Pg. 213. Concerns about brakes in 1956 Corvettes, ZAD-PL, (Oct 28, 1989).

Pg. 214. John Fitch takes over as Corvette team manager, John Fitch interview, (Nov 1997).

Pg. 214. Ed Cole makes decision to go to Sebring in 1956, KL-CASSSC, p. 50.

Pg. 214. "For the first time, USA's giant General Motors combine is officially taking part in international motor racing..." *Autosport*, (Feb 10, 1956).

Pg. 215. Team preparations for Sebring, KL-CASSSC, p. 50.

Pg. 215. "We were testing countless different components," John Fitch interview, (Nov 1997).

Pg. 215. Use of cerametallic brakes, KL-CASSSC, p. 50.

Pg. 216. Fitch problems with a slipping clutch, John Fitch interview, (Nov 1997).

Pg. 216. "Was less than we hoped, but more than we deserved..." KL-CASSSC, p. 50.

Pg. 217. "You talk about pure, unbelievable, exultant joy," Barney Clark, *Corvette Quarterly*, (Winter 1988).

Pg. 218. West coast Corvette racing activities, Bob D'Olivo interview, (April 23, 1998).

Pg. 218. RPO 684, KL-CASSSC, pp. 62-63.

Pg. 219. Zora breaking back in 1956, ZAD-PL, (Aug 29, 1989).

Pg. 219. Zora back to work wearing a kilt, ZAD-PL, (Sept 14, 1989).

Pg. 220. Early origins of SR-2, KL-CASSSC, p. 65.

Pg. 221. Zora working with Bob McLean, ZAD-PL, (Sept 14, 1989).

Pg. 222. Technical development of Corvette SS, Zora speech at SAE, (1958).

Pg. 222. Use of Mercedes 300 SL frame, KL-CASSSC, p. 75.

Pg. 222. Use of driver-adjustable mercury brake bias switch, ZAD-PL, (Oct 28, 1989).

Pg. 222. Fangio and Moss testing SS, ZAD-PL, (Sept 18, 1989).

Pg. 223. Mauri Rose and N.H. McCuen crashing second mule car, ZAD-PL, (Sept 18, 1989).

Pg. 223. Zora logging 2000 miles in testing the SS, ZAD-PL, (Sept 18, 1989).

Pg. 223. Zora's determination behind the wheel, Jim Rathmann interview, (Jan 23, 1998).

Pg. 224. SS racecar arrives late, not ready to race, ZAD-PL, (Sept 18, 1989).

Pg. 224. Heat problems with magnesium body, ZAD-PL, (Oct 21, 1989).

Pg. 225. Zora's plans to enter Le Mans, ZAD-PL, (Sept 18, 1989).

Pg. 226. "If we had enough time, we could have made a very good race car out of it..." John Fitch interview, (Nov 1997).

Chapter Fourteen

Pg. 229. Zora named director of high performance for Chevrolet, ZAD-PL, (Sept 13, 1989).

Pg. 230. Early interactions with Zora, Dick Keinath interview, (Nov 1998).

Pg. 230. "We'd sit around and ask where we could make things better," Dick Keinath interview, (Nov 1998).

Pg. 231. Zora's visits to the dynamometer cell, Larry Drake retirement party comments, (Jan 1975).

Pg. 231. Zora blowing smoke through an intake port model, Fred Frincke interview by Pete Lyons, (Oct 13, 1989).

Pg. 231. "Ed Cole called me up and asked me if I could run the racing operation..." Jim Rathmann interview, (Jan 23, 1998).

Pg. 232. SEDCO disbanded, Paul Van Valkenburgh, *Chevrolet = Racing*, Walter R. Haessner and Associates, (1972), p. 43.

Pg. 232. Terminator Corvette marine engine, Terminator brochure, ZADM.

Pg. 232. Payments to Jim Rathmann, Advance Marine build orders, (1958-1960).

Pg. 233. "That thing was a hunk of junk..." Jim Rathmann interview, (Jan 23, 1998).

Pg. 233. "It was a real challenge to make the W-engine into a real engine, Dick Keinath interview, (Nov 1998).

Pg. 233. Zora's clandestine meeting with Buck Baker, ZAD-PL, (Oct 27, 1989).

Pg. 234. Scaglietti aluminum body Corvettes, Carroll Shelby interview by Pete Lyons, (Jan 5, 1990).

Pg. 234. Bold engine designs, Fred Frincke interview by Pete Lyons, (Oct 30, 1989).

Pg. 235. If someone disagreed with Duntov too persistently," Fred Frincke interview by Pete Lyons, (Oct 30, 1989).

Pg. 235. "Zora was like a Baptist preacher," Gib Hufstader interview, (March 22, 1999).

Pg. 235. "He was 100 percent honest," Denny Davis interview, (July 11, 1997).

Pg. 236. Developing the 327, Dick Keinath interview, (Nov 1998).

Pg. 236. Chevy mystery engine, Dick Keinath interview, (Nov 1998).

Pg. 237. Tech transfer from mystery engine to 396, Ray Brock, *Hot Rod* magazine, (May 1963) p. 41.

Pg. 238. Zora hacking piano to pieces, EAD, (May 13, 1997).

Pg. 238. Zora's practical joke with party guest, ZAD-PL, (Oct 30, 1989).

Pg. 239. London Chop House, EAD, (May 24, 1997).

Pg. 240. "Zora couldn't boil water, but he could make a hell of a good martini," Lyle Tuck interview, (May 17, 1997).

Pg. 241. Linking performance with safety, Zora speech, Madison Avenue Sports Car Driving and Chowder Society, (Oct 9, 1958).

Pg. 243. Making safer, faster police pursuit vehicles, Zora speech, Michigan State Police, (March 17, 1958).

Chapter Fifteen

Pg. 249. Zora assigned to design Q Corvette, KL-CASSSC, pp. 93-95.

Pg. 249. Factors preventing the building of a running prototype mid-engined Corvette, ZAD-PL, (Oct 31, 1989).

Pg. 249. "If you have an automobile powered like lawn mower…" ZAD-PL, (Oct 28, 1989).

Pg. 250. Testing of other power plants in CERV I, R-car engine history, Fred Frincke interview, (Feb 20, 1964).

Pg. 250. CERV II radiator angles, ZAD-PL, (Oct 27, 1989).

Pg. 250. First use of fuel cell in racecar, ZAD-PL, (Oct 27, 1989).

Pg. 251. CERV I rear suspension, ZAD-PL, (Oct 27, 1989).

Pg. 251. Nicknamed "The Hillclimber," KL-CASSSC, p. 26.

Pg. 251. CERV I tested at Pikes Peak, ZAD-PL, (Oct 31, 1989).

Pg. 251. Zora's tire choices at Pikes Peak, GM memo, (Dec 6, 1960).

Pg. 252. Factors preventing CERV I from Indianapolis 500 eligibility, ZAD-PL, (Oct 28, 1989).

Pg. 253. "Rumors of a grand prix car from General Motors have now been confirmed…" *Competition Press*, (Sept 24, 1960).

Pg. 253. "A beautifully designed blue-white machine…" Bill Olmsted, *Riverside Press Telegram* (Nov 20, 1960).

Pg. 254. Stirling Moss testing CERV I at Riverside, Report on First Showings of the Rear-engined Chevrolet Engineering Research Vehicle #1, Product Information and Public Relations Department, Chevrolet Engineering Center, (Nov 20, 1960).

Pg. 255. Ed Cole with CERV I, Robert O'Brien "The American Sports Car Comes of Age," *Esquire* magazine, (Nov 1961).

Pg. 255. Zora's philosophy about driving CERV I, Mountain Climber Report, (Dec 6, 1960).

Pg. 255. Performance modifications to CERV I, KL-CASSSC, p. 131.

Pg. 255. Zora's speed run at GM Proving Ground, ZAD-PL, (Oct 31, 1989).

Pg. 256. Using false birth date on competition license application. USAC competition license forms (1958-1970), ZADM.

Pg. 256. Driving Maserati racecar at Lime Rock, Larry Shinoda interview, (Oct 25, 1997).

Pg. 257. Rumors about Zora driving at Indy 500 in 1960, Don Reilly, *Inside Auto Racing*, (Jan 1, 1960).

Pg. 257. Setting up Corvettes for Le Mans, Zora post-race report, (Aug 8, 1960).

Pg. 259. U.S. Air Force flying parts over from US, Briggs Cunningham retirement letter to Zora, (July 6, 1974).

Pg. 260. Rationale for building CERV II, Zora memo to Harry Barr, (Jan 3, 1962).

Pg. 262. Zora's reaction to swing axles on Corvair, ZAD-PL, (Aug 29, 1989).

Pg. 262. Building a competition Corvair, ZAD-PL, (Aug 29, 1989).

Pg. 262. Zora's court testimony regarding Corvair, ZAD-PL, (Aug 29, 1989).

Pg. 263. Zora rolling a Corvair, ZAD-PL, (Oct 27, 1989).

Pg. 263. "The 1965 Corvair came out with a more fundamental change in the form of a link-type suspension…" Ralph Nader, *Unsafe at Any Speed*, Grossman Publishers, New York, p. 37; Cole's debate with Ralph Nader on Phil Donohue show, Alvie Smith, *Hungry Eyes and Dirty Feet*, Memoirs of Alvie Smith, Cushing Malloy, Ann Arbor, (1996) p. 194.

Chapter Sixteen

Pg. 267. "Styling was pretty cocky…" Chuck Jordan interview, (April 24, 1998).

Pg. 268. Bill Mitchell background, Strother McMinn, "A Shark is Not A Grouper," *Automobile Quarterly*, (second quarter 1988) p. 132.

Pg. 268. Italian inspiration for Q Corvette design, KL-CASSSC, p. 95.

Pg. 270. "I thought that external design should reflect what car is." ZAD-PL, (Aug 28, 1989).

Pg. 270. Zora objections to split window design, David Barry, "The Day the Earth Stood Still" *Corvette Quarterly*, (Spring 1992) p. 18.

Pg. 271. "Mitchell got very red faced during these discussions," Chuck Jordan interview, (April 24, 1998).

Pg. 271. "I'm the designer and you're the engineer…" Larry Shinoda interview, (Oct 25, 1997).

Pg. 272. "When that car came out, I said to myself…" Chuck Jordan interview, (April 24, 1998).

Pg. 272. "I always thought the Sting Ray had too many phony scoops…" Dave Holls interview, (Nov 16, 1998).

Pg. 272. "After the big pissing contest, Zora was sort of banned…" Larry Shinoda interview, (Oct 25, 1997).

Pg. 272. "The design of that car— good, bad, mediocre—had an awful lot to do…" Chuck Jordan, Chuck Jordan interview, (April 24, 1998).

Pg. 273. "Mercedes has a star and everybody knows what Mercedes is…" ZAD-PL, (Oct 31, 1989).

Pg. 273. Background behind the four-seater Corvette, Larry Shinoda, Larry Shinoda interview, (Oct 25, 1997).

Pg. 273. "I am favoring the name Corvette much more than the Sting Ray…" Letter from Zora to Joe Callahan, (Sept 7, 1962).

Pg. 274. Front suspension on Corvette Sting Ray, KL-CASSSC, p. 140.

Pg. 274. Rear suspension on Corvette Sting Ray KL-CASSSC, pp. 140-141.

Pg. 274. "The Corvette must compete with all other sports cars in a market…" Zora SAE speech, (Sept 1962).

Pg. 275. Use of higher roll center on Sting Ray, ZADM.

Pg. 275. Birth of the Mako Shark, KL-CASSSC, p. 151.

Pg. 275. The ordeal of painting the Mako Shark, Dave Holls interview, (Nov 16, 1998).

Pg. 276. Power combinations on Mako Shark, KL-CASSSC, pp. 150-151.

Pg. 276. "The tendency of the rear wheels to spin freely on acceleration…," "1963 Corvette," *Road & Track*, (Oct 1962): 22-23.

Pg. 277. "Of course, the big news is the suspension…," "1963 Corvette Sting Ray," *Sports Car Graphic*, (Nov 1962) p. 19.

Pg. 277. "We all get together and discuss things, what is wrong and how to make it right…" Z. Arkus-Duntov, "The 1963 Corvette," Presented to Society of Automotive Engineering (Oct 8, 1962).

Chapter Seventeen

Pg. 281. Zora's development/testing of Z06, KL-CASSSC, p. 144.

Pg. 282. First Z06 race at Riverside, KL-CASSSC, pp. 163-164.

Pg. 282. "In 1963, Corvette will have slightly better but basically the same relative position…" Zora memo to Harry Barr, (April 1962).

Pg. 283. "Neither the resolution (AMA) nor the basic policy equates performance with racing…" Zora memo to Harry Barr, (Feb 13, 1963).

Pg. 285. Disc brake development on the Grand Sport, Lowell C. Paddock and Dave Friedman, *Grand Sport*, Motorbooks International, Osceola, Wisc., (1989) pp. 17-18.

Pg. 285. Grand Sport bodies lifting at speed, ZAD-PL, (Nov 22, 1988).

Pg. 288. Driving the Grand Sports through the streets of Miami, Bob Clift interview, (Jan 25, 1998).

Pg. 288. Running the Grand Sports in at Nassau airport, Bob Clift interview, (Jan 25, 1998).

Pg. 288. Designing a differential cooler, Gib Hufstader interview, (May 22, 1997).

Pg. 288. "It was all right. It certainly was light enough…" Carroll Shelby interview, (June 6, 1998).

Pg. 289. "The car was so light, yet powerful…" Dick Thompson interview, (Nov 14, 1998).

Pg. 290. "Since the news of Corvette participating was known to Ford…" Chevrolet memo from Zora to E.J. Premo, (Dec 16, 1963).

Pg. 292. Rationale in suggesting 4WD in CERV II, Paul Van Valkenburgh interview, (April 23, 1998).

Pg. 292. Duntov's four wheel drive patent on CERV II, Plural Drive Axle Vehicles with a Separate Torque Apportioning Drivetrain to Each Axle, U.S. Patent #3,411,601 (Nov 19, 1968).

Pg. 293. Use of cow tongue spoiler on CERV II, ZAD-PL, (Oct 28, 1989).

Pg. 294. Duntov relationship with Frank Winchell, Paul Van Valkenburgh interview, (April 23, 1998).

Pg. 294. Genesis of the GS2, Paul Van Valkenburgh interview, (April 23, 1998).

Pg. 295. Zora's take on his relationship with Winchell, ZAD-PL, (Oct 28, 1989).

Pg. 296. 4WD versus suction traction, Paul Van Valkenburgh interview, (April 23, 1998).

Chapter Eighteen

Pg. 299. "Zora managed by love," Roy Sjoberg interview, (June 9, 1999).

Pg. 300. Zora as a technological maestro, Dr. Ron Westrum interview, (April 8, 1999).

Pg. 301. "We often intentionally looked the other way," Paul King interview, (Nov 12, 1999).

Pg. 301. "He was able to do entrepreneurial activities inside of GM…" Roy Sjoberg interview, (June 9, 1999).

Pg. 301. "Normally in a business, if it's not in your budget, you don't work on it…" Walt Zetye interview, (May 10, 1998).

Pg. 302. "He would be talking to me in group meetings about camshafts…" Denny Davis interview, (July 11, 1997).

Pg. 302. "Between eras of CERV and exhaust emissions, we did more to develop engines…" Larry Drake, GM retirement party remarks, (Jan 13, 1975).

Pg. 302. "Zora was driven by more horsepower, more rpm, better handling, another speed record—that was his adrenaline," Herb Fishel interview, (March 11, 1998).

Pg. 303. Walt Zetye background, Walter C. Zetye biographical page.

Pg. 303. "They didn't like him that much at the plant…" Gib Hufstader interview, (May 29, 1997).

Pg. 304. "Zora was no more or less responsive than other executives I worked under…" Bob Vogelai interview, (Sept 3, 1999).

Pg. 304. "I realize that you must be an extremely busy man…" letter to Zora from John Bradshaw, Burlingame, California, (Dec 28, 1972).

Pg. 304. "Letters such as yours are indeed rare and lift our spirits…" Zora reply to John Bradshaw, (Jan 1973).

Pg. 305. Bill McLain background with Sidewinder air-to-air missile, John F. Fialka, "After Nearly 30 Years, Sidewinder Missile Is Still Potent, Reliable," *Wall Street Journal*, (Feb 15, 1985).

Pg. 305. "He'd walk into an engineering department and commandeer whatever he needed…" Ron Westrum interview, (April 8, 1989).

Ph. 306. "Lots of GM executives were there with their wives…" David E. Davis, Jr., *Automobile* magazine, (July 1996) p. 42.

Pg. 306. Zora social life involving Ed Cole, Jim Rathmann and the Astronauts, EAD, (May 24, 1997).

Pg. 306. Meeting Tony Lapine, Tony Lapine interview, (Oct 27, 1997).

Pg. 307. Rachel being treated for mental illness in a sanitarium, EAD, (April 13, 1997).

Pg. 307. Yura letter to Zora requesting car for Nicola Bulgari, Letter from Yura Arkus-Duntov to Zora, (Oct 28, 1970).

Pg. 308. Yura leaving Dreyfus to head Equity Growth Fund of America, *Finance* magazine, (Jan 1968).

Pg. 308. Yura meeting Daphne Bagley, Daphne Arkus-Duntov interview, (Oct 7, 1999).

Pg. 308. "It was a God awful," Tony Lapine interview, (Oct 27, 1997).

Pg. 309. Arnie Brown requesting time off to visit dentist, Tony Lapine interview, (Oct 27, 1997).

Pg. 309. Zora meeting woman in Italy, Tony Lapine interview, (Oct 27, 1997).

Pg. 309. "There was Zora in his room and he couldn't talk," Walter Keating interview, (Sept 26, 1998).

Pg. 309. Zora sketching apologies to Elfi, EAD, (March 1, 1997).

Pg. 310. Relationship with Steve McQueen, Letter from Zora to Steve McQueen, (Nov 4, 1966).

Pg. 310. Looking after a destitute Maurice Olley, Gib Hufstader interview, (March 22, 1999).

Chapter Nineteen

Pg. 313. "Roche took it as a religious mission that we would do everything we could to support safety," Alvie Smith interview, (March 6, 1998).

Pg. 314. Jim Premo's effort to stop Zora from contacting Cole, ZAD-PL, (Oct 20, 1989).

Pg. 314. "Zora was always in some kind of trouble," Alex Mair interview, (Sept 21, 1998).

Pg. 314. "We hopped in and drove faster and faster around the test track loop…" David E. Davis, Jr. quoted in *Corvette Quarterly*, (Winter 1992).

Pg. 315. Protecting Zora from the wrath of GM Chairman Donner, Alex Mair interview, (Sept 21, 1985).

Pg. 316. Origins of Mako Shark II, KL-CASSSC, pp. 204-205.

Pg. 318. "He now looking at me as member of styling group," ZAD-PL, (Oct 20, 1989).

Pg. 320. Zora's negative reaction to the third generation Corvette, ZAD memo to Alex Mair interview, (March 21, 1967).

Pg. 320. Opportunity to go to Opel, ZAD-PL, (Oct 31, 1989).

Pg. 320. "If Zora had a weakness, it was his commitment to the Corvette program…" Karl Ludvigsen interview, (Jan 8, 1998).

Pg. 320. Zora's "demotion," ZAD-PL, (Oct 31, 1989).

Pg. 321. Zora's reaction to Cole, ZADM.

Pg. 322. "We were building thousands of cars a day and a handful of Corvettes," Alex Mair interview, (Sept 21, 1998).

Pg. 323. Fixes to 1968 Corvettes for press preview, KL-CASSSC, p. 215.

Pg. 324. "Steve Smith article was what nailed it down," ZAD-PL, (Oct 31, 1989).

Pg. 324. Winner of *Car and Driver's* Best All Around Car nine of eleven years, *Car and Driver*, (May 1968).

Pg. 324. "Chevrolet's Corvette ranks just one notch below immortality…," *Car and Driver*, (May 1968).

Pg. 325. "We found it very flattering that Z. Arkus-Duntov was accompanying the car…" Zora quoting Frere in a letter to Bunkie Knudsen, (Dec 5, 1967).

Pg. 326. "When you drive the Corvette, bear in mind that the 300 hp/350 cubic-inch base car is the nicest by Corvette standards…" Zora memo to John DeLorean, (Feb 19, 1969).

Pg. 326. "St. Louis was one of the worst plants that GM had," John DeLorean interview, (Dec 4, 1998).

Pg. 327. Background of Zora's stroke, EAD, (March 28, 1997).

Chapter Twenty

Pg. 331. Roy Lunn background, "The Men From AVC," *Sports Car Graphic*, (August 1966) p. 57.

Pg. 332. Testing racing parts for analysis, Gib Hufstader interview, (May 29, 1997).

Pg. 332. LS8 homologation in January 1967, Richard Prince interview, (Feb 3, 2002).

Pg. 332. LS8 competition debut at 1967 12-Hours of Sebring, Richard Prince interview, (Feb 3, 2002).

Pg. 332. LS8 at 1967 Le Mans, Dean Batchelor, "Stars and Stripes at Le Mans," *Corvette Quarterly*, (Winter 1989): 36-40.

Pg. 333. Having LS8 certified as a FIA Group III touring car, KL-CASSSC, page 219-220

Pg. 333. Non-certified Corvettes finished better at Daytona, "24 Hours in the Thunderbowl" *Corvette News*, vol. 11 no. 4, (1968): 8-13.

Pg. 333. Tony DeLorenzo's support from Duntov, Tony DeLorenzo interview, (Sept 10, 1999).

Pg. 334. No one at Chevrolet was aware of a problem that would be caused by using 8-1/2" wheels on the car," Letter from Tony DeLorenzo to Ed Cole, (Feb 1968).

Pg. 334. "Although both problems could have been avoided if Tony would follow our advice…" Zora memo to Pete Estes, (Feb 27, 1968).

Pg. 335. Zora not a fan of big blocks, ZAD-PL, (Oct 31, 1989).

Pg. 335. The original Corvette ZR-1, KL-CASSSC, pp. 233-234.

Pg. 335. "They will make mincemeat of our small-engine Corvettes," ZAD memo to W. J. Dettloff, (Jan 8, 1969).

Pg. 337. Negotiations with BF Goodrich over Le Mans effort, Zora letter to Gerard Alexander, (April 4, 1972).

Pg. 337. Background on Bob Johnson/Dave Heinz Le Mans Corvette, Walt Thurn interview, (Nov 16, 1998).

Pg. 338. Zora's feeling that Greenwood often overreached himself in racing, ZAD-PL, (Oct 30,1989).

Pg. 338. Greenwood driving technique at Le Mans, John Greenwood interview, (Nov 9, 1998).

Pg. 339. Zora's assistance with Greenwood silhouette racers, John Greenwood interview, (Nov 9, 1998).

Chapter Twenty One

Pg. 343. Drivetrain unit on XP-882, Vehicle Power Unit and Drivetrain, U.S. Patent #3,580,350 (May 25, 1971).

Pg. 345. Production projections on XP-895, "My Plan for the Four-Wheel-Drive Corvette," *Vette* magazine Memorial Duntov Issue, (1996) p. 49.

Pg. 346. "They were giving him something like $20,000," John DeLorean interview, (Dec 4, 1998).

Pg. 346. Duntov refusing his bonus, "My Plan for the Four-Wheel-Drive Corvette," *Vette* magazine Memorial Duntov Issue, (1996) p. 51.

Pg. 348. Four rotor engine— "More like a set of Siamese twins than a single 4-rotor engine." "Corvette Four Rotor: The Betting Man's Choice to Replace the Sting Ray," *Car and Driver*, (Dec 1973).

Pg. 348. "It was more than a case of hooking two 2-rotor engines together," Gib Hufstader interview, (May 29, 1997).

Pg. 348. "This Wankel car is faster 0-100 mph than 454," "Corvette Four Rotor: The Betting Man's Choice to Replace the Sting Ray," *Car and Driver*, (Dec 1973).

Pg. 349. "I reproached myself for tying the Corvette with the rotary engine's thermodynamic inefficiencies…" "My Plan for the Four-Wheel-Drive Corvette," *Vette* magazine Memorial Duntov Issue, (1996) p. 51.

Pg. 349. Production speculation about the Aerovette, "The Mid-Engine Corvette? Chevrolet has finally decided to build it," Victor Appleton, *Road & Track*, (Feb 1977).

Pg. 351. Ed Cole post-retirement pursuits, Karl Ludvigsen, "Here Was A President, A Tribute to GM's Ed Cole," *Automobile Quarterly*, vol. 16 no. 2 (2nd quarter 1978).

Chapter Twenty Two

Pg. 356. "The world of performance was in a vertical dive in 1973/1974," Gib Hufstader interview, (May 29, 1997).

Pg. 357. "After so many years, the mold was set…The only true Porsche accepted by the cognoscenti is the 356-911…" Dave McLellan interview, (Jan 2, 1998).

Pg. 357. Zora burns a car on Pikes Peak, Dave McLellan interview, (Jan 2, 1998).

Pg. 357. "We knew that Dave might have been pretty sensitive succeeding Zora…" Gib Hufstader interview, (May 29, 1997).

Pg. 358. "You could never turn him off…" Ed Cole remarks at Zora retirement party, (Jan 13, 1975).

Pg. 359. "Zora has given a stimulus to us which is wonderful…" Bill Mitchell remarks at Zora's retirement party, (Jan 13, 1975).

Pg. 360. "You were always a sharp engineer…" Ray Brock retirement album letter, (July 5, 1974).

Pg. 361. "Zora has always been convinced in his heart of two things about himself and his life…" John Fitch retirement album letter, (July 5, 1974).

Pg. 361. "Well, you've really done it to us this time," Joe Oldham retirement album letter, (1974).

Pg. 361. "Anytime Zora had something he wanted to see in print, he would usually try me first…." Walt MacKenzie retirement album letter, (July 1, 1974).

Pg. 362. "Unfortunately, Zora, you've been severely hamstrung by your company's 'not *really* racing' policy," Don Yenko retirement album letter, (July 1, 1974).

Pg. 362. "Zora has forgotten more about automobiles than I shall ever know," Betty Skelton Frankman retirement album letter, (July 1, 1974).

Chapter Twenty Three

Pg. 366. "He knew the business, he knew cars," John DeLorean interview, (Dec 4, 1998).

Pg. 366. Configuration of early cars, *Automotive News*, (July 21, 1980) p. 2.

Pg. 366. "If the car has the same drawback now as described in the report…" Zora letter to DeLorean, (Oct 15, 1980).

Pg. 367. "After our conversation on the 24th of this month, it transpired that you did not plan to involve me…" Zora letter to DeLorean, (Feb 26, 1981).

Pg. 367. Zora's raise from DeLorean, letter from DeLorean to Zora, (April 15, 1981).

Pg. 367. "Before writers lay their hands on the cars for intensive testing…" Zora letter to DeLorean, (April 11, 1981).

Pg. 368. "The DeLorean is short of dramatic…" Zora letter to DeLorean, (June 30, 1981).

Pg. 369. "I understand that you are managing to surface above the water…" Zora letter to DeLorean, (May 2, 1982).

Pg. 369. DeLorean's arrest for fraud, racketeering and dealing cocaine, "The Bottom Line…Busted" Ed Magnuson, *Time* magazine, (Nov 1, 1982): 30-37.

Pg. 370. "Personally, I like him…" ZAD-PL, (June 24, 1989).

Pg. 371. Z system manifold, Z System advertisement (1970).

Pg. 372. Malcolm Bricklin background, "Bricklin's Back at the Car Table. And it's His Deal" Bill Lovell, *AutoWeek*, (July 2, 1984).

Pg. 372. "We lined up hundreds of dealers, a sales and service and parts operation…" Tony Cimenera interview, (March 26, 1999).

Pg. 373. First Yugos hit American shores, *Wall Street Journal*, (May 16, 1986) p. 6.

Pg. 374. Duntov Turbo Corvette, "Duntov Turbo Corvette—What's Red, White and Quick All Over?" Larry Griffin, *Car and Driver*, (Nov 1980): 81-83.

Pg. 374. Duntov association with Mr. Gasket, Jim Browning interview, (May 18, 1999).

Pg. 375. Teaming up with Triad on special Corvette, description of project paperwork, ZADM.

Pg. 375. Arkus Duntov Corvette, description of project paperwork, ZADM.

Pg. 376. Consulting for Energy Conversion Devices, Zora letter to Lionel Robbins, (Feb 24, 1981).

Pg. 376. Consulting for Buick Indy Engine program, memo from Zora to Bernard Santavy, (May 1989, Joe Negri, Sept 20, 2001).

Chapter Twenty Four

Pg. 380. Misadventures in flight school, ZAD-PL, (June 24, 1989).

Pg. 380. Speed record concept with CERV II, Larry Truesdale letter to Zora, (Dec 10, 1974).

Pg. 380. Zora's desire to take part in ZR-1 distance/ speed record attempt, Tommy Morrison interview, (March 2, 1998).

Pg. 380. Peter Gregg visit to Duntov household, Peter Gregg letter to Zora, (Aug 21, 1974).

Pg. 382. Assembly of former Le Mans winners at Williamsburg, Va., *Detroit News*, (April 26, 1975).

Pg. 382. "Loss of Yura for me like 75 percent of my life…." ZAD-PL, (Sept 16, 1989).

Pg. 383. Deaths of Asia Orley, Julian Hoffman and Vadim Gonsoff, EAD, (April 6, 1997).

Pg. 383. Rescuing historic engines from the scrap pile, Gib Hufstader interview, (Feb 20, 1999).

Pg. 386. "Rewriting history is wrong, regardless of the purpose…" Zora letter to Jim Perkins, (Oct 6, 1994).

Pg. 386. Duntov's lawsuit against Don Sherman, *Car and Driver* magazine, (Sept 13, 2001).

Pg. 386. "The Audi has front wheel drive…" Don Sherman, *Car and Driver*, (April 1979) p. 21.

Pg. 387. Dismissal of Duntov suit, State of Michigan, Circuit Court of Washtenaw County, Case # 81-22015 NZ, Opinion rendered by Honorable Patrick J. Conlin, (March 29. 1983).

Pg. 387. Duntov reaction to a *Road & Track* article praising the Nissan 300ZX, ZADM.

Pg. 387. Taking exception to a Robert Cumberford article in *Automobile* magazine, Zora letter to David E. Davis, Jr., (March 1995).

Pg. 388. "I sat with Zora for hours…" Jim Perkins interview, (March 30, 1999).

Pg. 388. Zora's plans for a mid-engined fifth-generation Corvette, Letter from Zora to Perkins.

Pg. 389. Zora's invitation to test drive a Dodge Viper, Roy Sjoberg interview, (June 9, 1999).

Pg. 389. "He never hit on her, but he lusted for her…" Carroll Shelby interview, (June 6, 1998).

Pg. 389. Modifying his BD5 airplane, Gib Hufstader, (March 22, 1999).

Epilogue

Pg. 396. "The fact that people like Duntov are different and more creative…" Bob Lutz interview, (April 5, 1999).

Pg. 396. "A Lockheed skunk works or something modeled after the old Chevy Research & Development…" Dave Cole interview, (May 11, 1999).

Index

Art Credits

About the Author

Jerry Burton has been close to the automotive scene all his life. He is well known in the Corvette world as the founding editor and current editorial director of *Corvette Quarterly* magazine. He also has written many performance-oriented ads for the Corvette and Chevrolet as a senior copy writer at the Campbell-Ewald advertising agency. It was in this capacity that he authored the Heartbeat of America themeline for Chevrolet in the mid 1980s.

Jerry was also a member of the founding board of directors of the National Corvette Museum and is a former editor at *AutoWeek* magazine in Detroit.

These activities helped spawn his acquaintance and his later friendship with Zora Arkus-Duntov and his wife Elfi. As Jerry came to know Zora personally, his desire to paint an accurate picture of this fascinating and complex man developed into the ultimate biography of *Zora Arkus-Duntov: the Legend Behind Corvette*.

Jerry Burton lives in Michigan with his wife Nancy and son Michael.

Selected Books From Bentley Publishers

Chevrolet

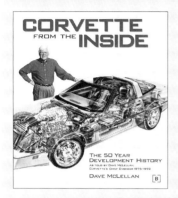

Corvette from the Inside: The 50-Year Development History *David R. McLellan* ISBN 0-8376-0859-7

Corvette Fuel Injection & Electronic Engine Management 1982–2001: *Charles O. Probst, SAE* ISBN 0-8376-0861-9

Corvette by the Numbers: The Essential Corvette Parts Reference 1955–1982: *Alan Colvin* ISBN 0-8376-0288-2

Chevrolet by the Numbers 1955–1959:The Essential Chevrolet Parts Reference *Alan Colvin* ISBN 0-8376-0875-9

Chevrolet by the Numbers 1960–1964: The Essential Chevrolet Parts Reference *Alan Colvin* ISBN 0-8376-0936-4

Chevrolet by the Numbers 1965–1969: The Essential Chevrolet Parts Reference *Alan Colvin* ISBN 0-8376-0956-9

Chevrolet by the Numbers 1970–1975: The Essential Chevrolet Parts Reference *Alan Colvin* ISBN 0-8376-0927-5

Corvette 427: Practical Restoration of a '67 Roadster *Don Sherman* ISBN 0-8376-0218-1

Camaro Exposed: 1967–1969, Designs, Decisions and the Inside View *Paul Zazarine* ISBN 0-8376-0876-7

Chevrolet and GMC Light Truck Owner's Bible™ *Moses Ludel* ISBN 0-8376-0157-6

Other Enthusiast Titles

Road & Track Illustrated Automotive Dictionary *John Dinkel* ISBN 0-8376-0143-6

Jeep Owner's Bible™ *Moses Ludel* ISBN 0-8376-0154-1

The Official Ford Mustang 5.0 Technical Reference & Performance Handbook: 1979–1993 *Al Kirschenbaum* ISBN 0-8376-0210-6

Driving

The Unfair Advantage *Mark Donohue* ISBN 0-8376-0073-1(hc); 0-8376-0069-3(pb)

Going Faster! Mastering the Art of Race Driving *The Skip Barber Racing School* ISBN 0-8376-0227-0

Driving Forces: The Grand Prix Racing World Caught in the Maelstrom of the Third Reich *Peter Stevenson* ISBN 0-8376-0217-3

A French Kiss With Death: Steve McQueen and the Making of Le Mans *Michael Keyser* ISBN 0-8376-0234-3

Sports Car and Competition Driving *Paul Frère* with foreword *by Phil Hill* ISBN 0-8376-0202-5

The Technique of Motor Racing *Piero Taruffi* ISBN 0-8376-0228-9

Engineering

Supercharged! Design, Testing, and Installation of Supercharger Systems *Corky Bell* ISBN 0-8376-0168-1

Maximum Boost: Designing, Testing, and Installing Turbocharger Systems *Corky Bell* ISBN 0-8376-0160-6

Race Car Aerodynamics *Joseph Katz* ISBN 0-8376-0142-8

BMW

BMW 3 Series Enthusiast's Companion™ *Jeremy Walton* ISBN 0-8376-0220-3

The BMW Enthusiast's Companion *BMW Car Club of America* ISBN 0-8376-0321-8

Volkswagen

Battle for the Beetle *Karl Ludvigsen* ISBN 08376-0071-5

Volkswagen Sport Tuning for Street and Competition *Per Schroeder* ISBN 0-8376-0161-4

Bentley Publishers also offers a comprehensive selection of Repair Manuals for Audi, Volkswagen, BMW and Porsche.